Karakoram Highway
the high road to China

John King

Karakoram Highway: the high road to China - a travel survival kit
    1st edition

Published by
    Lonely Planet Publications
    Head Office: PO Box 617, Hawthorn, Victoria 3122, Australia
    US Office: PO Box 2001A, Berkeley, CA 94702, USA

Printed by
    Colorcraft Ltd, Hong Kong

Photographs by
    John King (JK)
    Julia Wilkinson (JW)
    Cover: Road workers, Xinjiang, China (JK)

Published
    August 1989

National Library of Australia Cataloguing in Publication Data

    King, John (John S.)
    Karakoram Highway : the high road to China, a travel survival kit.

    Includes index.
    ISBN 0 86442 065 X.

    1. Karakoram Range Region - Description and travel –
    – Guide-books. 2. Karakorum Highway (Pakistan)
    – Guide-books. I. Title

    915.4'604

John King

John King grew up in the United States (last known address, San Francisco). In 1984 he quit his job and left for Asia and has been unable to settle down ever since. He has spent thirteen months in China at various times – as an English teacher (at the Chinese Academy of Science in Chengdu), photographer, and traveller – and five months in the Northern Areas of Pakistan. In past incarnations he has been a college physics teacher, an environmental consultant and a newspaper proofreader. He now splits his time among Hong Kong, England, and the United States as a freelance writer and photographer.

Lonely Planet Credits

Editor	Peter Turner
Maps	Graham Imeson
	Chris Lee Ack
Cover design, design & illustrations	Vicki Beale

Thanks also to Todd Pierce for additional maps.

Acknowledgements

Many people helped with this book in important ways, with information, hospitality and encouragement. All did so without complaint and with no motive except generosity. Some have probably been driven to the edge of madness by my endless questions.

The Pakistan Tourism Development Corporation (PTDC) gave information and logistical help on many occasions. Special thanks are due to Mr Ashab Naqvi (Director, P&P, Islamabad); to Tourist Information Centre managers Mr Zia (Abbottabad), Sheristan Khan (Balakot), Ijaz Ali (Besham) and Riaz Ahmed (Gilgit); and to Mrs Marietta Allen at PTDC London.

For taking time to tell me about Aga Khan programmes in the Northern Areas I am grateful to Robert D'Arcy Shaw, Director of Special Programmes, Aga Khan Foundation, Geneva; Shoaib Sultan Khan, General Manager, and Nabeel Malik, Business Manager, Aga Khan Rural Support Programme, Gilgit.

For the Geology section – and for suffering my layman's reinterpretations – I'm indebted to Dr Peter J Treloar of Imperial College of Science & Technology, London, and Dr Michael Searle of the University of Leicester. Tony Brown of Imperial College prepared the geology diagrams.

For good advice, the patience of a saint and the answers to ten thousand questions my warmest thanks go to Latif Anwar Khan of Chalt. For the most extraordinary hospitality, my gratitude to Mohammad Shuab Khan of Pokal. For data and quotations, for moral support, and for reviewing the entire manuscript, love and thanks to Julia Wilkinson.

For helpful research on short notice, thanks to Prem Samuel (Islamabad), Barry Girling (Hong Kong) and staff of the India Office Library, London.

On the road, the following people made

important contributions: Mokimjian (Kashgar); G M Baig, Sherbaz Ali Khan and Mushtaq Ahmed (Gilgit); Qurban Ali (Dasso), and Alex Reid (US). My friend Ferdy Ackermann of Switzerland offered not only excellent information but fresh viewpoints, and enlarged my own affection for the Karakoram; his death in an avalanche in Nepal in March 1988 is a profound loss for those who met him and those who might have.

Others who gave help and advice are: Ibrahim Baig (Sust), Izatullah Baig and Haqiqat Ali (Passu), Mohammad Jaffar and Mohammad Rahbar (Gulmit), Iftikhar Hussain (Ganesh), Ikram Beg (Gilgit), Muhammad Yusuf (Assistant Commissioner, Pattan), Adam Nayyar (Director of Research, Lok Virsa, Islamabad), Muhammad Zubair Usmani (Capital Development Authority, Islamabad), Christopher Rennie (British Council, Islamabad), Kurt Greussing (Austria), Chris Nielsen (US), Pat Lederle (US), Doug Pfeiffer (US) and Dr Lewis Owen (University of Leicester, UK). Cheers to John Callanan (UK) for his elegant maps of Kashgar and Karimabad highlights.

Lonely Planet correspondents who furnished helpful information are Dr George Moore (US Geological Survey), Dr Patrick Frew (Southland Hospital, Invercargill, NZ) and Wouter Tiems (Netherlands).

A Warning & a Request
Tourism is fairly new to the KKH region and it's growing like mad. Hotels and restaurants are sprouting in Sust, Hunza, Gilgit, Kohistan; prices are climbing; jeep roads are being pushed into remote valleys. If you find the book isn't quite right any more, don't get mad; instead, write to Lonely Planet – even a quick postcard – and help us make the next edition better.

Your letters will be used to help update future editions and, where possible, important changes will also be included as a Stop Press section in reprints.

All information is greatly appreciated and the best letters will receive a free copy of the next edition, or any other Lonely Planet book of your choice.

Abbreviations
People talk in initials along the KKH. Following are the most common abbreviations you'll hear.

AKRSP	Aga Khan Rural Support Programme.
CAAC	Civil Aviation Administration of China.
CBS	Community Basic Services Programme.
CITS	China International Travel Service.
C&W	NWFP Communication & Works Department.
GTS	Government Transport Service.
GPO	General Post Office.
IYHA	International Youth Hostel Association.
NAPWD	Northern Areas Public Works Department.
NATCO	Northern Areas Transportation Company.
NWFP	North-West Frontier Province.
PCO	Public Call Office.
PIA	Pakistan International Airlines.
PRC	People's Republic of China.
PTDC	Pakistan Tourism Development Corporation.
PTL	Pakistan Tours Ltd.
PYHA	Pakistan Youth Hostels Association.

Contents

Introduction

Between the central Asian desert and the plains of Pakistan is a geographical vortex that is rich with history, natural beauty and cultural diversity. In this 'collision zone' of the Indian and Asian continents, the Pamir, Kunlun, Hindu Kush, Karakoram and Great Himalaya ranges are knotted together and China, the USSR, Afghanistan, Pakistan and India all come within 250 km of each other.

In the 1960s and 1970s China and Pakistan jointly cut a road across these mountains, following a branch of the ancient network of trade routes called the Silk Road. In 1986 their mutual border was opened to travellers, completing an Asian 'high road' loop taking in Pakistan, China, Tibet, Nepal and north India.

The Karakoram Highway (KKH) con-nects the Silk Road oasis of Kashgar with Rawalpindi and Islamabad, Pakistan's capital, via the 4730-metre Khunjerab Pass, the semi-mythical Hunza Valley and the trading post of Gilgit. Despite half a dozen languages the region crossed by the highway has an identity of its own, defined by religion (almost everyone is Muslim), commerce (from the Silk Road era to present-day Kashgar-Gilgit barter trade), a demanding environment, and a sense of alienation from greater China or Pakistan.

Within reach of the KKH is some of the most mind-bending mountain scenery any-where and, in the Karakoram, the highest concentration of lofty peaks and long glaciers in the world, some virtually at the edge of the road. As the 20th-century

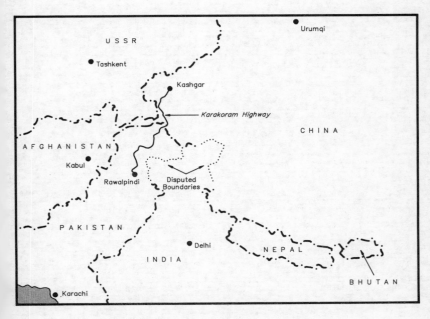

scholar-traveller John Staley has written: 'This is terrain in which even birds in flight are seen against a background of mountains.'

The region is also dense with history and artefacts, from the campaigns of Alexander the Great to the 20th century rivalry between the British and Russian empires. It was through here that Buddhism first reached China. In a sense history is still alive in the camel caravans of Xinjiang and the tribal traditions of Kohistan. Some of that history is disappearing before our eyes, in part because of the KKH itself.

Travel is cheap; overland transport from one end to the other can be as low as US$30. Theoretically you could make the 1200-km trip in 48 hours, but you might go crazy trying to do it in less than two or three weeks. Tourist development is accelerating but still mercifully modest outside Gilgit. And the Islamic tradition of hospitality can make visiting northern Pakistan a pleasure.

One thing KKH travel doesn't have is predictability. You may experience first-hand the fickleness of the Karakoram: steep and loose to begin with, shattered by KKH construction, always trying to bury the road. Landslides and rockfalls, floods and mud introduce unplanned delays. This is a frustrating place to be on a fixed schedule.

In Pakistan the highway can sometimes feel like a tunnel of ragged roadside bazaars, slapped together to take advantage of the money coming through, and not at all typical of what may lie half a km away. The best of the KKH is usually off the road.

This book describes what you can find within about half a day's village-hopping from the highway. It goes from north to south only because more people seem to go that way, and because that's the direction that prolongs the good weather in the best travelling season, autumn. Apologies to north-bound travellers.

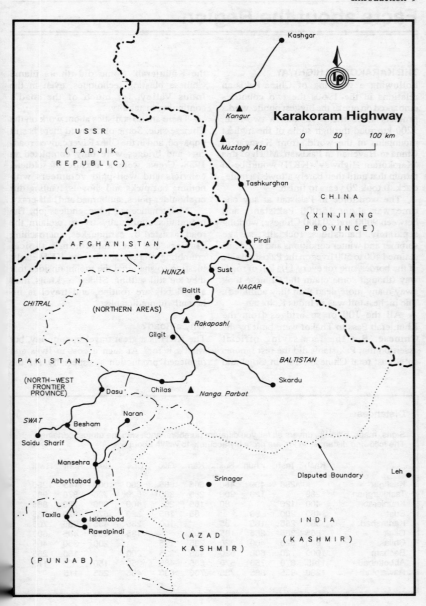

Karakoram Highway

0   50   100 km

Facts about the Region

THE KARAKORAM HIGHWAY

Following a warming of China-Pakistan relations in the 1960s the two countries embarked on one of the biggest public-works projects since the pyramids: a two-lane, 1200-km road through some of the highest mountains in the world, from Kashgar in China to Havelian in Pakistan. Much of this 'Karakoram Highway' (KKH) would be in terrain that until then barely allowed a mule-track. It took 20 years to finish.

The workforce in Pakistan at any one time was about 15,000 Pakistanis and between 9000 and 20,000 Chinese, working separately. Landslides, rockfalls, savage summer and winter conditions and accidents claimed 400 to 500 lives on the Pakistani side of the border, one for every 1 1/2 km of roadway (though some claim the Chinese took away many more dead than they admitted). The highest toll was in Indus Kohistan.

All the 100 or so bridges from the Khunjerab Pass to Thakot were built by the Chinese. But the face-saving official assertion that Pakistanis did the rest ignores an almost total Chinese effort in Gojal and the Khunjerab. Some old-timers blame Chinese blasting techniques, even in the Indus Valley, for much of the road's continuing instability.

There are no statistics about work on the Chinese side. Some of the road there is still unpaved, and in the Ghez River canyon road-cuts and bridges were only completed in 1988. Crews were a mixture of soldiers, convicts and well-paid volunteers with nothing but picks and shovels, hauling dirt on shoulder-poles, sunburned and half-crazy.

Maintenance is a huge, endless job. The mountains continually try to reclaim the road, assisted by earthquakes, encroaching glaciers and the Karakoram's typical crumbling slopes, and by the KKH itself: blasting so shattered the mountainsides that they are still settling. Slides, rockfalls, mud and floods are routine, and travel is inherently unpredictable.

Why a Road?

The KKH is a great travel opportunity, but what's it for? At such a cost in lives and displaced production – especially for the

Distances

Signs, maps, officials, drivers all tell you different numbers, each with the utmost certainty. The following distances in km are probably accurate to within about 5%.

	Kash	Tash	Khun	Sust	Kari	Gilg	Chil	Besh	Abbt	Rwpi
Kashgar		280	400	480	565	665	800	1000	1145	1260
Tashkurghan	280		120	200	285	385	520	720	870	985
Khunjerab	400	120		80	165	265	400	600	750	865
Sust	480	200	80		85	185	320	520	670	785
Karimabad	565	285	165	85		100	235	435	585	700
Gilgit	665	385	265	185	100		135	335	485	600
Chilas	800	520	400	320	235	135		200	350	465
Besham	1000	720	600	520	435	335	200		150	265
Abbottabad	1145	870	750	670	585	485	350	150		115
Rawalpindi	1260	985	865	785	700	600	465	265	115	

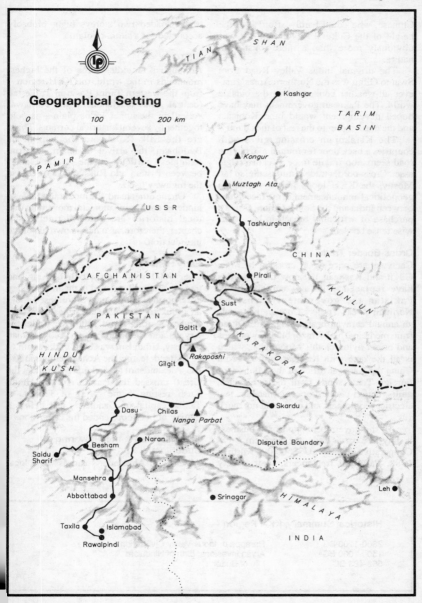

Chinese, who could hardly afford it at the height of the Cultural Revolution – it was obviously more than a mere joust with nature.

The original Indus Valley Road from Swat to Gilgit was the Northern Areas' first-ever all-weather connection to the outside world. The Pakistan government may have hoped development would bind Kohistan and the north closer to the rest of the country.

The Karakoram crossing gives both countries a back door for mutual aid, but the road seems too fragile to be a real strategic asset. Cross-border trade is minuscule, so far. Mostly, the KKH looks like a symbol: a geopolitical announcement in the face of ties between India and the Soviet Union; China's purchase of a friendly breach in her otherwise tense borders.

Cross-Border Trade

Caravans are once again crossing between Gilgit and Kashgar, but now diesel lorries have replaced yaks and camels. From Pakistan the government-sponsored Northern Areas Traders Cooperative sends an annual caravan bearing cigarettes, dried fruit, medicinal herbs, razor blades, woollens and bright nylon cloth ('Moonlight', which is all the rage with Kashgar ladies). From China the Kashgar office of the Ministry of Foreign Trade sends farm tools, bicycles, quilts, cotton cloth, crockery, matches, tea, electrical equipment and coal – but not much silk.

All the government-sponsored business is duty-free barter trade; the Northern Areas Cooperative did about US$500,000 worth in 1988. Pakistani freelancers, their rickety trucks loaded two storeys high, probably accounted for a similar volume.

HISTORY

Although it straddles some of the highest mountains in the world, the KKH region – from the western Tarim Basin in Turkestan (central Asia) to Gandhara (the Peshawar valley) in the upper Indus plain – is held together by several historical currents. These are the Silk Road and the spread of Buddhism; the arrival of Islam; imperial struggles, particularly the 'Great Game' between Britain and Russia; and of course the highway itself.

On the other hand, the mountains have so hindered communication and movement that local histories are quite distinct. Each chapter, therefore, also has its own historical introduction.

Early History

Over 4000 years ago a rich farming and trading culture flourished in the Indus Valley as far north as Gandhara, but collapsed under an influx of central Asian tribes known as Aryans, starting about 1500 BC. Under the Aryans and the later Persian Achaemenian Dynasty, Hinduism was born in the south.

After defeating the Achaemenians in 330 BC, Alexander of Macedonia (Alexander the Great) crossed the Pamirs and the Hindu Kush, resting in the spring of 326 BC at Taxila, capital of Gandhara, just before a mutiny of his troops ended his expansion.

The Silk Road & the Flowering of Buddhism

Allied with Alexander's successors a local

Historical Summary, KKH Region

2300-1700 BC	Harappa or Indus Valley Civilisation
1500-1000 BC	Aryan invasions; birth of Hinduism
563-483 BC	Life of Buddha

560-330 BC	Persian Achaemenian Dynasty
336-323 BC	Hellenic Empire of Alexander the Great
321-185 BC	Mauryan Empire; patronage of Buddhism under Ashoka
206 BC-220 AD	Chinese Han Dynasty; growth of Silk Road
70 AD-240 AD	Kushan Empire; spread of Buddhism on Silk Road
399-414	Fa-Hsien's journey from China to India
570-632	Life of Mohammed, founder of Islam & Arab Empire
618-907	Chinese Tang Dynasty; Silk Road flourishes
629-633	Hsuan Tsang's journey from China to India
711	Arab naval expedition to the mouth of the Indus
714?	Arab expeditions visit Tarim Basin & Indus Valley
752	Tang Dynasty displaced from Tarim Basin by Turks
870-1001	Shahi Dynasty; Hindu resurgence in Indus Valley
977-1186	Ghaznavid Dynasty in Afghanistan & north-west India
999-1211	Qarakhan Dynasty, Tarim Basin; appearance of Islam
1206-1227	Campaigns of Genghis Khan; start of Mongol Empire
1369-1405	Campaigns of Timur (Tamerlane)
1526	Babar takes Delhi; founding of Moghul Empire
1600	Charter granted to British East India Company
1755	Tarim Basin falls to Qing (Manchu) Dynasty
1757	Battle of Plassey (Bengal); beginning of Moghul decline
1799	Ranjit Singh founds Sikh Empire from Lahore
1838-1842	First Anglo-Afghan War
1846	First Anglo-Sikh War; creation of Kashmir state
1849	Second Anglo-Sikh War
1857-1858	Great Mutiny (Sepoy Rebellion); British Raj begins
1862-1875	Muslim rebellions in China
1877, 1889	British Agency at Gilgit opened, re-opened
1884	Xinjiang Province created under Qing Dynasty
1878-1880	Second Anglo-Afghan War
1882, 1890	Russia, then Britain, open Kashgar consulates
1895	Anglo-Russian agreement on Pamir boundaries
10 October 1911	Chinese Revolution; end of Chinese dynasties
7 November 1917	Russian Bolshevik Revolution
1931-1934	Muslim uprisings in Xinjiang
March 1940	Muslim League demands separate Pakistan
14 August 1947	Partition; independence of Pakistan & India
1 November 1947	Gilgit Uprising
1947-1948	India-Pakistan War; UN cease-fire January 1949
1 October 1949	Founding of People's Republic of China
7 October 1958	Martial law in Pakistan under General Ayub Khan
1960	Pakistan starts 'Indus Valley Road', Swat-Gilgit
1964	China and Pakistan talks on 'Friendship Highway'
September 1965	India-Pakistan War
March 1969	Martial law in Pakistan under General Yahya Khan
December 1971	India-Pakistan War; secession of Bangladesh
1974	Bhutto ends autonomy of Northern Areas princely states
5 July 1977	Martial law under General Zia ul-Haq
4 April 1979	Bhutto hanged
December 1979	Karakoram Highway finished
August 1982	Khunjerab Pass opens to official traffic & trade
30 December 1985	Zia lifts martial law
1 May 1986	Khunjerab Pass opens to tourism
17 August 1988	Zia dies in air crash
1 December 1988	Benazir Bhutto becomes prime minister

king, Chandragupta, founded India's first empire, the Mauryan Dynasty, which at its peak covered most of the subcontinent. The most famous Mauryan king was Ashoka (273 to 235 BC), a patron of the new philosophy of Buddhism, who developed Taxila as a centre for religious study.

After Ashoka's death, Hindu backlash and invasions by Bactrian Greeks, central Asian Scythians or Sakas, and Persian Parthians dragged Gandhara through 250 years of chaos.

Meanwhile in China the Han Dynasty was pushing its frontiers west and south over a growing network of trade routes that later came to be called the Silk Road. From the early Han capital of Chang'an (now Xian) a line of oases skirted north and south around the Takla Makan Desert to Kashgar. From there tracks ran west across the Pamir and Turkestan to Persia (Iran), Iraq and the Mediterranean, and south across the Karakoram to Kashmir. Caravans took silk, spices, tea and porcelain west and brought back wool, gold, ivory, jewels – and new ideas.

Bandits from Mongolia, Tibet and the little Karakoram state of Hunza made these expeditions dangerous, often impossible, and Han emperors spent vast resources policing the road. Most powerful was the nomadic Mongolian alliance known as Xiong-nu (possibly ancestors of the Huns who later terrified India and Europe).

Among the tribes driven south by the Han and the Xiong-nu, the Kushans made the most of it and, by the 1st century AD controlled an empire spanning Kashgar, most of the Karakoram, the Hindu Kush and northern India. Under the Kushan Dynasty, finally centred in Gandhara, Buddhism experienced an artistic and intellectual flowering and spread up the Indus into central Asia, China and Tibet. The Silk Road became as much a cultural artery as a commercial one.

In Gandhara, Buddhism found expression in an extraordinary fusion of Indian and Greek artistic styles. In monasteries across the Tarim Basin wealthy merchants and pilgrims commissioned works in another fusion of styles, Chinese and Indian, which reached its height during the Tang Dynasty from the 7th to 9th centuries.

The Kushans fell to the Sassanians in the 4th century, and Taxila was destroyed by the Hephthalites or White Huns in the 5th century. But pilgrims continued to travel overland to Gandhara and India, providing the only detailed accounts of the Karakoram at that time. The most well-known is the Chinese monk Fa-Hsien who, on a 15-year journey across Turkestan and the Karakoram to India, found Buddhism still dominant in early 5th century Gandhara. Hsuan Tsang, another monk-traveller in the 7th century, found it fading, carried on by monks who no longer understood their own scriptures.

Nourished by Kushan patronage and fertile soil along the Silk Road, Buddhism left an extraordinary record in western China and northern Pakistan, from the cave frescoes of Dunhuang (Gansu) and Bezeklik (near Turfan in Xinjiang) to the petroglyphs at Ganesh and Chilas, the bas-relief Buddha-figures near Gilgit and Skardu, and the fabulous trove of sculpture at Taxila.

After the 8th century a Hindu revival under the Shahi Dynasty probably pushed Hinduism as far north as Gilgit.

The Advent of Islam & the Decline of the Silk Road

An Arab navy reached the coast of what is now Pakistan in 711 and Arab armies from Persia visited Kashgar and Gilgit at about the same time, but it wasn't until the 11th century that Islam began to establish itself in this region.

Muslim Turkish raiders from Afghanistan, led by the warlord Mahmud of Ghazni, battered the Indus Valley in the early 11th century. Ultimately the Persian-influenced Ghaznavid Empire spanned Afghanistan and the north-west of the subcontinent, destroying the Hindu kingdoms of the Indus Valley and paving the way for a series of Turkish-Afghan sultanates that ruled from Delhi in the 13th and 14th centuries. Conversion to Islam was widespread, for pragmatic as well as spiritual reasons.

In Turkestan the Silk Road was fading along with the Tang Dynasty. The Tarim Basin fell to the Turks in the 8th century and then to a series of Turkic and Mongol kingdoms, among them the Qarakhan in the 11th and 12th centuries. The earliest appearance of Islam in Turkestan was under the Qarakhan.

In the early 13th century the Mongol armies of Genghis Khan controlled central Asia, and his successors began raiding south into the subcontinent. With the largest land empire in history cleared by the Mongols of bandits and boundaries, the Silk Road enjoyed a last burst of activity into the 14th century. Europeans, forced to take note of Asian power, also took an interest in Asia; Marco Polo made his epic journeys during this time. The subsequent eclipse of the Silk Road has been variously attributed to the arrival of Islam, the collapse of the Mongols and the drying up of oasis streams.

Of the Muslim invaders from central Asia the cruelest was Timur (or Tamerlane), a Turkish warlord from the western Pamirs who at the end of the 14th century savaged most of the Islamic cultural centres of Asia – including Kashgar and Delhi – in the name of 'purification'. Paradoxically, his capital city of Samarkand was one of the most splendid and cultured in Asia, full of his spoils.

The final nail in the Silk Road's coffin was the discovery in 1497 of sea routes from Europe to Asia around Africa by the Portuguese navigator Vasco da Gama. By this time the entire region now spanned by the KKH was Muslim, but it was in total disarray, fractured by quarrelling remnants of the Mongol empire in the north, petty chieftains in the mountains and Timur's successors and Pathan tribes in the south. A traveller wouldn't have stood a chance on any long-distance roads.

In 1526 Zahiruddin Babar, King of Ferghana and Samarkand and descendant of both Timur and Genghis Khan, marched into Delhi to found a line of Persian-speaking Turkish Muslim emperors of India known as the Moghuls (a corruption of 'Mongol'). For six generations, often harassed by Pathans west of the Indus, they presided over a 'Golden Age' of Islamic art, architecture, literature and music, across what is now Pakistan and north India.

Britain, Russia & the Great Game
In 1600 Queen Elizabeth granted monopoly trading rights in Asia to a small merchant group, the British East India Company. Starting with one-off expeditions to the Bay of Bengal for cotton and spices, within 50 years they had established a permanent presence on the subcontinent, trading under Moghul grants, gaining territory and influence by cunning and keeping it by force.

In 1757 the defeat of a Moghul viceroy at the Battle of Plassey in Bengal demonstrated the strength of 'the Company' at the expense of the Moghuls. A century later, a mutiny in the Bengal Army set off a two-year rebellion against the British. After it was put down, the crown in 1858 took control of Company territory, bringing the Moghul Empire to a formal end. The 'Raj' (Britain's Indian Empire) by then covered most of present-day India, through alliance or direct control. (The East India Company later distinguished itself by introducing opium to China, in exchange for tea.)

Meanwhile, in Turkestan, a Manchu army marched into Kashgar in 1755 and the Tarim Basin fell within China's Qing Dynasty for a century. A series of Muslim rebellions in the 1860s temporarily weakened its grip but in 1878 Qing authority was tightened and a formal province, Xinjiang ('New Dominions'), was created.

Westward, Russian expansionism triggered the Crimean War in 1853. Within a decade Russia was to take for herself an area the size of Europe between the Caspian Sea and the Pamirs, and start eyeing Xinjiang and Afghanistan.

The British, anxious about this (and ever eager to trade) set out to pacify the insecure north-west frontier. In 1839 they installed a hand-picked ruler of Afghanistan, which resulted in an uprising, a death-march from Kabul by the British garrison and a vengeful 'First Afghan War'. By the end of it Britain's man was murdered and his predecessor was back on the throne. This failure to either control or befriend the headstrong Afghan Pathans was repeated in an equally ill-fated 1878 invasion.

Pathans from west of the Indus, in the course of tormenting the Moghuls, had in 1799 given control of Lahore to an aggressive Sikh chief named Ranjit Singh. Over the next 40 years he carved out his own little military state across the Punjab, Kashmir, Hazara and Peshawar. A treaty barring expansion into 'Company' India was violated by his successors and in 1846 the British fought a short, bloody war with the Sikhs and annexed the Kashmir Valley, Ladakh, Baltistan and Gilgit. Renaming it 'the State of Jammu and Kashmir' they sold it to a Hindu prince, Gulab Singh, declared him the first Maharajah of Kashmir and thereby created a friendly buffer state on the Russian flank. A second Sikh War brought an end to the Sikh state, and Britain took the Punjab.

With a grip now on the 'Northern Areas' Britain began a kind of cat-and-mouse game with Russia across the vaguely-mapped Pamirs and Hindu Kush. Agents posing as scholars, explorers, merchants, even Muslim holy men, crisscrossed the mountains, mapping them, spying on each other, courting local rulers, staking subtle claims like dogs in a vacant lot. The British called it 'the Great Game', the Russians 'the Tournament of Shadows'.

In 1882 Russia established a consulate in Kashgar. A British Agency at Gilgit, opened briefly in 1877, was urgently re-opened after the Mir (ruler) of Hunza entertained a party of Russians at Baltit in 1888. Britain set up its own Kashgar office in 1890.

In advanced stages of the Game the British tried to persuade reluctant Afghan and Chinese authorities to assert a common border in the Pamirs, sealing Russia's southward moves. In 1890 Francis Younghusband (later to head a British incursion into Tibet) was sent to do some politicking with Chinese officials in Kashgar. On his way back through the Pamirs he found the range full of Russian troops, and was told to get out or face arrest.

This electrified the British, who raised hell with the Russian government and invaded Hunza the following year; at the same time Russian troops skirmished in north-east Afghanistan. After a burst of diplomatic manoeuvring an Anglo-Russian boundary agreement in 1895 gave Russia most of the Pamirs and established the Wakhan Corridor, the awkward tongue of Afghan territory that stretches across to meet Xinjiang.

The Pamir settlement merely shifted the focus of the Great Game toward Kashgar, where the two powers went on conniving over Turkestan. But in the chaos following the Chinese Revolution of 1911 the British were no match for Russian economic and political influence in western Xinjiang, despite Russian absence from Kashgar for almost a decade after the 1917 Bolshevik Revolution.

Autonomous Xinjiang & Muslim Pakistan

On both sides of the Karakoram the idea of a separate state had a strong appeal to Muslims living under non-Muslim rule. In 1865 Yaqub Beg, an officer from Tashkent, had briefly established an independent Turkestan. Muslims rose up in Xinjiang in the 1930s; in Khotan a short-lived Turkestan Republic was again declared. Soon after the 1949 founding of the Peoples' Republic of China, Xinjiang was made an 'Autonomous Region', a formality that has failed to calm things down.

As pressure for Indian independence grew after WW I, Muslim-Hindu disagreement over how to achieve it was echoed in communal violence in the 1920s and 1930s. The idea of a Muslim state was first proposed by the philosopher-poet Alama Mohammed Iqbal in 1930, and adopted in 1940 as a platform of the All-India Muslim League.

In the end Britain was forced to grant separate independence to a Muslim-majority Pakistan and a Hindu-majority India. With the approach of the formal date for Partition and the end of the Raj, 14 August 1947, Muslims fled westward and Hindus and Sikhs eastward, seven to eight million in each direction, probably the biggest mass population transfer in history. In hideous violence on both sides, perhaps 200,000 died.

As 14 August came and went, Maharajah Hari Singh delayed his decision on whether Kashmir should accede to India or Pakistan, hoping to remain free of both. At the end of October a band of Pathan tribesmen invaded Kashmir, having been told the Maharajah was about to join India. This he promptly did. A week later the Kashmiri governor was arrested at Gilgit and Muslim militiamen and soldiers there demanded to join Pakistan. The two new nations went to war, and a United Nations cease-fire in January 1949 gave each a piece of Kashmir, a temporary arrangement that after 40 years shows signs of becoming permanent.

India and Pakistan again fought over Kashmir in 1965 and 1971. The latter war was followed by the secession of East Pakistan, which became Bangladesh.

The Karakoram Highway

China, following its invasion of Tibet in 1950, occupied parts of Ladakh, Baltistan and the upper Shimshal Valley in the mid-1950s. All traffic across the border stopped. While the China-India border in Ladakh is still in dispute today, a thaw in China-Pakistan relations in 1964 under General Ayub Khan led to a border agreement, China's return of 2000 square km of territory and talk of a 'Friendship Highway' linking the two countries across the Pamirs and the Karakoram, via Hunza and Gilgit.

(According to an apocryphal story around Gilgit, General Ayub had politely declined a similar offer by Soviet Premier Bulganin to build a road through Ishkoman.)

The Pakistan Army had already started a road of its own in 1960, the 400-km 'Indus Valley Road' between Swat and Gilgit. In 1966 a China-Pakistan decision expanded it to a Havelian-to-the-border two-lane paved road, with Pakistanis working north from the Indus and the Chinese working south from the Khunjerab as well as to Kashgar on their own side. In 1968 the Indus Valley Road and a link to Havelian were finished, and joined by a bridge at Thakot. Between then and 1973, Chinese crews cut a road over the Khunjerab Pass to Gulmit, and in 1974 returned at Pakistan's request to help south of Gulmit. Chinese workers left in December 1979 and the KKH was declared complete (in Pakistan) in 1980.

In August 1982 the highway was formally inaugurated, the Northern Areas were opened to tourism (as far as Passu) and the Khunjerab Pass opened to official traffic and cross-border trade. On 1 May 1986 the Khunjerab and the entire road to Kashgar were opened to tourism. Joint Chinese-Pakistani survey teams were back in 1987, and there are now plans to widen the road.

GEOGRAPHY

The KKH threads its way through a 'knot' of four great mountain ranges: the Pamirs, the Karakoram, the Hindu Kush and the Himalaya, all of them part of the vast collision zone between the Asian continent and the Indian subcontinent. Here the ground rises higher, over a greater area, than anywhere else on the planet.

The Pamirs are a range of rounded, 5000 to 7000-metre mountains with prosaic names like Communism, Lenin and Karl Marx, stretching 800 km across the Tadjik Republic of the Soviet Union. With very broad, flat valleys nearly as high as the lower peaks, the Pamirs might be better described as a plateau. The valleys are treeless, grassy (*pamir* roughly means 'pasture' in local dialects), and often swampy with meandering rivers. The KKH crosses the eastern limb of the Pamirs, also called the Taghdumbash or Sarikol Pamir.

The Karakoram arches for 500 km along the border between China and Pakistani Kashmir, parallel to the Himalaya and cleanly separated from it by the trough of the upper Indus River. To a geographer the Karakoram reaches west to the Ishkoman Valley (beyond which it becomes the Hindu Kush) and south-east into Ladakh in Indian Kashmir. It's characterised by closely-packed, steep, jagged high peaks and deep gorges; immense glaciers (the longest outside the sub-polar regions) and lush high valleys. The world's second highest mountain, K2 or Mt Godwin Austen, is in Baltistan, and recent satellite data hint that it might in fact be *the* highest.

The 'Great Karakoram' is the range's high backbone, grouped in clusters called *muztagh* (Uyghur for 'ice mountain') from which the biggest glaciers descend. In northern Hunza is the Batura *Muztagh*, source of the Batura, Passu and Ultar glaciers; south-east is the Hispar *Muztagh* from which Nagar's glaciers flow; in Baltistan is the mighty Baltoro *Muztagh*, home of K2. This crest-zone is broken at only one point, by the Hunza River (accompanied by the KKH) in southern Gojal.

South of Gilgit the Indus River divides the Himalaya from the Hindu Kush, which extends over 800 km into central Afghanistan. The western anchor of the Himalaya is 8126-metre Nanga Parbat, which has defeated and killed more climbers than any other mountain in the world. Under the force of the collision that gave birth to the Himalaya, Nanga Parbat continues to rise at almost seven mm per year.

Statistics

The highest peaks near the KKH (approximate heights in metres, all in the Karakoram except as noted) are: Nanga Parbat (Himalaya, 8126), Rakaposhi (7790), Batura Peak (7785), Mt Kongur (Pamir, 7720), un-named (at the head of the Passu Glacier, 7610), Muztagh Ata (Pamir, 7540), Malubiting (7450), Haramosh (7400) and Ultar Peak (7390). In the Northern Areas alone there are about three dozen peaks over 7000 metres.

The Karakoram has four glaciers over 50 km long: Batura, Hispar, Baltoro and Biafo. The Batura comes right down to the KKH at Passu.

GEOLOGY

A trip along the Karakoram Highway reveals one of the world's greatest geological exhibits. The mountain chain comprised of the Himalaya, Karakoram and Hindu Kush Ranges was born 55 million years ago in a stupendous collision between India and Asia, a collision that is still going on today. The highway climbs right over the 'wreckage'.

According to the theory of plate tectonics, the earth's crust is made up of continent-sized slabs of rock (plates), afloat

Baltit Fort, Hunza Valley (JK)

on a more fluid layer (mantle). As a result of currents and upwellings from below, the plates move around, bump into each other, break up and re-form, all in ultra-slow motion.

About 130 million years ago, when dinosaurs still roamed the earth, the 'Indian Plate' broke away from a primordial super-continent that geologists call Gondwanaland (the ancestor of Africa, Australia and Antarctica) and drifted north toward another landmass called Laurasia, the 'Asian Plate'. Between the converging continents lay a wide, shallow sea called Tethys, and off the shore of Laurasia was a chain of volcanic islands, similar to present-day Indonesia or Japan.

In the collision that followed 75 million years later, the Indian Plate buried its leading edge under the Asian Plate, lifting it up. Both plates compressed and piled up against each other. Trapped in the middle, the small oceanic plate supporting the offshore island chain was flipped very nearly on end, and the Sea of Tethys was swallowed up.

Continents are not easily slowed down. India continues to plough northward (at about five cm per year), and the mountains are still rising, in some cases faster than erosion can wear them down. Frequent earthquakes across the region reveal the strains underneath.

From the Khunjerab Pass to Islamabad, the Karakoram Highway crosses the entire collision zone – the Asian Plate, the remnants of the offshore volcanic islands, and the Indian Plate. The evidence of this on-going encounter is easy to see, both on the grand

Geological map of northern Pakistan, showing the major rock units and thrust zones in the three 'plates' crossed by the KKH.

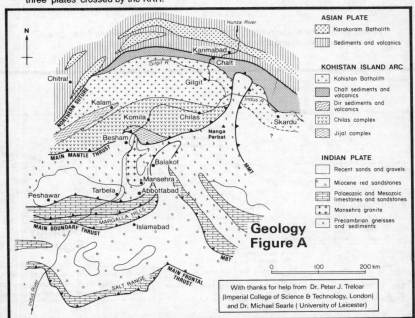

scale – in the size and sequence of the mountains – and up close, in the colours and patterns of road-side rocks and minerals.

The Asian Plate

From Khunjerab to Chalt (in the lower Hunza Valley) the road crosses old Laurasia, its former southern shore now heaved up into the Karakoram Range itself.

The geology from Khunjerab to Passu is dominated by dark and light-coloured metamorphic shale and limestone, seen prominently in the saw-tooth peaks around Passu. ('Metamorphic' refers to rocks re-formed from older ones deep in the earth's crust under high temperatures and pressures.) From Passu to Karimabad, the high spine of the Karakoram is composed mostly of 50-million to 100-million-year-old granite (the Karakoram Batholith in the diagrams), part of a vast body extending eastward for 2500 km along the India-Asia boundary, to Lhasa and beyond.

In the Hunza Valley itself is a variety of metamorphic rocks, with large red garnets very common. White marble bands are conspicuous around Karimabad. The famous ruby mines of Hunza are in the hills north of the river, between Karimabad and Hasanabad (although the 'rubies' offered to you by the urchins of Baltit are probably garnets).

The edge of the Asian Plate (called the Northern Suture or NS on the diagrams) is exposed near Chalt, in a multi-coloured jumble of sedimentary rocks, volcanic material, talc and greenish serpentine. Southward, the road crosses onto the eroded remains of the small oceanic plate that was pinned between India and Asia.

The Kohistan Complex

In the course of the continental collision, the plate bearing the old volcanic island chain was effectively up-ended, with the shallower ocean sediments and volcanic materials in

Vertical section in the vicinity of the KKH, showing major rock units and thrust zones in the Asian, Kohistan and Indian 'plates'. The diagram is schematic only.

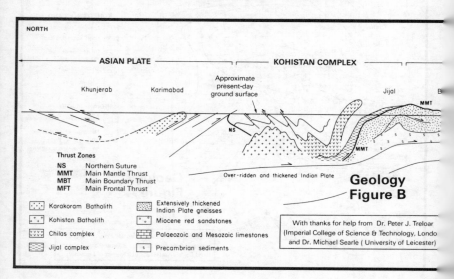

Geology Figure B

With thanks for help from Dr. Peter J. Treloar (Imperial College of Science & Technology, London) and Dr. Michael Searle (University of Leicester)

the north, and its very deep parts exposed in the south. Consequently the northern part of this so-called Kohistan Complex, from Chalt to Raikot Bridge (east of Chilas), is a mass of sedimentary and volcanic rocks. Dark patches are remnants of ocean-floor crust upon which the island chain was built. The area around Gilgit and the confluence of the Gilgit and Indus Rivers was invaded at a later stage by granites from a deep molten reservoir (the Kohistan Batholith in the diagram). At the confluence especially, hundreds of small intrusive granite sheets cross-cut one another.

By contrast, the southern part of this unit reveals rocks formed under conditions of extreme heat and pressure deep in the earth, ie beneath the old oceanic plate. Examples include the black-banded pinkish rocks seen just east of Chilas (the Chilas Complex on the diagrams), and garnet-rich outcrops between Pattan and Jijal that include some dark-red, nearly pure garnetites (Jijal Complex). Just west of the Shangla Pass, on the Besham-Swat road, are outcrops of the rare rock blueschist, which laboratory studies indicate can form only at depths of at least 25 km.

At Jijal the KKH crosses the boundary from the volcanic island complex to the Indian Plate. The green rocks at Jijal belong to Kohistan, and the contorted white and grey gneisses 100 metres south belong to the Indian Plate.

The Indian Plate

As it drove into and under Asia, the top of the Indian Plate was compressed and bulldozed back, most severely along the leading edge. Under the resulting compression the crust became fractured and sliced. Along certain fronts or 'thrusts', individual slices, some up to 10 km thick, slid southwards and upwards over originally higher rocks. The effect was to throw up great piles of material, some still visible as hill or mountain ranges.

The direct contact between Kohistan and the Indian Plate (called the Main Mantle Thrust or MMT in the diagrams) is not marked by a distinct chain of hills but does pass through the rugged terrain from Babusar Pass via Besham into the Swat Valley. The emerald deposits at Mingora, in Swat, are within this zone.

To the south, major thrusts are associated with escarpments (mountain fronts), eg the steep terrain between Abbottabad and Havelian (the Panjal Thrust in the diagram), the Margalla and Murree Hills along Islamabad's northern side (the Main Boundary Thrust or MBT in the diagrams) and the Salt Range, 100 to 150 km south of Islamabad (the Main Frontal Thrust or MFT in the diagrams).

The severest compression, right at the northern edge of the plate, tended to push up the oldest and deepest material, subsequently exposed by erosion. Thus, as you go southward the exposed surface gets younger. Material from deep in the plate's crust, where temperatures are high and rock is slightly plastic, tended to fold and deform, and the geology south as far as Mansehra is dominated by contorted and streaky metamorphic rocks from the plate's Precambrian 'basement' (more than 600 million years old). Precambrian slate outcrops are visible along the road between Mansehra and Abbottabad.

From here, south through the Taxila Valley to the Margalla Pass, the road crosses 600 million to 160 million-year-old Palaeozoic and Mesozoic limestones. At the road-cut through the Margalla Pass, the thrusting of these limestone strata, southward up and over younger rock, is well-exposed. South of Margalla, red rock outcrops indicate Miocene-age (about 20 million years old) sandstones, originally eroded from the embryo Himalayan chain.

Nanga Parbat

An unmistakable feature of the region is massive Nanga Parbat, 8126 metres high and rising by seven mm every year, faster than almost any other part of the Himalayan chain. Nanga Parbat sits atop a mass of ancient Indian-Plate rocks, sticking oddly northward into the volcanic-island material of the Kohistan Complex. Its unusual position and growth are still matters of active research; explanations involve the dynamics of the entire Himalayan system.

At the Liachar Valley, about four km upstream from the Raikot Bridge over the Indus (between Gilgit and Chilas), across from the KKH, you can see the grey Precambrian granite of the Indian Plate, hundreds of millions of years old, pushed over on top of river sediments less than 100,000 years old. This reversal is part of the continuing disruption as Nanga Parbat rises.

This geological instability, coupled with an earthquake, caused a colossal landslide near Liachar in 1841, which dammed up the Indus and created a lake stretching nearly to Gilgit. The remnants of the slide can be seen in a steep-sided, two-km-long ridge on the river's east bank. When the dam broke, the wall of water thundering down the canyon and out onto the plains of the Punjab washed away scores of towns and villages and drowned thousands of people, including an entire Sikh army battalion camped at Attock.

At another side valley just above Raikot Bridge, the boundary between the Kohistan Complex and the Indian Plate is visible. Across the river from the highway, a 100-metre stretch of jeep track passes from grey Indian-Plate granite, southward through a layer of brown garnet-bearing schists that formed a sedimentary cover to the granite, and into the greenish rocks of Kohistan.

Other Evidence of Geological Activity

Insistent reminders of the strains of mountain-building are the earthquakes that constantly jar the Karakoram. The worst in recent times struck near the Indus River village of Pattan, north of Besham, in December 1974. Pattan and many smaller villages virtually disappeared under collapsing hillsides. Between 5000 and 8000 people died, and tens of thousands were injured. Pattan has been entirely rebuilt with government and international relief money but, like many towns along the KKH, it continues to be at the mercy of its tormented surroundings.

In the same year, earthquakes probably triggered a mud and rock slide out of the Shishkat Valley in Gojal (Upper Hunza) that dammed the Hunza River. The resulting lake, extending to well above Passu, lasted so long before the river cut its way through again, that the once deep and fertile valley was virtually filled with silt and gravel, and is now a shallow, flat-bottomed wasteland. A section of the KKH, including a major bridge, was permanently buried, and had to be re-routed and re-built.

A happier consequence of geological activity is the high frequency of hot springs in the area. Relatively recent 'faults' or fractures permit easy upward movement of underground water that has been in contact with hot rock deep in the crust.

CLIMATE

The hottest months all along the KKH are June, July and August; the coldest are January and February. The wettest months are during the monsoon, mid-July to mid-September, with steady rain as far north as Kohistan and the Kaghan Valley and random summer storms as far north as Hunza; the same regions are also drizzly through the winter and early spring. The driest months are June, October and November in Pakistan, and anytime in Xinjiang. Winter snow is common from Kashgar to Gilgit and is enough to close the Khunjerab Pass from November through April.

When To Go?

Assuming you like sunshine and moderate temperatures, the best time to travel the KKH is from September to October, and a south-bound journey will stretch out the good weather. The next-best time is May to June, and a north-bound trip will prolong the pleasure. Summer is ferociously hot and dry in Kashgar, pleasantly warm and occasionally stormy in Gojal and Hunza, very hot and rainy from Kohistan south.

The Khunjerab Pass is formally closed to travellers from 30 November (31 October for tour groups) until 1 May. In several recent years heavy snow has closed it by mid-November.

Another consideration is that the KKH from Gilgit south is no fun during *Ramadan*, the Muslim month of fasting. Everyone is cranky and food is hard to find until sunset. In 1990 it's around 30 March to 29 April, in 1991 from 20 March to 19 April.

RURAL DEVELOPMENT

Most people living near the KKH are subsistence farmers or herdsmen. For their maize, wheat, barley, rice, fruit and (in Xinjiang) cotton, farmers depend heavily on irrigation, from wells and isolated streams around Kashgar or channelled glacial melt-water in the Northern Areas. Plots are tiny and harvests are meagre (though yields per hectacre are well above those in the rest of Pakistan). Herders, especially in Kohistan and the Northern Areas, make long migrations to pastures only accessible in summer. Little except fruit is exported from

the Northern Areas, where annual per capita income is estimated to be about US$150.

Into this setting the KKH has brought government grants, down-country developers, tourists and a kind of wealth, but it has also tended to unravel old traditions, social structures and community self-reliance. A social re-development effort initially funded by the private Aga Khan Foundation has had interesting results in the Northern Areas.

The Aga Khan Foundation

This foundation was started by the Aga Khan, spiritual head of Ismaili Muslims, to provide capital for health, education and rural development projects in certain low-income areas of Asia and Africa. Ismailis actually make up only a small fraction of its current beneficiaries, although it's obvious in northern Pakistan that the Ismaili community has provided the enthusiasm and energy necessary to get many AKF-funded programmes off the ground.

The main recipients of AKF (and now other) money in northern Pakistan are the Aga Khan Rural Support Programme, the Community Basic Services Programme, Aga Khan Health Services and Aga Khan Educational Services.

Aga Khan Rural Support Programme In 1974 when Prime Minister Bhutto ended the semi-autonomy of Hunza, Nagar, Swat and other Northern Areas princely states, the local rulers' traditional power to initiate collective works also ended. The central government's own public-works projects tended to be vast in scale and run from Islamabad. At the same time population growth was exceeding the capacity of the land under cultivation and forcing people into the towns for work. Village productivity and collective confidence seemed to be fading away.

The AKRSP was formed in 1982 to encourage a home-grown solution in the form of self-sustaining, cooperative village organisations that could carry out their own development projects. It offered starter loans, technical resources and management advice to any village that would form its own decision-making body, name its projects and commit itself to acquiring the necessary skills and saving its own money. AKRSP's role is to act as a catalyst only until the projects are self-managing.

The effects have been quite dramatic. Over 90% of the 600 to 700 villages in Hunza, Nagar, the Gilgit River watershed and Chitral now have their own village organisations with their own projects underway, and several hundred have begun second projects with their own money. The programme is also in an early stage in Baltistan, and projects in Xinjiang have at least been discussed. The work covers both Ismaili and non-Ismaili villages.

Nowadays significant AKRSP money also comes from private organisations such as Oxfam in the UK and the Conrad Adenauer Foundation in Germany, and from EEC, Dutch, Canadian, American and British overseas aid agencies.

First projects tend to be irrigation schemes and link roads; AKRSP signs sprout weekly by the highway, announcing new ones. Some of the more impressive ones close to the KKH are a 400-metre irrigation tunnel above Sust; a 45-km road being pioneered up the Shimshal Valley; an irrigation channel from the Batura Glacier at Passu; channels and new fields in impossible-looking places above Ahmedabad, east of Ganesh; the Karimabad-Aliabad link road; and an irrigation pipeline across the Gwachi Nala (Gwachi Canyon) south of Chalt.

If you're interested in these projects you can visit them, but don't expect a guided tour. AKRSP staff in Gilgit are spread too thinly to welcome casual visitors, but a good way to learn more about the programme is the video presentation, *Valleys in Transition*, which can be viewed by arrangement at the Gilgit Serena Lodge. The lodge, incidentally, is run by another Aga Khan outfit, Tourism Promotional Services, along with three other Serena Lodges in Pakistan and other top-end hotels around the world; the chairman of TPS is the Aga Khan's brother, Prince Amin.

Other Programmes Aga Khan Health Services has been operating a large network of minor medical clinics in northern Pakistan for several years and is setting up a primary health-care programme.

Aga Khan Educational Services now operates 130 schools in northern Pakistan (two prominent ones are the huge Girls' Academy on the west side of Karimabad and a school in Sher Qila in Punial). Most are for girls, and provide the main access to education for women in the Northern Areas. Both AKES and local government-run schools are involved in an AKF-funded teacher development scheme.

The Community Basic Services Programme is a joint effort by the Pakistan government and UNICEF, with heavy participation by Canadian agencies, to improve drinking water, sanitation and other facilities.

For More Information The Aga Khan Foundation is at 7 Rue Versonnex, PO Box 435, 1211 Geneva 6, Switzerland. AKRSP is at PO Box 506, Gilgit.

RELIGION

Although the Indus Valley saw the birth of Hinduism and an early flowering of Buddhism, both traditions were swept eastward by Islam. With the exception of small Christian and Hindu communities in Pakistan and scattered Buddhists in western China, nearly everyone from Turkestan to the Arabian Sea is Muslim, and a good deal of the flavour of KKH travel stems from this fact.

Islam – History & Schisms

In 612 AD Mohammed, a wealthy Arab of Mecca, began preaching a new religious philosophy, Islam, based on a revelation from God and incorporating elements of

Judaism, Christianity and other faiths. Islam translates loosely from Arabic as 'the peace that comes from total surrender to God'. God's will, as revealed to Mohammed, is put into words in the Koran. In addition to the creeds set out in the Koran, Muslims express their surrender in the form of daily prayers, alms-giving, fasting and pilgrimage to Mecca. In its fullest sense Islam is an entire way of life, with guidelines for doing nearly everything.

The appeal of this new faith fitted nicely with a latent Arab nationalism and by the end of his life Mohammed ruled a rapidly growing religious and secular dynasty. Within a century the Arab empire reached from Spain to central Asia.

At an early stage disputes over succession to the caliphate (rulership) split the community. When the fourth caliph, the Prophet's son-in-law Ali, was assassinated in 661 his followers and descendants became the founders of the Shia (or Shi'ite) sect. Others accepted as caliph another relative with more political clout, and this line has become the modern-day orthodox Sunni (or Sunnite) sect. In 680 a chance for reconciliation was lost when Ali's surviving son Hussain and most of his male relatives were killed at Karbala in Iraq by Sunni partisans. Today over 90% of Muslims worldwide are Sunni.

Among doctrines developed by the Shias was that of the *Imam* or infallible leader, who continues to unfold the true meaning of the Koran and provides guidance in daily affairs. Shias recognise an hereditary line of 12 legitimate Imams, ending in the 9th century (although *imam* is still used, more loosely, by modern Shias).

A division among Shias in the 8th century gave rise to another branch of Islam, the Ismailis (or Maulais), who disagreed as to which son of the sixth Imam should succeed. For Ismailis the line of Imams continues into the present. Their main surviving branch, the Nizari, numbers several million in pockets of Pakistan, India, East Africa, Iran and Syria, and its present leader and *hazir* (living) *Imam*, Prince Karim Aga Khan, is considered to be No 49.

Ismaili doctrines are more esoteric, and their practices less regimented, than those of Shias or Sunnis, many of whom consider them blasphemers. Prayer is a personal matter, the mosque is replaced by a community hall called a *jamat khana* ('meeting place'), and women are less secluded. The most obvious Ismaili activities along the KKH are very secular ones, in the area of rural development (see the section on Rural Development).

Islam along the KKH

Although an Arab expedition reached Kashgar in the 8th century, the earliest conversions to Islam in the Tarim Basin were by rulers of the Qarakhan Dynasty in the 12th century. Today most non-Chinese there are Sunni Muslims.

Almost simultaneously with the central Asia explorations an Arab naval force arrived at the mouth of the Indus, but likewise left little religious imprint. Islam only took hold in the Indus Valley after invasions from Afghanistan by Mahmud of Ghazni in the 11th century and later work by Pathan missionaries, who tended to convert by force. Today, people as far north as Chilas are all Sunnis, and more fervently so than their Kashgar cousins.

In between, travelling preachers brought Shi'ism from Persia and Ismailism from Afghanistan and central Asia, and concentrated on conversion by peaceful means. By the 13th century most people of the upper Gilgit River watershed were Ismaili, while Nagar and the Bagrot and Haramosh valleys became Shia. Hunza and Gojal, Shia at first, adopted Ismailism in the mid-1800s. Even today a few old carved Shia mosques can be seen there, a sharp contrast to the spanking green-and-white *jamat khanas*.

Gilgit is the only KKH town with sizeable proportions of all three sects, and it's always a bit on edge. In past years during the gripping Shia *Ashura* processions, Shias and

Sunnis have exchanged taunts, even gunshots. Ismailis and Shias are anxious about puritanical *Wahhabi* Sunni missionaries. Sunnis and Shias are ambivalent about Aga Khan-funded development work, even in their own villages. And in 1988 at the end of *Ramadan*, the Muslim month of daytime fasting, armed violence exploded in and around Gilgit, leaving several hundred dead.

Perhaps hardest for Muslims along the KKH are internal tensions between their traditions and the libertarian popular culture imported by southern Pakistanis and by tourists.

Prayers

In addition to congregations on the Friday sabbath, devout Sunni and Shia Muslims pray five times a day, in a mosque if possible. For Sunnis, prayers are at prescribed times: just before sunrise, just after high noon, late afternoon, just after sunset and before retiring. For Shias there are three fixed times – sunrise, noon and sunset – and the others are at one's discretion during the afternoon and the night. Ismailis consider prayer a personal matter and have no fixed times.

Just before fixed prayers a *muezzin* calls the faithful, traditionally from a high minaret, nowadays through a loudspeaker. The Arabic *azan*, or call to prayer, translates roughly as: 'God is most great. I swear there is no God but Allah. I swear that Mohammed is God's disciple. Come to prayer, come to security. God is most great.'

HOLIDAYS & FESTIVALS

National Holidays Banks and government offices may be closed in China or Pakistan (and the Chinese Embassy in Islamabad closes on Chinese national holidays). These are marked (•).

Holy Days In Islamic communities -- modern astronomy notwithstanding – *mullahs* or religious officials have formal authority to declare the beginning of each lunar month,

on the basis of sightings of the new moon's first crescent (this has its problems, as when Sunnis and Shias don't get the same moon reports). The Islamic lunar calendar begins about 10 days earlier each solar-calendar year, so future holidays can be estimated; but deference to the *mullahs* leaves them in doubt by a day or two until just beforehand. These holy days, observed in Pakistan and in a low-key way in Xinjiang, are marked (*) and are approximate dates only. They normally run from sunset to the next sunset.

There are also Chinese festivals in a very different lunar calendar. The only one you might notice in western Xinjiang is Spring Festival (Chinese New Year).

Seasonal Celebrations These are associated with planting, harvesting, annual migrations or local traditions. The most visible ones are noted here, marked (+); others are listed under Gojal, Hunza & Nagar, Gilgit, and Rawalpindi & Islamabad.

Weekly Holidays The Muslim sabbath is Friday; banks, businesses and government offices throughout the KKH region are closed, and Thursday or Saturday is often a half-day as well.

Major Holidays & Festivals

• 1 January (China)

New Year's Day. There are no festivities but banks, government offices and some shops are closed.

• Late January-Early March (China)

Spring Festival or Chinese (lunar) New Year. For Han Chinese this is the biggest holiday of the year and their only three-day break. There are no public events in Xinjiang other than some fireworks. Government offices (and the Chinese embassy in Islamabad) are closed.

+ Late February-Early March

First (Wheat) Ploughing or Sowing. Called *Taghun* in Gojal and *Bo Pho* in Hunza and Nagar, this is now only celebrated privately by a few farmers in the Northern Areas, usually with food and prayers in the field. Some plough in November-December and celebrate then.

+ 21 March

Nauroz ('New Days'), a spring festival and a Shia and Ismaili celebration of the succession of the

Prophet's son-in-law Ali. Polo matches may be held in Gilgit; in smaller Northern Areas villages there is lots of visiting, and sometimes music and dancing.

• 23 March (Pakistan)

Pakistan Day, celebrating the 1940 demand by the All-India Muslim League for an independent Muslim state.

* 30 March to 29 April (1990), 20 March to 19 April (1991)

Ramadan (also called *Ramazan* in Pakistan), the Muslim month of sunrise-to-sunset fasting. Non-Muslims, and Muslims who are travelling, are exempt; Ismailis generally don't take part. On the KKH, food and drink are hard to find during daylight between Rawalpindi and Gilgit. The best places for a foreigner are tourist hotels, Ismaili neighbourhoods in Gilgit, or anywhere in Gojal or Hunza (but not Nagar). Elsewhere most shops and restaurants are closed until sunset, and tempers are short.

April

Polo matches are common in Gilgit during April, but they may not be in 1990 and 1991 because of overlap with *Ramadan*.

* 29 April (1990), 19 April (1991)

Eid-ul-Fitr, celebrations marking the end of *Ramadan*. This is probably the closest thing to Christmas in the Muslim world, with family visits, gifts, banquets and donations to the poor. You'd be pretty happy too, if you'd just finished fasting for a month. Shops are usually closed for a day or two.

• 1 May (China & Pakistan)

International Labour Day. Banks and government offices are closed.

+ Late June-Early July

First (Wheat) Harvest. This is called *Chinir* in Gojal and *Ginani* or *Ganoni* in Hunza and Nagar, and is similar to First Sowing.

• 1 July (Pakistan)

Banks are closed but government offices and businesses are open.

* 5 July (1990), 25 June (1991)

Eid-ul-Azha, 'Feast of Sacrifice'. Those who can afford it buy and slaughter an animal, sharing the meat with family and with the poor. For the rich it's one-upmanship time. It's celebrated for two days by Shias and Sunnis, whose businesses may be closed. This is also the season for *hajj* (pilgrimage to Mecca).

* 5 August (1990), 26 July (1991)

Ashura, the 10th day of the month of *Muharram*.

Shias begin 40 days of mourning the death of Hussain at Karbala. In trance-like processions through Shia villages in the Northern Areas, sometimes led by a riderless white horse, men and boys pound their chests and chant the names of those killed at Karbala; some flail their backs with blade-tipped chains. It's a powerful, incomprehensible spectacle.

• 14 August (Pakistan)

Independence Day, the anniversary of the founding of Pakistan with the Partition of India in 1947. While banks and offices are closed, the real celebrations in the Northern Areas are on 1 November.

• 6 September (Pakistan)

Defence of Pakistan Day, commemorating the India-Pakistan War of 1965.

• 11 September (Pakistan)

Anniversary of the death of Mohammed Ali Jinnah, regarded as the founder of Pakistan.

* 24 September (1989), 14 September (1990), 4 September (1991)

Chehelum, 40 days after *Ashura*, with similar but smaller processions.

• 1 October (China)

National Day, celebrating the founding of the People's Republic of China in 1949, with pomp and ceremony elsewhere but, in Xinjiang, just a day or two off work.

* • 13 October (1989), 3 October (1990), 23 September (1991)

Eid-Milad-un-Nabi, the Prophet's birthday. In Pakistan, government offices, banks and some businesses are closed. In the Northern Areas the mountainsides are festooned at night with sawdust-&-kerosene fire-pots.

1 November

Northern Areas Independence Day or *Jashan-i-Gilgit* ('Gilgit Festival'), commemorating the 1947 uprising against the Maharajah of Kashmir when he decided to join India after Partition. The major event is a week-long polo tournament in Gilgit, starting on the 1st.

• 9 November (Pakistan)

Iqbal Day, honouring the poet Mohammed Iqbal, who in 1930 first proposed the idea of a Muslim Pakistan.

• 25 December (Pakistan)

Birthday of Mohammed Ali Jinnah, founder of Pakistan.

• 31 December (Pakistan)

Banks are closed but government offices and businesses are open.

Facts for the Visitor

VISAS, PERMITS & REGULATIONS

Bureaucrats: you can't live with 'em and you can't live without 'em. In Islamabad they're officious, suspicious and fond of implying that only they are keeping your plans from collapsing. In remote Pakistan they're unnervingly off-hand. In China they're just unpredictable.

There are isolated stories of hassles, mostly on arrival or departure. The moral in all of them has been: keep your papers in order and err on the side of caution. Here are a few tips.

(1) Get a visa before you get to the border; you can't enter China without one, and obtaining a Pakistan visa before you arrive will save a long paper-chase in Islamabad.

(2) Don't let anything expire, even by a day; it's just an excuse for impromptu 'regulations' and 'fees' you can't verify.

(3) Treat certain papers with reverence: entry-exit form, China customs declaration, Pakistan registration certificate and foreign exchange receipts.

(4) If you're staying more than 30 days in Pakistan, register with the police before the first 30 days are up.

Other important-looking cards and documents with seals, stamps, logos and plastic laminations may also come in handy. Smile through your clenched teeth as they shuffle, staple, stamp and sign.

China Visa

Everyone needs a visa to enter China, and you cannot get one at the border. Usual durations are one and three months from the date of *issue*; one-month extensions can be obtained in China. With the visa you can visit any 'open' city or region, and while in China you can get permits for some 'provisionally open' places.

Some visa offices ask for proof of onward or return travel, but they may back off if you tell them you're leaving over the Khunjerab Pass. All require one or two passport-size photos.

Where to Get It Visas can be obtained through the People's Republic of China Embassy or Consulate in your country, often by mail; for addresses see Embassies on page 31. However, policies vary wildly. In the US it can take weeks or months to get a visa good for a month, but it's dead easy to get a three-month visa in a few working days in Islamabad or Hong Kong.

In Islamabad go to the Chinese Embassy, where a three-month visa takes three working days and costs Rs 100.

In Hong Kong the cheapest source is directly from the Visa Office of the PRC Ministry of Foreign Affairs (tel 5-744083), China Resources Building, Wanchai; their entrance is on the west side just off Gloucester Rd. A three-month visa costs HK$50 and takes two working days.

Two Hong Kong agencies geared to independent travellers are in the Tsimshatsui area of Kowloon. They are Time Travel (16th floor, Block A, Chungking Mansions, 40 Nathan Rd, tel 3-666222, 3-7239993) and Phoenix Travel (6th floor, Milton Mansion, 96 Nathan Rd at Granville Rd, tel 3-7227378, 3-7233006). At Phoenix a three-month visa costs HK$80 and takes two working days; next-day and same-day service cost more.

You don't have to stick to the itinerary or entry/exit points you name in the application. Avoid listing big tourist cities (Beijing, Shanghai, Xian, Guilin) in big tourist months (May, August, September, October) and don't list Tibet.

Extensions Rules vary from year to year. You can get at least one one-month visa extension at the Foreign Affairs section of any Public Security Bureau office, for Y10 FEC. In Kashgar this office (called the Border & Administrative Office for Foreigners & Visitors) is on Shengli Lu.

Travel Permit Besides the hundreds of 'open' areas you can visit with just a visa, there are others you can go to by applying at Public Security Bureau offices for an 'Alien's Travel Permit'. Examples in the Kashgar area are Kara Kul Lake, Yarkand (Shache), Khotan (Hetian) and Kucha. Rules change all the time and PSB officers in remote areas don't always know what they are. If you have a place in mind, ask at every PSB office you see. Each permit is Y2 FEC.

Pakistan Visa
Everyone from European and English-speaking countries now needs a visa for Pakistan. The usual duration is three months from date of *entry*. Travellers who appear at the border with no visa may be given a free transit visa valid for 10 to 14 days. Extending this or any Pakistan visa involves a great convulsion of paperwork in Islamabad. In view of reported hassles, and rumblings

about new regulations, getting a visa in advance would be a very good idea.

The visa lets you go almost anywhere. Near the KKH there are a few permit-only areas such as the Misgar and Chapursan Valleys above Sust, and most places above 6000 metres.

Policies and prices are tit-for-tat, eg UK citizens pay huge fees in retaliation for the UK's stiff immigration laws, while Americans pay little or nothing in return for all those F-16s. All visas and extensions require two passport-size photos. Any demand for an onward ticket can usually be deflected by saying you're leaving over the Khunjerab Pass.

Where to Get It Visas can be obtained through the Pakistan Embassy or Consulate in your country, often by mail; for addresses see Embassies on page 31. You're slightly better off getting one at home, where you're more likely to get three months and avoid the headache of extensions.

Recently the Pakistan Consulate in Hong Kong was issuing visas only to Hong Kong

citizens. Travel agencies there might help; see the Getting There chapter for some. The closest alternatives are Bangkok and Beijing. In Beijing a one-month visa takes a few working days; it's free for Americans and Canadians, around Y10 for Australians and a whopping Y140 for UK citizens.

Foreigners' Registration Your visa is really just permission to *enter* Pakistan. When you arrive you get permission to stay, and after that permission to leave! This martial-law hangover keeps many civil servants employed.

On arrival immigration gives you an entry stamp and, if you're staying for more than 30 days, a paper called a Temporary Certificate of Registration, or 'Form C'. If you're staying for 30 days or less on an ordinary visa you just give Form C back when you leave, in exchange for an exit stamp.

If you stay more than 30 days you become a 'resident'. Before the 30 days are up you're supposed to register with the police. Most large towns have a Foreigners' Registration office. Bring two passport-size photos and Form C and they give you new papers: a Certificate of Registration and a Residential Permit. There's no fee.

In theory you turn everything in at your last town and get a pass which you show to immigration on departure. But in practice you can just save all the papers for immigration, and trade them for your exit stamp.

Travellers coming from China may not get Form C at Sust, but at if you leave the country at Islamabad or Karachi, immigration will want to see something, so you ought to register somewhere just to get the papers. On the KKH you can do it at Gilgit (the simplest), Abbottabad, Rawalpindi or Islamabad.

What if you don't bother? On my first trip I entered at Sust, got nothing and did nothing. At Karachi airport I wasn't allowed to leave the country until I wrote a letter on the spot, saying there'd been a big mistake and may I please be allowed to go.

If you're going to China they probably won't even ask for registration papers at Sust, although things may tighten up there with increasing tourist traffic.

Visa Extension or Replacement Islamabad is the only place to extend your visa or transit permit, or deal with an expired visa or lost papers (although if you're in Gilgit and time's running out the police might write a letter giving you a few extra days to get to Islamabad or the border).

Following are the steps in this paperchase. Allow at least a day. Bring two passport-size photos and the Temporary Certificate of Registration or Form C if you have one.

Fees vary with the diplomatic climate. Lately, extensions are free for Americans but several hundred rupees for Commonwealth citizens. There may be an extra Rs 20 charge to extend a transit permit. All decisions are at the officials' discretion.

Step 1: Your embassy might help, especially for lost or expired visas. Try to get a letter asking that your stay be extended.

Step 2: The Visa Section Office, Ministry of Interior, is in Room 605, Block R, Secretariat, Islamabad (Section Officer Mr M A Ashgar when I went). Ask for a letter recommending your visa be granted, and for how long.

They're open Sunday through Thursday; 9 am to 1 pm is best. From Rawalpindi a No 6 wagon on Haider Rd or a No 30 GTS bus at Adamjee Rd near Kashmir Rd goes to the Secretariat. From Aabpara take the No 6 wagon.

Step 3: The Regional Passport Office, Directorate of Immigration & Passports, is on Khyaban-i-Suhrawardy in Aabpara, next to the National Bank. Upstairs find the office of the Assistant Director (Mr Abdur Razzaq when I was there). With your letters and your fee you get a form saying your visa has been granted or extended.

Their hours are 8.30 am to 3 pm in summer (to 2 pm in winter), Sunday through Thursday. Take any inter-city bus.

Step 4: Go to the Foreigners' Registration office in the city where your hotel is. With the form from the Regional Passport Office, your Form C and two photos, they'll give you a Certificate of Registration and a Residence Permit. These are what you'll be asked for when you leave the country.

Crossing the Khunjerab Pass

The Khunjerab Pass is formally open to travellers from 1 May to 30 November (31 October for tour groups) but it may open later or close sooner on account of weather, and this is only decided at the last possible moment. Everybody sounds like they know when this will be but the *only* people who know are senior immigration or transportation officials near the border, and only within a week or so of the date. In both 1986 and 1987 it opened on time and closed early, by the middle of November.

During the winter the pass stays open for traders, officials and postal service. Pakistan immigration officials at Sust say off the record that they'd let you in or out at any time, but Chinese officials almost certainly wouldn't.

At least through late 1988, because of unfinished road-work between Kashgar and Tashkurghan, tour groups could cross only on the 1st, 2nd, 3rd, 16th, 17th and 18th of each month. There were no such limitations on individual travellers. Contrary to old rumours there is no such thing as a special permit to cross the Khunjerab Pass.

EMBASSIES

For foreign embassies in Pakistan see page 196.

Embassies & Consulates of the People's Republic of China

Australia & New Zealand

Embassy of the PRC, 247 Federal Highway, Watson, Canberra, ACT 2602, Australia (tel (062) 41 2448)

Canada

Embassy of the PRC, 511 St Patrick St, Ottawa K1N 5H3 (tel (613) 234-2706)

Hong Kong

Visa Office, PRC Ministry of Foreign Affairs, China Resources Building, Gloucester Rd (mail: 26 Harbour Rd), Wanchai (tel 5-744083)

Pakistan

Embassy of the PRC, Diplomatic Enclave, Ramna-4, Islamabad (tel 826667)

UK

Embassy of the PRC, 31 Portland Place, London W1N 3AH (tel (01) 636 1835)

USA

Embassy of the PRC, 2300 Connecticut Avenue NW, Washington, DC 20008

Embassies & Consulates of Pakistan

Australia & New Zealand

Embassy of Pakistan, 59 Franklin St, PO Box 198, Manuka, Canberra, ACT 2603, Australia (tel (062) 95 0021)

Canada

Embassy of Pakistan, 151 Slater St, Suite 608, Ottawa K1P 5H3 (tel (613) 238-7881)

China

Embassy of Pakistan, 1 Dongzhimenwai Dajie, Sanlitun Compound, Beijing (tel 522504, 522581, 522695)

Hong Kong

Consulate of Pakistan, Room 307-308, 3/F Asian House, 1 Hennessy Rd, Wanchai (tel (5) 274426)

UK

Embassy of Pakistan, 35-36 Lowndes Square, London SW1X 9JN (tel (01) 235 2044)

USA

Embassy of Pakistan, 2315 Massachusetts Avenue NW, Washington, DC 20008 (tel (202) 939-6200).

Consulate of Pakistan, 12 East 65th St, New York, NY (tel (212) 879-5800)

CUSTOMS & IMMIGRATION

Following are normal entry and exit formalities. For more on the KKH border post, see the Khunjerab chapter.

China

Arrival At immigration, fill out a health form and an entry-exit card; passports are inspected and stamped. China won't issue transit visas on the spot. At customs, fill out a form declaring money, cameras, radios and so on; you get a copy, which you must present on departure. Baggage inspection is usually cursory for foreigners but they like to see your high-tech stuff.

Departure At customs you turn in the declaration you filled out when you entered, and they may want to see those items again. You're not allowed to take out antiquities; purchase receipts can save arguments. At immigration, turn in the entry-exit card you got when you arrived, and get an exit stamp.

Pakistan

Arrival At immigration, fill out a health form and an entry-exit card. They give you an entry stamp and, at most ports of entry, a Temporary Certificate of Registration (Form C). If you don't have a visa they give you a transit permit free of charge, good for about two weeks. To stay longer you must get an extension in Islamabad.

At customs they ask if you're bringing in liquor (you're not supposed to). There are no other significant restrictions on what you can bring in, aside from firearms. One old regulation says you can't bring in more than one camera and five rolls of film, but it doesn't seem to be enforced any more.

If you arrive at Karachi and will fly on to Islamabad, get a few rupees after immigration: you'll have to pay a Rs 10 domestic departure tax.

Departure At customs, baggage inspection is usually cursory for foreigners. You're not allowed to export antiquities (if in doubt about something ask a museum curator or top-end tourist-hotel shopkeepers). Pakistan airport security may want to confiscate the batteries out of cameras, Walkmans, etc; save the hassle by putting them in checked baggage.

At immigration you present your entry-exit card, turn in your Form C (or if you stayed more than 30 days, your Certificate of Registration and Residential Permit) and get an exit stamp.

If you're flying out you'll need to pay the

departure tax – Rs 100 for tickets bought outside Pakistan, Rs 350 for those bought inside. Change the rest before immigration as there's no bank on the other side.

MONEY
Chinese Money

The formal unit of Chinese money is the *yuan* (Y), divided into 10 *jiao* or 100 *fen*. But when talking prices in Chinese, yuan is called *kuai* (*koi* in Uyghur), jiao is called *mao* (*mo* in Uyghur) and fen is still *fen* (pronounced 'fun').

There are two parallel currencies: *renminbi* (RMB) or people's money, and Foreign Exchange Certificates (FEC) or tourist money (*wai hui*, 'wye-hway' in Chinese). FEC is meant to be the basis for a separate visitors' economy, giving access to services and foreign goods normally off-limits to Chinese. But the distinction has faded and the dual system has become a black-marketeer's dream.

RMB comes in paper notes down to 1 fen and aluminium coins for 5, 2 and 1 fen. The tiny fen notes are hard to decipher; 5 fen is a green boat, 2 fen a blue aeroplane, 1 fen a yellow truck. FEC comes in notes only, down to 1 jiao.

In Kashgar, CITS and CAAC demand FEC. Hotels, restaurants and the bus station accept either, but at different rates reflecting current black-market values. In all non-tourist places RMB is the rule; many people in remote areas don't even know what FEC is.

It's not illegal for you to have RMB, only to get it on the black market. You often get RMB change when you tender FEC (a loss of purchasing power, and a good reason to avoid carrying big FEC notes).

Pakistani Money

The unit of Pakistani money is the *rupee* (Rs), divided into 100 *paisa*. Paper notes come in denominations down to Rs 1 and there are 50, 25 and 10 paisa coins. Try to avoid change in very worn or tattered notes as these may be refused later by others.

Top: Uyghur men at Id Kah Mosque, Kashgar (JK)
Bottom: 'Test driving' horses at the stock pens, Sunday Market, Kashgar (JK)

Top: Uyghur family near Id Kah Mosque, Kashgar (JK)
Left: Crowds going to the Sunday Market, Kashgar (JK)
Right: Roadworks in Ghez River Canyon between Kashgar and Tashkurghan (JK)

Foreign Exchange

In China you must go to the Bank of China; there's a branch in Kashgar. In Pakistan you can exchange at half a dozen domestic banks, the most competent being National Bank of Pakistan and Habib Bank. In Rawalpindi and Islamabad you can also go to the top-end hotels and to the offices of some foreign banks, including BCCI, Grindlays, Bank of America, Citibank and American Express.

What to Carry US dollar cash and travellers' cheques are by far the most widely accepted. In Kashgar and the Northern Areas, cash dollars are very welcome and can be exchanged unofficially when nothing else can, usually at elevated rates; as such they make good emergency money.

Banks accept travellers' cheques in most western currencies, and cash in some. US dollar and pounds sterling cheques are easiest to cash. American Express cheques are very familiar, though this familiarity has led to some fraud; now some Pakistani banks are uneasy about them. You're probably safe if you've got a bundle of them and the purchase receipt.

Rates Approximate exchange rates are as follows. Chinese rates are the same everywhere; Pakistani rates aren't.

US$1 = Y3.70 FEC = Rs 19
£1 = Y6.10 FEC = Rs 33
A$1 = Y2.70 FEC = Rs 17
C$1 = Y2.80 FEC = Rs 16

US$1 is *unofficially* equivalent to about Y4.80 RMB. For those entering or leaving Hong Kong, US$1 = HK$7.8 and £1 = HK$13.

Save your exchange receipts in China to avoid a scene at customs. Save them in Pakistan because they can be helpful when buying airline tickets and possibly reconverting rupees.

You can't officially trade yuan in Pakistan or rupees in China, though Bank of China at Pirali might give you RMB for rupees. At the China-Pakistan border you're normally given US dollars which you change again on the other side.

Reconversion When you leave China you can usually change both FEC and RMB back to hard currency, but you're supposed to show exchange receipts. At Pirali, before entering Pakistan, if you've got mostly FEC and less than about Y100 of RMB they'll exchange it all; no FEC or lots of RMB (especially without receipts) can cause problems. With receipts you can also reconvert at the Bank of China in Hong Kong.

Unspent rupees can be reconverted by

1 Yuan Foreign Exchange Certificate

1 Yuan Renmibi

authorised branch banks at customs and immigration facilities; few other banks in Pakistan will do it. Officially you're not allowed to sell back more than Rs 500 without permission from the State Bank of Pakistan, but I've done more without trouble. I've never been asked for exchange receipts, but it can't hurt to have them.

If you fly out of Islamabad or Karachi, reconvert before immigration as there's no bank on the other side. Save Rs 350 for international departure tax.

The Black Market

In China, because FEC gives access to foreign goods, people will offer their RMB at lopsided rates for your FEC, despite the risk of punishment. Aside from occasional threats to phase out FEC, the government has done little about the trade, probably because even high-level officials take part in it.

In Kashgar it's a Uyghur business, and they trade US dollars as well. Unfortunately some dealers have learned to cheat. For suggestions on avoiding rip-offs, see Kashgar – Information.

In Pakistan some shopkeepers will buy US dollars at slightly elevated rates, but for you it's more of a convenience than a way to boost spending power, and hardly deserves to be called a black market.

Getting Money from Home

The only places near the KKH where you're likely to succeed at this are Rawalpindi, Islamabad and Urumqi. Banks in Rawalpindi suggest you arrange a telex or telegraphic transfer of funds from your home bank. A simpler way is to have someone post a bank draft to you at a reliable address, such as your embassy.

If you have a major credit card you might be able to get cash or travellers' cheques with it at a western bank. One traveller who used his Master Card to buy travellers' cheques at Bank of America in Islamabad waited one day and paid US$15 for a telex to verify his card. Others say you can get up to Y3000 FEC with a card at Bank of China in Urumqi.

Along the KKH credit cards aren't of any other use except in a few shops and top-end hotels in Rawalpindi and Islamabad.

Tipping

If you're flush enough to give a tip, you'll find it expected in Islamabad (about 10%), appreciated in Rawalpindi, Abbottabad and Gilgit, and possibly returned in remoter areas, where it runs counter to the Muslim obligation to be hospitable. In rural China tips are unheard of.

COSTS

With modest self-control you can spend three weeks on the KKH for under US$10 a day; with some effort you can keep it to US$6. This includes a *total* ground transport cost (Kashgar to Rawalpindi) of about US$30, daily per-person accommodation (double rooms) of US$1.50 to US$2, and about US$2 each for food. It means staying in lower-cost hotels, eating local food, and travelling by bus. Rooms and food are lower in the north, much higher toward Rawalpindi.

Overland travel with no detours between Kashgar and Hong Kong adds about US$70 plus accommodation and food; by air, add about US$400. See the Getting There chapter for more on links to and from Kashgar.

You can push costs lower by staying in dorms or a tent, self-catering when you can, hitch-hiking, travelling overnight, or using the black market. Bargaining is appropriate in bazaars in both countries. It's useless in restaurants and Chinese hotels but sometimes works in bottom-end Pakistani hotels.

TOURIST INFORMATION
China International Travel Service

CITS is the government travel agency, responsible for looking after foreign tourists (mostly groups). They'll do piece-work such as booking flights and hotels, but always at tourist prices and usually with a service charge. They're generally less than thrilled about helping cost-conscious independent travellers.

Kashgar CITS rents jeeps, and their package trips are the only legal way to get to some remote areas. And the Uyghur staff there are friendly sources of local information.

Head Office
6 East Chang'an Avenue, Beijing (tel 75-7181)
Urumqi
People's Square, Urumqi (tel 25794)
Kashgar Branch
Chini Bagh Hotel

Overseas CITS offices are at:

Hong Kong
27-33 Nathan Rd, Tsimshatsui, Kowloon (tel 3-667201)
6th floor, Swire House, Chater Rd, Central (tel 5-250897)
UK
4 Glentworth St, London NW1 (tel (01) 935 9427)
USA
Suite 465, 60 East 42nd St, New York, NY 10165 (tel (212) 867-0271)

Pakistan Tourism Development Corporation

PTDC is the promotional arm of the Tourism Division, Pakistan Ministry of Culture, Sports & Tourism. Among other efforts, they operate a string of up-scale motels in the Northern Areas and maintain Tourist Information Centres in several towns, with brochures, advice and sometimes jeeps to hire. The Rawalpindi and Islamabad centres are useful only as sources for brochures but some of the regional ones are managed by helpful and intelligent people. PTDC's group-tour affiliate is Pakistan Tours Ltd (PTL).

Head Office
Hotel Metropole, Club Rd, Karachi-4 (tel 515593)
Islamabad Office
No 2, Street 61, F-7/4, Islamabad (tel 828814)
PTL
Flashman's Hotel, The Mall, Rawalpindi (tel 64811, 65449)

Tourist Information Centres near the KKH:

Rawalpindi
Flashman's Hotel, The Mall (tel 64811, 66231)
Islamabad
Tourism Division, College Rd, F-7/2
Taxila
PTDC Motel, opposite Taxila Museum
Abbottabad
Club Annexe, Jinnah Rd (tel 2446)
Besham
PTDC Motel (tel 92)
Balakot
PTDC Motel (tel 8)
Naran
PTDC Motel
Saidu Sharif
Swat Serena Hotel (tel 4215, 4604)
Gilgit
Chinar Inn, Babar Rd (tel 2454, 2562)
Skardu
K2 Motel (tel 104)

Overseas PTDC offices:

Canada
Suite 202, 2678 West Broadway, Vancouver, British Columbia V6K 2G3 (tel (604) 732-4686)
UK
Suite 433, 52-54 High Holborn, London WC1V 6RL (tel (01) 242 3131)
USA
Suite 508, 303 Fifth Avenue, New York, NY 10016 (tel (212) 889-5478)

TREKS & TOURS
Trekking in China

The only way to pre-arrange a short trek in China is with the 'help' of China International Travel Service (CITS), whose main aim is to make money from group tourists while keeping them on a short leash. Through any other official channel you'll just be told there are few places foreigners can go in Xinjiang, etc, etc. The Chinese Mountaineering Association, which handles expeditions, might be a source of some information.

The CITS head office is at 6 East Chang'an Avenue, Beijing (tel 75-7181); the Kashgar branch is at the Chini Bagh Hotel. The Chinese Mountaineering Association is at the All-China Sports Federation, Tiyu Guan Rd, Beijing. They also have a Kashgar office on Jiefang Nan Lu, with knowledgeable staff and a good but grossly overpriced map of the Muztagh Ata and Kara Kul area.

If you're keen to trek in the Chinese Pamirs the simplest way is probably just to go and improvise. For an example, see the Kara Kul section.

Trekking in Pakistan

Rules & Regulations The Pakistan Ministry of Culture, Sports & Tourism defines 'trekking' as foot-powered exploration of remote areas no higher than 6000 metres. The ministry's inventoried treks are in either 'open' or 'restricted zones'. In open zones need no permits and get no official support; routes and arrangements, and guides if you want them, are up to you.

Restricted zones include sensitive areas and anything above 6000 metres. Travel here is expensive and full of red tape; you need a ministry permit and a government-approved guide or liaison officer. Permit requirements include per-head fees, a detailed application, and briefing and debriefing sessions in Islamabad.

For a booklet with regulations and some trek suggestions, and for enquiries on permits, guides and current restricted zones contact Mr Taleh Mohammad, Assistant Chief for Operations, Tourism Division, College Rd, F-7/2 (in the central area of Jinnah Market), Islamabad (tel 827015).

Where To Go Along the KKH, open trekking zones are in *certain* parts of the following: Shimshal and the Batura *Muztagh* (the crest zone in Hunza-Gojal); Hopar, Hispar, the north side of Rakaposhi and Chalt-Chaprot (Nagar); Naltar, Ishkoman, Yasin, Bagrot and Haramosh (Gilgit area); across the Shandur Pass into Swat and Chitral; the Skardu area; Nanga Parbat; and the Kaghan Valley.

The small trips described in the regional chapters are in open zones. The popular big treks are described in the Tourism Division's booklet and in brochures from the Pakistan Tourism Development Corporation (PTDC), but a better source of ideas might be private

agencies listed here or local outfits identified in the regional chapters.

A reliable but slightly dated and not very detailed source of information on trekking in Hunza-Gojal is Hugh Swift's *The Trekker's Guide to the Himalaya & Karakoram* (London, Hodder & Stoughton, 1982); it has gone out of print but Sierra Club Books may print a new edition in 1989. A book by Gojal author Haqiqat Ali, *Trekker's Guide to Hunza*, is good for ideas but several experienced mountaineers claim some of his detailed routes may be unreliable.

Equipment It's best to bring your own. Trekking equipment is not manufactured in Pakistan, and the most you can hire or buy are the bits left behind by expeditions. Guides, agencies and a few shops in Gilgit and Skardu may have tents, pads, stoves and mountaineering gear. Sleeping bags are scarce.

Guides For short, low-risk treks the best bargain is probably a local shepherd with a little English, or a student home for the holidays, who may be content with under Rs 100 a day for trail-finding and possibly some carrying and cooking.

Agencies in Gilgit and Skardu have English-speaking guides with enough experience and reliability for modest treks, though they won't necessarily be from the area. Local freelance guides typically charge Rs 100 to Rs 150 a day for basic services (trail-finding, transport, accommodation, food and cooking) but can adapt to low-budget requirements. Most will gladly provide evidence of their experience. Some agencies and freelancers are mentioned in the regional chapters.

The best professional and government-accredited guides expect Rs 150 to Rs 300 a day, but tend to prefer big groups and long trips.

Trekking Alone Some people who've taken long treks alone don't recommend it. Villagers in remote areas can be suspicious of solo foreigners and may be tempted to take advantage of them. You may be driven mad by children demanding sweets, pens or money; some may even throw stones if you refuse.

Other Options Some agencies noted here offer packages for fishing trips, pony treks, jeep safaris or bicycle trips. A few can provide support for white-water boating; stretches open for rafting or kayaking include the Hunza from Aliabad to Gilgit, the Indus from Jaglot to Thakot, the Swat from Bahrain to Saidu Sharif and the Kunhar from Naran to Kaghan.

Agencies & Guides in Pakistan

The following outfits can help you with your own plans or sell you packages for KKH trips, special-interest tours and treks as long as two months. They're all expensive compared to local help, but are experienced and responsible. For some local agencies, see the Gilgit chapter – Trips Beyond Gilgit.

Adventure Pakistan (Travel Walji's Ltd) (tel 823963, 828324), 10 Khyaban-i-Suhrawardy, PO Box 1088, Islamabad . They also have an office on Babar Rd in Gilgit (tel 2663).
Himalaya Nature Tours (tel 822925, 828732), M/6 Dossul Arcade, 47 Blue Area, F-6, Islamabad.
Karakoram Tours (tel 829120), 1 Baltoro House, Street 19, F-7/2, Islamabad.
Nazir Sabir Expeditions (tel 853672), PO Box 1442, Islamabad.
Pakistan Tours Ltd (an affiliate of PTDC) (tel 64811), Flashmans Hotel, The Mall, Rawalpindi.
Qurban Ali, Mountain Guide, PO Box 519, Gilgit.
Sitara Travel Consultants (tel 66272, 64750), 25-26 Shalimar Plaza, PO Box 63, Rawalpindi.

Overseas Agencies

The following are some of the bigger overseas agents with packages for multi-week KKH trips, special-interest tours and treks in China or Pakistan. This is an expensive way to go.

Encounter Overland (tel (01) 370 6845), 267 Old Brompton Rd, London SW5, UK
Exodus Expeditions (tel (01) 870 4814), 100 Wandsworth High St, London SW18 4LE, UK
Hann Overland (tel (01) 834 7337), 268-270 Vauxhall Bridge Rd, Victoria, London SW1V 1EJ, UK
InnerAsia Expeditions (tel (800) 551-1769 or (415) 922-0448), 2627 Lombard St, San Francisco, CA 94123, USA
Karakoram Experience (tel (0533) 833903), 16 Parvian Rd, Leicester LE2 6TS, UK
Mountain Travel (tel (415) 527-8100), 1398 Solano Avenue, Albany, CA 94706, USA
SCT China Travel (tel (0223) 311103), 10 Rose Crescent, Cambridge CB2 3LL, UK
Voyages Jules Verne (tel (01) 486 8080), 10 Glentworth St, London NW1, UK
World Expeditions (tel (02) 264 3366), 377 Sussex St, Sydney, NSW 2000, Australia

GENERAL INFORMATION
Post

Receiving Mail International service is fairly dependable for letters to Kashgar, Gilgit, Rawalpindi and Islamabad, and to smaller towns if the address is well-known. Parcels – especially books or magazines – are less likely to make it.

Big-town GPOs will hold letters at poste restante for months. I picked up a postcard in Kashgar that had just missed me a year earlier, and the Kashgar GPO has even returned unclaimed mail. Kashgar charges 2 mao per letter; it's free elsewhere. American Express card (and travellers' cheque?) holders can have mail held at American Express in Rawalpindi or Islamabad.

In China where family names come first – and even in Pakistan – check under your given name too.

Sending Mail International service is good for letters and parcels from Kashgar, Gilgit, Rawalpindi and Islamabad. They're usually happy to frank letters on the spot, eliminating the possibility of stamp theft.

Except for printed matter, outgoing parcels generally must be sewn into cloth bags in both countries – a tedious job, though it probably helps them survive the trip. All require customs declaration forms and a postal inspection, so leave the bag open when you take it in.

Services & Rates - China You can buy stamps with RMB. Overseas airmail letters up to 10 grams are Y1.10 (except Y0.40 to Hong Kong). Airmail postcards are Y0.90 and aerogrammes are Y1. Parcels under one kg can go at low 'small packet' rates, up to Y10.80 for 1/2 kg to one kg by surface mail, plus Y0.20 per 10 grams for airmail. Rates for parcels over one kg depend on the country of destination. Registration is Y0.50 extra.

Services & Rates - Pakistan Overseas airmail letters up to 10 grams are Rs 6 to Europe and Rs 7 to America, Australia and New Zealand; airmail postcards are Rs 4 and Rs 4.30. Aerogrammes are Rs 5. The lowest parcel rate is for printed matter by surface mail, from Rs 15 for one kg to a maximum of Rs 55 for five kg; these must be left unsealed and marked 'book post'. Ordinary parcel rates are Rs 34.30 per kg for surface mail, plus Rs 12 per 1/4 kg for airmail.

Telephone & Telegraph

International calls can be made from government-run telephone exchanges and from top-end hotels in Kashgar, Gilgit, Abbottabad, Rawalpindi and Islamabad. The exchanges are usually open 24 hours a day. The connections can be surprisingly good; your biggest problem may be the man in the next booth screaming his lungs out down a domestic line.

Domestic calls can be placed from exchanges, most hotels and, in Pakistan, the PCOs (public call offices) in most towns.

Some Pakistani shopkeepers run unofficial PCOs. In the big cities of Pakistan, the enquiries number is 17.

Domestic and international telegrams can also be sent from the main exchanges.

Time

All China officially runs on Beijing time. But Kashgar, 3500 km away, runs on (unofficial) 'Xinjiang time', two hours earlier; visitors have to keep track of both. A single time-zone also covers all of Pakistan.

This would be easy enough except that in summer China (along with the US, Canada, Britain, Australia and New Zealand) sets its clocks ahead one hour, but Pakistan doesn't. Thus China and Pakistan are four hours apart from mid-May to mid-September, and three for the rest of the year. (Hong Kong doesn't set clocks ahead either, but soon may.)

The following table shows some standard – ie winter – time differences, with summer differences in parentheses.

The time in ... is this many hours earlier (–) or later (+) than the time in ...

	China	Xinjiang (official)	Pakistan (unofficial)
San Francisco	–16	–14	–13(–12)
New York	–13	–11	–10(–9)
Toronto	–13	–11	–10(–9)
London	–8	–6	–5(–4)
Islamabad	–3(–4)	–1(–2)	0
Beijing	0	+2	+3(+4)
Hong Kong	0(–1)	+2(+1)	+3
Sydney	+2	+4	+5(+6)
Wellington	+4	+6	+7(+8)

KARAKORAM 40

Rs.1.60 پاکستان PAKISTAN

SNOW LEOPARD Panthera uncia

PAKISTAN TOURISM CONVENTION 1987 پاکستان Rs.150

Each country switches to summer time on its own schedule, so in early spring and early autumn expect other one-hour differences to come and go.

Electricity

Electricity in both countries is 220 volts, 50 cycle AC; some hotels have 110-volt shaver outlets. On the KKH, lower Hunza, Nagar and most tributary valleys aren't yet 'electrified' except by generators; most other regions have hydroelectric ('hydel') stations in their side canyons. Gilgit's power supply is the flakiest.

Business Hours

In Pakistan nearly everything official is closed on Friday, the Muslim sabbath, and often for a half-day on Thursday or Saturday. In Xinjiang the Chinese-imposed day of rest is Sunday; a few offices may take a half-day off on Saturday. Business hours are variable and are listed under individual towns.

HEALTH
Immunisations

If you arrive from an area infected with cholera or yellow fever, both China and Pakistan require certification of immunisation; there are no other health requirements for tourists. For your own peace of mind you might consider shots or boosters for cholera, typhoid and tetanus-diphtheria. Doctors differ over the value of immune serum globulin (gamma globulin) against hepatitis-A.

If you're going through Hong Kong a convenient place for shots is the Port Health Office (tel 5-722056), Centre Point Building, 2nd floor, 181 Gloucester Rd, Wanchai – across the road from the China visa office.

Hospitals

There are hospitals at Kashgar, Karimabad, Gilgit, Abbottabad, Rawalpindi and Islamabad, and clinics in many smaller towns.

Medical Kit

A kit to solve most routine problems might include tweezers, scissors, antiseptic, plasters (band-aids), a few gauze pads, adhesive tape, moleskin (for foot blisters), elastic bandage (for sprains), aspirin, water-purification tablets (or iodine tincture bought locally), Lomotil (for diarrhoea) and malaria pills. Options include sunscreen, lip salve, bug repellent, foot powder, vitamins and a broad-spectrum antibiotic like tetracycline or penicillin. You can get Lomotil over the counter in Hong Kong.

Problems

Diarrhoea The most common problems on the KKH are diarrhoea and associated digestive-tract infections, including dysentery and giardia. A few days of simple diarrhoea is a normal reaction to jet-lag, stress or new foods; the main problem with it is dehydration. Eating bland foods and drinking lots of lightly salted water for a few days should take care of it. Lomotil or Imodium plugs you up but isn't a good long-term solution.

Drinking silt-laden glacier melt water, no matter how clean, can give you temporary runs too.

If diarrhoea lasts more than a few days or is bloody you may have amoebic dysentery, which needs proper treatment. If you have a fever too, you may have bacillary dysentery, which is treated quite differently. If diarrhoea is yellow and frothy and you feel bloated or burpy, you might have giardia, a common parasite in Pakistan.

Amoebic dysentery and giardia can be treated with metronidazole (Flagyl); avoid Enterovioform or Mexaform, which can have serious side-effects.

Hepatitis The risk on the KKH is hepatitis-A or infectious hepatitis, from contaminated water, food or utensils. Symptoms include fever, nausea, loss of appetite, fatigue, depression, very dark urine, yellowing of skin or eyes, sometimes liver pain (under the rib cage). The only treatment is healthy food and lots of rest, usually weeks of it, and no alcohol for even longer.

An unusual strain of hepatitis was epidemic around Kashgar in 1987 and many eating places were shut down for cleaning. Authorities claimed it was under control by mid-1988, but the need for caution is obvious.

Malaria Malaria is spread by infected mosquitoes; along the KKH you're at risk south of about Gilgit, in all but the coldest months. For strains found in Pakistan a weekly 500-mg tablet of chloroquine (common brands Nivaquine and Aralen) kill any parasites in your bloodstream. You must start it two weeks before entering a malarial area and keep it up for six weeks after leaving. Nivaquine is available over-the-counter in Hong Kong. Avoid Fansidar, used for chloroquine-resistant strains (there aren't any in Pakistan) which can have severe side-effects.

Mountain Sickness The low oxygen above about 3000 metres can cause headaches, dizziness, nausea and sleeplessness, especially if you're dehydrated or exerting yourself. Even the bus trip from Kashgar to the Khunjerab Pass, climbing to 4730 metres in two days, can bring it on. You're less likely to suffer if you drink plenty of water, eat high-energy snacks and avoid alcohol and cigarettes. Most people acclimatise after a few days.

If the symptoms appear when you are trekking at high altitude, do not ascend further. If symptoms worsen or there is no improvement after a few hours, then descend. Unwary trekkers have died by ignoring worsening symptoms and then continuing to higher altitudes, from where it is difficult to descend quickly.

Dehydration & Heat Exhaustion You breathe and sweat away body water very fast in the mountains as well as the desert. Dark urine and not much of it are signs you're dehydrated, though you may not feel very thirsty.

In the hot plains around Kashgar, if you're faint and sweaty and your pulse is very rapid you may have heat exhaustion. Rest in a cool place for at least a few hours and drink lots of water with salt in it. The next stage, with hot, dry skin and fever, is heatstroke, which is dangerous.

Precautions

Drinking Water Don't drink tap water. The best way to purify water is five to 10 minutes of boiling (more at high altitude). Boiled water is easy to find in Kashgar and eastward; thermos flasks are in every room and on every table. In Tashkurghan and in Pakistan it's not so easy.

You can stick to tea and name-brand soft drinks or carry your own water. If you can't boil it, iodine treatment kills bacteria, amoebae and giardia, and is safe for *short-term* use unless you're pregnant or have thyroid problems. The tidiest way is with tablets like *Potable-Aqua* or *Globaline*. The cheapest way is with tincture of iodine, which you can find in Pakistani pharmacies; use two drops per litre. With either, wait $1/2$ hour before drinking the treated water.

Chlorine treatment doesn't kill amoebae or giardia. Some pocket filters trap amoebae and giardia but none can stop a hepatitis virus, and after a while many clog up or breed their own bugs.

Sad to say, even glacier-fed mountain streams can carry giardia, unless you're right at the glacier's snout or above all possible grazing areas.

Utensils A good hepatitis defence is to carry your own utensils. Restaurant chopsticks ('hepsticks') may be the worst culprit; if you're stuck with nothing else, soak them in boiling hot tea. You can buy your own in Chinese department stores.

Food Common sense will keep you out of the grottiest places. Avoid raw vegetables and fruit you can't peel. Even the wonderful dried apricots of Hunza should at least be washed because of the way they're handled.

FOR WOMEN TRAVELLERS

Travel in Muslim Pakistan is hard work for women. Islam is a man's world, in which women are simultaneously subordinate and precious. A man keeps his wife and daughters out of sight (or at least out of reach) of other men – in the house, in the veil or shroud called *purdah*, in special sections of buses, in 'family' areas of restaurants.

Because most Muslim men are prohibited from what westerners think of as normal interactions with women outside the family, their view of 'other' women is mostly fantasy, stoked by films, magazines and pop culture. Western women tend to be regarded as vaguely cheap; at best they're ignored or patronised. Their questions are answered to male companions; when they're alone they're asked, 'Where is your husband?'.

Standing up for yourself can produce confusion, loss of attention or laughter, although refusal to eat in the family section or sit at the front of the bus is usually tolerated.

To make matters worse the sexuality suppressed in traditional culture is inflamed by films full of full-hipped women, guns and violence. Although even mild harassment is rare, it's possible anywhere. In Pakistan the least troublesome places are Ismaili areas and the big cities.

Wearing a local-style *shalwar qamiz* defuses things a bit. But it's an unfortunate fact that women are better off travelling with someone else, especially in newly-developed areas like Indus Kohistan.

Paradoxically, women travellers are more likely to get a look into people's private lives. Even in very traditional households women may ask other women in, feed them, show them around if there are no men about.

China, even Muslim Xinjiang, may be a relief in this respect. Chinese men are at least deferential. Uyghurs seem equally uninterested in men and women foreigners, except for their money.

CULTURAL CUES
Hospitality

In Islam, a guest – Muslim or not – has a position of honour not quite understood in the west. If someone visits you and you don't have much to offer, as a Christian you'd be urged to share what you have; as a Muslim you're urged to give it all away. Traditionally in Hunza, guests are seated higher than the head of the household. In several places I've been the only one eating in a room full of hungry-looking spectators.

In the Northern Areas this is a constant source of pleasure, some embarrassment, and temptation. Most people have little to offer *but* their hospitality, and a casual guest could drain a host's resources and never hear a word about it. If someone makes an offer of food, tea or a visit, and doesn't persist after you decline, then he probably can't afford to share much. On the other hand if he does persist, especially in his own home, you may be rude to decline!

Pulling out your own food or offering to pay someone for a kindness will probably humiliate him. All you can do is enjoy it, and take yourself courteously out of the picture before you become a burden.

In China, at least on the tourist trail, reflex generosity is rare. Uyghurs mainly ignore you in Kashgar. Han Chinese officials, attendants and drivers are generally beastly to everyone. This lack of warmth is probably what makes China travel so much harder to put up with.

Clothing

To a Muslim, shorts (even short sleeves) and tight clothing are roughly equivalent to walking around in your underwear: they look funny on men and are scandalous on women. In any event long, loose clothing is much more comfortable in a Punjab summer. For women a light scarf covering the head is appropriate in places like mosques or people's homes. Conservative western clothes are common in Islamabad.

Eating With Your Left Hand

The left hand is considered unclean, and handling food with it is revolting to most Muslims. It's an acquired skill to break off bits of chapatti with only the right hand and not everybody bothers, but no-one raises food to their mouth with the left hand. (Many westerners recoil at the thought of eating with either hand, but even the grottiest cafe has a washstand somewhere.)

Shaking Hands

With Pakistani men the handshake is as essential to conversation as eye contact or a smile in the west. Don't be offended if someone offers you his wrist; he just considers his hand unclean at the moment, for example if he has been eating with it. If he presents his left hand, you may have just been insulted.

If you try to shake hands with someone in China they may act as if you've just tried to kiss them.

DANGERS & ANNOYANCES

To people living on next to nothing the dollars and expensive baggage of foreign visitors can be too much to resist. The main problem for travellers on both sides of the border is petty theft, but most of it is avoidable with common sense.

In Kashgar the Chini Bagh Hotel swarms with Uyghur money-changers who'll push your door open and walk in if you let them, and the Seman Hotel attendants are not very good about locking doors. I've heard no stories of theft in Hunza or Gilgit, but a few about the villages around Nanga Parbat and Chilas and plenty about Darel and Tangir. A further Kashgar pitfall is getting fleeced by money-changers; for some tips on this see Kashgar – Information.

Sexual harassment of western women can occur in any sizeable town in Pakistan, including Gilgit, but almost never in the open. There are some obvious places to avoid if you're alone, like passenger Suzukis late at night. Shorts and cycling suits just raise Pakistani men's blood pressure. More serious are stories of assaults on women cyclists in northern Indus Kohistan; the entire region from Chilas to Thakot is a good place to keep a modest profile.

PHOTOGRAPHY

Customs

A Pakistan customs regulation says you can bring in only one camera and five rolls of film, but I've had no trouble with many more. Registering equipment with customs at home is not only proof against paying duty twice but gives you a piece of paper, full of government stamps and camera serial numbers, to wave around if trouble arises.

Restrictions & Etiquette

In China it's forbidden to photograph military sites, factories, airports, railway stations and bridges, and often there are people nearby who'll collar you and take your film. You're not supposed to take pictures from aeroplanes but I've never seen a CAAC hostess swoop down on anybody. The insides of museums and temples are often off-limits. Some older Chinese shy away from cameras but nearly everyone loves having their kids photographed.

Prohibited subjects in Pakistan are military sites, airports, major KKH bridges and, above all, women. To Muslims, especially in rural areas and even among Ismailis, it's an insult to photograph any woman older than a child. If a husband or brother is nearby it's risky as well. Women photographers may get lucky if they've established some rapport. Pakistani men, on the other hand, are irrepressible in front of a camera, and quick to ask you for a copy.

Hazards

Heat To avoid getting home and looking at 35 rolls of magenta photos of central Asia, keep film away from heat. If you buy one of those ultra-light 'survival blankets' – just a sheet of aluminised mylar – cut out a patch and line a stuff-sack with it. Film will stay cool inside through the fiercest summer day. Be careful where you buy film too; some shops proudly display their film in the window – and cook it.

Condensation If it's very cold outside you can avoid ruinous moisture on film and inside the camera by putting it in a plastic bag *before* going indoors and leaving it there till it's warm.

Dust Parts of the highway in China are a wallow of fine dust that gets into everything. Bag it all up; and a rubber squeeze-bulb is good for blowing dust from inside the camera.

Cold Camera batteries get sluggish in down-jacket weather. Keep the camera inside your coat and keep some spare batteries warm in your pocket.

X-Rays One dose of the x-rays for inspecting carry-on baggage won't harm slow or medium-speed films, but the effects are cumulative and too much of it will fog your pictures. I don't trust the machines at Chinese airports, and in Hong Kong the x-rays for *checked-in* baggage are notoriously strong. Lead 'film-safe' pouches help but the best solution is hand inspection. Officials hate you for it but in Pakistan and China they'll do it if you persist. Having all your film in one or two clear plastic bags makes it easier.

Film & Processing

Western-brand colour print film and processing are available in Rawalpindi, Islamabad, Gilgit and Kashgar. In Rawalpindi a 36-frame roll is about Rs 50; processing is about Rs 10 a roll plus Rs 3 a print. Going north, prices rise and reliability drops. Kashgar prices are 30% to 40% higher, and processing is still dicey there.

Colour slide film can be bought and processed in Rawalpindi and Islamabad, but it's three times as expensive as prints. There's little slide film elsewhere on the KKH. Kodachrome cannot be processed in China or Pakistan.

Black & white is cheap and common in China. It's rare and of doubtful quality in Pakistan, and processing costs more than for colour.

Mailing film from anywhere in China or Pakistan is asking for trouble. You can safely mail it from Hong Kong, or process it there. A Kodak centre is on Des Voeux Rd near Pedder St in Central (all done locally except Kodachrome, which goes to Australia and takes at least three weeks). A Hong Kong source of cheap, fresh film is Kwong Tai Photo Supplies on Stanley St near Pottinger St in Central.

ACCOMMODATION

Hotels are mostly state-run in China, mostly private in Pakistan, and with the growth of KKH tourism they now come in all cost and comfort ranges. Pakistan has other options too: government rest houses, a few youth hostels and campsites, railway retiring rooms (theoretically only for holders of 1st-class tickets) and the ultra-cheap travellers' stops called *serais* or *muzaffar khanas* ('resting places') where a rope-bed without privacy, security or bedding is just a few rupees.

There are some bottom-end places where foreigners can't stay because the owner (or the state) is too indifferent, embarrassed or proud to adjust to western demands. In Pakistan some save face (theirs and yours) by saying they have no 'Form D', the hotel-register form the government requires for keeping track of us.

Two areas beloved by middle-class Pakistani tourists – the Kaghan Valley and the hill-station towns of the Galis, north of Rawalpindi – get so crowded in summer that they're worth avoiding unless you have a booking or a tent. Off-season, on the other hand, they have some of the best hotel bargains in Pakistan.

Many 'hotels' in Pakistan are just eating-places. The *Jamil Hotel & Restaurant* in Sust and the *Rakaposhi View Hotel and Restaurant* in Ghulmet are food-tents!

Government Rest Houses

These include some of the best bargains on

the KKH. Also called Circuit Houses, Inspection Bungalows or Dak Bungalows (*dak* means a stage of travel), most are two or three-unit guest houses run by government agencies for staff on business. But they're available to tourists (at higher rates) if no-one else is using them. The best are in isolated, idyllic locations and each has a *chowkidar* (caretaker) living nearby who can also prepare meals by arrangement, at extra cost.

Most of the ones near the KKH are run by the Northern Areas Public Works Department (NAPWD), the North-West Frontier Province Communication & Works Department (C&W) or Forestry Districts. A booking is a good idea, just a chit from a regional office to show the *chowkidar*. Or you can drop by and take your chances; some *chowkidars* will let you in if there's room. The best rest houses and their booking offices are noted in the regional chapters.

Youth Hostels

The Pakistan Youth Hostels Association (PYHA) (tel 881501), 110-B/3, Gulberg-III, Lahore, runs several hostels near the southern KKH. Most have 20 to 50 gender-segregated beds, and yards where you can pitch a tent. They serve no meals but have cooking facilities.

Fees are Rs 15 per bed plus charges for bedding, bikes and so on. You're supposed to be a member of PYHA or the International Youth Hostel Association (IYHA) and you may not be able to join on arrival at a hostel. Booking isn't essential but it might help in the high-use summer months; call PYHA or inquire with PTDC. At least some are open only in the tourist season.

There are hostels in the Kaghan Valley (Balakot, Sharan, Naran and Battakundi), Abbottabad (Mandian), the Galis (Bhurban and Khanaspur) and Taxila (close to the museum). There are said to be others at Thandiani (the hill station area near Abbottabad) and Rawalpindi (near Ayub Park) but I couldn't find them.

Camping

In Xinjiang you can't pitch a tent with any security around larger towns but with a travel permit you can camp at places like Kara Kul and below Muztagh Ata.

In Pakistan you can camp all over the place. Hotels will often let you pitch a tent in their yards or on the roof and use their toilets for a small fee. In Hunza and Gilgit there are private tent-sites and an up-scale one run by PTDC. You can even camp in Islamabad, at Aabpara's super-cheap Tourist Campsite.

Vandalism is not a problem in tent-sites or on most trekking routes but don't leave things loose near villages in the Nanga Parbat and Chilas area, or anywhere in Indus Kohistan.

Booking Ahead

Booking a few days ahead can be useful at government rest houses or hostels but KKH travel is too unpredictable for long-range plans. Most middle and bottom-end hotels don't even take bookings and even an arrangement in writing is apt to get screwed up.

FOOD

Food on the KKH is as varied as its ethnic groups. Eating can be a pleasure in Kashgar, Hunza and Rawalpindi. In Gilgit it's dreary, and in Indus Kohistan you won't go hungry but you may go mad from non-stop curried mutton and chapatti. Local specialities are described in the regional chapters.

Vegetarians can get by in big-town produce markets, Kashgar's Chinese restaurants, Hunza and Gilgit cafes and most places in Rawalpindi-Islamabad. Some hotels will stir something up for you, especially if you buy the ingredients.

In Pakistan Tuesday and Wednesday are 'meatless' days, when mutton and beef are not sold at market (the reasons are economic, not religious). Restaurants mostly have chicken then.

In bigger towns the cook may sometimes add a side dish you don't remember ordering.

It's partly goodwill but of course you'll have to pay for it!

In 1987 and 1988 an unusual strain of hepatitis was epidemic in western Xinjiang, and in Pakistan gut infections are common with foreign travellers. See the Health section for hygiene suggestions.

Alcohol

In Kashgar, Chinese beer, wine, brandy and spirits are available in Chinese restaurants and big department stores, although Muslim Uyghurs rarely drink (in public).

Pakistan is officially dry but non-Muslim foreigners can drink in special lounges at top-end hotels in Rawalpindi and Islamabad. You can get a liquor permit, as long-term residents do, but elsewhere on the KKH there isn't much liquor to get with it.

In Hunza some people still brew *mel*, a coarse grape wine, and a powerful mulberry brandy called *arak*. This so-called 'Hunza water' may be offered to you by friends or hustlers.

Ramadan

Ramadan is the Muslim month of sunrise-to-sunset fasting. Non-Muslims, and Muslims who are travelling, are exempt; Ismailis generally don't take part. On the KKH, most restaurants and food shops from Rawalpindi to Gilgit are closed until sunset. The best places to find food and drink are tourist hotels, railway or bus stations, and anywhere in Gojal or Hunza (but not Nagar).

BOOKS

If you can't find these at home, many are available as reprints in Pakistan bookshops.

Guidebooks

Other Lonely Planet guidebooks with some information on Pakistan's Northern Areas and western Xinjiang, and lots on the rest of Pakistan and China, are *Pakistan - a travel survival kit* and *China - a travel survival kit.*

Ali, Haqiqat, *Trekker's Guide to Hunza* (Ferozsons, Rawalpindi, 1987). Introduction to Hunza and Gojal treks by a Passu guide, with Burushaski and Wakhi glossaries and good advice on cultural awareness. Several experienced mountaineers say some route descriptions may be unreliable.

Shaw, Isobel, *An Illustrated Guide to Pakistan* (Collins, London, 1988). A compact guide to Pakistan by a knowledgeable ex-expatriate who's obviously fond of the place. It's especially good on Rawalpindi-Islamabad and Hazara.

Shaw, Isobel, *The Pakistan Handbook* (Century, London, 1989). An encyclopedic version of *An Illustrated Guide to Pakistan*, with information on Northern Areas treks.

Swift, Hugh, *The Trekker's Guide to the Himalaya and Karakoram* (Hodder & Stoughton, London, 1982, now out of print but Sierra Club Books may put out a new edition in 1989). A concise and practical trekker's handbook, including a good medical appendix and glossaries of Chitrali, Burushaski, Balti and Urdu words. It's somewhat general and out of date on Hunza-Gojal.

Health

Schroeder, Dirk, *Staying Healthy in Asia, Africa, & Latin America* (Volunteers in Asia Press, Stanford, 1988). The perfect take-along medical handbook – small and easy to use, covering prevention, basic first-aid, and advice on just about anything you might catch. If you can't find it write to Volunteers in Asia, PO Box 4543, Stanford, California 94305, USA.

History & Culture

Danziger, Nick, *Danziger's Travels* (Paladin, London, 1988). An account of the attempt to follow the Silk Road, from Turkey through China. It includes chapters on Xinjiang and Pakistan's Northern Areas, and describes the author's desperate attempts to get a visa to cross the Khunjerab Pass, before the highway was open to international traffic.

Dupree, Nancy Hatch, *Gandhara; An Instant Guide to Pakistan's Heritage*. Just a PTDC pamphlet on the history of the Taxila area but a cut above anything else they've got; available from PTDC in Rawalpindi or Islamabad.

Fa-Hsien, *A Record of Buddhistic Kingdoms* (Clarendon Press, Oxford, 1886; reprint by Lok Virsa, Islamabad, no date). The Buddhist monk's own account of his 5th-century pilgrimage across Xinjiang, the Karakoram, Indus Kohistan, the Taxila Valley and on to India; available in some Rawalpindi-Islamabad bookshops.

Fairley, Jean, *The Lion River: The Indus* (John Day, New York, 1975). A detailed and elegant book about the Indus River and the people along it, from Tibet to the Arabian Sea.

Keay, John, *The Gilgit Game* (John Murray, London, 1979). A very readable account of the explorers and oddballs who played in the 'Great Game', the imperial rivalry between Britain and Russia across the Pamirs, Hindu Kush and Karakoram in the late 1800s.

Keay, John, *When Men & Mountains Meet* (John Murray, London, 1977). The predecessor to The Gilgit Game, with gripping and often hilarious stories of the Europeans who penetrated the western Himalaya in the early 1800s.

Knight, E F, *Where Three Empires Meet* (London, 1894). Travels of a Victorian journalist in Kashmir, Ladakh and the Northern Areas, including an exciting but lopsidedly British-colonial version of the 1891 'campaign' in Hunza.

Murphy, Dervla, *Full Tilt* (John Murray, London, 1965). The first quest of the now-legendary eccentric Irish traveller: a solo bicycle journey from Ireland to India, including Afghanistan and the Northern Areas. Hair-raising adventures described in a matter-of-fact, almost deadpan, tone.

Murphy, Dervla, *Where the Indus is Young* (Century, London, 1977). Her account of a winter spent with her young daughter in Baltistan.

Schomberg, Colonel R C F, *Between the Oxus & the Indus* (London, 1935; reprint Lahore, no date). Detailed chronicles of 19th-century Gilgit and Hunza by an acidic and opinionated British officer who found the landscapes nobler than the people.

Staley, John, *Words For My Brother* (Oxford University Press, Karachi, 1982). The culture, politics, religious traditions and recent history of pre-KKH Chitral, Kohistan, Gilgit and Hunza. Staley and his wife studied and travelled here in the 1960s. This scholarly but affectionate book is my favourite on the Northern Areas.

Stein, Sir Aurel, *On Alexander's Track to the Indus* (Macmillan, London, 1929). Stein, a Hungarian-English archaeologist renowned for his central Asian expeditions between 1900 and the 1940s, was the first westerner into some parts of Kohistan. He also traced the footsteps of earlier travellers including Alexander the Great and the pilgrim Fa-Hsien.

Younghusband, Sir Francis, *The Heart of a Continent* (John Murray, London, 1896; reprint by Oxford University Press, Hong Kong, 1984). The adventures in Kashgar and the Karakoram of one of Britain's foremost players in the Great Game.

Petroglyphs

Dani, Dr Ahmad Hasan, *Human Records on Karakorum Highway* (Islamabad, 1983). A paperback guide to rock inscriptions along the KKH from Mansehra to the Khunjerab Pass, by a Pakistani researcher who has translated many of them; available in Pakistan bookshops.

Jettmar, Dr Karl, *Rockcarvings & Inscriptions in the Northern Areas of Pakistan* (Lok Virsa, Islamabad, 1984). By a German colleague of Dani, it's stuffy but illuminating; available in Pakistan bookshops.

Fiction

Kipling, Rudyard, *Kim* (Macmillan, London, 1899). The master storyteller's classic epic of India during the Great Game.

Geology & Geography

Mason, Kenneth, *Abode of Snow* (Dutton, New York, 1955). Mason was a well-known Himalayan explorer. Chapter 3 introduces the geography of the Karakoram.

Miller, Keith, ed, *Proceedings of the International Karakorum Project* (two volumes) (Royal Geographical Society, London, 1984). Staggering detail on the Karakoram's geology and geography and their overlap with disciplines as diverse as architecture and cultural anthropology; based on an expedition in 1980 and later studies.

Miller, Russell, *Continents in Collision* (Time-Life Books, New York, 1983). An illustrated laymen's introduction to plate tectonics and the birth of the Himalaya.

Islam

Guillaume, Alfred, *Islam* (Penguin, New York, 1956). Dry as dust but dense with information on history, doctrine and practice.

MAPS
Contour Maps

The best for detail are the US Army Map Service U-502 series at 1:250,000 (2½ km per cm). They're black & white copies of colour maps last revised in 1962 so they don't show the KKH and other roads. Along the KKH, only Pakistan sheets seem to be available: NI 43-1 (Churrai, covers northern Indus Kohistan), NI 43-2 (Gilgit), NI 43-3 (Mundik, covers Skardu), NJ 43-14 (Baltit,

covers Hunza and Gojal) and NJ 43-15 (Shimshal, covers the Khunjerab area). Sources include:

US Library of Congress, Geography & Map Division, Washington, DC 20540, USA. U-502 sheets are about US$8 each plus postage. You can order by mail; write for an index.

Edward Stanford Ltd International Map Centre, 12-14 Long Acre, Covent Garden, London WC2E 9LP, England, tel (01) 836 1321. Maps can be ordered by mail or with a major credit-card number. U-502 sheets are £5 each. They can send a description and grids of their India, Pakistan, Nepal and Himalaya maps.

The Survey of Pakistan has coloured topographic maps at 1:1,000,000 (10 km per cm). Two of them cover the KKH: NI-43 (Kashmir) and NJ-43 (The Pamirs). These are £5 per sheet from Stanford's. Two capital-area bookshops that might have them, for about Rs 60 per sheet, are London Book Company (tel 823852, Kohsar Market, north-east sector F-6, Islamabad) and the Book Centre (tel 65234, Saddar Rd in Saddar Bazaar, Rawalpindi).

An alternative is the coloured ONC aeronautical chart series at 1:1,000,000. Two maps cover the KKH: ONC G-6 and ONC G-7, but precision is lower and many place-names are obsolete. They're £6 per sheet from Stanford's.

Large universities often have map libraries where you can order photocopies (in person, not by mail), eg Doe Library at the University of California, Berkeley, USA.

Regional Maps

The most gorgeous of all are finely-detailed three-colour contour maps, at 1:50,000 (500 metres per cm), of the north slopes of Rakaposhi (Minapin) and Nanga Parbat, by Deutscher Alpenverein (DAV), £7.50 each from Stanford's. Survey of Pakistan has 1:500,000 contour maps of Hunza (NJ-43/SW), £5 from Stanford's, and of the China-Pakistan border, £2.50 from Stanford's.

PTDC has brochures on the KKH and the Silk Road, the Northern Areas, Trekking,

Hunza, the Gilgit Valley, Skardu, Swat, the Kaghan Valley and Taxila, but the tiny maps are of little use for finding your way around.

The China Mountaineering Association (Jiefang Nan Lu, Kashgar) has an excellent map of roads and villages near Muztagh Ata, Kara Kul and Mt Kongur, seriously overpriced at Y30.

City Maps

PTDC's tourist map of Rawalpindi and Islamabad, for sale at the Tourist Information Centres in both cities, is good for Islamabad but not much help in Rawalpindi. There's no PTDC map of Gilgit.

The Survey of Pakistan's *Islamabad & Rawalpindi Guide Map* at 1:30,000 (300 metres per cm) is quite detailed, although many street names are out of date. It's Rs 20 at the London Book Company, the Book Centre or other shops in the capital area.

CITS has a rough Kashgar map but it's so old even the location of CITS is wrong (as well as Public Security, Bank of China and others).

Other Maps

The Capital Development Authority in Islamabad has a good map-brochure, *Trekking in the Margalla Hills*, showing walks and rest houses in the hills behind Islamabad. PTDC might have it, or go to CDA on Khyaban-i-Suhrawardy (south G-7, west of Aabpara) and ask for the Public Relations Office, room 31.

WHAT TO BRING

Of course, bring as little as you can; get it to the bare minimum and then cut it in half. You can pick up many items en route, in Kashgar, Gilgit or Rawalpindi.

Pack An internal-frame or soft pack takes less of a beating on buses; a 'convertible' (with a suitcase-type handle and a flap to hide the straps) looks respectable when you need to.

Clothing For the range of KKH conditions

and the potential for cold-weather exertion, many light layers work better than a few heavy ones. On the China-Pakistan bus you'll need your warmest clothing in any season. Rain can strike in Pakistan at any time but especially July and August.

Shorts (and even short sleeves) on women are very offensive to conservative Muslims. This is a problem in summer, but the solution is long, loose, light shirts, trousers or skirts. The locally-worn baggy trousers and long shirt (*shalwar qamiz*) are very comfortable, and can be made cheaply in the bazaars of Karimabad, Gilgit, Abbottabad or Rawalpindi. Women might also take a light scarf to cover their heads in places like mosques or people's homes. In big cities conservative western dress is common.

Shoes Light walking shoes are adequate for all but long or snowy treks. You could get away with gym shoes except at monsoon time.

Camping Gear For one-off trips you can find tents, pads and cooking equipment in Gilgit. Sleeping bags are hard to find along the KKH.

Gifts Some easy-to-carry, well-received gifts are postcards and flower and vegetable seeds from home.

Other Besides the usual take-alongs, good KKH ideas are eating utensils, water bottle, sunglasses, sunscreen, lip salve, a light day-pack, thermal long-johns, plastic bags, compass. You can buy tampax in Hong Kong. For a suggested medical kit see page 39, and for photography pre-requisites see page 42.

Half a dozen passport-size photos will save you trouble in case of paperwork, though it's possible to get them en route. A lightweight aluminised-mylar 'space blanket' is good for emergency warmth, though it's a poor sleeping bag as perspiration turns it wet inside.

Things You Can Find in Kashgar, Gilgit & Rawalpindi Books and magazines (not Kashgar), toilet paper, instant coffee, candles and matches, batteries (but not as good as those in Hong Kong or at home), laundry soap, old-style razor blades, shampoo, aspirin.

Getting There

The northern end of the KKH is at Kashgar in China's Xinjiang Autonomous Region, accessible from outside Asia by air or by rail plus bus through China, most likely via Hong Kong. Its official southern end is at Havelian in Pakistan's North-West Frontier Province, but for practical purposes it's at Islamabad, the capital. Islamabad and its sister-city Rawalpindi are within easy reach of international air routes, most via Karachi, and by rail from southern Pakistan. There are limited overland connections from India and Iran.

Flying Cheaply

Discounted fares of all kinds – excursion, APEX, round-the-world and others – are available from travel agencies and student travel services (where non-students can do almost as well). Even among discounters the range is very wide, so shop around. Some reputable big-city agencies are:

Australia Flight Centre, 50 offices across Australia; tel (03) 663 1304 (Melbourne), tel (02) 235 3166 (Sydney).
STA (Student Travel Australia) with offices in all state capitals; tel (03) 347 6911 (Melbourne), tel (02) 212 1255 (Sydney).
Canada CUTS (Canadian Universities Travel Service), 24 offices across Canada; tel (800 toll free) 972-4004 (BC), 272-5615 (Alberta), 667-1141 (Sask), 268-9044 (South Ontario).
UK Student Travel Association (tel (01) 581 1022), 74 Old Brompton Rd, London W7.
Trailfinders (tel (01) 938 3366), 42-48 Earls Court Rd, London W8.
USA Student Travel Network, nine offices across the USA; tel (213) 934 8722 (Los Angeles), tel (415) 391 8407 (San Francisco), tel (212) 486 9470 (New York).

On the US coasts, Sunday-paper travel sections have classified ads for discount agencies. In London, discount travel is big business, with hundreds of 'bucket shops' advertising in the *Sunday Times* travel section or the 'What's On' section of *Time Out* magazine. You're probably safest if they're licensed by the International Air Transport Association (IATA) or a national association.

Unless you get an odd bargain it's cheaper (though more time-consuming) to book only to Hong Kong or Karachi and make the rest of your arrangements from there.

Prices here are approximate, low-season, discounted economy fares. Because the KKH can make a mockery of schedules and because tickets are cheap in Asia, one-way fares are given. Fares to Hong Kong are 20% to 30% higher in high travel season (July, August and September in North America and Europe, January and December in Australia and New Zealand); fares to Pakistan are not very seasonal.

Kashgar

TO KASHGAR
Air

The choice of carriers and the ease of getting China visas makes Hong Kong the sensible first stop. Cheap fares to Hong Kong are around £300 from London, US$350 from San Francisco, A$610 from Sydney, and C$560 from Vancouver.

Several carriers link Hong Kong to Guangzhou (Canton), Beijing or Shanghai, from where you can fly to Kashgar via Urumqi on CAAC, China's national airline. But flying across the border is very expensive compared to the same distance inside China; you can pay domestic fares and avoid the HK$100 airport departure tax by taking an overnight boat, morning hoverferry or fast train to Guangzhou and flying from there the same day.

From Hong Kong the lowest fares into

China are on CAAC (called CNAC in Hong Kong). Because they give no discounts to travel agents the cheapest tickets are probably direct from the CNAC ticket office (tel 5-8401199) at 17 Queens Rd, Central. The Chinese name for Kashgar is *Kashi*.

The PRC government-run China International Travel Service (CITS) can make arrangements at higher prices; their Kowloon office (tel 3-667201) is at 27-33 Nathan Rd in Tsimshatsui, and their Central-District office (tel 5-250897) is on the 6th floor of Swire House at Chater Rd and Pedder St.

Hong Kong to Guangzhou on CAAC is HK$300, Guangzhou to Urumqi about HK$1900 and Urumqi to Kashgar HK$800 (Y378 FEC). The frequency of flights depends on the season and your connecting city, from daily in summer to weekly via Guangzhou in winter.

Overland

The marathon land journey from Hong Kong to Kashgar is by rail to Urumqi (4900 km, 4¹/2 days) and by bus from there, parallel to the old Silk Road along the northern edge of the Takla Makan desert (1480 km, 3¹/2 days). Few people in their right minds would do the whole thing at once, considering not only comfort but all there is to see en route.

The train from Hong Kong to Guangzhou is about HK$40 (local) or HK$170 (express). From Guangzhou to Urumqi by 'hard sleeper' (the minimum comfortable class for multi-day trips) is about Y200 FEC; you may be able to get 'Chinese price' of about Y120 RMB if you can get local or overseas Chinese to buy your tickets.

The daily bus from Urumqi to Kashgar is Y38.30 RMB; buy your ticket at Urumqi's long-distance bus station no sooner than three days in advance (and no later for a good seat). There is said to be a bus from Turfan too. En route you can get off at Korla, Kucha (with a travel permit) or Aksu, but you might wait days before another bus comes through with an empty seat. Baggage goes on the roof and may be inaccessible for the whole trip,

so plan your carry-ons. The bus makes meal-stops but, except for lots of delicious Hami melons, the food is very basic.

In 1992 a rail line is expected to be finished between Urumqi and Alma Ata in Soviet Kazakhstan, raising hopes for a new long-distance overland link from the USSR.

FROM KASHGAR
Air

You can only fly to Urumqi, in a creaking Russian Tupolev-154, for Y378 FEC. In summer there's a flight every day, in winter three a week. For bookings and airport transport see under Kashgar. From Urumqi there are connections to most big cities of China, and to Hong Kong via Beijing, Shanghai or Guangzhou. Urumqi-Guangzhou is Y900 FEC, Guangzhou-Hong Kong Y140 FEC.

Buying Airline Tickets in Hong Kong

Hong Kong is a good place for cheap airfares, but a good place to get ripped off too. Three reliable travel agencies geared to independent travellers are in the Tsimshatsui area of Kowloon:

Phoenix Travel (tel 3-7227378), 6th floor, Milton Mansion, 96 Nathan Rd (at Granville Rd).
Time Travel (tel 3-666222, 3-7239993), 16th floor, Block A, Chungking Mansions, 40 Nathan Rd.
Hong Kong Student Travel Bureau (tel 3-7213269), 10th floor, Star House (by the Star Ferry from Central).

Fares out of Hong Kong are volatile, but here's a rough idea: Karachi HK$2550, Sydney HK$3150, London HK$2900, San Francisco HK$3200, New York HK$3500. When you leave you'll need HK$100 cash departure tax.

Overland

From Kashgar it's three to 3¹/2 days in a bus to Turfan (1330 km) or Urumqi (1480 km) and onward by train (4¹/2 days and 4900 km if you go to Hong Kong). See Kashgar – Getting There & Away for booking and schedule information to Turfan and Urumqi.

You can get off at Korla, Kucha (with a travel permit) or Aksu, but you might have to wait days for another bus with an empty seat.

The long rail journey from Urumqi to Guangzhou is about Y200 FEC tourist price or about Y120 RMB Chinese price, for a 'hard sleeper' berth. If you want to visit Turfan, do it first and then go to Urumqi; even if you have no interest in Urumqi, the chances of getting a hard sleeper are much better at the beginning of the line.

If you're headed for Hong Kong, you can go through customs and immigration at Guangzhou station and get a non-stop train (about Y80 FEC), or take a cheap local train to the border at Shenzhen. An appealing alternative is an overnight boat down the Pearl River from Guangzhou's Zhoutouzi Wharf (*Zhoutouzi Matou*, 'jo-toh-dzih mah-to'), about Y60 FEC for a dormitory berth.

Islamabad

TO ISLAMABAD
Air
Some airlines serve Islamabad directly but most go to Karachi, from where you hop to Islamabad on Pakistan International Airlines (PIA), the national carrier. Going via Karachi is cheaper because there are more ways to get there and because domestic tickets cost about 30% less if you buy them in Pakistan. There are five to eight Karachi-Islamabad flights a day including cheap red-eye specials on most nights.

Approximate low-season one-way fares to Karachi are: £200 from London, US$700 from San Francisco, US$500 from New York, A$770 from Sydney and C$880 from Vancouver. Karachi to Islamabad is about Rs 1000 (night coach) to Rs 1300.

Train
A rail crossing from Iran at Nokkundi in the far west of Baluchistan province has been closed since the overthrow of the Shah. Although you cannot leave Pakistan by train, you can come in this way, from Delhi to Lahore.

But you can reach the KKH from all over Pakistan. Most trains to the capital area go to Rawalpindi; for information on some connections and fares see the following From Islamabad section. A spur of the Rawalpindi-Peshawar line goes to Havelian, the official southern end of the KKH.

Overland
Depending on the political situation in the Indian Punjab you may be able to take a bus from Delhi to Lahore, in a convoy with military escort, three days in each month. There is no other way to cross overland from India.

FROM ISLAMABAD
Air
There are some international departures from Islamabad but most go from Karachi. Fares via Karachi tend to be lower, and it's easy to get there on PIA, especially their cheap night coaches.

India-bound travellers can go to Delhi from Lahore (the cheapest route, Rs 715 plus departure tax), and to Bombay from Karachi, with PIA or Air India. Book early; flights to Delhi can fill up weeks ahead. You can't get a ticket unless you have an Indian visa (for this see Rawalpindi & Islamabad – Visas, Permits & Paperwork).

Buying Airline Tickets in Rawalpindi & Islamabad The airlines have booking offices in Islamabad's Blue Area, on The Mall in Rawalpindi and in top-end hotels, but these are expensive places to buy tickets. Travel agents get their tickets at around 9% discount and can pass most of that on to you if you ask.

Travel agents are thick as flies in Rawalpindi's Saddar Bazaar and Islamabad's Blue Area. Some offer great deals and tell you later about their 'commission'. You have a better chance of an honest deal if they belong to IATA; look for the sticker in the window. Some good ones are:

Shakil Express, north side of Haider Rd between Canning & Kashmir Rds, Saddar, Rawalpindi (the oldest agency in Pakistan).
Rohtas Travel Consultants (tel 63224, 66434), 60 Canning Rd between Bank and Adamjee Rds, Saddar, Rawalpindi.
Travel Walji's Ltd (tel 823963, 828324), 10 Khyaban-i-Suhrawardy, Aabpara, Islamabad.

You can do even better with PIA flights (except to the Northern Areas). General Sales Agents (GSAs) deal exclusively with one airline and get discounts of around 12%, but these are a greedier lot. Some reliable PIA GSAs in Saddar Bazaar are Green Hill Travel (south-east corner of Haider & Canning Rds) and Services Travels (north side of Haider Rd between Saddar and Kashmir Rds).

With these discounts and the agencies' own further scams you can improve on airline prices by 10% to 30%. Typical approximate discounted fares are: Delhi, Rs 650; London, Rs 5000; New York, Rs 6500. A PIA night coach to Karachi can be as low as Rs 800.

Paying for Airline Tickets You can't just walk in with travellers' cheques or a wad of rupees. If you buy a ticket in Pakistan, for a flight leaving Pakistan, you can only pay in cash rupees you've exchanged from foreign currency. You prove this by furnishing foreign exchange receipts totalling at least the amount of the ticket. Without these, no matter how much cash you already have, you'd have to exchange an amount equal to the full price, just for the receipts. They don't have to be connected with buying the ticket; any obtained in the last three months will do.

Even if the agency gives you a big discount, they need receipts for the un-discounted price. They keep the receipts, but it doesn't matter because Pakistan customs don't need to see them.

Departure Tax The Rs 10 departure tax for domestic flights is included in the ticket price if it was bought in Pakistan. International tickets normally don't include the outrageous Rs 350 departure tax for tickets bought in Pakistan (Rs 100 otherwise). You must have this on hand at check-in when you leave the country.

Train
You can't leave Pakistan by rail. The Lahore-Delhi line is off-limits to foreigners, though you can come *from* India this way. The rail crossing to Iran is closed, but you can get away very cheaply to the rest of the country.

Pakistan Railways offers discounts of 50% for students (with identification) or 25% for tourists. For either one, get a certificate from the PTDC tourism office (if there's one in town) and take it to the Divisional Superintendent of Railways at the station. If he happens to be around, he'll give you a letter to present at the ticket window. You must go through this at every town where you buy a ticket.

Trains are Ordinary or Express. Classes are 2nd (hard or soft seats, no compartments), 1st (soft seats, open compartments), and Air-conditioned (closed compartments); long-distance runs also have sleepers. First-class tickets can be booked ahead, while 2nd-class are usually sold a few hours before departure.

Trains leave from Rawalpindi station in Saddar Bazaar, not from Islamabad. The Rawalpindi booking office (tel 72303 or 65704) is at the station and ticket windows are open 24 hours a day. The Islamabad booking office is at Aabpara, on Khyaban-i-Suhrawardy near Bank of America. Schedules are posted at stations or you can buy a timetable on the platform.

Peshawar Three express trains, two rail-car shuttle trains and many slow ones go to Peshawar every day. The trip takes four hours. Second class is Rs 15 and 1st class (express) is Rs 29.

Lahore & Quetta Five express trains depart for Lahore each day. The trip takes six hours and costs Rs 24.50 2nd class, Rs 47 1st class. One of these, the Quetta Express at 6 am, goes on to Quetta, a 31-hour trip; 2nd class is Rs 114, 1st class Rs 220, sleeper Rs 360. There is a twice-weekly train, taking 26 hours, from Quetta to the Iranian border post at Taftan.

Karachi There are four daily express trains to Karachi, for Rs 121 2nd class, Rs 234 1st class, Rs 380 sleeper; the trip takes 25 to 29 hours.

Overland
The India-Pakistan border, except for one road between Lahore and Delhi, is closed to foreigners. On the 2nd, 12th and 22nd of each month a convoy of Turkish or German buses leaves from Lahore's International Hotel and crosses to Delhi via Wagah, with a police escort through the Indian Punjab, and no stop in Amritsar. Tickets are US$20 or equivalent. To book (at least a day ahead) pay a deposit to the drivers, on the bus or in the hotel coffee shop; hotel staff will not help you. If you have a vehicle you may be able to join the convoy. Foreigners cannot cross the border on foot.

The Iranian border is open at Taftan in Baluchistan (Zahedan in Iran). From Quetta, Taftan is an exasperating bus ride (daily) taking one to two days, or a more comfortable 26-hour train ride (twice a week). The train departs Quetta on Sundays and Wednesdays and cost Rs 320 for 1st class and Rs 90 for 2nd class. Border formalities are tedious and money-changers are devious. Americans and Britons cannot enter Iran.

Getting Around

AIR

Pakistan International Airlines (PIA) has flights linking Gilgit, Skardu and Islamabad, in propeller-driven Fokker Friendships. For the prolonged and stunning views of the western Himalaya and High Karakoram, these government-subsidised flights may be the best airfare bargains in the world. Between Islamabad and Gilgit, 8126-metre Nanga Parbat, 8th highest in the world, is straight out the window (on the right north-bound, left south-bound).

Because the flights require near-ideal weather they're often cancelled, so all bookings are effectively standby; for booking information see under Rawalpindi or Gilgit. If the flight is cancelled you're wait-listed for the next one.

Schedules are seasonal. In summer Islamabad-Gilgit (Rs 255) departs one to three times a day, Islamabad-Skardu (Rs 310) once or twice a day. Gilgit-Skardu (Rs 175) is weekly. There are two tourist-priority seats on each flight, so if PIA says it's full go to PTDC for a 'special booking'. The only concessions are for residents of the Northern Areas.

Another air-approach to the KKH is from Islamabad to Saidu Sharif in the Swat Valley (Rs 220), from where it's a few hours by bus to Besham in Indus Kohistan.

HIGHWAY TRANSPORT

Although you can take a train up to the southern end of the KKH or a plane into the middle of it, the cheapest and easiest way to get around is on the road itself. Long-distance buses cover the whole thing, and in Pakistan village-hopping is easy; buses will stop almost anywhere for a passenger. Here's what you can ride and what they're called in the book.

Bus Pakistan government buses, called GTS (Government Transport Service) in the south, are stodgy grey or blue diesels. Up north GTS is NATCO (Northern Areas Transportation Company), with red-and-white long-distance coaches connecting Rawalpindi, Gilgit, Skardu and the China border.

Private Pakistani buses are rolling works of art: glittering, chrome-sequinned vintage Bedfords, decorated with poetry, Koranic passages, F-16 jets and laminated photos of the Aga Khan, and equipped with blue-tinted windows and musical horns.

Chinese buses, all government-run, are marginally maintained, tired old crocks, equipped with bad-tempered drivers.

Van NATCO and private operators in Pakistan run 15-seat Toyota Hi-Ace or 21-seat Toyota Coaster vans on set regional

and long-distance routes. They're faster but more expensive than buses.

Wagon Old 15-seat Ford wagons are common in Pakistan, privately operated on set regional routes.

Datsun Private Datsun pickup trucks equipped with seats for 10 to 12 are common regional transport in Kohistan. NATCO runs a few 4WD pickups to remote Northern Areas villages.

Suzuki The most common local transport in northern Pakistan is the converted Suzuki light-duty pickup, holding eight to 10.

Jeep Four-wheel-drive passenger-cargo jeeps serve remote villages in the Northern Areas. They're said to seat seven but I was once on one with 24 people attached to it. Jeeps and land-cruisers can also be hired.

Local Transport In Kashgar local transport is by pony-cart; in Rawalpindi add motor-rickshas, taxis and horse-carts.

Schedules

Only government buses run on genuinely fixed schedules. Nearly everything else goes when it's full, so departures can be lengthy affairs. Chinese buses seem to be repeatedly packed, fuelled and repaired after everyone is on board.

Concessions

A 50% student discount is available from NATCO between Gilgit and Rawalpindi (except for their once-a-day 'deluxe' service), with a maximum of four discount tickets for each departure.

Hire Your Own

When there's no passenger service, you can often hire your own vehicle and driver. In Pakistan a private hire is called a 'special', and it's a great bargain if you've got enough friends to fill it. If you just want a seat be sure

you're not hiring the whole vehicle; all drivers understand 'no special'.

Jeeps can be hired from CITS (Kashgar), PTDC (Gilgit, Kaghan Valley and Rawalpindi) or privately (Gilgit). They may be hard to find in summer or on short notice. Gilgit rates are about Rs 10 per km plus Rs 150 a night; Kaghan Valley and 'Pindi rates are higher. Kashgar CITS charges Y70 FEC per half-day.

A Gilgit agency, Pamir Tours, offers a Toyota Corona, with or without a driver, for Rs 600 a day plus fuel and oil. To drive it yourself you need an International Driver's Licence and a Rs 5000 security deposit.

Segregation of Women

On most passenger transport in Pakistan, women and family groups are seated separately. Western couples are often asked to rearrange themselves or sit apart, not to force Muslim habits on foreigners, nor just for the women's comfort, but because Muslim men are often acutely uncomfortable sitting next to a strange woman.

CROSS-BORDER BUSES

For many people the whole point of visiting the KKH is the demanding and spectacular trip between Xinjiang and the Northern Areas over the Khunjerab Pass. Except for tour-group vans and occasional lorries, a bus is the only way to do it.

China-to-Pakistan travellers ride buses of the Xinjiang Tourism Authority from Kashgar to the Pakistani border post of Sust; these buses return empty as far as the Chinese border post of Pirali. Pakistan-to-China travellers ride NATCO from Sust to Pirali, and the Chinese buses from there to Kashgar; NATCO returns empty to Sust. (This asymmetrical arrangement has its problems: if China doesn't send as many buses as Pakistan, travellers pile up at Pirali, which has very few comforts.)

The Kashgar-Sust trip normally takes three days south-bound and two north-bound, though Chinese bus breakdowns are not uncommon. From June to early October a bus goes each way every day if it's reasonably full; early or late in the season there are usually at least two per week. The pass is closed to travellers by 30 November (31 October for tour groups), sooner if snow is heavy; it reopens 1 May.

For information on schedules, costs, bookings and border formalities see the chapters on Kashgar-Tashkurghan and the Khunjerab Pass.

RAIL

Pakistan's rail system ends where the KKH begins. You can start or finish your trip with a three-hour, Rs 7 train trip between Rawalpindi and Havelian, the official southern end of the highway, but that's about all.

HITCH-HIKING

There's no better view of the Karakoram than from the top of a lorry. Hitching is possible in both China and Pakistan, and sometimes to or from Kashgar with Pakistani traders.

Although some drivers just like the company, others hope for the equivalent of the bus fare. There are no central loading yards in KKH towns, though Besham has a big repair yard. Nobody knows the thumbs-up sign; just try waving.

Quite a few Pakistani lorries drive off the road every year. Have a good look at your driver! Gojal people say some are fond of the Chinese wine that can be found at Sust, and there are stories of Pathan speed-freaks on the long-hauls.

BICYCLES

The KKH looks like a harrowing but spectacular trip for a super-fit cyclist. Xinjiang roads are awful for jeeps, let alone bikes, but the highway in Pakistan, while rarely level, is paved in most places, at most times. Travellers have taken bikes both ways across the Khunjerab Pass, though most are urged to pack them on top of a bus, or see the wisdom of it at almost 4730 metres.

Pakistan has no rules about bringing bikes in or out, though you're expected to mention it on your visa application. Getting a bike into China seems to depend on where you enter, and is probably easier with the mythical 'CITS permit'.

Most people who have cycled the KKH rate Indus Kohistan (Chilas to Besham) their least favourite part. The people are poor, anarchic and suspicious of outsiders, and men tend to have distorted ideas about western women. The intervals between food and rest are awkward, and summer weather is scorching.

Excellent sources of current information are the 'rumour books' at three Northern Areas hotels, in which travellers leave their own advice and warnings. The best of these is at the Mountain Refuge Hotel at Sust, with separate books on China and Pakistan. Also see the one at Tourist Cottages in Gilgit. The most entertaining one is at the Batura Inn in Passu.

Kashgar & Tashkurghan

The Tarim Basin is a 1500-km-long depression covering most of southern Xinjiang Autonomous Region in China. It consists almost entirely of a hostile desert called Takla Makan (Uyghur for 'Desert of No Return') with a string of oases round the edge.

Kashgar (Chinese name Kashi or Ka-shih) is one of these oases, at the western end of the desert in a cul-de-sac formed by the Tian Shan ('Celestial Mountains'), the Pamirs and the Kunlun Range.

But because it was a hub of the world's most famous overland trade route system – the Silk Road, linking China, India and the Mediterranean – and a crossroads for invading armies, Kashgaria (the historical name for the western Tarim Basin) has bristled with activity for over 2000 years.

History

Kashgaria's terrain, people, languages and religion have more in common with the adjacent republics of the Soviet Union, or even with the Northern Areas of Pakistan, than with China. But over the centuries Imperial China has come again and again to control its frontiers or police the Silk Road. History in the Tarim Basin is mainly about conflicts between the Chinese and the indigenous nomad tribes.

The Han Dynasty was already here in the 1st century AD, protecting its new trade routes to the west, but the prospering Silk Road oases fell to northern nomadic warrior tribes, Mongols and later Turks. The Emperor's power was not reasserted until the Tang Dynasty, China's golden age in the 7th and 8th centuries. Even then, empires were jostling each other; in the 8th century an Arab expedition reached Kashgar, and a Tang army crossed the Pamirs and occupied Gilgit and Chitral for several years, trying to cope with Arab and Tibetan expansion.

Tang control in Kashgaria was ended in

752 by the Turks, and the area was ruled by a succession of tribal kingdoms – Uyghur, Qarakhan and Karakitai, ancestors of present-day Uyghurs – for more than four centuries. It was during the Qarakhan Dynasty in the 11th and 12th centuries that Islam, spreading east from Persia (Iran), first took hold here. Qarakhan tombs are still standing in Kashgar and nearby Artush.

In 1219 Kashgaria fell to the Mongol Empire of Genghis Khan. In a realm reaching almost to the Atlantic, few boundaries or local conflicts impeded travel, and for another century the Silk Road flourished. Marco Polo journeyed to China during this time. In the late 1300s a Turkish warlord of Samarkand, Timur (called Tamerlane in the west), sacked Kashgar in the course of a rampage across Asia to purge it of Mongol 'impurities'. Until the 1700s Kashgaria was under the control of his descendants or various Mongol tribes.

In 1755 China was back, in the form of a Manchu army, and Kashgar became part of the Qing Dynasty. One of China's favourite tales of tragic love concerns the fourth Qing Emperor, Qian Long. Having put down a revolt led by an Uyghur princess named Xiang Fei, he had her brought to the Forbidden City as a concubine – and promptly fell in love with her. Within two years of arriving in Beijing, she committed suicide.

Resentment of Qing rule often boiled over in local revolts. In 1847 Hunza, then an independent Karakoram state, helped the Chinese put down a revolt in Yarkand. During the 1860s and 1870s a series of Muslim uprisings erupted across China. In 1865 Yaqub Beg, a military officer from Tashkent (now in the Soviet Uzbek Republic), seized Kashgaria, proclaimed an independent Turkestan and made diplomatic contacts with Britain and Russia. Within a few years, however, a Qing army had re-

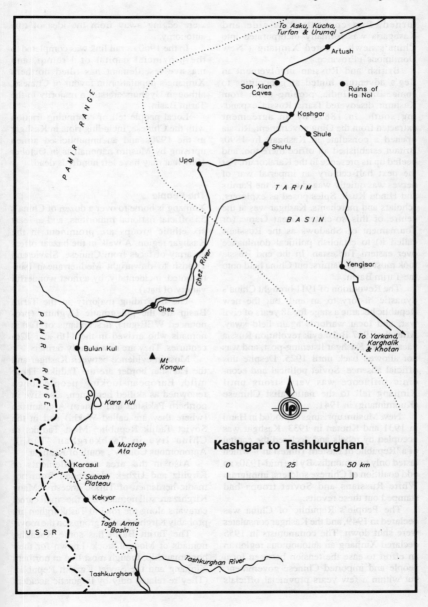

To Asku, Kucha,
Turfan & Urumqi

Artush

San Xian
Caves

Ruins
of Ha Noi

Kashgar

Shule

Shufu

Upal

PAMIR   RANGE

TARIM

Ghez River

BASIN

Yengisar

Ghez

Bulun Kul

Mt Kongur

To Yarkand,
Karghalik
& Khotan

Kara Kul

PAMIR   RANGE

Muztagh
Ata

Kashgar to Tashkurghan

Karasul

Subash
Plateau

0   25   50 km

Kekyor

USSR

Tagh Arma
Basin

Tashkurghan

Tashkurghan River

turned, Beg committed suicide and Kashgaria was formally incorporated into China's newly created Xinjiang ('New Dominions') Province.

British and Russian involvement in Beg's adventure hinted at geopolitics to come. British India, probing north from Kashmir, discovered Tsarist Russia, expanding south. In 1882, by an agreement extracted from the Qing government, Russia opened a consulate in Kashgar. In 1890, Britain established an office there too, and beefed up its presence in the Karakoram. For the next half-century an imperial war of nerves was quietly waged across the Pamirs and Hindu Kush. Spies posed as explorers, scholars and merchants. Kashgar was at the centre of this so-called Great Game (or Tournament of Shadows as the Russians called it) to establish political dominance over eastern Turkestan. In the end Russia took most of the Pamirs, but China held onto the Tarim Basin.

The Revolution of 1911 brought China's dynastic history to an end, but the new Republic became a stage for 38 years of civil war, and local warlords again held sway. After the 1917 Bolshevik revolution Russia vacated her Kashgar listening-post, and was not allowed back until 1925. Despite this official absence, Soviet political and economic influence was very strong until Xinjiang fell to the nationalist Chinese (Kuomintang) in 1941.

New Muslim uprisings exploded in Hami in 1931 and Khotan in 1933. Kashgar was occupied by rebels and declared the capital of a 'Republic of Eastern Turkestan' – which lasted only two months. By the mid-1930s an odd coalition of Chinese soldiers, immigrant White Russians and Soviet troops had stamped out these revolts.

The People's Republic of China was declared in 1949, and the Kashgar consulates were shut down. The communists in 1955 declared Xinjiang an autonomous region in an effort to ease the tension between local people and imported Chinese government, but within a few years provincial officials were edging away from the idea of true autonomy.

In the 1960s a rail link was completed to the provincial capital of Urumqi, and massive resettlement has tilted northern Xinjiang's population in favour of Chinese, although Uyghurs are still a majority in the Tarim Basin.

Local people tell of continuing friction with the Chinese, including riots in Kashgar in the 1970s and an unpublicised armed uprising by Muslim nationalists in October 1981 that may have left hundreds dead.

The People

Xinjiang is home to over a dozen of China's 55 official national minorities, and at least six ethnic groups are prominent in the Kashgar region. A walk in the bazaar offers an array of faces from Chinese, Slavic and Turkish to downright Mediterranean (surmounted, incidentally, by a most wonderful variety of hats).

The overriding majority in the Tarim Basin are the phlegmatic Uyghurs (pronounced WEE-gur), descendants of Turkic nomads who arrived in the 11th and 12th centuries. They are now mainly farmers.

Most in evidence between Kashgar and the Pakistan border are the Tadjiks. These mild, European-looking people, once renowned as skilled herdsmen, also live in northern Pakistan and eastern Afghanistan (where they are called Wakhi) and in the Soviet Tadjik Republic. Most Tadjiks in China live in Tashkurghan 'Tadjik Autonomous County', south of Kashgar.

Also in this area are settlements of Kirghiz and Uzbek, descended from nomadic herdsmen of Turkic ancestry. Many Kirghiz are still nomads, and the small camel caravans along the road to Tashkurghan are probably Kirghiz family groups on the move.

The Tarim Basin has some Kazakhs, nomads of Mongol stock, known for their horsemanship, though most live in northern Xinjiang and the Soviet Kazakh Republic. (They're related only by linguistic accident to the Russian frontiersmen called Cossacks.)

It's a surprise to encounter the occasional Russian here, looking for all the world like a visitor from 1950s Eastern Europe. They're descendants of White Russian troops who fled after the 1917 revolution. Han Chinese are still a small minority in southern Xinjiang; most are to be seen in government offices.

The official language is Mandarin Chinese and each tribe has its dialect, but the speech of the marketplace, and Xinjiang's *lingua franca*, is Uyghur (also called Turki). Uyghur is written in both Arabic and Latinised scripts, the latter introduced for a time in an unpopular attempt to reduce illiteracy.

With the exception of the Chinese and Russians, everyone is Sunni Muslim, although, on the whole, not as obviously devout or self-conscious about it as their brethren in Pakistan.

KASHGAR

Some things in Kashgar haven't changed since medieval times. City transport is by pony-cart. Old town blacksmiths, lumbermen and cobblers work by hand. In surrounding fields the loess soil bears wheat, maize, beans, cotton, and fruit in profusion: melons, grapes, pomegranates, peaches and apricots. Id Kah Mosque stands over the town as it has since 1442. Even after two millennia it's still just a big market town, from impromptu street-corner negotiations to the perpetual bazaars and the hotel-room deals with Gilgit traders.

In other ways the past is clearly gone, and not just the jingling camel caravans. Most obvious are the aggressive changes since 1949. The old town walls have been torn down, factories and schools (even a university) have gone up. Stodgy, Stalinesque municipal buildings – and now the first high-rise – dominate the town's centre. The most striking symbol is the huge statue of Mao Zedong, itself an anachronism now, even among the Chinese.

The British and Russian consulates, for half a century the nerve centres of the Great Game, were closed in 1949. The British office, known as Chini Bagh (Uyghur for Chinese Garden), was first occupied in 1890 by George Macartney. In 1898 he imported a bride from his native Scotland, and over the next 20 years Catherine Macartney made Chini Bagh an island of gardens and European stateliness. A 15-minute walk away was the Russian Consulate, never blessed with a Lady Macartney. The imperial rivalry across the Pamirs was matched by personal rivalries across town – for information, Chinese sympathies, even Silk Road antiquities.

These days the Great Game is played elsewhere in Asia, and both consulates are reincarnated as tourist hotels. Chini Bagh is a melancholy place, neglected and seedy; the Russian consulate is now the stoic and crumbling 'old wing' of the Seman Hotel.

Kashgar's future may imitate its past. Barter trade across the Soviet border resumed in 1983. In 1988 China agreed to finish a rail link from Urumqi to Soviet Kazakhstan, and floated a plan for Special Economic Zones around Kashgar and other towns. Considering the attraction that existing SEZs have for China's entrepreneurs, it's not hard to imagine a new high-tech Silk Road crossing the Tarim Basin.

Orientation

Kashgar is built around two perpendicular main streets and a perimeter road. Official (Chinese) street names are given here. The compass direction is often part of the name; *bei, nan, dong, xi* mean respectively north, south, east, west. The main streets out from the centre are Renmin Dong Lu and Renmin Xi Lu (East and West People's Road), and Jiefang Bei Lu and Jiefang Nan Lu (North and South Liberation Road). The perimeter road – at least on the north-west – is Shengli Lu (Victory Road).

The heart of town depends on who you are. For Uyghurs it's Id Kah Mosque and the main bazaar; for Chinese it's probably the Mao statue. For a budget traveller it's the

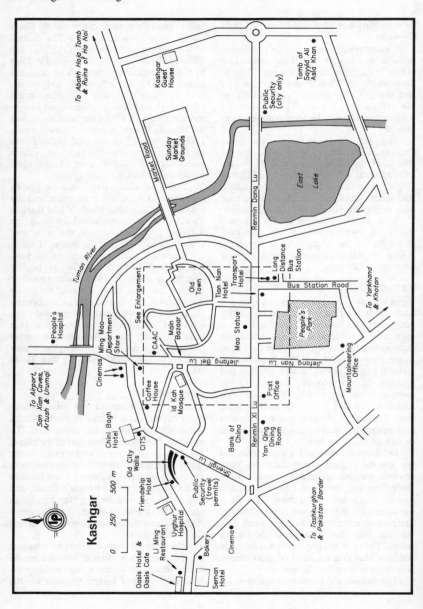

Kashgar

0   250   500 m

To Abakh Hoja Tomb & Ruins of Ha Noi

Kashgar Guest House

Market Road

Tuman River

To Airport, San Xian Caves, Artush & Urumqi

People's Hospital

Cinemas

Ming Mao Department Store

CAAC

Coffee House

Chini Bagh Hotel

CITS

Old City Walls

Friendship Hotel

Public Security (travel permits)

Uyghur Hospital

Bakery

Li Ming Restaurant

Oasis Hotel & Oasis Cafe

Seman Hotel

Cinema

Id Kah Mosque

Main Bazaar

Old Town

See Enlargement

Tian Nan Hotel

Transport Hotel

Long Distance Bus Station

Renmin Dong Lu

East Lake

Tomb of Sayyid Ali Arslan Khan

Public Security (city only)

Bus Station Road

Mao Statue

People's Park

Jiefang Bei Lu

Jiefang Nan Lu

Mountaineering Office

Post Office

Bank of China

Yan Qing Dining Room

Renmin Xi Lu

Shengli Lu

To Yarkhand & Khotan

To Tashkurghan & Pakistan Border

western outskirts, where the middle-range hotels are. The Sunday Market grounds are east of town.

If you've just arrived on the long-distance bus, it's a long walk to any of the major hotels except the Tian Nan. In front of the bus station you can hire a pony-cart to the Chini Bagh Hotel, Seman Hotel or Kashgar Guest House for about Y1 per person. The bus from Pakistan sometimes stops first at Chini Bagh, where most Pakistanis prefer to stay.

If you arrive by air a CAAC bus brings you to the airline office on Jiefang Bei Lu. From here you can walk to Chini Bagh; or from Id Kah Mosque, a block away, you can catch a pony-cart to the Seman for 5 mao if you bargain.

Information

Tourist Offices China International Travel Service (CITS), the government tourist agency, is on the grounds of the Chini Bagh Hotel (second building on the left inside the gate). They'll give you a Kashgar map and a rundown of standard tourist sites but not much more. But this is one place to hire a jeep for a day-trip outside the city or a dash to the border.

The Chinese Mountaineering Association, a government liaison for expeditions, is now open to tourists too. This may not be the place to arrange a trip to the mountains but they do have some information, including an excellent map of roads, trails and villages around Muztagh Ata and Mt Kongur, for an outrageous Y30. They are on Jiefang Nan Lu and have an English sign.

Maps & Other Information The CITS map (also available at the main hotels) has out-of-date locations for CITS itself, the Public Security Bureau, Bank of China and the post office. But it comes in handy for showing pony-cart drivers photos of places you want to visit.

The best source of useful information is probably the neighbourhood around the Seman and Oasis Hotels. The *Oasis Cafe*

(not the Oasis Restaurant) has a good bulletin board, and wall-to-wall westerners at breakfast and every evening. But its lease is perpetually in doubt, so it may have moved by now.

Time A recurring problem for visitors is clock time. All China is supposed to run on Beijing time. For Kashgar, 3500 km away, this is ludicrous, and Kashgaris simply do things according to their own 'Xinjiang time', two hours earlier than Beijing time. You, alas, must run on both times, always asking which is intended (*Beijing shijian? Xinjiang shijian?*).

Business Hours Normal hours are 10 am to 2 pm and 3.30 to 7.30 pm (Beijing time), Monday through Saturday, with variations as noted. Many local shops are open Sundays and closed Mondays.

Post & Communications The post office is on Renmin Xi Lu about 250 metres west of the main intersection; take the left door. Downstairs are stamp counters and two yellow mailboxes; the left one is for international mail. The stamp section is also open during siesta-time and on Sundays. Upstairs is Poste Restante, staffed by a conscientious young man who speaks good English and can help with all international postal matters. There's a 2 mao charge for each letter you pick up.

The centre entrance is the Telephone and Telegraph office. You can call and cable overseas from here.

Bank The only place to cash travellers' cheques is the Bank of China on Renmin Xi Lu, 300 metres west of, and across from, the post office. It's easy to miss, a small brown building set back behind a gate with a tiny English sign. They accept travellers' cheques and cash in most currencies, paying only FEC. They also buy back FEC, but only give US dollars. Exchange rates are uniform throughout China. The office closes at 6.30 pm, and at 2 pm on Wednesdays.

CAAC The CAAC ticket office is on the east side of Jiefang Bei Lu, about 150 metres north of Id Kah Square. This is also the terminus for the airport bus.

Police A city Public Security Bureau is on Renmin Dong Lu, past East Lake.

Travel Permits & Visa Extensions The regional Public Security Bureau, officially the Border & Administrative Office for Foreigners & Visitors, is on Shengli Lu opposite an ornamental pool. One-month visa extensions are Y10 FEC. If you're south-bound and your visa is about to expire, extend it here to avoid big problems at the Pirali border post. Travel permits, to towns not freely open to foreigners, are Y2 FEC.

Hospitals The main Chinese hospital is People's Hospital (*Renmin Yiyuan*) on Jiefang Bei Lu north of the river. There's a hospital of traditional Uyghur medicine on Seman Lu about $^1/_2$ km east of the Seman Hotel.

Film & Processing You can get print film (Fujicolor and Chinese black & white) in the big department stores on Jiefang Bei Lu. Colour processing is available on Renmin Xi Lu opposite the Bank of China and on Renmin Dong Lu across from the Mao statue. For black & white, look for the small 'Kodak' sign on the south-west corner of the intersection near the Seman Hotel.

Newspapers & Magazines Forget it – even *China Daily* seems to get here only in travellers' rucksacks.

Black Market Money-changing in Kashgar is a Uyghur business. Dealers are thick as flies outside the hotels and in the bazaar, and you'll be asked to change money – both FEC and US dollars – until you're sick of it. Some dealers are learning how to cheat, and the following comments may help you avoid rip-offs.

Trade a round sum, for quick mental calculations. Fold it up in a pocket, to avoid fumbling in an open wallet. Tell him what you have, but don't pull it out (some claim they want to check it for counterfeit). Insist on his money first, and take your time counting it. Ignore his pleas to hurry, even walking slowly along to avoid drawing a crowd. Once you're sure it's right, don't let him re-count it; give him your little wad, and split.

Oddly enough, the black market – though it's illegal – is a *de facto* part of the local economy. Anywhere that tourists go, in government-run hotels like the Seman, even in the bus station, you can pay in either currency but the RMB price is higher than the FEC price.

The Sunday Market

Once a week Kashgar's population swells by 100,000, as people stream in to the Sunday Market – surely the most mind-boggling market in Asia, and not to be missed. By sunrise the roads east of town are a single-minded sea of pedestrians, horses, sheep, braying donkeys, bikes and motorcycles, pony-carts and push-carts, everyone shouting *boish-boish!* ('look out, coming through!'). In arenas off the road, men 'test-drive' horses or examine the teeth of huge Bactrian camels (you can take one away for about US$200). A wonderful assortment of people sit by their rugs and blankets, clothing and boots, hardware and junk – and, of course, hats. It's a photographer's paradise; bring three times as much film as you expect to use.

It's a 10-minute walk from the Kashgar Guest House, but over an hour from the Seman Hotel. Pony-carts are plentiful outside the Seman on market-day, and you shouldn't have to pay more than Y1 each. Ask for *Yenga Bazaar* (New Market) or *Yekshenba Bazaar* (Sunday Market).

Abakh Hoja Tomb

The best example of Muslim architecture in Kashgar is an elegant mausoleum built in the

Top: Old Mosque in old town district, Kashgar (JK)
Bottom: Karakul (Black Lake), between Kashgar and Tashkurghan (JK)

Top: Kirghiz men on the Kashgar to Tashkurghan road (JK)
Bottom: Boot sellers at the Sunday Market, Kashgar (JK)

mid-1600s for the descendants of a Muslim missionary named Muhatum Ajam. With its tiled dome and four minarets, it resembles a brightly coloured, miniature Taj Mahal. There are more than 70 graves, including the small ones of children, beneath the tiled stones in the main chamber. These include Muhatum Ajam's grandson Abakh Hoja, a local Uyghur aristocrat sometimes called the 'patron saint of Kashgar'.

Its most celebrated occupant is Abakh Hoja's grand daughter Ikparhan, widow of a Yarkandi prince and better known to Chinese as Xiang Fei (Fragrant Consort). In 1759 she led Uyghurs in an unsuccessful revolt against the Qing Emperor Qian Long, and was then taken off to Beijing as an imperial concubine. There the Emperor fell madly in love with her. Two years later, while Qian Long was out of town, his mother the Empress Dowager – perhaps worried about her son's emotional stability – ordered Xiang Fei to commit suicide. Her body, according to legend, now rests here, and an old sedan chair in the mausoleum is said to be the one that bore her home.

The tomb is a half-hour bike ride or a two-hour walk north-east of town; a pony-cart round-trip shouldn't be more than about Y5. Admission is a few mao. Avoid going at lunch-time, as you may not find anyone to let you in.

Three Immortals Caves, Ruins of Ha Noi & Mor Pagoda

Twenty km north of Kashgar is one of the area's few traces of the flowering of Buddhism, the Three-Immortals (*San Xian*) Caves, three grottoes on a sandstone cliff, in one of which some peeling frescoes can be made out. Unfortunately the cliff is too sheer to climb, so it's a bit of a disappointment.

At the end of a jarring 30-km drive north-east of town are the ruins of Ha Noi, a Tang Dynasty town built in the 7th century and abandoned in the 12th. Little remains except a great solid pyramid-like structure and the huge Mor Pagoda or stupa.

You can visit both of these sites in half a day, in a jeep hired from CITS or your hotel, for Y70 FEC.

Id Kah Mosque

The big yellow-tiled mosque is one of the largest in China, with courtyard and gardens that hold 8000 people. From its minarets the *azan*, or call to prayer, is cried through a loud-speaker. It was built in 1442 as a smaller mosque on what was then the outskirts of town. During the Cultural Revolution,

Id Kah Mosque, Kashgar (JK)

China's decade of political anarchy from 1966 to 1976, Id Kah suffered heavy damage, but has since been restored.

It's acceptable for non-Muslims to go in. Local women are rarely seen inside – public prayer is a men-only affair – but western women who go in for a look are usually ignored if they're modestly dressed (arms and legs covered and a scarf on the head). There are also more than 90 tiny neighbourhood mosques throughout the city.

In front of the mosque is Id Kah Square, swarming on sunny days with old men in their high boots and long black coats, and faceless women with brown veils over their heads.

Bazaars

East of Id Kah Square, behind the first row of buildings, is the main bazaar, a dusty labyrinth of blacksmiths, farriers, carpenters and jewellers; teashops, bakeries and noodle-shops; and vendors of everything, including hats of every description.

On the south side of the square is the night market, the best place in town to sample Uyghur food. There are two covered cloth markets, one north of the square and one off Jiefang Bei Lu.

The Old Town

Sprawling across a hill east of the main bazaar is a complex of narrow passages and adobe buildings that seems trapped in a time warp. Off Jiefang Bei Lu, along the north side of the hill, are several streets with bright new buildings in traditional Uyghur style. Other old neighbourhoods are north-west and south-west of Id Kah.

City Wall

At the east end of Seman Lu a 10-metre-high section of the old wall – actually inner and outer walls, at least 500 years old – is still standing. Construction around, on and in it makes access impossible; clearly there's no pressure to preserve it.

Tomb of Sayyid Ali Asla Khan

Probably the oldest historical site within the city limits is this tomb of a ruler of the Qarakhan Dynasty in the 11th century. At the end of Renmin Dong Lu (2½ km from the centre of town), turn right and go ½ km more; the tomb is on your right.

People's Park

South of the Mao statue is People's Park (*Renmin Gongyuan*), a huge, weedy arboretum with ponds, pathways and an avenue of tall poplars, a good place for a picnic. Admission is one mao. East of the park, 200 metres down a back lane, is an old tomb, now quite smashed up, with its blue tiles stripped off. According to local people it may have been for a local *imam* or religious leader in the 19th century.

East Lake

Just outside town along Renmin Dong Lu is a man-made lake lined with willows – another candidate for a picnic or a peaceful walk among the weeds. In the summer you can rent little boats here.

Pigeon Swap

You may notice flocks of pigeons wheeling over the city, signalled from house-tops with flags, whistles or hoots. Pigeon-raising is big here, and on warm evenings young men gather on a side-street north of the main bazaar to buy and sell pigeons by the light of oil lamps and candles. It's an oddly solemn scene.

Places to Stay – bottom end

All bottom-end and mid-range hotels have dorm beds for Y3 to Y5 RMB. Once the main cheapo in town, the *Renmin Hotel* at Renmin and Jiefang Lu no longer welcomes foreigners.

Through the second gate west of the Mao statue, at the end of a huge yellow building, is a little government guest house (*zhaodaisuo*). Noisy doubles/triples/quads are Y6/4/3 RMB a bed. One day they said 'no foreigners', another they showed me a room.

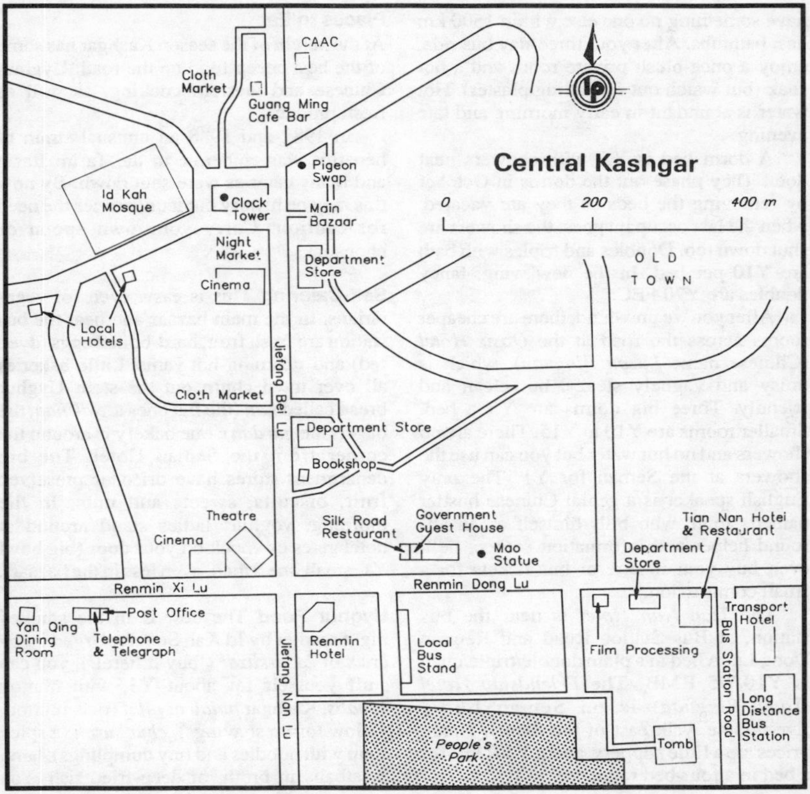

Central Kashgar

0   200   400 m

There's a hotel at the bus station, the *Jiaotong Lushe* (Transport Hotel). They told me 'no foreigners' but others have stayed there. A dorm bed is about Y3 RMB. Go out the back door of the station, turn left, left again, and right; the entrance faces away from the street.

Places to Stay – middle

Listed here are FEC prices. Mid-range hotels accept RMB too, but RMB prices, reflecting black-market rates, are about 30% higher.

The *Chini Bagh Hotel* shows little of its splendour as the old British Consulate. Dorm beds are Y4 and Y5; beds in smaller rooms are Y6 to Y10. The friendly manager speaks English. A shower building built in 1986 hasn't been cleaned since then. Water is occasionally hot for an hour each morning. This is where most Pakistani traders stay, and Uyghur money-changers loiter everywhere.

The Russian consulate is now the crumbling old wing of the *Seman Hotel* ('sih-MAHN'), also called *Lao Binguan* (the Old Hotel). Nothing seems to have been repaired since the Russians left, but they have something no one else within 1500 km has: bathtubs. After your three-day bus ride, enjoy a once-plush private room and a hot soak (but watch out for falling plaster). Hot water is abundant in early morning and late evening.

A dorm bed is Y5, with showers next door. They phase out the dorms in October by removing the beds as they are vacated; when the last occupant goes, the showers are shut down too. Doubles and triples with bath are Y10 per bed. In the new wing, fancy doubles are Y70 FEC.

After you've unwound, there are cheaper rooms across the road at the *Oasis Hotel* (Chinese name *Luzou Binguan*), which is noisy and vaguely sleazy, but clean and friendly. Three big dorms are Y5 a bed. Smaller rooms are Y10 to Y15. There are no showers and no hot water but you can use the showers at the Seman for Y1. The only English speaker is a genial Chinese hustler named 'John' who bills himself as an all-round helper and information source; he'll even buy your theatre or bus tickets for a small commission.

The *Tian Nan Hotel* is near the bus station, at Bus Station Road and Renmin Dong Lu. A bed in a plain double/triple/quad is Y10/7/5 RMB. The *Friendship Hotel* (*Youyi Binguan*) is on Seman Lu, a five-minute walk east of the Seman Hotel; prices are a little slippery, about Y5 RMB for a bed in a four-bed room.

Places to Stay – top end

The *Kashgar Guest House*, also called *Xin Binguan* (the New Hotel), is a spacious, quiet compound in the eastern 'suburbs'. It's priced for tour groups, but triples (Y15 a bed) and quads (Y10 a bed) are not outrageous. Only FEC are accepted. Its biggest drawback is that it's about three km out of town.

In 1989 construction was to begin on a huge four-star hotel on the shore of East Lake, a joint venture between the Chinese government and the Aga Khan's Tourism Promotion Services.

Places to Eat

At the height of the season Kashgar has some of the best cheap food on the road: Uyghur, Chinese and western cooking, as well as fresh produce.

In 1987 and 1988 an unusual strain of hepatitis was epidemic in the Tarim Basin and many eateries were shut down. By now this may be history but it underlines the need for caution. Carry your own spoon or chopsticks.

Self-Catering This is easy, even for vegetarians. In the main bazaar and near the bus station are fresh fruit, hard-boiled eggs (dyed red) and steaming-hot yams. Little bakeries all over town churn out the stout Uyghur bread called *nan* (the flat ones are *ak nan*, the bagels are *gurdah*); one bakery is around the corner from the Seman Hotel. The big department stores have dried or preserved fruit, biscuits, sweets and nuts. In the morning, yoghurt ladies stand around at hotel gates or knock on your door (big bowl Y1, small one 5 mao, even less in the bazaar).

Uyghur Food The best is in the smokey night market by Id Kah Square. Urged on by cries of *kaza-kaza!* ('buy it here!'), you can stuff yourself for about Y3, with mutton *kebabs*, Kashgar *pulau* or *pilaf* (rice, mutton, yellow turnip shavings), *chuchureh* (a spicy soup with noodles and tiny dumplings), lamb meatballs in broth, or deep-fried fish. You can eat *laghman* or *la-mian* (meat, vegetables and chillies on a bed of boiled noodles), or *so-mian* (Chinese *chao mian*, noodle bits fried with meat and vegetables), while you watch the noodles being thrown by hand. It's no place for a vegetarian, though.

There are some grotty Uyghur cafes near the Seman Hotel, mostly hang-outs for the local youth. The food doesn't compare to what's available in the night market.

Chinese Food There's plenty of this, one of the few consolations for an exiled bureaucrat. Pork is replaced by mutton in deference to Muslims.

The *Tian Nan Restaurant*, behind the hotel of the same name, is very Chinese, complete with red-faced cadres throwing back white spirits. It's an obvious favourite of officials and their families. The food is excellent, and good value for the money. There's no English menu so point, or visit the kitchen. A big dinner is Y4 to Y5 per person.

The *Si Lu Fandian* (Silk Road Restaurant), a tiny whitewashed building with no sign, adjoins the government guest house (second gate west of the Mao statue, in the rear of the yard). Food is overpriced but good; eat well for Y6 to Y7.

The *Yan Qing Canting* (Yan Qing Dining Room), just east of the bank and across the street, serves Mongolian-style hotpot, *shui-yan-rou* ('water-salt-meat'). In the middle of the table is a brass pot with a chimney up the middle; coals underneath keep broth in the pot nearly boiling. You add herbs and salt and dip in rice noodles, cabbage and meat slivers till they cook; you can drink the broth afterward. Big mess, great fun – a good group meal for Y6 each plus beer.

The small *Li Ming Fandian* (Break of Dawn Restaurant) is across from the Seman Hotel and always wall-to-wall with hungry westerners. Favourites are braised eggplant, egg-and-tomato, and chips; fill up for Y3 to Y5 per person. With similar prices, the *Oasis Restaurant*, beneath the Oasis Hotel, has a big selection (including vegetarian) but cranky, unpredictable service.

Both the *Seman Hotel* and *Kashgar Guest House* serve big, somewhat meaty set meals at 2 and 7.30 pm (Beijing time), Y5 at the former and Y12.50 at the latter. The Kashgar Guest House is said to have a second dining hall for Uyghur food.

Western Food The main source of good (but high priced) western food, including breakfast and vegetarian dishes, is the *Oasis Cafe*, at the end of the Oasis Hotel building. In the evening it's a pub. You didn't come all this way for cheesecake or Irish coffee, but if you need an antidote for burn-out, it's here. It's also a good place for travellers' information.

Unfortunately, manager Tafir's lease is perpetually in doubt (too bourgeois?) so by now this good place may be gone or relocated. Recent travellers report the appearance of pizza and quiche at the Friendship Hotel.

Alcohol Local and Qingdao beer are available in non-Uyghur restaurants, and department stores carry beer, Chinese wine, brandy and white lightning. You can even get cocktails at the Oasis Cafe. Enjoy it here: you can't get alcohol in Pakistan.

Entertainment
In an old colonnaded theatre at the main intersection, a sort of vaudeville programme plays to enthusiastic local audiences on most week-nights: Uyghur music, Kazakh dances, theatre pieces, even 'Chinese rock'. Tickets are a few mao at the window or a few yuan from touts, or ask at your hotel.

There are four cinemas in town: one beside the old theatre, one by Id Kah Square, and outdoor cinemas south-east of the Seman Hotel and at the corner of Renmin Bei Lu and Shengli Lu.

On summer evenings the Seman Hotel has a kind of outdoor beer-garden, where the local in-crowd is to be seen.

Things to Buy
For serious shopping go to the main bazaar and the Sunday Market; Sunday Market prices tend to be lower. The citizens of Kashgar have been selling things for 2000 years, so be prepared to bargain. It helps to listen in on what local people are paying for the same things (a good reason to learn to count in Uyghur).

Leather Boots Not very practical unless you're on horseback, but at Y30 to Y40 they're one of the best deals in China.

Fur Hats The big Russian-looking ones with ear flaps are Y25 to Y100. But look them over: some ear flaps don't come down, some hats have fleas, some smell like yak's breath when they're wet.

Musical Instruments Beautiful long-necked stringed instruments run the gamut from junk to collector's items, and include the two-string *tutar*, larger three-string *komuz*, small long-necked *tambur* and the elaborately shaped *ravap*, with five strings and a lizard-skin sounding board.

Rugs There are dealers in the bazaar and some bargains in small shops, but there seem to be more and better ones in Urumqi (eg, the covered market a few blocks north of the Overseas Chinese Hotel). Locally, the best are said to be in Khotan.

Getting There & Away

Air You can only fly to or from Urumqi, in an old Russian Tu-154 propeller job. It's Y378 FEC and you can book up to three days ahead. There are no discounts. The schedule varies with the season: daily during summer and down to three flights a week in winter. The CAAC ticket office is on the east side of Renmin Bei Lu, north of Id Kah Square. An airport bus leaves from the ticket office two hours before departure.

Bus Almost everything goes from the long-distance bus station (the 'Kashgar International Bus Station' as the sign says). The ticket window inside is open from 8 am to 10.30 pm (Beijing time). Avoid early afternoons; the ticket office sometimes closes for lunch, which can create a large, bad-tempered crowd.

An English-speaking Chinese woman named Xia Liu works here as a liaison for foreigners. She's the only one who'll give you any comfort, especially in the maddening exercise of getting a bus to Pakistan. Find her to check rumours: out the back, turn right, in the last door on the right, and right again into her office.

Except where noted these are FEC prices but, as with hotels, they'll accept RMB at a higher price. Student discounts (pay in RMB but without the mark-up) are available with a student card.

Pakistan Nothing's certain about this trip, except that it goes to the Pakistan border post of Sust, via Tashkurghan and the Khunjerab Pass, about 500 km. It normally takes three days. From June to early October at least one bus goes every day if it's reasonably full. Late in the season this drops to two buses per week, on Tuesdays and Fridays. The trip costs Y77 FEC and you can book up to three days in advance.

But snow, landslides or just too many empty seats may lead to multiple re-schedulings, often without warning or logic. The best you can do is check frequently at the station, no matter what your ticket says or what you heard yesterday.

The Pass is formally closed for the winter by 30 November (31 October for tour groups) but it may be closed sooner on account of weather, and this is only decided at the last possible moment. The only people who can tell you about this with any certainty are upper-level immigration or transportation officials who work near the border, and only within a week or so of the date.

The bus is supposed to leave at 9.30 am (Beijing time) but rarely does. Some buses may leave from Chini Bagh and you may even be able to buy your tickets there. Baggage goes on the roof, exposed and out of reach for the whole trip, so plan your carry-ons. There aren't many food stops, so bringing a day's water and plenty of snacks is a good idea. Count on cold nights.

If the buses have stopped for the season but you're desperate to cross the border, Pakistani traders at Chini Bagh may have space in a truck or may charter their own bus; you can also hire a jeep from CITS.

Note that the trip *from* Pakistan *to* Kashgar is not simply the reverse of this one; see the chapter on the Khunjerab.

Tashkurghan Take the Pakistan bus, or the weekly local bus that leaves Wednesday morning and stops overnight in Bulun Kul. It returns every Friday morning, with no overnight stop. The fare is Y29.40. If you pause here en route to Pakistan you run the risk of not finding a seat on the next bus through.

Turfan & Urumqi This trip (1330 km to Turfan, 1480 km to Urumqi) takes three to 3$^1/_2$ days. Turfan is Y35.50, Urumqi Y38.30, and you can book up to three days ahead. A bus goes daily at 8.30 am (Beijing time). Baggage goes on the roof and may be inaccessible for the whole trip, so plan your carry-ons. The bus makes meal stops, but the pickings are sometimes slim.

The Turfan stop is actually at the railway station of Daheyon, one of the most dismal and lonely places on earth. From there local buses and cars-for-hire go to Turfan.

Aksu, Kucha, Korla These are stops on the way to Turfan and Urumqi, and are respectively one, 1$^1/_2$ and 2$^1/_2$ days east of Kashgar. You need a travel permit for Kucha. Aksu is Y12.20, Kucha Y18.80 and Korla Y26.60. One problem with stopping over in these places can be getting a seat on the next bus out.

Artush Catch a bus by People's Hospital (*Renmin Yiyuan*). They run all day long, take about an hour and cost Y1.50 RMB.

Shache, Yecheng, Hetian (old names: Yarkand, Karghalik, Khotan) Ask for tickets by the Chinese name. You may have to produce a travel permit from Public Security. Buses leave every two hours all day for Shache (Y5) and Yecheng (Y6.60). There is one bus each morning to Hetian (Y13.20).

Jeep Toyota Land Cruisers can be hired from CITS at Y1.50 per mile (about Y0.93 per km) and Y150 for each overnight stop beyond the first. Food and lodging are extra, and the driver pays his own. An overnight trip to Sust

is Y1162 FEC. With six passengers this works out to 2$^1/_2$ times the bus price, and more control over stops for food, photos and bodily functions. Book ahead, especially during summer.

Hitch-hiking Travellers report lifts in lorries to Pirali for Y40 RMB (same as the bus) and in jeeps for about Y70 RMB. But from Pirali you'll have to wait for an empty seat on a bus.

Lhasa This is difficult but possible. It seems easier coming out than going in. The shortest time I've heard is two weeks, but the average is three to six weeks. Plenty of people try it; so many foreigners accumulated in one remote Tibetan town that Public Security had to arrange a bus to move them all on!

There are said to be Tibetan truck drivers at Chini Bagh, but I've never seen any. You can take a bus to Yecheng and talk to truckers on the highway south of town. You may find them nervous about official punishment; there are many police check-posts, and some are very thorough. If you're discovered at one near Kashgar – such as Yecheng – you'll be sent back, and possibly fined.

Transport may include bus, truck, donkey, yak and your own feet, and the trip is likely to cost Y200 to Y300. In small places with no obvious food, wait for the standard meal-times of 11.30 am and 5.30 pm and the streets may suddenly fill with Chinese going to a canteen, cups and chopsticks in hand. After September the cold is severe, and there are stories of travellers freezing to death in the backs of trucks or by the roadside.

Getting Around

Bicycle Rental To prevent unauthorised journeys out of town, Public Security has ended bike rental for foreigners, eliminating the cheapest and most versatile way to get around Kashgar. The Seman Hotel, Oasis Hotel and Kashgar Guest House were renting one-gear clunkers for 5 to 6 mao per hour, about Y5 for the day; deposit required. Inside the second gate west of the Mao statue, a genial old Chinese man who speaks no

English was charging less and not asking for a deposit. Maybe good sense will prevail again.

Pony-cart This is the commonest way to get around. A few drivers are always outside the Seman and Chini Bagh, eager to take as much of your money as they can. Locals pay three or four mao from the Seman to town, five to the bus station, six or seven to the Sunday Market; you'll probably have to pay more. They're restricted to the back streets during the day.

If you hire your own, set the price and destination before you go. Drivers have no integrity where foreigners are concerned; prices change in mid-journey and rides end early. Squeezing one for a rock-bottom price is a sure way to make this happen. Of course, don't pay till you get there, and try to have exact change.

How much? It's a buyer's market. Ask him (*konch-pul?*) and offer half as much. If he says no, start walking, and almost certainly someone will take your offer. (This may not work at 6 am when you are off to the bus and he's got the only cart!)

There is also a kind of pony-cart 'shuttle'. Some carts have coloured signs with horse-head logos and a number, and certain stops have similar signs, including the Seman, Chini Bagh, People's Hospital, Id Kah Mosque, the long-distance bus station and the Sunday Market road. Each cart is supposed to stick to a certain route, but they don't always. When it's working, each hop is one or two mao, no bargaining necessary.

Local Buses There's a local bus station at the west end of the athletic field opposite the Mao statue, but the buses mainly go to outlying counties.

Jeeps Four-wheel-drive jeeps can be hired from CITS, directly or through the Seman Hotel or Kashgar Guest House. There's also a Municipal Taxi Company on Renmin Dong Lu near East Lake. A Land Cruiser (holds 6 to 8) is Y70 FEC per half-day. If you go out

all day with a Chinese driver, settle the question of his lunch and nap, or you may pay for two hours hanging around town!

Beyond Kashgar

OPEN CITIES

The only cities on the western Tarim Basin that are officially open (no travel permit required) are Kashgar, Artush and Aksu (other open cities in Xinjiang are Korla, Turfan, Urumqi, Shihezi, Hami and Changji). Nearby towns still off-limits to foreigners are Shufu, Shule and Yengisar.

Artush

Artush (Chinese say 'Ah-tu-shih'), an hour's ride north-east of Kashgar, is a Kirghiz market town and the centre of a Kirghiz Autonomous Region. It has a large bazaar, heavy on cloth and clothing. It is locally famous for its figs, 'the pride of Artush', best in late summer or early autumn. Also here is the tomb of Sultan Sadiq Bughra Khan of the 11th-century Qarakhan Dynasty, reputedly the first local ruler to convert to Islam.

There are some small hotels, and plans afoot to build more. Buses go to Artush all day long, from near People's Hospital (*Renmin Yiyuan*) on the north side of town, for Y1.50 RMB.

Aksu

Aksu, once a major Silk Road oasis, is now a rather boring administrative town, a full day's ride from Kashgar and normally the first overnight stop on the way to Turfan and Urumqi.

PERMIT REQUIRED

Towns on the western Tarim Basin that you can visit with a travel permit are Yarkand (called Shache by the Chinese), Karghalik (now Yecheng), Khotan (Hetian) and Kucha. You can apply for a permit (Y2 FEC) at the Border & Administrative Office for Foreigners & Visitors on Shengli Lu.

Yarkand, Karghalik & Khotan

These were stops on the Silk Road branch along the south side of the Takla Makan Desert, and from time to time were little kingdoms unto themselves. The craftsmen of Khotan were celebrated throughout Asia for their rugs, silk and carved jade – and to some extent, still are. The 4th-century Chinese pilgrim Fa-Hsien described Khotan as a highly developed centre of Buddhism, with no fewer than 14 large monasteries.

The odds of getting permits to these places are greater – but the odds of seeing what you want, smaller – if you make expensive arrangements through CITS. Several daily buses go to Yarkand and Karghalik (ask for tickets by their modern names, Shache and Yecheng) and one bus each day to Khotan, the most distant at about 500 km. You may be asked to show travel permits in order to get tickets.

Kucha

Kucha was another oasis and mini-kingdom on the northern side of the desert, and a major Buddhist centre. Hsuan Tsang, a Chinese traveller of the 7th century, wrote about the delicate frescoes at the stone monastery-temples of nearby Kizil, which were subsequently ransacked (in 1906) by the German archaeologist Albert von le Coq. Kucha is two days by bus from Kashgar, on the way to Turfan and Urumqi. With a travel permit you'll have no trouble getting a ticket, but once there you may have difficulty getting to Kizil.

KARA KUL

Many travellers come to Kashgar hoping to visit nomads in the pastures around Kara Kul, also called Karakol Lake (Chinese, *Kalakuli Hu*). This must be one of the most beautiful places in western China, the deep blue waters (*kara kul* is Uyghur for 'black lake') lying nearly in the laps of two Pamir giants, 7540-metre Muztagh Ata to the south and 7720-metre Mt Kongur to the north-east.

With a tent you can spend days at the lake

or on the flanks of Muztagh Ata. You could be invited into a Kirghiz yurt (a cylindrical tent-house used by nomads all over Central Asia) but you might have to settle for a CITS mock-up, or the nearby road-workers' camp. The CITS staffers at the yurt-camp are a friendly lot; they can suggest hikes and tell you what countries have expeditions on the mountain. A yurt space, if available, is Y15; they also prepare good meals, but at tour-group prices.

Go between June and early September; at other times you won't find much but an icy wind and a few wild horses. The lake is at 3800 metres and nights are below freezing even in summer. CITS is not always there, so you'll need a few days' worth of food.

There's no Kara Kul bus. You can buy a ticket to Kara Kul (about Y20) on the bus to Pakistan or on the local bus to Tashkurghan (every Wednesday) but you may be asked to show a travel permit, since this is not an open area. You arrive at Kara Kul on the morning of the second day. Going back, flag down a long-distance bus (if it's running, it goes by some time after 2 pm Beijing time) or the local from Tashkurghan (Fridays only, passing some time after noon, Beijing time).

If this sounds like too much trouble, CITS can arrange it all – jeep, food, accommodation, base-camp treks – for an astronomical fee.

KASHGAR TO TASHKURGHAN

To the Chinese the road from Kashgar to the border is the China-Pakistan Highway (*Zhong-Pa Gong Lu*, 'China-Pak Big Road'). After 80 km across the flats and a sharp 70-km climb, it runs for 250 km to the border in a high valley through the eastern Pamirs. Tashkurghan is about 280 km from Kashgar.

This is a region of sublime scenery and extremes of weather. It is a 2000-year-old passage for trade, plunder and religious ideas, and a geopolitical vortex even now. But the journey between Kashgar and the border is easily ruined by uncertain schedules, rude officials, demented drivers, buses that fall to pieces and cold nights. And the road itself is subject to landslides, mud, fine dust and shattering corrugations that, as one traveller put it, 'will leave your kidneys in your toes'. It's easy to waste all your attention on anger, discomfort and disappointment.

As you leave Kashgar the main attraction, rising straight up from the plain, is the luminous rampart of the Pamirs. About 1¹/₂ hours down the road is tiny Upal, a regular food-stop in either direction. While you're buying your samosas, bread and melons, keep an eye on your bags.

Three hours from Kashgar you enter the canyon of the Ghez River (Uyghur, *Ghez Darya*), with wine-red sandstone walls at its lower end. The scattered adobe houses are the same colour, and during heavy rainstorms the Ghez itself runs red. The white giant to the south is Mt Kongur, at 7720 metres the highest peak near the road until you reach Pakistan's Hunza Valley.

Upstream of the check-post at Ghez the canyon grows steep and lifeless, forbidding even on a sunny day. This is the segment where road construction and frequent landslides have made travel to and from Pakistan so unpredictable in recent years. The road is cut into sheer walls, or inches across huge tilted plains full of boulders. It's not hard to see why the work went so slowly.

At the top of the canyon the landscape changes abruptly. The Ghez, just before dropping into the canyon, seems to lose its way in a huge wet flood plain. This terrain is typical of the entire Pamir Range: high, broad, treeless valleys strung between glacier-rounded mountains, with rivers often pooling into shallow lakes. The word *pamir* refers to pasturage, the valleys' main historical use. Marco Polo came through here seven centuries ago and wrote, 'a lean beast grows fat here in 10 days'. The corridor from here to the Pakistan border is a pamir valley, the Sarikol Valley. The mountains on either side are called the Taghdumbash (or Sarikol, or Chinese) Pamir.

Half an hour south, at the foot of Mt

Kongur, is the Kirghiz settlement of **Bulun Kul**, a night stop south-bound and a lunch stop the other way. In a ragged road-house, a dorm bed is Y4 RMB and fried vegetables are Y1.50. Fill your water bottle from the tea urn, as there's no other hot water. At 3700 metres nights are very cold. Toilets are outside the compound on the north side. North-bound lunch is mutton soup or fried veggies for Y2 and *nan* bread at five times the Kashgar price.

About 1¹/₂ hours south of Bulun Kul, nestled between Kongur and Muztagh Ata, is **Kara Kul** (or Karakol Lake), or properly Lesser Kara Kul, as there's a bigger lake of the same name 150 km north-westward in the Soviet Union. In clear weather a good photographic view of Kara Kul is from the south end of the basin, as the road climbs the shoulder of Muztagh Ata.

Although quite imposing, **Muztagh Ata** (Uyghur for Father of Ice Mountains) looks deceptively small, not the 7540-metre giant on the map. This may be because all the available vantage points are themselves over 3300 metres high.

The high ground west of Muztagh Ata is the **Subash Plateau**. Along here, the highway makes its closest approach to the USSR, about 10 km to mountain passes into the Soviet Tadjik Republic. From an intersection near some bleached old truck-stop buildings called **Karasul**, several jeep tracks go that way. At the turn of the century this area was still in dispute, never having been properly mapped, and this was one of the major issues fuelling the Great Game.

About a ¹/₂ hour south is a police check-post at **Kekyor**. From there, across the vast, marshy **Tagh Arma Basin**, it's about two hours to Tashkurghan. If you're lucky, the trip from Kashgar has taken 14 hours; north-bound, 12 hours is about the best.

TASHKURGHAN

In the Uyghur language, *tash kurghan* means stone fortress. The ruins of a huge mud-brick fort still stand on the edge of town, and although this one is estimated to be about 600 years old, local legends say Tashkurghan has been a citadel for over 2300 years. The Greek philosopher-scientist Ptolemy (90 to 168 AD) mentioned Tashkurghan in his *Guide to Geography* as a stop on the road to China. The Chinese Buddhist pilgrim Hsuan Tsang wrote about its fortress in the 7th century, when it was the furthest frontier outpost of the Tang Dynasty.

Nowadays Tashkurghan is the administrative centre of a 'Tadjik Autonomous County' stretching from Muztagh Ata to Pirali, and home to most of China's 20,000 Tadjiks. About 5000 of them live in the town. If you feel giddy, it's because Tashkurghan is about 3600 metres above sea level.

Travellers deliberately stopping for a day here will have more options for moving on if they're north-bound.

Information & Orientation
There's only one main street, lined with poplars and compounds with big gates. A small bazaar is on a side street 300 metres beyond the bus station. A department store, post office and Bank of China are about one km away, at the other end of the street; they keep rather slack business hours.

Things to See & Do
The single attraction here is the massive, crumbling fort at the north-east corner of town, on the only hill in the flood plain of the Tashkurghan River. Most of its multi-layered walls and battlements are still intact. Development beneath the fort makes it hard to reach. The easiest way is through the schoolyard just west of the Pamir Hotel; if that's closed, go up the alley east of the hotel and climb the wall next to the toilets. Follow the hill to your right.

Places to Stay
Tashkurghan is a night stop in either

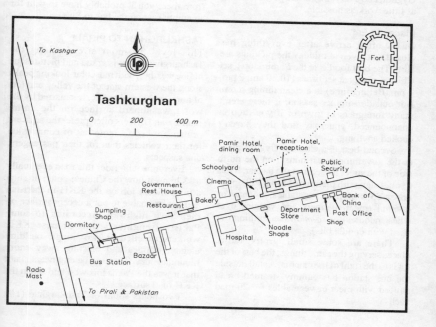

Tashkurghan

0   200   400 m

To Kashgar

To Pirali & Pakistan

Fort

Pamir Hotel, dining room
Pamir Hotel, reception
Schoolyard
Cinema
Public Security
Government Rest House
Bakery
Department Store
Bank of China
Post Office
Shop
Dumpling Shop
Restaurant
Noodle Shops
Dormitory
Hospital
Bazaar
Bus Station
Radio Mast

direction. You'll probably be deposited in the dormitory at the long-distance bus yard, a huge room full of head-to-toe beds. Passports are collected for registration, and returned next morning in exchange for the Y4 bed charge (FEC only). A hotel under construction in the yard looks set to open in 1989. Toilets are at the back of the yard.

If the dorm is full, bus passengers might also stay at a government rest house called *Shi Ping Gongsi Lushe*, about 400 metres down the road, for Y4 RMB per bed in a four-bed room.

The 'prestige' address is the *Pamir Hotel* at the other end of town. There's no English sign, but the first building inside the gate is white with a blue border and a red '1965'. Beds in dusty doubles/quads are Y15/6, and Y6 in a huge dorm (all FEC; RMB prices somewhat higher). They also have 'luxury' doubles with attached bath for Y40 to Y50 FEC. Management is Chinese, staff is Uyghur, and everybody is dedicated to doing as little work as possible.

Places to Eat

Buses often arrive after everything has closed, and even at midday the pickings are slim. The best food is at the Pamir Hotel, set Chinese meals at set times (10.30 am, 2 pm, 7 pm, Beijing time) in a clean dining room. But outside summer season, if there aren't many foreigners in town or if you drop in unannounced, you may find they haven't cooked anything.

Second-best is a Chinese-Uyghur place at the government rest house, on the north side of the street just east of the bazaar. It has a small sign with pictures of food. Fill up for under Y3, with fried vegetables, *laghman* or *la-mian* (meat, peppers and veggies over wheat noodles) or *so-mian* (same thing but fried with noodle bits).

There are some small, grotty Tadjik places serving the same things; the best of the lot is to the right of the cinema. A stall outside the bus station has gummy steamed bread stuffed with meat or vegetables for 20 mao each.

In 1987 and 1988 hepatitis was epidemic in southern Xinjiang; if you've arrived without chopsticks, order hot tea (*cha*) and soak theirs.

To the left of the cinema is a bakery that sells hot bagels (*nan* or *gurdah*) for 25 mao, and the bazaar has fruit, vegetables and (arrivals from Pakistan, take note) beer.

Getting There & Away

Kashgar A local bus goes every Friday morning for Y29.40, without a night stop. You can also try for a seat on the bus from Pirali, bringing travellers from Pakistan. There's one every day in summer, fewer at the beginning and end of the season. Or hitch a lift on the highway; truckers usually expect about the price of a bus ticket. Jeeps returning empty from Sust will be happy for the extra income, probably Y50 to Y100 per person.

Pakistan You might get a lift to Pirali but from there you'll probably have to wait for an empty seat on the bus to Sust.

TASHKURGHAN TO PIRALI

This level 3 1/2-hour stretch is grand along the Tashkurghan River is grand and picturesque in fine weather, with muscular-looking peaks along the western side of the valley and lots of horse and camel traffic. It's marred by the worst washboard surface on the entire journey, and drivers often prefer the adjacent dry stream-beds — more out of compassion for their vehicles than for their passengers, one suspects.

Everyone who rides this road eventually asks himself how the Chinese could do such a magnificent job on the KKH in Pakistan and yet be unable to put a decent surface on their own highway. According to some Pakistani engineers, the Chinese KKH workers excelled at two things: building elegant bridges and blasting away entire mountainsides. These same engineers claim that it was the Pakistanis who laid down the KKH road surface.

Two hours south of Tashkurghan (1 1/2

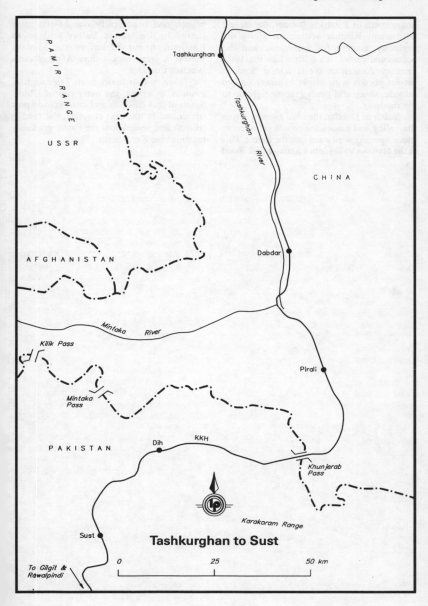

Tashkurghan to Sust

0   25   50 km

To Gilgit &
Rawalpindi

hours north of Pirali) is **Dabdar**, the largest permanent Kirghiz settlement along the highway. Except for a mosque and the occasional camel, it's a little like the 19th-century American west: adobe houses, brown ponies with bright blankets parked outside, sheep and goats grazing right up to the roadway.

South of Dabdar, the road sweeps across the valley and passes the mouth of an enormous opening westward into the Pamir. This is the **Mintaka Valley**, once a major Silk Road branch and historically one of the main routes to the Hunza Valley and on to Kashmir. About 75 km up the Mintaka Valley, a jeep track enters Afghanistan's Wakhan Corridor.

Three to four hours from Tashkurghan, **Pirali** is, in effect, the outer rim of China. South of this customs and immigration post (described in the next chapter), the road is smooth and sealed, and the Pamir gradually becomes the Karakoram.

The Khunjerab Pass

At 4730 metres the road over the Khunjerab Pass is said to be the highest public highway in the world. *Khunjerab* is Wakhi (Tadjik) for 'Blood Valley'; nobody is quite sure where the name came from, although the area swarmed with Wakhi and Hunza bandits until the 1890s, stalking caravans between Kashgar and Kashmir.

A steady trickle of horseback commerce crossed the Khunjerab until the 1950s, when China-Pakistan hostility closed the border. But relations improved and by the mid-1960s the two countries had agreed to cooperate on a Friendship Highway over the mountains. Work began in 1966, and the KKH was inaugurated in 1980. In August 1982 the Pass was formally opened to official traffic and cross-border trade. It was opened to tourism at a media event on 1 May 1986, though travellers had long since discovered it.

The crossing is not only between countries but between two of the world's major mountain ranges, the Pamir and the Karakoram. In the 120 km from Pirali to Sust the transition is evident, from the rounded *pamir* valleys to the deep, angular gorge of the Khunjerab River.

The alpine region between Pirali and the Pakistan security post at Dih is the only habitat of the rare, big-horned Marco Polo sheep, of which there are now only a few hundred in the world. The Pass is also home to ibex, Himalayan marmot, brown bear, fox and, according to some, snow leopard. Both countries have set aside game preserves too. On the Pakistan side, in a 20 km by 100 km strip along the border called the Karakoram National Park, hunting has been banned and grazing restricted since 1975, though little money and manpower have been allocated for surveys or enforcement. On their side the Chinese have established the Tashkurghan Game Preserve.

Time Zones

You reset your watch here, but it's not simple. All China runs on Beijing time, and the people of Xinjiang sometimes work by unofficial local time, two hours earlier. But Beijing (and Xinjiang) set their clocks ahead one hour during the summer, and Pakistan doesn't. The upshot is that from mid-May to mid-September Pakistan time is two hours earlier than Xinjiang time and four hours earlier than Beijing time. For the rest of the year, Pakistan is one hour earlier than Xinjiang and three hours earlier than Beijing.

PIRALI

There is no town at Pirali ('peer-a-LEE'), just China customs and immigration, a Bank of China and, in the summer season, a small guest house, noodle shop and post office. The whole place is just 200 metres long, with official buildings south of the gate and everything else north. A public toilet is about 100 metres west of the gate. The guest house is Y10 FEC per bed (Y5 RMB for locals) but foreigners are encouraged to move on. There's nothing to do but deal with border formalities.

Leaving China

At customs you turn in the declaration form you filled out when you entered China; baggage is inspected, usually cursorily for foreigners. Go next to the bank (just a desk in customs) because at immigration they keep your passport until the bus leaves. If you have mostly FEC and less than about Y100 of RMB, they'll exchange it all. No FEC or lots of RMB (especially without receipts) may cause problems, so share with your bus-mates. The bank only gives US dollars (at Sust they'll accept dollars but not FEC or RMB).

At immigration, turn in your passport and the entry-exit card you received when

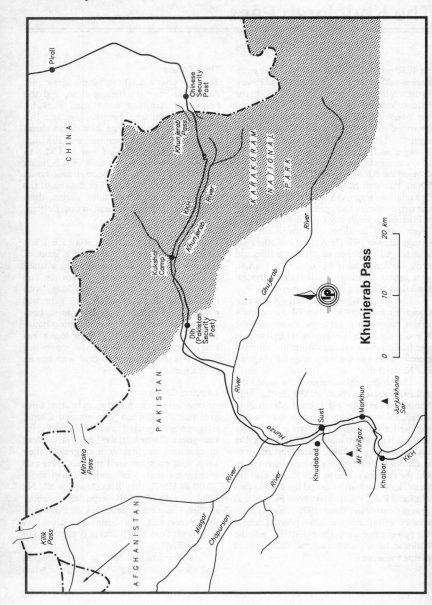

Khunjerab Pass

Top: Long distance bus station, Kashgar (JK)
Bottom: Tadjik children, Tashkurghan (JK)

Top: Khunjerab Pass from the Pakistan side (JK)
Bottom: Customs and immigration post, Pirali (JK)

you entered China. Passports are returned as you re-board the bus.

Officials here have occasionally used expired visas and lost customs-declaration or entry-exit cards as excuses for impromptu fines. Officials demanded US$50 from one traveller whose visa had expired the day before, and the bus was sent on to Sust without him. He refused to give in and they finally settled for Y20 to issue a visa extension.

If you have no Pakistan visa, you'll get a transit permit at Sust. No Pakistan travel documents are issued at Pirali.

Entering China

After casual Sust, procedures here seem stuffy and tedious. Queue up and pay Rs 2 for an entry-exit card and health form; they'll only take rupees. Passports are inspected and stamped. Unlike Pakistan, China does not issue transit visas on the spot.

At customs you fill out a form declaring money, cameras, radios, watches, etc; you get a copy back, which you must present when you leave China. Baggage inspection is usually cursory for foreigners but they like to see your cameras, Walkmans and other high-tech stuff.

The Bank of China (a desk at the end of the room) accepts most major currencies and gives you FEC. The rate is uniform all over China. They may also give you RMB for your Pakistani rupees (if not you can trade with south-bound travellers in Kashgar). Get some of your FEC in small bills (Y5, Y1, 10 mao) because you'll only get change in RMB between here and Kashgar.

Getting There & Away

If you're north-bound, a Chinese bus normally leaves when formalities are completed, although some travellers have been stranded here overnight or longer, or discovered that their bus only goes as far as Tashkurghan. The fare to Kashgar (380 km, including a night stop at Tashkurghan) is Y44 FEC plus a baggage fee, paid on board; to Tashkurghan it's Y15. *Don't pay this in RMB.* It's illegal to bring RMB into China, and if

the driver tells a customs officer, yours may be confiscated (elsewhere RMB is OK).

Occasionally jeeps that take tourists to Sust may give you a lift back to Kashgar. The rate will depend on supply and demand, anything from Y50 to Y150 per person.

PIRALI TO SUST

The Khunjerab has historically been admired for pastures rather than passage, and from Pirali to the Pass you are likely to see herds of shaggy wild yaks or domesticated *dzu*, a cross between yak and cow. A few km short of the top, at the outermost Chinese security post, the People's Liberation Army counts you and looks you over; say goodbye (or hello) to China.

The Pass itself is long and flat. At the summit are border markers, a plaque commemorating the August 1982 opening, and a huge tacky red gate recently installed by the Chinese. It's possible to come up here on a day-trip from Sust. At this point you are about 400 km from Kashgar and 860 km from Rawalpindi.

Scattered down the Pakistan side are deserted concrete buildings with sculpted gables: hostels for Chinese KKH workers, built in the late 1960s when the road was being laid to Gulmit. At **Kukshal**, about 45 minutes below the Pass, the ruins of a Chinese work-camp straddle the river at a large side-canyon.

Below Kukshal the valley walls are 'black, crumbling rock' (this is how the Uyghur words *kara koram* translate) and the river cuts through deep beds of gravel, the residue of repeated mud and rock slides. It's easy to imagine a big slide damming up the river. Between Kukshal and Dih is a shallow lake that formed behind such a slide in September 1987.

About 50 km below the Pass (35 km from Sust) is the Pakistan security outpost of **Dih**, which is just a few buildings and a gate. If you're coming from China you'll get a casual looking-over – and a warm welcome that may bring tears to your eyes.

It's an hour from Dih to Sust, through

some of the narrowest gorges on the KKH. Below the Misgar and Chapursan valleys, whose streams rise near the Afghan border, the Khunjerab River becomes the Hunza River.

SUST

Although it's mainly a customs and immigration post, Sust ('sost'), at 2700 metres, has long walks, grand scenery, even a hot spring. You can also visit the Khunjerab Pass from here, as a day-trip.

Local people are mostly Wakhi (Tadjik) and speak the Wakhi language; officials also speak English. Nearly everyone from here to Hunza is Ismaili Muslim, followers of the Aga Khan.

The opening of the Pass has forced development on Sust, and hotels are popping up faster than the services to support them. Electricity only arrived in 1987, and although the hotels have toilets, Pakistanis here seem to prefer the open system.

There are plenty of hotels. If you arrive late at night from Kashgar, and your driver takes you to an expensive place and says it's the only one in town, tell him to drive to immigration and let you choose for yourself.

Orientation

Along the road are only tourist facilities. Customs, immigration, post office, bus ticket office, cafes and some hotels are clustered near the gate. The bank and more hotels are about 3/4 km in the Pakistan direction, with other hotels further out both ways. Customs and immigration will eventually move to a new site about one km upstream.

Most people never see the village itself, on a ledge above the highway. Across the river (via a small bridge just upstream) is the village of Khudabad. The razor-sharp ridge above Khudabad is Mt Kirilgoz (5450 metres); the big peak straight down the road into Pakistan is Jurjurkhona Sar (5790 metres).

By an odd twist of the KKH here, you go north-west to China and south-east into Pakistan.

Information

Post A small post office, set back from the road near customs, sells stamps and aerogrammes; you can also cable or telephone within Pakistan. Hours are 9 am to 4.30 pm, closed Fridays.

Bank The one-room National Bank of Pakistan is across from the Khunjerab View Hotel. They accept US dollars and pounds sterling (cash or travellers' cheques), and sometimes other currencies. They claim to be open from 9 am to 2 pm and from 3 to 6 pm, but morning is the best bet. If they're closed you might be able to exchange a few dollars (cash) at immigration or with your hotel manager. There is no other bank from here to Gilgit authorised to do foreign exchange.

If you're China-bound you can sell back your rupees here or at the Bank of China in Pirali, or exchange them with south-bound travellers in Kashgar. Pakistan banks normally will not buy back more than Rs 500 per person.

Shops There are two small general stores near immigration and one near the bank, with biscuits, jam, fruit, toilet paper and the like.

Hospital A clinic in the village dispenses medications and first aid. Near the Mountain Refuge Hotel is a gravel track; about 400 metres along it, turn left, and the clinic is the last gate on the left before a big walled yard.

Hot Wash There is a *hammam* (a kind of barber shop and bath-house found all over Pakistan) next to the Hotel Shaheen. For Rs 5 you get a bucket of hot water and a bar of soap in a grotty private stall; this is usually for men but they'll make arrangements for women. For Rs 4 you can get the closest shave of your life.

Customs & Immigration

This is probably the most casual border post in the country. The police inspector in charge of immigration is a jester who may never give you a straight answer. For serious questions, ask his subordinates.

Entering Pakistan At immigration you fill out an entry-exit card and get an entry stamp as soon as you arrive. If you don't have a Pakistan visa you may be postponed until morning, when they'll issue transit permits, free of charge, for 10 to 14 days, no more. If you want to stay longer you must get an extension in Islamabad.

After you've cleared immigration your bags are inspected at customs. For foreigners this usually consists of: 'What's in there? ... OK'.

Most Pakistan ports of entry give you a document called a Temporary Certificate of Registration (Form C), which you must present when you leave the country. And if you're staying more than 30 days you're supposed to register with the police and trade Form C for a residence permit. But immigration at Sust may not give you Form C unless you ask. If they don't, save yourself later headaches and visit the Foreigners' Registration office in Gilgit.

Leaving Pakistan It's easiest to stay at Sust the night before you go. You must have a bus ticket before going through customs; the ticket office opens at 8 am. At customs you show your ticket and your baggage. At immigration you present your entry-exit card or fill out a new one, and get an exit stamp. The bus normally leaves by 11 am.

You must have a China visa or you'll be sent back from Pirali. China does not issue transit visas at the border. Keep Rs 2 to pay for an entry-exit card when you enter China at Pirali.

Day-Trip to the Khunjerab Pass

This is no picnic; the air up there is very thin, very dry and very cold, but it feels like the top of the world. Check with immigration; they'll keep your passport while you're gone. You can hitch-hike, beg a lift on the bus to Pirali or hire a Suzuki (about Rs 600, with room for eight to 10 people).

But have a clear idea how you're getting back down! Unless you take a Suzuki, the only reasonably certain rides back are the buses from Pirali (if there are any): the full

Marco Polo Sheep

Chinese bus, which usually crosses the Pass between noon and 3 pm (Pakistan time) and the empty Pakistani bus, usually crossing between 3 and 6 pm. Ask immigration to verify with Pirali that there is a bus that day. Take plenty of water.

Hot Spring

Six to eight km upstream from Sust (one km downstream from the petrol pumps), rock piles mark a steep short path to the river, where there are three pools near the bank that are deep enough to sit or lie in. One has a wall around it and is arranged to provide a steady flow (so you can even do your wash without ruining it for others). You have to tell immigration you're going, and if your group includes women, one of them is apt to come along. A Suzuki is about Rs 50 for the round-trip but also agree on how long he'll stay - or stay away - while you soak. 'Hot spring' is *theen kook* in Wakhi, *garem chashma* in Urdu.

Hikes Above Sust

At the intersection by the hospital, turn right on a path through fields to Upper Sust on the plateau above, and continue into Sust Nala (a *nala* is a tributary canyon). The compact houses and walled fields, the poplars and fruit orchards, and the dramatic canyon are very different from the scene along the road.

If instead you go straight at the intersection you'll come to an impressive village project to irrigate and plant new land. A gravel road passes fields of saplings and new water channels (if you shortcut up, take care with fragile channel walls and sluice gates). Three steep km from the hospital is the bottom end of a 400-metre irrigation tunnel, dug by villagers in 1985 and marked with stone tablets. This is one of hundreds of self-help projects in the rural Northern Areas, started with the aid of the Aga Khan Rural Support Programme (AKRSP).

From here you can take several excellent walks above Sust Nala, with fine views of the Hunza River valley. A trip into or above the nala can take a half to a full day.

Khudabad

Across the Hunza River is Khudabad village and the narrow Khudabad Nala. A footbridge spans the river 1 1/2 km upstream of Sust, and a walk to the village and back takes an hour. The nala can be a full day's trek.

Chapursan & Misgar Valleys

These valleys, dropping from near Afghanistan's Wakhan Corridor, are said to be very beautiful and their villages still very traditional. Unfortunately they are in a Restricted Area; for information about permits, inquire at the office of the Northern Areas Administrator in Gilgit.

Places to Stay – bottom end

The *Mountain Refuge Hotel & Restaurant* is the best deal in town. It's cheap and clean, the food is good and there are 'rumour books' for Pakistan and China, the best source on the KKH for current information and warnings from other travellers. Older rooms are Rs 20 a bed (Rs 15 with your own sleeping bag); new 'luxury' doubles are Rs 80.

The *Hotel Shaheen* nearby (a green sign in Urdu says 'hotel' in English) is Rs 15 a bed. The otherwise pricey *Khunjerab View Hotel* has a big, dirty, cold dormitory for Rs 20 per bed.

Left of customs, the *Tourist Lodge* has triples with toilet and cold shower for Rs 25 per bed, and outrageously overpriced 'luxury' doubles for Rs 175. Right of customs, the *Khunjerab Highway Hotel* has barren rooms with attached toilets for Rs 30 per foreigner (Rs 15 for Pakistanis). Next to immigration is the *Al Zaman Hotel*, a seedy, loud place where a rope bed is Rs 15.

About 1 1/2 km toward the Pass, opposite the footbridge, is the blue *Sar-Clean Hotel*. It was closed when I visited but locals said it was Rs 40 to Rs 70 for a double.

Most hotels will let you pitch a tent and use their toilets and water for a fraction of the room cost. In fact, you could throw a bag down almost anywhere, but keep in mind that most open space near the road is used as a toilet too.

...ces to Stay – middle

...e *Dreamland Hotel*, several km out of ...wn in the direction of Gilgit, is said to have ...bles for about Rs 80 to Rs 100. It's in a ...ely setting, but too far to walk.

...ces to Stay – top end

...e big *Khunjerab View Hotel* (also called ... *Khunjerab Inn*) at the east end of town ...s chilly carpeted doubles with toilet and ...d shower for Rs 150 or whatever they feel ...e charging that day, subject to bargaining ...slack times.

Places to Eat

Most hotels have basic Pakistani road-food: *gosht* (curried mutton), *dhal* (overcooked lentils), chapatti and tea. The *Khunjerab View* serves fairly good Pakistani food (but the tea tastes like dishwater).

The *Mountain Refuge* has sit-down Hunza-style dinners – rice, thick noodle soup, meat and vegetables – for Rs 20. This is normally for guests only; if you're staying elsewhere see them in advance. They also serve western-style breakfast.

The *National Hotel* is not a hotel but a

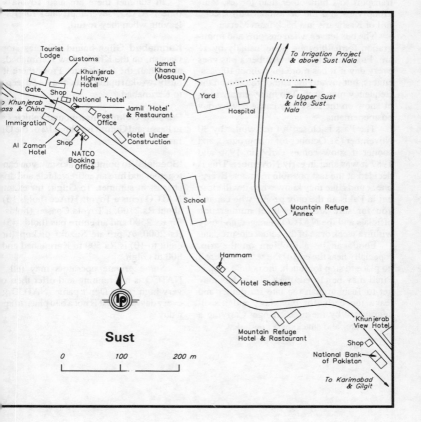

Sust

0   100   200 m

cheerful, grotty local hangout. The *Jamil Hotel & Restaurant* is neither a hotel nor a restaurant, but a little food-tent with good tea, soup and snacks; try their chicken soup in a glass.

Getting There & Away

Kashgar The government-run Northern Areas Transport Company (NATCO) runs buses to Pirali; from there, Chinese buses take you to Kashgar. The 135-km trip to Pirali takes 3½ to 4½ hours and costs Rs 170 (the same distance within Pakistan would be about Rs 30). This is the only transport to China other than lorries, tour-group vans and the occasional *hajj* special full of Kashgaris just back from Mecca.

The bus leaves when customs and immigration formalities are done, usually by 11 am. From June to early October a bus goes every day if it has more than about 10 passengers, but toward the end of the season the frequency may drop. Too many empty seats or snow on the Pass may cause day-by-day postponements.

The Pass is closed for the winter by 30 November (31 October for tour groups), and sooner if snow comes early; in 1986 and 1987 it was shut in early November. This is decided at the last possible moment. Everyone sounds like they know when it will close but in Pakistan the only people who can tell you for sure are upper-level immigration officials and the NATCO manager, and only within a week or so of the actual closure date.

Food can be a problem on the trip, especially near the end of the season. There's no place to stop for lunch; the noodle shop at Pirali may be closed; the Chinese bus may get to Tashkurghan too late for dinner and leave too early for breakfast; and it's all aggravated by the time change. Carrying a day's water and snacks is a good idea.

Above all, prepare yourself with a se of humour. China is a jolt after the re hospitality of the Northern Areas, Chin bus drivers are madmen, and the road bey Pirali is terrible.

Gilgit This takes four to five hours. NATCO bus leaves daily from near custo at 6 am in summer, 7 am in spring autumn and 8 am in winter. Loading departure is a noisy, boisterous busine seemingly repeated in front of every ho and hotel in town, for an hour or more. fare is Rs 30, paid on board.

In summer there are also Toyota v (one NATCO, several private) for Rs leaving when they're full.

Karimabad Gilgit-bound vehicles stop Ganesh, on the KKH below Karimabad, about half the Gilgit fare. From there it dusty two-km uphill walk or a Rs 50 jeep r to Karimabad.

Passu & Gulmit Gilgit-bound vehicles s in Passu and Gulmit for about ¼ of the Gi fare.

'Specials' To points in Pakistan, you can together and hire an entire vehicle and driv at least in summer. To Gilgit, for examp NATCO rents a Toyota HiAce (holds 15) about Rs 2100, a Toyota Coaster (holds   for Rs 2500 and an entire bus (holds 45) Rs 2600. A private Suzuki pickup (ho eight to 10) is Rs 500 to Karimabad and 800 to Gilgit.

Some private operators may tell y NATCO is not running and offer their o very high rates. Don't panic: NATCO g every day, and Sust is not a bad place to spe a day.

e region known locally as Gojal
(o-JAHL' or 'gu-JAHL') extends south
m Sust for about 60 km to where the
unza River turns west. This is the only river
at cuts across the high spine of the
arakoram, and it does so in southern Gojal.

a result the High Karakoram is more
cessible here than anywhere else on the
KH. At Passu and Gulmit several major
aciers reach nearly to the highway.

'The scenery is stern and impressive, but
o gloomy and harsh to be really sublime,'
rote the British explorer Reginald
homberg in 1935. Mountains with
zor-edge summits and bare walls drop
eer to the river, and the wind drives up the
lley even on brilliant days. Nevertheless,
you are fit, this is the place to climb up and
t a feeling for the highlands. The clearest
d most storm-free weather is in early
tumn.

The river picks its way among great fans
alluvium brought down by the smaller
reams; most villages are built on these
rtile deposits. The larger tributaries also
rry down soil and rocks, but often suddenly
d destructively. Huge floods have
riodically destroyed river-front fields and
chards. In 1974 a mudslide from Shishkat
ala backed up the Hunza River for 20 km,
spite Pakistan Air Force attempts to bomb
loose. The resulting lake lasted for over
ree years, during which time the once deep
lley literally filled up with sand and gravel,
aving much of it grimmer than when
homberg saw it.

Gojal is usually described as upper
unza. Like the people of Hunza proper,
ojalis are Ismaili Muslims and were loyal
ubjects of the Mir of Hunza. But their
ersian-influenced language is unrelated to
unza speech, and the people are Wakhi
adjik), descendants of nomadic herdsmen
om what is now eastern Afghanistan,
hina's Tarim Basin and the Soviet Tadjik

Republic. They're probably the most
warm-hearted people on the KKH, with easy
greetings and hospitality for both men and
women.

Celebrations & Holidays

Once an important part of life, community
celebrations are giving way to 'progress'.
But some are still held in Gojal, either Ismaili
holidays or very old seasonal rituals.

Late February
> *Kitdit*, the 'First Festival', for the coming of
> spring. Houses are decorated and there are public
> gatherings with food, music and dancing.

Early March
> *Taghun* ('sowing' in Wakhi). Families celebrate
> privately when the first seeds are cast, offering
> prayers and preparing *samn*, a sweet delicacy
> made from fermented wheat flour.

21 March
> *Nauroz* ('New Days'), a Shia and Ismaili festival
> celebrating the succession of the Prophet's son-
> in-law Ali. In Gojal this is a spring festival too;
> villagers visit one another and there may be music
> and dancing.

Early July
> *Chinir*, the first (wheat) harvest. Farmers may
> celebrate privately, as at first sowing, and there
> are some community celebrations too.

11 July
> *Taqt Nashina* ('taking of the seat'), the day the
> present Aga Khan assumed leadership of the Is-
> maili community. In Gojal this may include
> parades, games, music, dancing and fireworks on
> the mountain-sides.

*13 October (1989), 3 October (1990), 23 September (1991)
> *Eid-Milad-un-Nabi*, the Prophet's birthday.
> Some businesses may be closed.

18 November
> First Aga Khan visit to Gojal in 1987, celebrated
> in Gojal only. Festivities are similar to *Taqt
> Nashina*.

13 December
> Aga Khan's Birthday, celebrated by Ismailis with
> gatherings and speeches.

* approximate dates

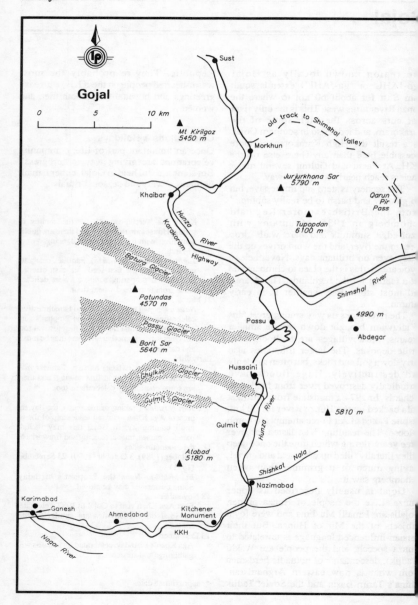

Gojal

0   5   10 km

Sust

Mt Kirilgoz
5450 m

Morkhun

old track to Shimshal Valley

Jurjurkhona Sar
5790 m

Qarun
Pir
Pass

Khaibar

Hunza

Karakoram

River

Highway

Tupopdan
6100 m

Shimshal River

Batura Glacier

Patundas
4570 m

Passu Glacier

4990 m

Passu

Abdegar

Borit Sar
5640 m

Ghulkin   Glacier

Hussaini

5810 m

Gulmit   Glacier

Hunza   River

Gulmit

Atabad
5180 m

Shishkat Nala

Nazimabad

Karimabad

Ganesh

Ahmedabad

Kitchener
Monument

KKH

Nagar River

UST TO PASSU

everal village projects supported by the
KRSP (see Facts About The Region – Rural
evelopment) are visible along the highway,
ncluding a tree plantation at **Morkhun** and
rigation channels and new orchards just
uth of **Khaibar**.

As the valley widens near Passu the
ghway crosses a makeshift girder bridge
er the **Batura Glacier** stream. The glacier
elf comes nearly to the road, although its
rty grey ice looks more like rocky soil. Its
wer end is accessible on a day-hike from
assu. This is one of the larger glaciers of the
arakoram, extending 60 km back into the
uster of 6000-to-7000 metre peaks called
e Batura Muztagh.

The Batura advances and retreats from
ear to year. In 1976 its 30-metre-high front
ound up the original Chinese bridge (the
ins are still visible nearby), which was then
placed by the 'permanently temporary'
rder bridge. There are also two jeep bridges
ross the Hunza River, one for access to the
her side and one to complete a KKH bypass
xt time the glacier eats up the highway.

East of the bridge is the yawning
imshal Valley, once one of the remotest
aces in the old state of Hunza. It was from
per Shimshal, even in the last century, that
nza raiders plundered caravans heading to
ashmir. In 1985 an Aga Khan-funded road
as begun and will eventually reach 45 km
Shimshal village at the valley's head; so
r it's advancing at about five km a year.

Ten minutes from the bridge, at the north
d of Passu, is a windy plain full of
oken-down buildings. From 1968 until
79 this was a camp for Chinese KKH
orkers. Now it's a Pakistan Army
stallation, for KKH maintenance and for
ountain training. In the corner of the camp
e Batura Inn occupies a few whitewashed
ildings.

ASSU

tting between the black Batura Glacier and
e white Passu Glacier, this is the place to
p if you like to walk. Passu, at 2400

metres, is the base for many dramatic
day-hikes, overnights and long treks.

Although it's one of the oldest
settlements in Hunza and Gojal, a kind of
geographical curse has prevented Passu from
growing into a town. As glaciers in the
Shimshal Valley periodically dammed the
Shimshal River and then broke, floods have
gradually torn away Passu's river-front land.
The 1974 mudslide at Shishkat Nala in
southern Gojal created a lake that submerged
parts of the village and choked the valley
with sand and gravel. Passu at one time had
extensive orchards, a polo field and nearly
five times its present population, all on land
that is no longer there.

Information & Orientation

The present village is below the Passu Inn,
where KKH buses usually stop. Buses will
also drop you at the Batura Inn, about 800
metres north along the road, or the Shisper
View Hotel, about 1 1/2 km south. There is no
clear village centre.

The nearest post offices are in Sust and
Gulmit. Telephone calls within Pakistan can
be placed from the Passu Inn. The village has
a tiny dispensary.

Trekking

Though many fine treks start from Passu,
only day-hikes and a few overnight trips are
described here. All can be done on your own,
with minimal equipment.

Several local people are good sources of
information about trips: the village's three
hotel owners, Izatullah Beg (Batura Inn),
Ghulam Mohammed (Passu Inn) and Azim
Shah (Shisper View Hotel), who can also
come up with occasional tents, sleeping bags
and other items; Haqiqat Ali on natural
history and Wakhi culture; and Kamar Jan on
treks (he is the *chowkidar* at the government
rest house).

If you want assistance you can get it
through your hotel. For trips of more than a
day into the Shimshal Valley, or extended
treks anywhere, an experienced guide is
recommended; some of the best live right in

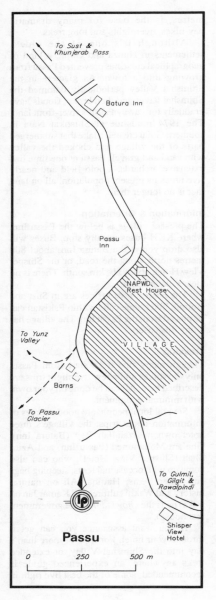

To Sust &
Khunjerab Pass

Batura Inn

Passu
Inn

NAPWD
Rest House

To Yunz
Valley

V I L L A G E

To Passu
Glacier

Barns

To Gulmit,
Gilgit &
Rawalpindi

Shisper
View
Hotel

Passu

0   250   500 m

Passu. As a rule, guides expect Rs 150 to [Rs] 300 per day. For other trips, a knowledgeab[le] local person can be hired as a porter, to sho[w] you the best trails and help with cooking a[nd] carrying, for around Rs 100 per day.

Glacier Views An easy trail goes to the la[ke] below the Passu Glacier, from the stone bar[n] on the KKH about 500 metres south of t[he] Passu Inn. Better views of this beautif[ul] glacier are from the trails to Yunz Valley a[nd] Passu Gar.

The toe of the Batura Glacier is four k[m] north of the Batura Inn, either along the KK[H] or over the adjacent low plateau. The view[s] improve as you climb the moraine (glaci[al] rubble) along its south side.

Yunz Valley The massive caramel-coloure[d] rock behind Passu is called Skazart (Wak[hi] for 'High Yellow'). A vigorous six to seve[n] hour loop climbs to the Yunz Valley behi[nd] Skazart, offering excellent views of bo[th] glaciers. There is no water along this trail.

South of the Passu Inn, high on the ro[ck] wall, is an old water channel. Where t[he] channel comes to ground level the tra[il] begins, immediately climbing up the wall [to] the right (if you end up at the Passu Glaci[er] lake, you began too far to the left). From t[he] Yunz Valley a 1½-hour detour goes to [a] view-point over the Hunza River. At the en[d] of the valley, bear left by some shepherd[s'] huts and descend to the moraine beside t[he] Batura Glacier. At the toe of the glacier cro[ss] the low plateau to the right, back to Passu.

An overnight option is to climb the fa[r] side of Yunz Valley onto 4300-metr[e] Patundas ('Arid Plain'), the first rise on t[he] ridge that separates the Passu and Batu[ra] Glaciers.

Passu Gar This hike climbs to shepherd[s'] huts along the south side of the Passu Glacie[r.] The trip is 3½ to 4½ hours out and two [to] three hours back. The trail leaves the KK[H] at a highway sign ½ km beyond the Shispe[r] View Hotel, and the huts are about two hou[rs] beyond the bottom of the glacier.

An option from here is a steep traverse ward Borit Sar (Borit Peak), with almost 0° views of the Passu Glacier, Ghulkin acier to the south, Borit Lake below and e Karakoram crest behind. This adds at st 1½ hours to the trip.

orit Lake A walk from Passu to Borit Lake d back takes four to five hours. From the ssu Gar trail, branch left near the bottom the glacier. At the south-east corner of the ke are fields, orchards and the simple *Borit ke Hotel* (eight beds, Rs 20 each during the mmer). The once-big lake has grown ampy and brackish (*borit* is Wakhi for lty') over the years, possibly because the derground seepage that feeds it has creased as the glaciers have receded.

A return option is to walk 20 minutes wn the jeep road to the KKH and hitch-ke back (eight to 10 km to Passu). The lake so makes a good overnight stop on a walk m Passu to Gulmit.

rabad & Hussaini This trip crosses the nza River on two long suspension idges, and has fine views of the Passu and ulkin Glaciers from the other side. It takes ur to five hours from Passu to Hussaini, s a hitch-hike or walk back (eight to 10 along the KKH or via Borit Lake).

From the KKH, at the first hairpin turn st the Shisper View Hotel, a trail drops to e river; stay to the right of the hamlet low. The first bridge is about an hour wnstream, with no obvious trail. The idge is just a cluster of steel cables with nks and branches woven in, and it's hair-ising to cross on a windy day. On the far e the trail forks at a pile of stones; continue aight on. Climb toward the canyon walls d cross the ravine as high as possible, to e small village of Zarabad. A dramatic rrow track then crosses a sheer rock face the second bridge.

Hussaini, on the other side, is in a hollow low the KKH. It has a warm spring by the er's edge, too small to get into and usually rrounded by jolly Hussaini women doing

their wash. On the north end is a gleaming white shrine to Shah Talib, a Muslim missionary active around the 14th century. A path climbs to the highway near the shrine.

Abdegar East across the river is a 4900-metre ridge offering the best views of all: a panorama from Sust to Shishkat, the entire length (over 20 km) of the Passu Glacier, and the highest peaks of the Batura Muztagh. This is an overnight trip, and only for the very fit. It's probably best done in early autumn when the risk of sudden storms is low, but it would be a good idea to talk to local people before you go.

Cross the footbridge toward Zarabad and on the far side take the left fork, which climbs, via tiny Kharamabad village, steeply up a side canyon. At the top, a full day's strenuous hiking away and almost as high as the Khunjerab Pass itself, is a shallow pass called Abdegar, a sublime (though very cold) place to see the sun come up.

Shimshal Valley It's quite feasible to take a day-hike up the new Shimshal Valley road, but stay away on rainy or windy days, when there is a high rockfall hazard. You can also hire a jeep to the end of the roadway (ask at your hotel). For a longer trip, unless you're a world-class mountaineer, take a local guide with experience in this difficult terrain. From the KKH, at the hairpin turn about 1½ km beyond the Batura Inn (and also from near the Batura Bridge), a track crosses a jeep bridge and enters the valley.

Places to Stay

The spartan but cheerful *Batura Inn* occupies a corner of the old work camp, and started out in 1974 as a canteen for Chinese officers. Four-bed dorms are Rs 15 a bed; doubles with toilets are Rs 40 and Rs 50. Izatullah Beg's food is abundant and delicious, and he has a small shop too. Check out the 'rumour book' here, very good on the Passu area and very entertaining.

The *Passu Inn*, right above the village, has singles/doubles for Rs 40/75. Owner

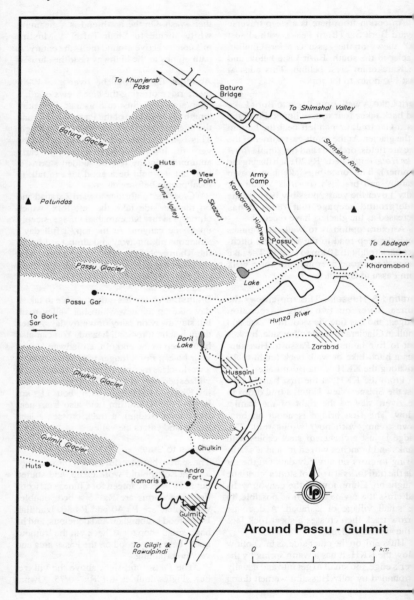

Around Passu - Gulmit

0   2   4 k.m.

Ghulam Mohammed also has a cheaper annex in the village, built in traditional Hunza style with a raised communal sleeping area around a central stove.

The isolated *Shisper View Hotel* is on the highway right below the Passu Glacier. Owner Azim Shah has comfortable singles/doubles with toilets for Rs 40/75, and service and food are good. It closes in late autumn; don't let the bus go till you've tried the gate as it's 1 1/2 km to the village.

An *NAPWD Rest House* is across the highway from the Passu Inn. Doubles are Rs 50. Take a chance, or book through the Administrative Officer, Office of the Chief Engineer, NAPWD (tel Gilgit 2515) Bank Rd, Gilgit.

The people of Passu are said to be planning their own tourist hotel, to be built on the KKH north of the village.

Getting There & Away

Gulmit Flag down anything; it shouldn't be more than Rs 5. Or how about walking? It's 16 km along the KKH, or 14 km via Borit Lake and Hussaini.

Karimabad Gilgit-bound buses go to Ganesh, on the KKH below Karimabad, for Rs 8 to Rs 10.

Gilgit Flag down a bus or van from Sust by your hotel. A bus is Rs 22, van Rs 30. If there are enough people to fill it, a wagon from Passu can be arranged through your hotel for about Rs 30.

Sust The NATCO bus from Gilgit passes sometime after 1 pm and costs Rs 6. Private vans may come by after 11 am and cost Rs 10.

Getting Around

Local jeeps or wagons can be hired through your hotel. A jeep ride up the new Shimshal Valley road is Rs 200 to Rs 250.

GULMIT

Gulmit ('GULL-mit'), with a library, a

museum and the mir's traditional second home, is the closest thing to a town in Gojal and its unofficial capital. It's very picturesque in spring and early summer when the fruit trees bloom. There are many good walks, though less monumental than Passu's.

Information & Orientation

Gulmit is centred on its old polo field, 700 metres up a track from the KKH, although several hotels are down on the highway, south of the turn-off.

There is a small post office behind the *jamat khana* (prayer hall). For medications or routine matters, go to the government dispensary (the Health Centre is for children and maternity care). A police post is opposite the KKH turn-off.

Cultural Museum

A unique collection of Hunza history is packed into a dusty traditional-style house near the Marco Polo Inn. It contains maps, musical instruments, domestic utensils, gemstones, a stuffed snow leopard, and firearms, including the matchlock gun said to have injured the British commander at the Battle of Nilt in 1891. If the museum isn't open, knock at the house next door or ask at the Marco Polo Inn. Admission is Rs 5.

Library

Adjacent to the *jamat khana* is a library with a good collection of English-language books on history, education and religious studies. If it's closed the librarian, Mohammed Rahbar, can be contacted at the Tourist Cottage.

Old Gulmit

The mir's palace is at the north end of the polo field. Until about 15 years ago the Mir of Hunza lived here for three months of the year, presiding over local *durbars* or councils; now it's rarely used. For a look inside, ask at the Tourist Cottage.

A tight cluster of houses to the left of the palace is the original village. The tallest one is said to be Gulmit's oldest, probably 100 to 200 years old; before the palace was built the mir stayed here on his Gulmit sojourns. To the left of this are the carved lintels of an old Shia mosque, from the early 1800s before Gojalis converted to Ismailism.

Trekking

Only day-hikes and some overnight options are described here; all can be done with minimal equipment and no assistance. If you want information or a guide for a long trek, four Gulmitis with good reputations as guides are Ayub Khan, Safar Beg, Tajran Shah and Haider Ali. In giving advice the robust Gulmitis tend to grossly underestimate walking times for a downlander!

Kamaris, Andra Fort & Gulmit Glacier A twisting jeep track behind Gulmit climbs for an hour to the village of Kamaris, with views up and down the valley. A half-hour walk north-east from Kamaris brings you to the ruins of Andra Fort, built about 200 years ago to defend Gulmit in Hunza's war with the neighbouring state of Nagar. Ask local people for Andra Gelah ('geh-LAH').

The jeep track continues past Kamaris for another hour, north-west to the base of the Gulmit Glacier. A long-day or overnight option is to continue on the footpath along the south side of the glacier, an area known locally as *Zherav or Jerab*, where there are some shepherds' huts. High winds increase the rockfall hazard along here.

Ghulkin Village From Kamaris a footpath crosses the stream below Gulmit Glacier, then becomes a jeep track up to Ghulkin village, and returns to the KKH. The entire loop back to Gulmit takes four to five hours.

Ghulkin Glacier, Borit Lake & Passu From Ghulkin a footpath crosses the grey Ghulkin Glacier to Borit Lake, two hours away. It's about 1 1/4 km across the glacier; although the way is marked by a rock pile on the south moraine and a big cleft in the north moraine, it's easy to lose your bearings. Kids in Ghulkin will show you across for a few

rupees. Ask in Gulmit about seasonal conditions on the glacier.

Borit Lake is altogether about five hours (about 12 km) from Gulmit via Kamaris, or two to three hours (about eight km) via the KKH to Ghulkin or Hussaini. You can spend the night at the lake, hitch-hike back from Hussaini or walk on to Passu. The little *Borit Lake Hotel* (eight beds, Rs 20 each during the summer) is at the south-east corner of the lake. Passu is about two hours from the lake (closer to three if you walk on the KKH).

Shishkat Nala A three-hour loop goes down the far side of the Hunza River past Shishkat Nala (locally it's called Baltbar) and returns on the KKH. Shishkat is the source of the 1974 slide that dammed the Hunza River for three years.

Cross the suspension bridge below the Horse Shoe Motel and turn right along the river. One to two km downstream you can see the original KKH section leading to the Friendship Bridge that is still buried under 25 metres of lake sediment. On both sides of Shishkat Nala the track passes Nazimabad village. Cross back on the new KKH bridge at Lower Nazimabad.

Places to Stay – bottom end

The *Tourist Cottage*, on the highway, has a Hunza-style dorm (mattresses in a raised sleeping area, stove in the middle) for Rs 25 each, and doubles with shared toilet for Rs 100 (negotiable outside tourist season). If it's closed, ask in the village for the owner, Abdul Bari. By request they'll serve Hunza whole-wheat bread and home-made apricot jam at breakfast, and (for a price) traditional Hunza and Gojal dishes for dinner. This is a good place for information on local trips.

You can pitch a tent at the otherwise pricey *Marco Polo Inn* or the *Village Hotel*.

A run-down *NAPWD Rest House* (Northern Areas Public Works Department), with doubles at Rs 50, is at the north end of the polo field. Book this through the Administrative Officer, Office of the Chief

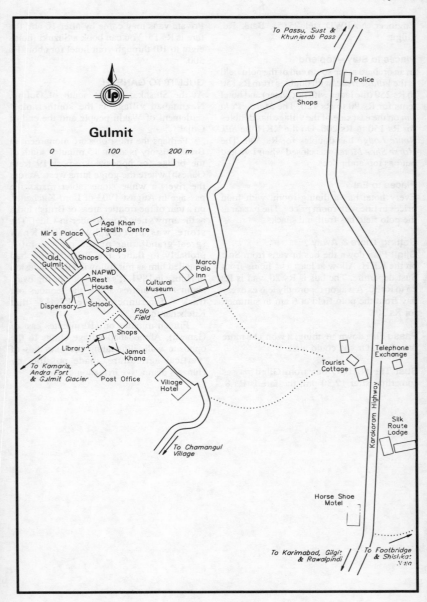

Gulmit

0   100   200 m

To Passu, Sust &
Khunjerab Pass

Police

Shops

Mir's Palace

Aga Khan
Health Centre

Shops

Old
Gulmit

Shops

NAPWD
Rest
House

Marco
Polo
Inn

Cultural
Museum

Dispensary

School

Polo
Field

To Kamaris,
Andra Fort
& Gulmit Glacier

Library

Shops

Jamat
Khana

Post Office

Village
Hotel

Telephone
Exchange

Tourist
Cottage

To Chamangul
Village

Karakoram Highway

Silk
Route
Lodge

Horse Shoe
Motel

To Karimabad, Gilgit
& Rawalpindi

To Footbridge
& Shishkat
N ua

Engineer, NAPWD (tel 2515), Bank Rd, Gilgit.

Places to Stay – top end

In an orchard at the south end of the polo field is the *Village Hotel* with doubles from Rs 150 to Rs 250 (the latter with hot water) and hotel tents for Rs 90 to Rs 120. The *Marco Polo Inn* on the east side of the village has doubles for Rs 150 to Rs 200. On the KKH the *Silk Route Lodge* has doubles for Rs 300. The *Horse Shoe Motel* was closed when I visited but has top-end prices.

Places to Eat

Every hotel has a dining room, with food prices in line with room prices. The bazaar at the polo field has fruit and snacks.

Getting There & Away

Gilgit Flag down the bus or vans from Sust on the KKH. Allow at least 1^{1}/2 hours from Sust departure. The bus is Rs 20, van is Rs 25 to Rs 30. A wagon reportedly leaves every day from the polo field at 6 am in summer, for Rs 30.

Passu Flag down anything; it won't be more than Rs 5. Or you could walk.

Sust The NATCO bus from Gilgit passes sometime after 12.30 pm; the fare is Rs 8.

Private vans may come by after 10 am; the fare is Rs 15. You can book a Suzuki (holds eight to 10) through your hotel for about Rs 300.

GULMIT TO GANESH

At the Shishkat Bridge south of Gulmit, Nazimabad village is the southernmost settlement of Wakhi people and the end of Gojal.

Perhaps the most obscure monument in British history is about 15 minutes south of the bridge (or opposite km-post 19 from Ganesh) where the gorge turns west. Across the river, a white stone tablet marks the passage in August 1903 of Lord Kitchener, on a tour of the frontier areas of British India as the army's new Commander-in-Chief. The stone was erected by Nazim Khan (great-grandfather of the present mir), probably to flatter the British, who had installed him as mir following their invasion of Hunza in 1891. It's even with the highway, about three metres above the tenuous old track – forerunner of the KKH – that Kitchener took.

Fifteen minutes on (10 minutes east of Ganesh), Ahmedabad village clings to the opposite wall, illustrating the extremes of 'vertical agriculture' made possible by Hunza's distinctive irrigation channels.

Hunza & Nagar

For pure natural beauty, the Hunza Valley is the centre-piece of the KKH. In spring everything is green shoots and white blossoms in endless tiers, and autumn is a riot of yellow poplars, reddening orchards and maize drying on rooftops. Above are broad brown mountain sides and higher yet, the snowy peaks.

Added to this, for a westerner, is a kind of mythology about Hunza's isolation and purity, spawned by James Hilton's 1933 novel *Lost Horizon*, nourished in films about the lost kingdom of Shangri-la, and fostered in the 1970s by media stories of extraordinary health and longevity.

The KKH itself has put an end to Hunza's isolation, and the Garden-of-Eden image ignores a rather bloody and disreputable history. But this hardly alters its appeal. Western visitors find more in common culturally with Hunzakuts than with anyone else in Pakistan, and the feeling seems mutual.

'Hunza' is commonly (and inaccurately) used in reference to the entire broad valley below Baltit. Two former princely states, Hunza and Nagar ('NAH-gar'), with a shared language and shared ancestry, face one another across this valley. Hunza, including its one-time satellite, Gojal, extends north and north-east to the China border.

The smaller but more populous Nagar actually occupies more of the main valley, the entire south side and some of the north side near Chalt, and includes 7790-metre Rakaposhi and the lower Hispar Glacier. Although it has enjoyed less media-fame, Nagar is home to some of the best treks in the Karakoram.

The Valley

Hunza-Nagar is a place of great 'geo-drama'. The very edge of the ancient Asian continent is exposed near Chalt (see Facts About The Region – Geology). The continuous sweep from the valley floor to the summit of Rakaposhi (which seems to loom everywhere) is a reminder of the river's deep slice across the Karakoram.

Snaking across the slopes are Hunza's hallmark, the precision-made stone channels on which its life depends. Carrying water from canyons to fields and orchards as much as eight km away, they have transformed a dry valley with few horizontal surfaces into a breadbasket. Their paths on the high rock faces are revealed by thin lines of vegetation, and patches of green can be seen on the most improbable walls and ledges.

Irrigation sustains orchards of Hunza's famous apricots, as well as peaches, plums, apples, grapes, cherries and walnuts; fields of corn and wheat; and the ever-present poplars, a fast-growing source of fodder, firewood and timber.

History

The Hunza Valley lies on a branch of the Silk Road from Kashgar to Kashmir. Just east of Ganesh a cluster of boulders called the Sacred Rocks of Hunza bears prayers, pictures and graffiti scratched in by passers-by over a period of 2000 years.

The origins of the Hunza-Nagar kingdom are lost in legend; local people say it began about 900 years ago. In perhaps the early 1600s the king divided the realm between two sons. They immediately fell to fighting and one killed the other. Over the years their royal descendants have continued the feud, even as they intermarried. Until a century ago, murder was a routine solution to questions of succession.

Arab armies brought Islam to the south of Pakistan in the 8th century, and most of the country was Muslim by the 14th century. Locally, Shia missionaries were probably still at work in the 1600s. In the mid-1800s Hunza's ruling family and most of their subjects converted to Ismailism.

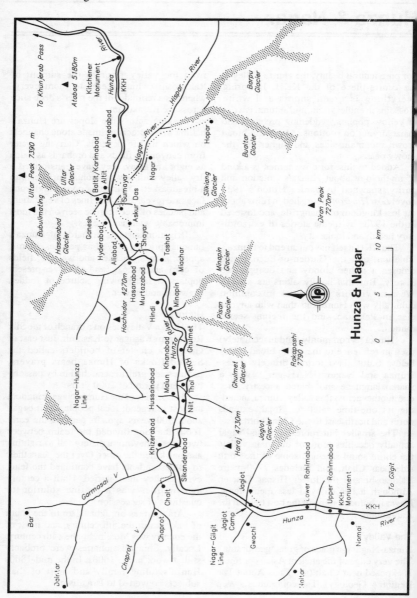

The 'Pacification' of Hunza & Nagar In the early 1800s Hunza had a political tilt toward China. Annual tributes of gold dust went to the governor of Xinjiang, and in 1847 the mir (ruler) helped put down a rebellion in Yarkand. At the same time, the valley's modest agricultural output was supplemented by raids on Kashgar-Kashmir caravans and by slave-trading.

Yaqub Beg, who proclaimed an independent Turkestan republic in Xinjiang in 1865, put a temporary end to the caravan raids. This economic blow led Hunza and Nagar to declare allegiance to the British-aligned Maharajah of Kashmir, probably for the subsidy they got in return. Kashmiri troops occupied Chalt.

In 1886 Safdar Ali Khan became Mir of Hunza by murdering his father and three brothers (his father had inherited the throne in the same fashion). Within two years he conspired to eject the Kashmiris from Chalt, resumed the caravan raids and played host in Baltit Fort to a party of Russian 'explorers'.

British India, spreading north from Kashmir, had grown aware of Russia expanding into Central Asia. Hunza began to look like a liability, and Britain decided to improve supply lines from Kashmir and to re-open its old agency at Gilgit. The Crown's representative was Captain Algernon Durand, who apparently believed that, to counter foreign influence in India, sooner or later all its frontier tribes would have to be subjugated or bought off.

In 1889 Durand visited Mir Safdar Ali Khan of Hunza and Mir Zafar Khan of Nagar and proposed British access up to Shimshal and an end to the caravan raids, in exchange for more subsidies. Both agreed, but the irrepressible valley men couldn't control themselves. The following year Hunza plundered a Kirghiz camp in the Pamirs, and in 1891 Uzar Khan, eldest son of the Mir of Nagar, began making threatening noises towards the British. Moreover he had just had two of his 12 brothers murdered and was plotting against the others.

Durand moved troops to Chalt and built a sturdy bridge across the Hunza River. The mirs protested, but they were already undone: both royal families were increasingly terrorised by Uzar Khan and both mirs had already advised several sons and nephews to take refuge with the British. Durand in fact arrived at Chalt with Uzar Khan's youngest brother Sikander.

On 21 December 1891 a British-Kashmiri force crossed the river and next day, at Nilt, encountered Uzar Khan's Hunza-Nagar irregulars at a fort beside a deep ravine. After dynamiting the gate the invaders rushed in, and the defenders fled through hidden passages beneath the fort. The British, despite some casualties, congratulated themselves on a splendid little fight.

Durand, seeking a view of the action, had stood up and received a shot in the groin – made, he later discovered, of a garnet slug encased in lead, standard issue in Hunza. The gun allegedly used for this deed is in the Gulmit museum.

Then it was discovered that the men of the valley had destroyed the trails by which they escaped across the ravine, and had regrouped in a stronger position on the other side. For 17 miserable days the British, unable to advance, sat in the fort trying this and that. Finally a party of Kashmiris slipped out at night and stormed the far side before breakfast. After that, opposition evaporated. Zafar Khan surrendered at Tashot and Durand's army marched into Baltit.

While they languished at Nilt, the British had received, and rejected, an appeal for negotiations from Safdar Ali, who then fled into Xinjiang with Uzar Khan and several hundred others.

Arriving at Baltit Fort, the mir's castle, the British found most of its treasure already gone, though they ransacked what was left. The spoils from years of plunder included antique chain armour, a Parisian music box, Dutch engravings, even a European armchair, as well as an extensive library and a cache of guns, powder and garnet bullets.

Overlooking superior British firepower

Shepherds' summer hut at Ultar Glacier, Hunza (JW)

and the embarrassing layover at Nilt, a London *Times* correspondent, E F Knight (who had already forsaken his objectivity by volunteering for a command at Nilt), declared the episode 'one of the most brilliant little campaigns in military history'.

The ageing Zafar Khan was reinstated as ruler of Nagar; his grandson is the present Mir of Nagar. As ruler of Hunza the British installed Nazim Khan, Safdar Ali's stepbrother and the great-grandfather of the present Mir of Hunza. Uzar Khan was sent back by the Chinese authorities and jailed in Kashmir. Safdar Ali was allowed to stay in Xinjiang and died a poor man at Yarkand in 1930.

A British garrison stayed at Aliabad until 1897, after which Hunza and Nagar carried on in relative peace for three-quarters of a century.

After Partition Within weeks of the formal partition of India and Pakistan in August 1947, an uprising in Gilgit against the Maharajah of Kashmir, who had opted to join India, brought Hunza and Nagar into Pakistan. But they remained semiautonomous until 1974 when Prime Minister Bhutto – probably mindful of the political sensitivity of the future KKH – declared them merged with Pakistan, reducing the mirs from sovereigns to district officials.

The People

Although Nagaris and Hunzakuts have common ancestors, there is no consensus on the place of their origin; scholarly suggestions include Kashmir, Baltistan, Persia, Russia and Mongolia. A persistent legend is of descent from Alexander the Great ('Sikander') or some of his soldiers who are said to have stayed behind in the 4th century BC. There isn't much to support this but it's startling to occasionally see Mediterranean features, sandy hair and blue eyes.

Most people here still think of themselves as subjects of their mirs, rather than as Pakistanis. They are not fond of the downland Pakistanis that the KKH has

brought, but even in remote areas are very hospitable to foreigners.

The two kingdoms also have a common language, Burushaski, but nobody is sure where that came from either. Wakhi is spoken in upper Hunza (Gojal); in lower Nagar (in common with Gilgit) Shina is also used. Many people speak Urdu and English.

Hunza and Nagar once also shared the Shia Islamic faith, but in the last three or four generations Hunza has become almost entirely Ismaili (except for Ganesh and a few other pockets). Older shamanistic beliefs also linger, especially about mountain spirits or fairies who supposedly live on the highest peaks and behave capriciously toward humans. You can still see children and young women with dark eye make-up, to ward off spirits that may enter the eyes and other body orifices.

Dress Hunza men and women wear the long shirt and baggy trousers called *shalwar qamiz*. The women's outfits are brightly coloured and many wear embroidered pillbox caps with a *dupatta* or shawl thrown over them. Men wear the distinctive Hunza wool cap, essentially a tube of cloth with the edges rolled tightly up, and in cold weather they may put on the *chogha*, a handsome embroidered woollen cloak with oversize sleeves.

Aga Khan Programmes

The loss of sovereignty in 1974 deprived Hunza, Nagar and other areas of the mirs' traditional power to initiate public works. Since then the private Aga Khan Rural Support Programme (AKRSP) has helped build an alternative infrastructure by which villages carry out their own revenue-producing projects, the most visible being new irrigation schemes and link roads. AKRSP signs sprout weekly by the roadsides, announcing new projects.

Other programmes include Aga Khan Health Services (AKHS), establishing minor-medical and primary-care projects, and Aga Khan Educational Services

(AKES), concerned school operation and teacher development. The Community Basic Services Programme (CBS) is a joint project between the Pakistan government and UNICEF to provide, among other things, rural drinking water and sanitation facilities.

These programmes are at least partially funded by the Aga Khan, the spiritual leader of Ismaili Muslims, though they cover non-Ismaili villages as well.

Celebrations & Holidays

Traditional seasonal festivals are hard to find now, though they are held privately. Locals speak of the 'dreamful times' when people enjoyed community gatherings, music, dancing, courtship, and a little drink. Ismaili holidays are big events in Hunza. Nagaris and people of Ganesh celebrate Shia holy days, to which non-Muslims are usually not welcome.

Late February or early March
  Bo Pho, the first wheat sowing. Families may celebrate in their fields, with food and prayers.

21 March
  Nauroz ('New Days'), a general spring festival, and a Shia and Ismaili celebration of the succession of the Prophet's son-in-law Ali. People visit family and friends, and there may be music and dancing. In Chalt, there are sometimes polo matches.

*30 March to 29 April (1990), 20 March to 19 April (1991)
  (Nagar, Ganesh): *Ramadan*, a month of daytime fasting. Food is hard to find in Shia villages during the day (but not in Hunza).

*29 April (1990) (Nagar, Ganesh), 19 April (1991)
  Eid-ul-Fitr, the end of *Ramadan*. This may include elaborate meals, visits to relatives, exchange of gifts.

Late June or early July
  Ginani, the first harvest. Before cutting the first wheat, farmers may celebrate in their fields. Community celebrations may include music and dancing, the slaughter of sheep and, in Chalt, sometimes polo.

11 July (Hunza only)
  Taqt Nashina ('taking the seat'). Ismailis celebrate the day the present Aga Khan became leader of their community; there may be games, music, dancing, fireworks.

*5 August (1990), 26 July (1991) (Nagar)
  Ashura. Shias mourn the death of Hussain; in village processions men and boys perform ritual self-punishment.

*14 September (1990), 4 September (1991) (Nagar)
  Chehelum, 40 days after *Ashura*, with similar processions.

*13 October (1989), 3 October (1990), 23 September (1991)
  Eid-Milad-un-Nabi, the Prophet's birthday. Some shops may close; fireworks.

23 October (Hunza only)
  The Aga Khan's first visit to Hunza in 1960; similar to *Taqt Nashina*.

13 December (Hunza only)
  The Aga Khan's Birthday, celebrated by Ismailis with gatherings and speeches.

21 December
  Tumishaling, a festival of renewal, celebrating the death of the evil cannibal-king Shiri Badat of Gilgit. According to local legend he put the writing on the Sacred Rocks of Hunza with his bare fingers. His daughter plotted with his subjects to trap him in a pit and burn him to death. In memory of this, bonfires are still built in some villages, and people carry fire from their own homes; there may also be music, dancing and the slaughter of sheep or goats.

Late December
  Nosalo. This usually begins at *Tumishaling* and goes on for 15 days. Each household slaughters a sheep or goat and hangs it up for all to see. This practical occasion assures a winter supply of protein and fat, and is soon enough to allow the meat to dry without spoiling.

* approximate dates

GANESH

Most travellers know Ganesh ('GAHN-ish' or 'GUN-ish') only as the bus stop for Karimabad, and see only the fly-blown shops by the KKH. But this is probably the oldest settlement in Hunza-Nagar, and despite the indignity of being cut to pieces by a great S-turn of the highway, it has a lovely old village centre full of classic Hunza architecture.

Ganeshkuts used to be famous for their raids against Nagar. In the 1800s Ganesh was the main Hunza hold-out against Ismailism and is today 100% Shia. With cultural ties to Hunza and religious ties to Nagar, nobody gives Ganesh credit for much any more.

Information & Orientation

The bus drops you at a clutch of cafes, shops and a hotel, near a monument to KKH construction-worker 'martyrs' (casualties). A narrow side-road climbs to Karimabad, high above. Have a rest and a cup of tea at the Yadgar Hotel before the dusty two-km hike, or yield to temptation and take a jeep for an outrageous Rs 50.

Buy your cigarettes here; at the urging of the Aga Khan, no Ismaili shops carry them (though lots of Ismailis smoke).

Things to See

Older Ganeshkuts frown on outsiders, but if you ask around you may be welcomed into the village, one of the least modernised in Hunza. Around a central pond are several richly carved wooden mosques, probably 100 to 200 years old, each donated by a clan of Ganesh; and an old watchtower from the days of war with Nagar, made of loosely mortared stone in a wood framework.

A few hundred metres west across the fields a flag-decked *ziarat* (shrine) to an early Muslim holy man named Bulja Toko (who never came to Hunza, but was featured in a villager's dream). On Fridays food is left here for poor people to take.

Two km west on the KKH the sister-village of Tsil Ganesh has an *imam barga*, a religious meeting hall, with a roof built in striking Balti-Tibetan style.

Places to Stay & Eat

If you're just passing through and don't want to haul your bags to Karimabad, the *Yadgar Hotel & Restaurant* has mouldy rooms for Rs 20 to Rs 25 a bed, and basic meat, chapatti and tea. About 150 metres west up the KKH, the *Ruby Hotel & Restaurant* has beds for Rs 15. East of the Yadgar, the *Karakoram Hotel & Restaurant* is not a hotel but has food. About 1 1/2 km west on the KKH the Pakistan Tourism Development Corporation is building a motel, likely to be top-end like their others.

Getting There & Away

Gilgit Wagons leave from Ganesh at 7 and 8 am, for Rs 20. Others come down from Karimabad or loop around from Aliabad in the morning. A NATCO bus steams through late in the morning but may not stop if it's full; it's Rs 14 to Gilgit. Vans from Sust tend to be full.

Sust The NATCO bus from Gilgit passes after 10 am and is Rs 14. Private wagons and vans come through as early as 8 or 9 am and are about Rs 20. Chartered wagons from Karimabad may pick you up.

Getting Around

Local passenger Suzukis ply the KKH between Ganesh and Aliabad (Rs 2) and sometimes as far as Murtazabad (Rs 3); check the fare first to be sure it's not a 'special' (for hire).

BALTIT & KARIMABAD

Baltit has always been the capital of Hunza. It consists almost entirely of Baltit Fort and a compact village at its feet. The fort was the royal palace until 1960, when structurally sounder quarters were built in Karimabad, just below. Karimabad (named for Prince Karim, the present Aga Khan) is just a modern extension of Baltit, with hotels, cafes and a bazaar.

Orientation

All the facilities of Karimabad are along a single road that climbs from Ganesh at one end, and at the other end weaves down the valley to rejoin the KKH two km west of Aliabad. A jeep track just above the Hilltop Hotel crosses under an aqueduct and descends to Altit village, and a track near the Rainbow Hotel leads up to Baltit.

Information

Tourist Office There isn't one, but a local shopkeeper named Mujibullah has made sketch-maps of local villages and roads, and he's a good source of information. His general store is at the lower end of the bazaar.

Post & Telephone A small post office is across the channel from the New Hunza Tourist Hotel. Calls within Pakistan can be made from the Telephone Exchange on the road down to Ganesh.

Bank The National Bank of Pakistan here isn't authorised to exchange foreign currency; the nearest banks that do are in Sust and Gilgit. Most hotel *wallahs* will accept US dollar cash in payment, and some may exchange dollars for rupees. Karimabad's cheerful local tycoon, Mr Ali Gohar Shah, will trade dollars over a cup of tea. His shop is a few paces up from the Karimabad Hotel, or you can find him in his own Mountain View Hotel.

Bookshop The little Hunza Book Centre, just beyond the Rainbow Hotel, has a few reprinted works on Hunza history and culture, as well as some charming educational posters. Manager Ibrahim Khan normally opens it from 9 am to 4 pm.

Hospital A 15-bed Civil Hospital is on the road to Ganesh, opposite the Mountain View Hotel.

Things to See

The trips described here can all be done on your own. You can get reliable information on trails from the Hilltop and Park Hotel managers; Alex Reid, mountain-guide instructor and part-time American 'resident' of Karimabad (ask at the Park Hotel); and Iftikhar Hussain, a guide from Ganesh (ask at the Yadgar Hotel).

In July and August thunderstorms may roll through. Many streams are swollen then, and dicey to cross.

Baltit Fort

Baltit Fort, on a throne-like ridge in front of Ultar Nala, was probably built 500 to 600 years ago, and was the royal residence until the previous mir moved out. It was built in Tibetan style for a princess of Baltistan (hence its name) who married a mir, and she brought her own artisans to do the work.

To go inside, ask one of the ageing bodyguards at the gate of the new palace in Karimabad; it costs Rs 10. The track to Baltit begins near the Rainbow Hotel. About 100 metres up, turn right at the polo field; 150 metres further, turn right on a path that runs under a house; then turn right again. Kids here are always trying to sell 'rubies' (garnets) to the tourists.

From the basement you climb through several storeys of mostly empty rooms that were cleared out by Safdar Ali as he fled to China, then looted by the British and, since it was vacated, by everyone else. From the roof, where the mir held his councils, the view of the valley is superb. On the roof is a kind of Tibetan-style skylight usually seen atop religious or ceremonial places.

Around Karimabad

Above the Park Hotel a road leads to the modern residence of the Mir of Hunza. Just beyond the aqueduct near the Hilltop Hotel a right turn takes you to a cemetery, with good low-altitude valley views for the sedentary. About one km out on the Aliabad link road is Hunza's pride and joy, the surprisingly modern, fort-like Aga Khan Girls' Academy, dedicated by the Aga Khan himself in 1987.

Altit Fort

The small fort at Altit, with its carved lintels and window-frames, is older than Baltit. In front is an apricot orchard, and behind is a vertical 300-metre drop to the Hunza River. It's a three-km walk from Karimabad; cross under the aqueduct above the Hilltop Hotel, descend on a jeep track and cross the stream from Ultar Nala. An alternative route is via Mominabad. Anyone in the village can find the watchman with the keys ('fort' is *gela*, 'geh- LAH'). This also costs Rs 10.

Mominabad

An old caste system persists in the Northern Areas, in which musicians and other craftsmen rank low. In the past they were often segregated in their own villages. Mominabad, though quite ordinary-looking, was such a village, and its people even speak their own language, Beriski. A path leads there from the topmost turn on the Ganesh road, and continues down to Altit.

Sacred Rocks of Hunza

About 1½ km east of Ganesh on the KKH are several stony rises marked by a sign with this name (which was probably invented at the Ministry of Tourism). The rocks, with pictures and writing from as early as the 1st century AD, are a kind of 'guest book' of the valley. In addition to local traditions they tell of Buddhist pilgrims, kings of the Kushan Empire at Taxila, a 6th century Chinese ambassador, 8th century Tibetan conquerors and even KKH workers!

Channel Walks

It's amazing how many irrigation channels come out of a single canyon, and how far they go. A three or four-hour walk along the main channels (gotsils) from Ultar Nala is a good way to see Hunza (but avoid the more delicate side-channels).

Climb to Baltit, past the polo field; instead of turning off on the path under the house, go straight on beside the channel. The main path goes down-valley all the way to Hyderabad Nala. There, scramble down the stream-bed to the link road and turn back toward Karimabad. Shortly you can drop down to another channel which goes all the way back, even passing several hotels. By now, however, you may have 'canal fever', and you can go right on around Karimabad, past Mominabad, to the channel's headworks behind Baltit Fort. Try out your Burushaski in the hamlets en route, and you may be asked in for tea.

Both channels distribute water from Ultar. There are two more above these, and at least two on the other side of the nala. The velvety appearance of the Ultar water is the result of minute flakes of mica.

Melishkar & Dulkar

These are adjacent summer-pasture villages about 300 metres above Altit; Melishkar is said to be the highest village in Hunza. This is a fairly demanding climb on a twisting jeep track (or a parallel footpath) through friendly hamlets and gravity-defying terraced fields. The climb offers huge, high views of the valley.

Take the jeep track toward Altit but just before you get there, branch left for the trail up. The trip from Karimabad takes three to four hours, the return about two. The best views are from a promontory above Melishkar called Tok. Bring water.

A return option, taking about the same time, is from just above Melishkar, right across the slopes toward Ultar Nala. The path is just below the upper water channel and points toward Baltit Fort. A trail then descends a ravine along the east side of Ultar and comes round into the wide bowl formed by the nala behind Baltit. Cross the foot-bridge and climb to the far side, where the path leads into the village. (The reverse trip has a gradual ascent but no easy landmarks, so it's possible to lose the trail across to Melishkar.)

Ultar Nala & Ultar Glacier

A climb to the Ultar icefall is a good way to get an appreciation for the vertical scale of things here. It's a rigorous six to eight-hour day-trip, and the sort of thing you might want to spend several days on. Some people hire a local guide (for around Rs 100 per day), which is useful but not necessary.

Ultar Nala is a dramatic slash in the valley wall. You enter it from the top of Baltit village; instead of the final right turn to the fort, turn left and immediately right. An indistinct trail climbs the moraines beside Ultar Glacier; steep bouldery sections alternate with little meadows.

Three to four hours above Baltit is a large meadow at the foot of the rumbling blue-white icefall and set in an amphitheatre of peaks. One black pinnacle, Bubulimating or Bubuli's Peak (named for an unfortunate

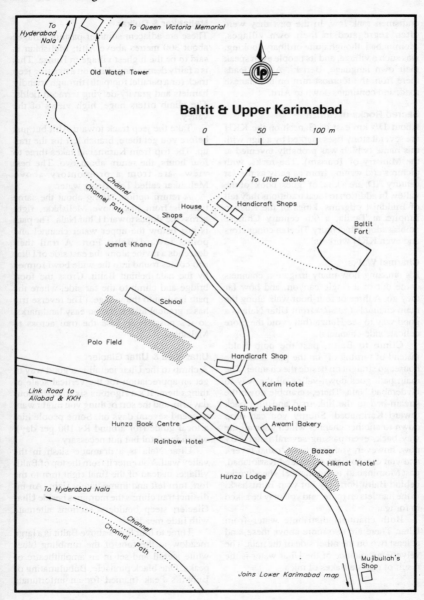

To Hyderabad Nala

To Queen Victoria Memorial

Old Watch Tower

Baltit & Upper Karimabad

0   50   100 m

Channel

Channel Path

To Ultar Glacier

House

Shops

Handicraft Shops

Baltit Fort

Jamat Khana

School

Polo Field

Handicraft Shop

Karim Hotel

Link Road to
Aliabad & KKH

Silver Jubilee Hotel

Hunza Book Centre

Awami Bakery

Rainbow Hotel

Bazaar

Hikmat 'Hotel'

Hunza Lodge

To Hyderabad Nala

Channel

Channel Path

Mujibullah's Shop

Joins Lower Karimabad map

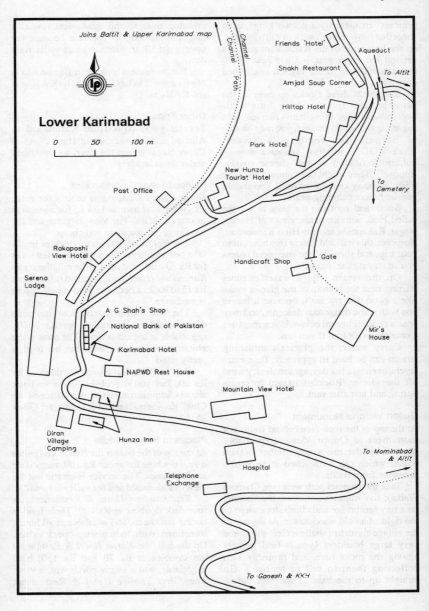

Joins Baltit & Upper Karimabad map

Channel

Channel Path

Friends 'Hotel'

Aqueduct

To Altit

Shakh Restaurant

Amjad Soup Corner

Hilltop Hotel

Lower Karimabad

0   50   100 m

Park Hotel

New Hunza Tourist Hotel

To Cemetery

Post Office

Rakaposhi View Hotel

Handicraft Shop

Gate

Serena Lodge

A G Shah's Shop

National Bank of Pakistan

Mir's House

Karimabad Hotel

NAPWD Rest House

Mountain View Hotel

Diran Village Camping

Hunza Inn

To Mominabad & Altit

Telephone Exchange

Hospital

To Ganesh & KKH

princess left there by a demon king), is so sheer that snow doesn't stick to it. To its right, on the backbone of the Karakoram and 4½ vertical km above you, is Ultar Peak (7390 metres), still one of the highest unclimbed mountains in the world.

Shepherds drive flocks up here in the summer, and live in stone huts until September. If you bring items like tea, salt, sugar, cigarettes or matches, you may be able to bargain for fresh milk (*mamu*, 'mah-MOO'), yoghurt (*dumanu-mamu*), buttermilk (*diltar*) or soft cheese (*burus*, 'broose'). They might even show you some trails, and they know them best! You should inquire before camping nearby.

South and up from the huts is a ridge called Hon, with immense views of Hunza, Nagar, Rakaposhi and the High Karakoram. However, this will add four to five hours onto your trip, and shouldn't be attempted unless you're staying the night.

On the return trip, a water channel starting near the bottom of the glacier looks like a good trail but isn't, because it leaves you with some dangerous descents, and may pose a rockfall hazard below. If you must use a channel, walk in it if you can.

Carry water; the glacier's thrashing stream can be hard to approach. Take extra layers, even on a hot day, against the icy wind off the glacier. Rockfall hazard increases during and just after rain.

Queen Victoria Monument

At the top of the rock face behind Baltit is a monument to Queen Victoria (probably erected by the mir's grandfather Nazim Khan) which can be reached in an hour's scramble from Baltit.

Take the channel path west (see Channel Walks); five minutes out, cross the channel on a tiny footbridge and climb stone steps to the right of an old watchtower. At the top of the village climb to a shallow cleft with some very large boulders (you'll find garnets among the rocks here, and probably kids collecting them to sell to tourists). Go straight up to the base of the cliff before

crossing over to the monument; avoid a diagonal crossing of the face because the uppermost Ultar water channel spills right down it.

The monument's name in Burushaski is *Malikamu Shikari* ('mah-li-KAH-mu shi-KAH-ree').

Other Trips

Several good trips from Karimabad to Aliabad and Murtazabad in Hunza, and to Upper Nagar across the river, are described under those headings.

Places to Stay – bottom end

Diran Village Camping is strictly for tents, Rs 10 for your own and Rs 15 for a mattress in one of theirs. The view is great and the food is good, abundant and cheap.

The *Hunza Inn* has grotty doubles for Rs 20 a bed and better ones with attached toilet for Rs 50 a bed and up. Up the hill, the seedy *Karimabad Hotel* has dorms and triples from Rs 15 to Rs 25 a bed. The food at both places is mediocre.

The *New Hunza Tourist Hotel* has plain doubles/triples with toilets for Rs 70/75, negotiable in the off-season. The cook is the gloomiest fellow in Hunza but his food is pretty good.

An *NAPWD Rest House* has doubles for Rs 60, but you'd probably have to book ahead (Administrative Officer, Office of the Chief Engineer, Bank Rd, Gilgit, tel Gilgit 2515).

Places to Stay – middle

At the top of the bazaar the *Hunza Lodge* has sunny doubles for about Rs 100, negotiable at slack times. The service is erratic but the view of Rakaposhi and the valley is fantastic.

The *Rainbow Hotel & Restaurant* has four dark doubles at Rs 100. Their food is boring but cheap, and available at all hours, sometimes with Indian soap-opera videos. Up the hill, the *Karim Hotel & Restaurant* has doubles at Rs 70 and Rs 150, both negotiable, and a sunny porch with a view. The *Silver Jubilee Hotel & Restaurant*, closed when I was there, is said to have some doubles for Rs 80.

The distant *Village Hotel*, on the Aliabad link road near the Aga Khan Academy, has doubles for Rs 100.

Places to Stay – top end

The *Mountain View Hotel* (tel 17) has singles/doubles for Rs 175/200, making it Karimabad's most expensive. The mir's own *Rakaposhi View Hotel* (which doesn't have a view of Rakaposhi) has doubles for Rs 160.

The *Park Hotel*, with singles/doubles for Rs 130/150, leans toward groups, but check out their Hunza-style dinner (see Places to Eat). Just up the road is the *Hilltop Hotel & Restaurant* (tel 10), which is favourite of tour groups and has hot water, electricity and a gift shop. Singles/doubles cost Rs 125/175.

The concrete megalith near Diran Village Camping was started by PIA, who got cold feet in 1985 and sold it to Tourism Promotion Services, owned by the Aga Khan's brother. It will eventually be a hulking four-star *Serena Lodge*, like the one in Gilgit (which TPS also runs).

Places to Eat

Hunza Food Hunza food is closer to western food than anything else on the KKH. Typical items are potatoes, rice, *daudoh* (a noodle soup with egg, corn and other vegetables, thickened with whole wheat flour) and *phitti* (thick whole wheat bread). Oil and spices are used sparingly.

Milk products include yogurt and *diltar*, a cultured buttermilk left after yogurt is churned for butter. A soft cheese called *burus* ('broose') settles to the bottom of *diltar* kept warm for several days; it's very easy on upset stomachs. *Kurut* is a sour, hard cheese made by boiling and drying *diltar*.

The *Park Hotel* offers a set Hunza dinner in the owner's home. The Rs 30 price is high but the food is very good. The *New Hunza Tourist Hotel* has a fairly good Hunza-style meal for Rs 20, though the menu never changes. At either place, if you're not a guest, make arrangements in the morning.

Local people say *phitti* isn't sold because it takes so long to make, but some hotels serve it for breakfast and you can often special-order it through the hotel or from villagers. Your hotel *wallah* can arrange for yoghurt in the summer when milk is plentiful.

Fruit Most of the Northern Areas' dried fruit comes from here, and dried Hunza apricots are found in bazaars all over Asia. There are at least 22 varieties of apricots, and the best trees are said to be heirlooms. Apricot season is July and early August. Early autumn produce includes peaches, plums, apples, grapes, cherries and walnuts. A great travel snack is dried mulberries. If you're China-bound this is a good place to stock up for the trip.

Cafes In the bazaar there are at least five little 'stay-and-dines' with tea, soup, meat and chapattis. My favourites are the breezy *Amjad Soup Corner* (try his peppery chicken soup, *murghi kai*) and the humble *Hikmat Hotel* (with authentic *daudoh* for Rs 3 a bowl). Others are the *Shakh Restaurant*, *Friends Hotel* and *Awami Bakery & Restaurant*.

Alcohol Despite Muslim prohibition and disapproval from the Aga Khan, some Hunzakuts carry on pre-Muslim traditions by brewing a rough grape wine called *mel* and a potent firewater called *arak* from mulberries. This so-called 'Hunza water' is hard to find, though it may be offered to you by friends or hustlers.

Things to Buy

Hunza wool (*patti* or *pattu*) is renowned for its durability, though it's already being displaced by factory-made imitations. You can find some cloth and clothing here; the best deals are in the bazaar's small general shops. The selection, however, is much larger in Gilgit.

Several souvenir shops have local handicrafts at high prices. The best of these is run by the Karimabad Women's Welfare Centre and is just inside the gate to the mir's house. Two tiny shops are along the path just before Baltit Fort, and one is outside the Hilltop Hotel.

Getting There & Away

Gilgit Wagons leave from the upper bazaar (near Hunza Lodge) between 7 and 8 am, for Rs 20; in summer there are at least three a day. Wagons are often available by arrangement with your hotel. All go first to Jamat Khana Bazaar at Gilgit's west end, and then to the general bus stand.

Other vans leave from Ganesh and Aliabad about the same time, and sometimes scout Karimabad for passengers. Buses and vans from Sust will stop in Ganesh and Aliabad if they have space.

Aliabad, Hasanabad & Murtazabad Passenger Suzukis go to Aliabad from Ganesh for Rs 2, and will probably go from Karimabad when the link road is fully paved. Some go to Murtazabad for Rs 3. For-hire Suzukis to Hasanabad or Murtazabad should be about Rs 30 to Rs 40. Or catch a Gilgit-bound wagon.

Sust The cheapest way is potluck at Ganesh: NATCO comes through after 10 am (Rs 14) and private wagons after 8 or 9 am (about Rs 20). There's nothing convenient or reliable from Karimabad except a wagon hired through your hotel (this is probably the only way to catch the Kashgar bus the same day).

Upper Nagar Walking from Karimabad to Nagar village, via the Sacred Rocks and the jeep road up the east side of the Nagar Valley, takes about three hours; to Hopar, five to six. A footpath over the ridge on the Nagar side of the KKH bridge shortens the trip a bit. Most afternoons, a NATCO pickup and various passenger jeeps come through Ganesh en route to Nagar, and sometimes Hopar. Jeeps can also be hired through your hotel.

Alternatively, take a Suzuki or early-morning Gilgit-bound wagon to the jeep road just beyond Hasanabad Nala, cross the suspension bridge and walk up the Nagar side. Afternoon passenger jeeps from Gilgit to Nagar village sometimes go this way, but they're usually *very* full.

ALIABAD

Aliabad's bazaar, strung loosely for 1½ km along the KKH, is a local transport hub (the Karimabad link road joins the KKH two km west), a minor administrative centre and the base for some hikes up Hasanabad Nala. It hasn't got a lot of character.

Information & Orientation

There's a post office at the far eastern end 200 metres beyond the petrol station. In the centre of the bazaar is a police post, and beside it a road to a 20-bed civil hospital. The Habib Bank is not authorised to do foreign exchange.

Gemstone Corporation

Beside the Dumani View Hotel is the Northern Areas showroom for the government-sponsored Gemstone Corporation of Pakistan, which coordinates exploration, mining and selling of precious and semi-precious minerals. The hills behind Aliabad and Murtazabad are known for their ruby mines, and rubies feature in the display of stones and jewellery here. A nice trip if you fancy gems or have a few thousand dollars to spend.

Hasanabad Glacier

In a sense this is the perfect KKH excursion: step off the highway and walk up a gradual trail through varied terrain, with good views of high country and glaciers, and an option for good camping just hours away. No guide is needed.

Three km west of Aliabad is the deep Hasanabad Nala. Take the trail up the right side, from near a small highway engineer's camp. About three hours in, past the snout of the Hasanabad Glacier and roughly even with the tributary Muchutsil Glacier on the other side, is a camping spot near a huge boulder. Small summer-time side streams are said by locals to be clean.

Hachindar

Several trails also go up the left side of Hasanabad Nala. Turn left after three km into the first side canyon, left again after 3 1/2 to four more km, and climb up to the beautiful pastures called Hachindar. The walk is about five hours one way. Water is available but purity is unknown. There's good camping here, and you may meet shepherds with whom you can barter for food.

Places to Stay

The *Prince Hotel & Restaurant*, east of the police post in Aliabad, has dorms and triples at Rs 15 a bed. In summer they have tents for Rs 25 a bed. West of the police post, the *Delux Hotel & Restaurant* has a dorm and doubles for Rs 30 a bed. You can pitch your own tent at either place for Rs 10.

Opposite the Delux, down the path from a yellow-and-black PTDC sign, is a *PTDC Tent Site*, open in summer only. A two-bed tent is Rs 30 a bed, or pitch yours for Rs 20; toilets and washrooms are nearby.

The *Dumani View Hotel* has immaculate singles/doubles for Rs 150/200, with attached bath, hot running water, carpets and soft beds. (Some locals will tell you 'Dumani' is the Shina name for Rakaposhi, but Shina speakers say this is nonsense.) West of town, a *Rakaposhi Inn* is under construction.

Places to Eat

The bazaar has cafes with soup, tea, sweets, or meat and chapatti. A cheerful soup-tent across from the Prince Hotel has delicious seasoned chicken soup for Rs 1 a glass. The *Delux Hotel* is a NATCO-bus lunch stop and the mixed Pakistani and Hunza food is fairly good. The fairly clean *Prince Hotel* has mediocre Pakistani food and ersatz *daudoh*.

Getting There & Away

In the early morning Aliabad crawls with wagons and Suzukis. At least two vans (and reportedly a bus) go to Gilgit daily between 7 and 8 am. NATCO and private vehicles come through between Sust and Gilgit.

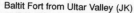
Baltit Fort from Ultar Valley (JK)

Suzukis go to Ganesh (and soon to Karimabad) all day for Rs 2; some may go to Murtazabad for Rs 1.

MURTAZABAD

Murtazabad ('MOOR-ta-za-bahd') is among the few villages in Hunza with a sizeable Shia population. Its attractions are several hot springs and a quiet little hotel. The village centre is just off the KKH eight km down-river from Aliabad.

Things to See

One km east of the village centre is a roadside quarry from which porcelain clay was once mined. A small steam vent is identifiable from the yellow sulphur crust on the clay. A mud bath in the hot, smelly clay is considered locally to have great medicinal value.

From a disused crushing mill across the KKH a path leads out to the bluff and down a short way to a hot spring overlooking the river. Local people use it for bathing (room for one at a time, men and women at different times). The landowner has considered building a shelter and charging a small fee.

'Hot spring' in Burushaski is *garum bul*, (gah-ROOM bool), while in Urdu it is *garem chashma*.

Places to Stay & Eat

In an orchard 100 metres east of the village centre is the small *Eagle Nest Hotel*, coarse but clean, overpriced but a nice retreat. A double is about Rs 120, probably negotiable, and it has a restaurant.

Getting There & Away

From Ganesh (and soon Karimabad) passenger Suzukis come to Aliabad for Rs 2, and sometimes to Murtazabad for Rs 3. For-hire Suzukis between Murtazabad and Ganesh should be Rs 30 to Rs 40.

UPPER NAGAR

That part of Nagar visible from Karimabad is strung together by a jeep road from the Murtazabad-Shayar suspension bridge up to the glaciers at Hopar. Much of it is in the shadow of its own peaks, giving it a slightly gloomy atmosphere. But this also gives Nagar heavier snows and more water, and so while it's more densely populated and cultivated than Hunza, there's no need for Hunza's meticulous irrigation and husbandry.

Information & Orientation

Opposite Ganesh the Nagar (sometimes called Hispar) River joins the Hunza River. About 12 km upstream the valley divides, south to the fertile Hopar Nala and south-east to the remote Hispar Nala. Hopar's glaciers reach nearly to this confluence.

In addition to the main jeep road from the KKH at Murtazabad, a road leaves the KKH near the Sacred Rocks east of Ganesh and climbs the dry east side of the Nagar River. At a small bridge one branch continues toward Hispar Glacier and the other crosses to join the main road near Nagar village. Above here the track is marginal, but future improvements will make Hopar accessible from Ganesh by tourist wagons.

Except for simple rest houses at Nagar village and Hopar, which also has food and camping, this area has few of the conveniences found along the KKH. Reliably clean water is rare at lower levels. Transport is erratic unless you walk or hire a jeep.

Murtazabad to Sumayar

At the promontory just down-river from Hasanabad Nala a jeep track drops from the KKH to a suspension bridge across the Hunza River. Except for the crossing, it's a fairly level two-hour walk to Sumayar, with wide views of Hunza and a close look at the people and villages of Nagar.

Askur Das has a tea shop and a tiny restaurant, and villagers claim there's a room to rent for about Rs 15 a bed. Other lodging options include going back (if it gets late and you can't catch a ride on the KKH, walk to the Eagle Nest Hotel in Murtazabad); camping at the high pastures in Sumayar Nala; or pressing on to Nagar village, three hours beyond Sumayar.

Top: Hunza River Valley near Gulmit and Passu (JK)
Bottom: Typically decorated lorry seen all over Pakistan (JK)

Top: Ultar Glacier and shepherd huts above Baltit Fort, Hunza Valley (JK)
Left: Tibetan-style tower on the roof of Baltit Fort (JW)
Right: The view from the roof of Baltit Fort (JW)

There are unconfirmed stories of stone-throwing kids along here but Nagaris dismiss them as 'Hunza propaganda'.

Sumayar Nala

This is the narrow canyon you look straight into from Karimabad, just right of the Nagar Valley. Camping is not advisable near Sumayar village, but it's excellent at the meadows three hours up the nala, with views of 7270-metre Diran Peak and the Silkiang Glacier. In summer you may find shepherds here. A footpath leaves the road near the powerhouse and initially follows the powerhouse channel. In the afternoon after freezing nights (in autumn, winter and early spring) there is a rockfall hazard in the nala.

When the Nagar River is low (mostly in winter) a makeshift footbridge crosses it, just where it joins the Hunza River; this way, it's only a one-hour hike from Ganesh to Sumayar. Footpaths descend to this point from the Nagar end of the KKH bridge and from the jeep road above Sumayar. At other times the easiest access is via Murtazabad (a third route, from Ganesh up to the Nagar River jeep bridge and back down, is a long, dry three to four hours).

Nagar Village

This little place was the capital of the state of Nagar, and the old mir still lives here. It has a few shops, a hospital and a police post where visitors' papers are sometimes checked. There are no obvious places to eat. An *NAPWD Rest House* has doubles for about Rs 60 (book through the Administrative Officer, Office of the Chief Engineer, NAPWD (tel Gilgit 2515), Bank Rd, Gilgit.

On foot this is about three hours from Karimabad (up the east side of the Nagar River), five from the KKH at Murtazabad, and three on to Hopar. After the hard-scrabble agriculture below, the stretch from here to Hopar is fertile and lovely in spring.

Hopar

Hopar refers to a cluster of villages, around a natural bowl at a bend of the Bualtar Glacier,

five to six hours' walking from Karimabad and a very long day's hike from Murtazabad. Opposite Hopar the white Bualtar is joined by the Barpu Glacier.

At the south end of the bowl are a rest house and tent-camp. At the *Hopar Hilton* tent-camp you can pitch yours or take a bed in one of theirs (about Rs 20, negotiable). The two-room *NAPWD Rest House* (double for Rs 60, meals by arrangement) should be booked ahead in Gilgit in the summer. In the off-season the manager, Shah Ban, lives in Ratal village, about one km down the valley.

From Hopar you can hike up along the Bualtar, or cross it and climb to the summer villages along both glaciers. The managers of both the rest house and the Hilton can help with information (including glacier crossings) and local guides. This is also the base for longer treks into the region of high, glacier-draped peaks called the Hispar Muztagh.

Getting There & Away

Via Murtazabad Take a Suzuki or an early-morning Gilgit-bound wagon to the jeep road just beyond Hasanabad Nala. There is no regular service crossing to the Nagar side here. Afternoon passenger jeeps from Gilgit sometimes go this way, but they're usually very full. Most go only to Nagar village.

Via Ganesh Most afternoons (but at varying times) a NATCO 4WD pick-up and various passenger jeeps go to Nagar village via Ganesh and the east side of the Nagar River; some may go to Hopar. Jeeps can also be hired in Ganesh and Karimabad.

From Nagar village, passenger jeeps and the NATCO pickup leave between 6 and 8 am, stopping at Ganesh on their way to Gilgit. Jeeps occasionally go from Hopar too.

MINAPIN

Down-river from Murtazabad the KKH crosses into Nagar, over a Chinese bridge with little stone lions. Just on the Nagar side, at Pisan, a jeep track turns east, 40 minutes' walk to Minapin. Literally at the foot of Rakaposhi, Minapin is the start of a glacier-side climb to one of the mountain's expedition base camps, and to longer treks toward Diran Peak.

Minapin has an *NAPWD Rest House*, on the east side of the stream. A double is about Rs 60, with meals by arrangement. Book ahead if you can with the NAPWD Administrative Officer in Gilgit. There is no camping in the village and the closest alternative is a 1 1/2-hour walk west to Ghulmet.

Rakaposhi Base Camp via Minapin Glacier

The well-used trail starts behind the rest house. The first few km are quite steep, up the Minapin Glacier's terminal moraine to the path along its west side. The path gives wide views of the glacier, and eventually of the entire Rakaposhi-Diran crest-line. A hut three to four hours makes a good day-hike destination; the next one is at the base camp, four hours higher. From the base camp, 1500 metres above Minapin in a vast meadow overlooking the glacier's upper icefields, Rakaposhi (7790 metres) is south-west and Diran (7270 metres) is south-east.

This trek is best done between July and September when days are long and water is available, but even then, plan on cold nights. Rakaposhi is also subject to unexpected, chilling storms. Unless you stay the night at Minapin and are in good shape, the meadow is perhaps better as a two-day climb.

A red bear is said to visit the meadow occasionally and raid campers' food supplies. There are no stories of harm to humans; just don't eat in your tent (which leaves the smell of food) or store food there.

Minapin villagers have come to expect employment as guides on this route, and it's not a bad idea. Young students who've grown up here and speak good English can tell you a lot. Beyond the upper meadow, a guide who knows the area is essential. As a very rough guideline, experienced guides expect Rs 150

to Rs 300 per day; local people may be satisfied with Rs 100 a day to show you the way and help with carrying and cooking.

GHULMET

The starting point for another Rakaposhi climb is the village of Ghulmet (pronounced 'ghool-MET'; this spelling is used instead of the often-seen 'Gulmit', to avoid confusion with the village in Gojal). At its eastern end is Ghulmet Nala, out of which Rakaposhi rises in a single unobscured sweep, begging to be photographed. In fact, a thoughtful sign points out this stupendous view, in case you overlook (underlook?) it.

At the nala's edge is a flag-decked tent-camp, the *Rakaposhi View Hotel & Open-Air Restaurant*; with basic food and space in a tent for Rs 10, this is the cheapo climbers' colony. By mid-October, like a travelling circus, it's been taken down.

Three km west, in Ghulmet Das, are two very seedy roadside hotels with beds for Rs 10 and basic meat-and-chapatti meals. The *Rakaposhi Inn* has a small blue sign; next door, the *Muhammadi Hotel* has no sign. There are no shops along the road.

Rakaposhi Base Camp via Ghulmet Glacier

Although there's a base camp up this trail (used by a Japanese expedition in 1979) and the views are outstanding, it's said to be a long, steep hike with no water and poor camping on the way. It seems better as a rigorous day-trip. The trail begins behind the hamlet of Yal east of Ghulmet Nala and climbs a high ridge between the Ghulmet and Pisan Glaciers. As with the Minapin hike, July through September are best, and even then cold storms can blow in. For more information ask at the Rakaposhi View; the owner is a retired guide, and climbed with the Japanese team.

THOL

The nala and village west of Ghulmet are called Thol ('tole'). A prominent landmark is

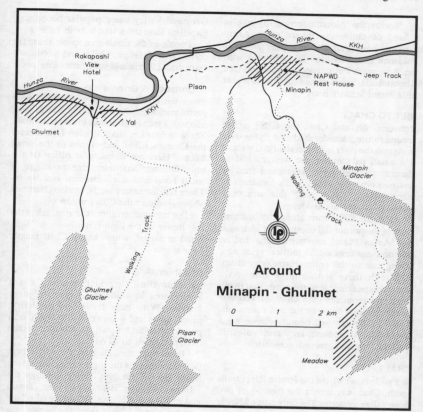

a blue-roofed shrine to Shah Wali, a Muslim preacher from Afghanistan who settled here in perhaps the 1600s. Roadside flags remind travellers to leave a few coins for its upkeep.

Of more interest is a small old house about 30 metres from the shrine. Made in traditional style, of stones fitted in a wood frame, it has a carved wooden door and a 'skylight' in the Balti-Tibetan style of Baltit Fort. Local people claim this was Shah Wali's house.

NILT

West of Thol (or about 20 minutes' ride east of Chalt) are the nala and stone fort that nearly derailed the British invasion of Hunza-Nagar in 1891. A path to the fort on the south side of the KKH is east of a stone tablet reading 'Mountaineering Institute & Alpine Club'. About 300 metres up the path, the fort is a nondescript low structure now used as residences. Although you can't get very close, the vantage point does give a sense of the British predicament.

Nearby, the 'Mountaineering Institute' is a kind of clubhouse where some Army officers have run training programs for Pakistani mountaineers. It's affiliated with the Adventure Foundation of Pakistan (see Abbottabad). Local mountain guides report little useful activity here.

NILT TO CHALT

Between Nilt and Chalt the KKH arches around fertile Sikanderabad as if flying over it. Across the river is Khizerabad and west of it a small nala marks the western end of Hunza. Further west, scratched into or fastened onto the valley walls hundreds of metres high, is the 'road' that was once Hunza's link to the outside.

Here the KKH runs along the southern edge of the primordial continent of Laurasia, the 'Asian Plate' into which the Indian subcontinent crashed 55 million years ago, giving rise to the entire Himalayan chain. Although there's no simple line, Asia (roughly speaking) is to the north, and to the south are remnants of a chain of volcanic islands trapped between the two continents. Rocks in the exposed boundary zone are a confusion of sedimentary and volcanic material, talc and greenish serpentine.

CHALT

In a wide bowl where the Hunza River turns south, Chalt sits across the mouths of two large valley systems. The only part of Nagar north of the river, this is probably the most well-endowed area from Kohistan to the Chinese border, in terms of weather, water, firewood, pasture and tillable land per person. The Mir of Nagar still keeps a house here.

The Chaprot Valley, with some fine day-hikes, has brought out the poet in visitors and residents alike. The misanthropic explorer Schomberg called it 'lovely, more beautiful than any other valley in the Gilgit Agency'. Safdar Ali, the Mir of Hunza at the time of the British invasion, said Chalt and Chaprot were 'more precious to us than the strings of our wives' pyjamas'. The grander but drier

Garmasai Valley has a popular hot spring. Excellent long treks start in both valleys.

People in the Chalt area speak Shina (in common with Gilgit, Chilas and Kohistan), Burushaski, Urdu and sometimes English.

Information & Orientation

From the KKH, one km west of a lonely petrol station, at the east end of a large rock outcrop, a jeep road crosses the river to Chalt. Three to four km along it a left fork crosses the Chaprot River and climbs to the small bazaar. Here are shops, post office (at the only intersection), telephone exchange, a small hotel and a government rest house. There is a dispensary on the road to Garmasai Valley, just past the Chaprot turn-off.

For information about the area, ask at the rest house or the high school – or in Bank Road in Gilgit, where many Chalt people have shops.

Ghashumaling

Ghashumaling ('ga-SHU-ma-ling') is a lovely area in a lower Chaprot tributary canyon. With easy trails and mulberry, peach, apple and walnut orchards, even local people come up for picnics. A walk can take from two hours to all day.

From the intersection by the post office, take the path past the high school and up the south side of Chaprot Valley, through the village of Rahbat. Bear left into the canyon and cross a footbridge. At the head of the canyon, about 12 km from the bazaar, are pine forests and the small Kacheli Glacier. A return option is via Chaprot village and the jeep track down the north side of the valley.

Chaprot Valley

From the bazaar, take the jeep road across the Chaprot River and turn left by some shops. About 150 metres up take the left fork, which climbs the north side of Chaprot Valley. It's an hour's walk to Chaprot village (actually a collection of hamlets). From there it's three to four hours on a mule-track through summer villages to pastures at the head of the valley, a good overnight destination. This is

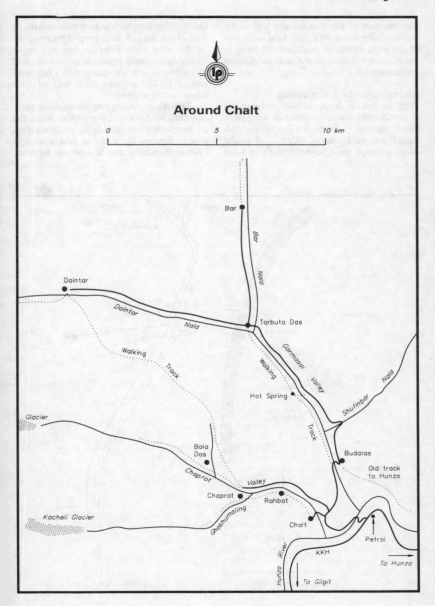

Around Chalt

0   5   10 km

Bar

Bar Nala

Daintar

Daintar Nala

Torbuto Das

Walking Track

Garmasai Valley

Walking Track

Hot Spring

Shutinbar Nala

Glacier

Bola Das

Chaprot

Budalas

Old track to Hunza

Chaprot Valley

Kacheli Glacier

Ghashumaling

Rahbat

Chalt

Petrol

Hunza River

KKH

To Hunza

To Gilgit

also the start of a five to six-day trek to the Naltar Valley north of Gilgit, said to be one of the most beautiful medium-size treks in the Northern Areas. In the summer, horses can be hired at Chaprot.

Garmasai Valley & Hot Spring

From the bazaar, cross the river and turn left as for Chaprot, but at the next fork keep right into Garmasai ('gar-ma-SAY') Valley, also called Bar or Budalas Valley (and easily confused with the Chaprot village of Bola Das!). After four km the jeep road crosses to Budalas on the east side; keep to the footpath on the west side. Four to five km up, a footbridge crosses from the other side, and 25 metres on is a hot spring with a low wall around it. The sulphur smell will tell you when you've arrived.

This is a popular spring for its therapeutic qualities; in April and September when the air temperature is just right, you may find people from as far away as Ishkoman and Chitral. Typically they'll soak for an hour,

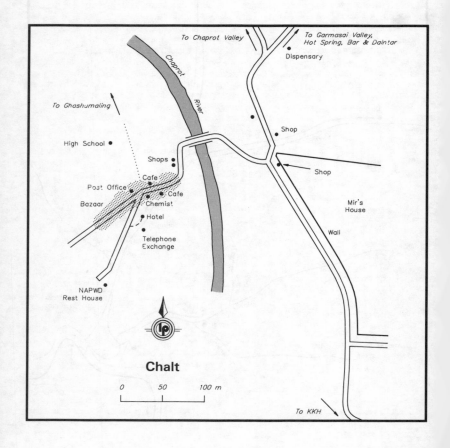

Chalt

0   50   100 m

then climb into a mound of blankets, drink hot tea, and sweat for several hours before going home. If you find local people there, note that the men and women soak separately.

About 100 metres upstream is some level ground for camping, by the remains of a house said to have been built by a British political officer from Gilgit.

'Hot spring' in Burushaski is *garum bul*, 'ga-ROOM bool'; in Shina it is *dato uts*, 'DAH-to oots'; in Urdu it is *garem chashma*.

A return option is to cross the footbridge and descend on the east-side jeep road for a side trip up Shutinbar Nala. For a longer trip, continue up-valley from the spring to Torbuto Das village at the confluence of the Bar and Daintar Nalas. Northward is Bar village (10 km from the spring), the trail-head for long treks to the upper Batura Glacier. Westward is Daintar village (about 15 km from the spring), from which a one or two-day walk crosses back over into Chaprot. You can also pick up the Chaprot-to-Naltar trek at Daintar, or a longer one into the Ishkoman Valley.

Shutinbar Nala

On the east side of Garmasai Valley, about three km upstream from the Budalas jeep bridge, the road briefly enters Shutinbar Nala. It's a steep eight to 10 km to a glacier at its head, and there are said to be abandoned ruby mines in the canyon.

Places to Stay & Eat

A small hotel 50 metres down the left fork in the Chalt bazaar has rope-beds for Rs 10; simple meals can be arranged.

An *NAPWD Rest House*, in an apricot orchard 100 metres past the hotel, has comfortable doubles with attached bath for about Rs 60, and meals can be arranged. The *chowkidar* lives nearby. Book it through the NAPWD Administrative Officer in Gilgit.

Besides hotel and rest-house food, there are two smokey cafes in the bazaar; food is basic but abundant. A new hotel is planned,

across the Chaprot River from the bazaar; inquire at the Golden Peak Inn in Gilgit.

Getting There & Away

From Karimabad, get off Gilgit-bound buses at the jeep road near the petrol station. From Gilgit, in addition to buses and jeeps to Hunza, Nagar and Sust, Chalt-bound jeeps and vans often leave in the early morning from Bank Rd and from near the Haidry Tea Shop off Rajah Bazaar, and a beat-up red wagon goes from Bank Rd every afternoon, for Rs 10.

Occasional passenger jeeps and the daily red wagon go from Chalt to Gilgit, usually between 7 and 8 am.

Getting Around

Local cargo jeeps, most frequent in summer, ply the roads from Chalt to Chaprot village, and to Bar village.

CHALT TO GILGIT

Below Chalt the Hunza River turns south. Ten minutes' ride down-river from the Chalt turn-off, road cuts above the highway are early 1960s attempts at a KKH by Pakistan Army Engineers. Across the river is the KKH's precarious precursor, a now-abandoned jeep road that follows the oldest caravan trails.

A few minutes southward the highway passes two grimy cafes and a road-maintenance base called Jaglot Guar (Jaglot Camp). Two or three km later, a jeep road climbs up to Jaglot village, the starting point for another Rakaposhi base camp trek, a day's climb up the north side of Jaglot Nala toward 4730-metre Haraj Peak, Rakaposhi's western arm. Accommodation in the area is scarce, though one of the cafes at Jaglot Guar has rope beds for Rs 10. For more trail information try Adventure Pakistan or the Tourist Cottages in Gilgit. (Note that there's another Jaglot on the KKH south of Gilgit.)

Across the river from Jaglot is an imaginative AKRSP irrigation scheme by the villagers of Gwachi: where a channel down the Gwachi Nala was impossible they have suspended a water pipe right across it, thin as a filament as seen from the KKH.

About 25 minutes down-river from Chalt, at the south end of Rahimabad village – and almost exactly midway between Kashgar and Rawalpindi – is a monument to KKH workers, topped with an old pneumatic rock-drill used for setting explosives. In Urdu script on the pedestal are the words of Pakistan's favourite philospher-poet, Alama Mohammed Iqbal (who in the 1930s first proposed a Muslim state in India): 'God has given man integrity, faith, and a strong mind, and if he sets himself to it he can kick a mountain to powder or stop a river in its tracks.'

Two minutes south of the monument the highway crosses a nala on a Chinese bridge decorated with the characters for 'double happiness'. Across the Hunza River is Nomal, the base for day-trips and treks into the beautiful Naltar Valley (described in the chapter on Gilgit).

As the road comes out into the basin where the Hunza River joins the Gilgit River, the view back up the Hunza Valley is dominated by 7140-metre Kampire Dior, 70 km north on the crest of the Karakoram. Dainyor, at the confluence, is the southernmost Ismaili village on the KKH.

Gilgit

Gilgit is the hub of the KKH: services, information, food and comfort; transport in every direction; easy access to over half the KKH in Pakistan, from the Khunjerab Pass to Chilas, and a web of valleys fingering Rakaposhi, Nanga Parbat and other giants. Not surprisingly it swarms with travellers, trekkers and mountaineers from May to October.

The scenery around Gilgit town (at 1500 metres) is austere and brown, except for riotous springtime peach blossoms and the autumn colours of fruit trees and poplars. But, typical of the Karakoram, the higher you go the better it looks; many glacier-fed valleys above 2000 metres harbour pine and juniper forests and luxuriant meadows.

Gilgit is headquarters for the 70,000 square km Northern Areas, a federally administered quasi-province extending north-east to the Khunjerab; north and west up the Gilgit River into the Hindu Kush; south-east up the Indus River to Baltistan and the highest peaks of the Karakoram; and south to Nanga Parbat. For the Pakistan government it's a ticklish place, bordering on India, China and Afghanistan (and the Soviet Union just beyond).

History

Prior to the 1800s Gilgit's past is mostly legends and inherited recollections. By the 1st century AD it was part of the Buddhist Kushan Empire at Taxila (near Rawalpindi), and remained Buddhist after the Kushans' demise in the 3rd century. The Chinese pilgrim Fa-Hsien found hundreds of active monasteries on his way from Xinjiang to Taxila in 403 AD. A few traces remain, including the great bas-relief Buddha on a cliff-face west of Gilgit and pictures scratched onto riverside rocks at Chilas.

Sanskrit inscriptions on a rock in the Gilgit 'suburb' of Dainyor list local Tibetan rulers of the 7th and 8th centuries. In the 8th century a Tang Chinese army occupied Chitral and the Gilgit Valley for three years before the Tibetans drove them out. According to the Dainyor stone, local rulers in turn expelled the Tibetans.

By the 10th century Gilgit was overrun by the Shins, an aggressive tribe from the lower Indus Valley, probably Hindu. Not much is known about them, but they imposed their language, Shina, on everyone else, and it's still the common speech.

Islam appeared in the south in the 11th century and migrated up the Indus over the next 300 years; during this time missionaries also came overland from Afghanistan and Persia. Gilgit's last non-Muslim ruler (until 1842) was the cruel Shiri Badat; legend says he was a cannibal, who ate a baby every day. His successor is credited with cleaning things up and introducing Shia Islam here.

In the early 1300s one Taj Mughal, a chieftain from north-east Afghanistan, conquered most of the upper valleys of the Gilgit River. To commemorate his victory at Gilgit he built a stone monument above nearby Jutial, and it's still there, in remarkably good shape. He went about converting everyone up-river of Gilgit to Ismailism.

During the following centuries the Silk Road fell out of use and Gilgit became an isolated backwater, with local tribe-states continually snatching it from one another. Its last local ruler was a tyrant named Gauhar Aman, who distinguished himself by selling a sizeable part of Gilgit's population into slavery.

He was turned out in 1841 by Dogra tribesmen of Kashmir, on behalf of the Sikh Empire in the Punjab, but they proved so disagreeable that Gauhar Aman had no trouble taking Gilgit back again in 1848. He fortified the town (a remnant is the yellow tower at the present militia barracks) and ruled till he died 10 years later.

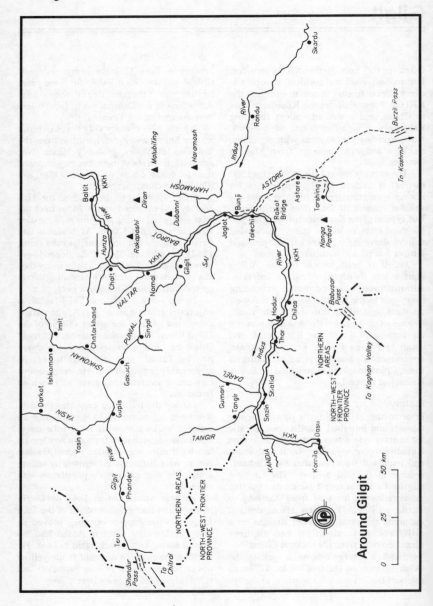

Around Gilgit

0   25   50 km

After that the Dogras came back, under new management. In 1846 the British won the first of two quick wars with the Sikhs and annexed Sikh territories in the Kashmir Valley, Ladakh, Baltistan and the vassal state of Gilgit. Packaging them up as 'the State of Jammu and Kashmir', they sold it for Rs 750,000 to a Dogra prince named Gulab Singh and declared him the first Maharajah of Kashmir. Thus Muslim Gilgit again found itself with a Hindu master, who received grudging tributes from local rulers in the upper Gilgit Valley (and occasionally from Hunza and Nagar) and maintained his garrisons.

Then Britain discovered the Russians snooping in the Pamirs and Afghanistan, and began to have doubts about the good sense of the Maharajah. In 1877 Kashmir was put under control of the Indian Foreign Office and a British 'political agent' arrived in Gilgit to look over the Kashmiri governor's shoulder. This proved very awkward, and the Agency was closed down after a few years – only to re-open in 1889 as Britain's anxiety mounted. The new 'PA' was a no-nonsense soldier named Algernon Durand, who lost no time in taking charge and putting everyone in their places.

Soon after his Hunza campaign of 1891 (see Hunza & Nagar – History) Durand put a garrison at Chilas to control the Babusar Pass to the Kaghan Valley, one of two tenuous supply routes for Gilgit (the other was the Burzil Pass to Kashmir). The troops had barely arrived when Indus Valley tribesmen attacked and nearly overran them. This inspired some quick improvements to the Chilas Fort, which still stands today, occupied by the police department (and resented as much as ever by the anarchic Chilasis).

Gilgit, like Kashgar, was an outpost in the Great Game, the imperial hide-and-seek between Britain and Russia, well into the 20th century. A succession of political agents managed by grace or guile to stay in charge, and in 1935 Britain actually leased back the entire Agency from Kashmir. A local militia,

the Gilgit Scouts, was raised, dressed in their own tartan, and drawn heavily from sons of local royalty. They were probably as much a warning to the Russians and a vehicle for intrigue, as a defence force.

Partition & the Gilgit Uprising In the 1930s and 1940s demands mounted both for Indian independence and for a separate Muslim homeland. In the end Britain agreed to split the empire into two countries, a Muslim-majority Pakistan and a Hindu-majority India.

An awkward problem was the hundreds of princely states with direct allegiance to Britain, who theoretically stood to regain their original sovereignty. Most were coaxed to join India or Pakistan. Kashmir - with a Hindu ruler, a Muslim majority and its lovely vale beloved by both Hindus and Muslims - was the biggest hot-potato of all. Maharajah Hari Singh, hoping for his own independence, stalled.

Two weeks before the 14 August 1947 end of the empire, the last political agent handed over the Gilgit Agency to a new Kashmiri governor, Ghansar Singh. As 14 August came and went, Gilgit held its breath while the Maharajah dithered. Then, on 26 October, a band of Pathan Afridi tribesmen from the North-West Frontier Province marched into Kashmir proclaiming a *jihad* or holy war, and everything came unglued. Hari Singh fled to Delhi, acceded to India and asked for military help. India accepted, subject to an eventual vote by the people of Kashmir.

Several groups had expected this. A clique of Muslim officers in the Maharajah's own army, led by Colonel Mirza Hassan Khan, had conspired to seize Kashmir for Pakistan, but word had got out and Hassan was transferred to Kashmir's 'Siberia', the Bunji garrison south of Gilgit. Meanwhile, Major Mohammed Babar Khan of the Gilgit Scouts and several fellow-officers (and, according to some, their British commander) had hatched a rebellion of their own.

Within days of the Maharajah's decision

a mob collected in Gilgit from neighbouring valleys. The governor called Bunji for help, and who should be among the reinforcements but Colonel Hassan. On 1 November Babar Khan arrested Ghansar Singh and the rebels asked to join Pakistan. Within a few days the Scouts, and Muslim soldiers of the Kashmiri army, joined an already ongoing war with India. In the following months the Scouts took Baltistan and Hassan got to the outskirts of Srinagar.

The fledgeling Indian Air Force at one point bombed Gilgit, no easy task in the narrow valleys. Gilgitis like to tell the story of the Scouts' pipe band, who mocked the Indian pilots by defiantly tootling up and down the airfield the whole time.

In January 1949 the war ended with a United Nations cease-fire. Pakistan was given temporary control over what is now the Northern Areas, and a slice of western Kashmir it calls *Azad* (Free) Kashmir; India got Ladakh and the Kashmir Valley. The cease-fire line across Kashmir became the *de facto* border.

The memories of the 'Uprising' are still alive in Gilgit. Babar and Hassan are buried in the town's maple-shaded municipal park, Chinar Bagh. One of Babar's sons is a chief of police; one of Hassan's sons is a local politician and several others run the Mt Balore Motel. A Pakistani officer later put in charge of Babar and Hassan has become something of a local villain in Hunza: Brigadier Aslam, purveyor of the Shangri-La resorts.

Of course it's not 14 August but 1 November that Gilgit celebrates as Independence Day, with spontaneous music and dancing and a week-long polo tournament. One of the best polo teams every year is from the Gilgit garrison of the Northern Light Infantry, descendants of the Gilgit Scouts.

After Partition India and Pakistan again fought over Kashmir in 1965 and 1971; the latter war also led to the secession of East Pakistan as Bangladesh. Pakistan stands officially by its position that, until the referendum promised by India is held, Kashmir doesn't belong to anyone. But the chances of reunifying Kashmir by any means seem to have faded away.

Meanwhile the Northern Areas are in limbo. To make them a province would concede the status quo of a divided Kashmir. They are instead a 'Federally Administered Area' with a chief officer answering to a special ministry in Islamabad. Although the government is generous with development money, Northerners cannot, for example, vote in national elections or take cases to the Supreme Court. Having fought to join Pakistan, many now feel excluded and exploited.

The Burzil Pass was closed by the 1948 cease-fire, leaving only the Babusar Pass to link the Northern Areas with the rest of Pakistan. It's surprising to realise that Gilgit was only firmly linked to the outside world some 20 years ago, by a civilian air corridor and the first stages of the KKH.

The People

The Shins provide a major pedigree in the Gilgit Valley and Indus Kohistan and their language, Shina ('shee-NAH'), is spoken by everyone. Gilgit's crossroads position has filled its bazaar (and enlivened its genetic pool) with people from all over Asia, and forced Gilgitis to be multi-lingual. It is not unusual to hear Uyghur, Wakhi, Burushaski, Pushto or even Persian; Urdu and English are widely spoken.

All brands of Islam are represented: Ismailis in the Gilgit and Hunza valleys; Shias in Nagar, Bagrot and Haramosh; Sunnis in Chilas and southward; and all of them in Gilgit town, where sectarian tension is just below the surface. In 1988 Sunni-Shia hostility exploded here, touched off when Shias celebrated the end of *Ramadan* a day earlier than Sunnis; gun battles raged all over the Gilgit area, and hundreds are said to have been killed.

Festivals

Late February – Early March

First (Wheat) Sowing. In remote valleys like Bagrot, farmers, before breaking ground, may celebrate in their fields with their families and neighbours.

21 March

Nauroz ('New Days'), a spring festival and a Shia and Ismaili celebration of the succession of the Prophet's son-in-law Ali. In Gilgit there may be polo, but many shopkeepers close down and celebrate in their home villages.

April

Polo matches are often held in Gilgit or the upper Gilgit Valley during this month, but they may not be common in 1990 and 1991 because of overlap with *Ramadan*.

*30 March to 29 April (1990), 20 March to 19 April (1991)

Ramadan, a month of daytime fasting for Shias and Sunnis. Restaurants and markets are closed until sunset, and people are cranky. Foreigners can find food at tourist hotels and in Ismaili neighbourhoods such as Jamat Khana Bazaar.

*29 April (1990), 19 April (1991)

Eid-ul-Fitr, two days of celebrations at the end of *Ramadan*, including feasting and gift-giving. Many shops are closed.

Late June – Early July

First (Wheat) Harvest. In remote valleys some farmers have private ceremonies, similar to First Sowing.

*5 August (1990), 26 July (1991)

Ashura, the 10th day of *Muharram*. Shias mourn the death of Hussain at Karbala. In an awesome and horrific procession through the west end of Gilgit, led by a riderless white horse, men and boys pound their chests and chant the names of the dead at Karbala; some flail their backs with blade-tipped chains. Shia-Sunni hostility has sometimes flared up at this time, and armed police now watch from the rooftops. In other Shia villages smaller processions may be held.

*14 September (1990), 4 September (1991)

Chehelum, the end of the 40 days of mourning that starts with *Ashura*, with similar but smaller processions.

*3 October (1990), 23 September (1991)

Eid-Milad-un-Nabi, the Prophet's birthday. Some shops are closed. At night, sawdust-and-kerosene firepots light up the hillsides above town.

1 November

Uprising Day or *Jashan-i-Gilgit*, 'Gilgit Festival'. This is the biggest event of the year, celebrating the 1947 uprising against the Maharajah of Kashmir, and the normally reserved Gilgitis let their hair down. People stream into town for a week-long tournament of thunderous 'no-rules' polo (northerners say the game was invented here), kicked off by a tartan-clad pipe band and much good-humoured pomp.

*15 December

Nos. In Bagrot and Haramosh every household slaughters a goat and hangs it up for all to see, thus insuring a winter food supply, and in time for the meat to dry without spoiling. In Bagrot *Nos* is an occasion for music and dancing.

* approximate dates

GILGIT

The KKH has dragged Gilgit into the mainstream, but it's been slow to catch on. Public services aren't multiplying nearly as fast as hotels; electricity is intermittent and water supplies are still vulnerable to the weather.

The Gilgit bazaar, while not as colourful or traditional as Kashgar's, is eclectic and lively; good Hunza wool garments alone make it worth a look. The shopkeepers, from all over Pakistan and Xinjiang, are part of its attraction. In search of a sale or a chat, it's their 'Muslim duty' to ask you in and serve you sweet tea till your kidneys burst.

The town wakes up early, to *muezzins* in scores of mosques, calling the faithful to dawn prayers. Plaintive and charming for the first few days, the overlapping, amplified chants are before long a nuisance to the average infidel. The faithful probably cope by going to bed early; except for a few cafes and barbershops, the bazaar is dark soon after sunset.

There are very few local women on the streets. Young men, fed on cinematic stereotypes, often seem unable to take foreign women seriously. There are stories of low-level sexual harassment, eg in passenger Suzukis after dark. More often, women are simply patronised or ignored.

Orientation

Gilgit is about 10 km west off the KKH. The road first passes through the cantonment at Jutial (these tidy military sectors are a common colonial holdover in large towns of India and Pakistan). Bus passengers are

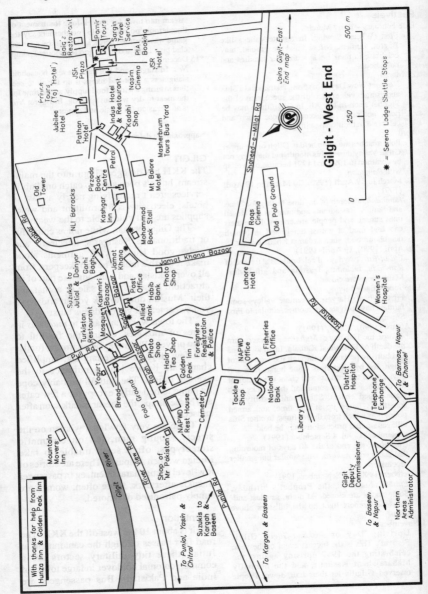

Gilgit – West End

With thanks for help from
Hunza Inn & Golden Peak Inn

0   250   500 m

= Serena Lodge Shuttle Stops

Map labels:

Baig 2 Restaurant
Pamir Tours
Sargin Travel Service
JSR Plaza
PIA Booking
JSR 'Hotel'
Prince Tours (Taj 'Hotel')
Nasim Cinema
Jubilee Hotel
Pathan 'Hotel'
Indus Hotel & Restaurant
Kadahi Shop
Masherbrum Tours Bus Yard
Old Tower
Petrol
Pirzada Book Centre
Mt Balore Motel
NLI Barracks
Kashgar Inn
Mohammad Book Stall
Suzukis to Jutial & Dainyor
Garhi Bagh
Jamat Khana
Jamat Khana Bazaar
Jamat Khana Bazaar
Photo Shop
Post Office
Habib Bank
Lahore Hotel
Sadar Bazaar
Mosque/Kashmiri Bazaar
Turkistan Restaurant
Allied Bank
Foreigners Registration & Police
Raas Cinema
Old Polo Ground
Photo Shop
Haidry Tea Shop
Golden Peak Inn
NAPWD Office
Fisheries Office
Women's Hospital
Pull Rd
Rajah Bazaar
Yogurt
Bread
Polo Ground
Tackle Shop
National Bank
Cemetery
NAPWD Rest House
District Hospital
Telephone Exchange
River View Rd
Shop of Mr Pakistan
Library
Gilgit Deputy Commissioner
Suzukis to Kargah & Baseen
Punial Rd
Northern Areas Administrator
Hospital Rd
Shaheed-e-Millat Rd
Joins Gilgit-East End map
To Punial, Yasin & Chitral
To Kargah & Baseen
To Baseen & Napur
To Barmas, Napur & Channel
River Gilgit
Mountain Movers Inn

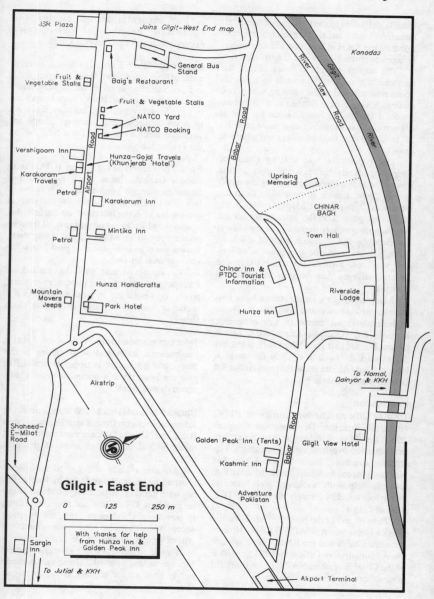

JSR Plaza

Joins Gilgit-West End map

Konodas

Fruit & Vegetable Stalls

General Bus Stand

Baig's Restaurant

Fruit & Vegetable Stalls

NATCO Yard

NATCO Booking

Road

Vershigoom Inn

Karakoram Travels

Hunza-Gojal Travels (Khunjerab Hotel)

Petrol

Airport

Karakorum Inn

Mintika Inn

Petrol

Mountain Movers Jeeps

Hunza Handicrafts

Park Hotel

Airstrip

Shaheed—E–Millat Road

Babar Road

River View Road

Gilgit River

Uprising Memorial

CHINAR BAGH

Town Hall

Chinar Inn & PTDC Tourist Information

Riverside Lodge

Hunza Inn

To Nomol, Dainyor & KKH

Babar Road

Golden Peak Inn (Tents)

Gilgit View Hotel

Kashmir Inn

Adventure Pakistan

Gilgit - East End

0   125   250 m

With thanks for help from Hunza Inn & Golden Peak Inn

Sargin Inn

To Jutial & KKH

Airport Terminal

usually delivered to the east end of the Gilgit bazaar. A back road also comes from further north on the KKH at Dainyor, via suspension bridges over the Hunza and Gilgit Rivers.

The airport is east of town. From the terminal it's a 15-minute walk to a roundabout near the end of the runway, where you can catch a passenger Suzuki into the bazaar for Rs 1 (if you do find Suzukis for hire at the terminal, it shouldn't cost more than Rs 20 to take a full load of riders anywhere in town).

The bazaar is just a long chain of shopping streets through the core of the town. The Gilgit River flows along the north side of town. Beside it, north-east from the bazaar, is Chinar Bagh ('Maple Garden'), the municipal park. The flat ground across the river is appropriately named Konodas, Shina for 'Scrubby Plain'. South-west of town, up Bank Rd, are regional government offices and services. Further up the hillside are several villages, the biggest of which is Barmas.

Many of Gilgit's larger streets have two names, one common and one official. These include (official name in parentheses): Airport Rd (Quaid-i-Azam Rd), Jamat Khana Bazaar (Sir Aga Khan Rd), Bank Rd (Khazana Rd; *khazana* is Urdu for 'bank'), Hospital Rd (Alama Iqbal Rd) and Babar Rd (Abdur Rabh Mishtar Rd).

Information

Tourist Offices The local office of PTDC (Pakistan Tourism Development Corporation) (tel 2454, 2562) is at the Chinar Inn, on Babar Rd overlooking Chinar Bagh. The smiling manager, Riaz Ahmed Khan, has Northern Areas brochures and information, and can help with bookings, jeep hire and group tours. Oddly enough, there is no PTDC map of Gilgit.

To book any of the Northern Areas Public Works Department (NAPWD) Rest Houses between Chilas and the Khunjerab Pass, see the Administrative Officer (tel 2515), Office of the Chief Engineer, NAPWD, on Bank Rd across from the National Bank.

For information on guides and equipment needed for out-of-town excursions, see Trips Beyond Gilgit.

Business Hours Except as noted, government offices open from 9 am to 1 pm and 2 to 5 pm Saturday through Wednesday, and 9 am to 1 pm Thursday. Banks open from 9 am to 1 pm Monday through Thursday, and 9 am to noon Saturday and Sunday. Shops are variable; some even open for a half-day on the Friday sabbath.

Post The General Post Office (GPO) is in Saddar Bazaar. Hours are 8 am to 2 pm Saturday through Wednesday. A window at left front sells stamps. Poste restante is around back, in the last room on the left; this is also the place to get outgoing mail franked on the spot, to avoid the risk of stamp theft. On the street in front, the blue post-box is for international letters.

To mail out parcels, go in the centre door. Except for flat things like papers, everything has to be sewed up in cloth (about Rs 5 a metre in Saddar or Kashmiri Bazaar cloth shops).

Telecommunications You can place international calls and send cables at the Telephone Exchange in upper Hospital Rd, past the hospital. It's open 24 hours a day, seven days a week.

Banks National Bank of Pakistan is off Bank Rd, two blocks up from Rajah Bazaar. Habib Bank and Allied Bank are next door to each other in Saddar Bazaar, west of the post office.

All are a little allergic to travellers' cheques because of past fraud by foreigners, but with good identification you should have no problem. US dollars and pounds sterling, in travellers' cheques or cash, are the most acceptable. If all else fails, some merchants will offer a good rate for US dollars cash.

Habib, at least, doesn't give encashment receipts unless you ask. These can come in handy later, eg for airline-ticket paperwork.

Top: Local children with typical kohl-coloured eyes, Hunza (JW)
Left: Chalt Village, Hunza Valley (JK)
Right: Shia Muslim mosque from the days before the Hunza people converted to
       Ismailism (JK)

Top: Children of Farphu Village, Bagrot Valley (JK)
Left: Men chat on the Karakoram Highway, Hunza Valley (JK)
Right: Altit Fort, Hunza Valley (JW)

To be of any use they must have the amounts in both currencies, the exchange rate, an official signature and the bank's stamp.

If you're south-bound this is the last place to change money (except possibly US dollars cash) until Abbottabad; north-bound, no banks will do foreign exchange until Sust.

PIA The PIA booking office is at the rear of JSR Plaza at the east end of Cinema Bazaar.

Bookshops & Newsstands The best-known bookshop in the Northern Areas is G M Baig's Mohammad Book Stall (tel 2409) in Jamat Khana Bazaar. Baig, a 'republisher' of books on the region (some of them unavailable elsewhere), historian, raconteur and self-styled 'cultural consultant', also sells antiques, postcards and daily copies of *The Muslim*, the closest thing to a newspaper.

Dad Ali Shah's Hunza Handicrafts, in front of the Park Hotel on Airport Rd, has some books among the curios, clothing and camping gear. The Pirzada Book Centre in Cinema Bazaar carries *Time* and *Newsweek*.

Libraries In a lane off upper Bank Rd is the Gilgit Municipal Library, the Northern Areas' only public library. It has almost 20,000 volumes, mostly in English, heavy on colonial tastes and modern Americana, and a great 'adventure & travel' section. You can browse through *Time*, *Newsweek* and English-language Pakistani papers in its baywindowed reading room, once the home of the early British political agents (whose photographs line the walls). Head Librarian Ashraf Ali and Assistant Librarian Sherbaz Ali are themselves good sources of local knowledge. April to October hours are 11 am to 5 pm Sunday to Thursday, and 8 am to noon Friday; in winter they open and close earlier.

There is also a small library in the Ismaili Study Centre, by the *jamat khana* or prayer hall in Jamat Khana Bazaar.

Foreigners' Registration & Police A Foreigners' Registration office is at the police post in Saddar Bazaar, opposite the big mosque. If you're south-bound and didn't get a Temporary Certificate of Registration (Form C) from Sust immigration, or if you're planning to be in Pakistan more than 30 days, registering here and getting a residence permit will reduce paperwork hassles later on. If you're heading for China, Sust immigration officials may not care whether you've registered.

Hospitals The District Hospital has entrances in upper Hospital Rd and Bank Rd. There is also a Women's Hospital nearby, with female doctors. Foreign women can be treated at either place, but the District Hospital has more specialists. Gilgit has a few overworked private physicians (there are two near the general bus stand), suitable if you already know what you need.

Photo Shops & Studios You'll need passport-size photos for Foreigners' Registration. There is a small studio a few doors west of the police station and another on the west side of Jamat Khana Bazaar. Three prints are about Rs 20, ready in one day.

Major-brand colour print film is available at these and other shops, but it's often overheated from being displayed in the windows. The Serena Lodge sells film that has been kept cool. No-one sells slide film.

Hot Wash If your hotel won't heat up a bucket of water, you can wash at one of the little *hammams* all over town. These barbershop-cum-bathhouses are easily recognisable by the lines of towels drying outside. Rs 5 gets you soap, towel and bucket in a tiny booth with hot water on tap; bring your own towel if a recycled one doesn't appeal to you. Normally men-only, some will clear the premises for women customers. They're open early and late, and closed only one day a month.

Around Gilgit

Besides the original political agents' house

(now the old wing of the Municipal Library), a few other traces of Gilgit's history can still be found.

In the middle of the NLI barracks (Northern Light Infantry, once the Gilgit Scouts) a yellow tower is all that remains of fortifications built by Gauhar Aman in the 1850s. Unfortunately the sentries won't let you go in, or even photograph it, but you can see it from the gate at the east end of Saddar Bazaar. There are old photos of it in Karim Jan's photo shop in Pull Rd.

Near the Golden Peak Inn in lower Bank Rd is a sad old British cemetery, overgrown and surrounded by barbed wire. Among those buried here are Captain George Hayward, a British explorer who was murdered in Yasin in 1870 by a son of Gauhar Aman. Ask in the shop across the street for the key to the gate ('key' is *chabi*, 'chah-BEE', in Urdu).

On the west side of Chinar Bagh is a rather touching memorial to those who rose against the Maharajah of Kashmir in 1947. On either side are the graves of the Uprising's heroes, Mohammed Babar Khan of the Gilgit Scouts and Mirza Hassan Khan of the Kashmir Infantry.

The Kargah Buddha A survivor from Buddhist times is the large standing Buddha carved on a cliff-face in Kargah Nala, west of Gilgit. It probably dates from the 7th century, and is in a style also found in Baltistan. Local stories have it that the figure is in fact a man-eating giant who terrorised the valley until it was pinned to the wall by a passing holy man.

From Rajah Bazaar walk about 300 metres out along Punial Rd, catch a Rs 2 passenger Suzuki toward Baseen village and get off at Kargah (or it's a five-km hike). Walk 10 minutes up the jeep road on the east side of Kargah Nala to a steep gully on your left; the Buddha is high above the far (south) side of the gully. Approach it along vague paths through the fields.

Going up the north side of the gully (which is called Shukogah) you reach the village of Napur. Nearby are the ruins of a monastery and stupa, where Buddhist texts on birch-bark (now called the Gilgit Manuscripts) were found in the 1930s. A return option, with good views of the valley, is to continue on this high path to Barmas village, and then down into Gilgit.

A transport alternative is to hire a Suzuki (holds eight to 10, about Rs 100 return). Ask at your hotel or try Pamir Tours or the Hunza Inn.

Jutial Nala & Channel Walk The Gilgit Valley is actually rather grand, but it's impossible to appreciate it from town. A fairly easy hike from Jutial along the water channel high on the valley wall gives a superb panorama that includes Rakaposhi and other snowy peaks.

From Saddar Bazaar catch a passenger Suzuki to Jutial (Rs 2) and go to the end of the line, just below the Serena Lodge. Walk up past the Serena entrance; the road turns right after about 1/2 km and then left into the main road up the nala. Climb till you see a stream going off to the right; this is the headworks of the water channel, which among other things is Gilgit's water supply. The channel has a stout outer wall, good for walking.

Several km along, you can scramble up the rock face to the monument erected by Taj Mughal in the 1300s. At Barmas village, near some water tanks, descend into Gilgit along what becomes Hospital Rd. From the Serena to the bazaar takes under two hours.

One option is to first walk into Jutial Nala, about two hours up to pine forests and excellent views of Rakaposhi. Another is to continue along the channel to Napur and the Kargah Buddha (about two hours beyond Barmas).

If there's been more than a few hours of rain in recent days, *stay away* from this walk as the hillsides are very prone to rockslides.

Dainyor A small village at Gilgit's back door, Dainyor makes a good day-trip for some interesting historical items. From

Saddar Bazaar, passenger Suzukis go to Dainyor's bazaar on the KKH for Rs 2. The trip there, over two spectacular bridges, is half the fun; some Gilgitis claim that the bridge over the Gilgit River is the longest jeepable suspension bridge in Asia, although the one over the Hunza River is more hair-raising.

Overlooking the Hunza River is a *ziarat* or shrine to a 14th-century Muslim preacher named Sultan Alib. On its roof is a classic Balti or Tibetan-style wooden 'skylight' like the one on Baltit Fort in Hunza. Nearby villagers will show you inside, and ask you to leave a few coins for upkeep. The black flag over it denotes a Shia holy place. Get off the Suzuki when it tops the climb on the east side of the Hunza River, and double back on a path above the road; or it's two km back from the Dainyor bazaar.

The 'Chinese cemetery' is a peaceful, melancholy place with the graves of 88 Chinese KKH workers who never made it home. From the bazaar walk 1½ km south on the KKH; it's on the left behind a large yellow gate.

In the village is a huge rock with Sanskrit inscriptions about a line of Tibetan princes who ruled here in the 7th and 8th centuries. It's on the property of one Rafid Ullah, who has now somewhat obstructed it with walls, but he's willing to show it to visitors, perhaps encouraged with a few rupees for his trouble. From the bazaar walk one km north along the KKH (if you cross a bridge you've gone too far) to a jeep road on the right, with an AKRSP sign by it. Go up the road about ¾ km and ask for him by name; his house is on the left, off the road. If you get lost, ask for the 'old writing stone': *likitu giri* ('lee-KEE-too gee-ree') in Shina, or *girminum bun* ('geer-MEEN-oom boon') in Burushaski.

According to local people there are other inscriptions and an excavation of a 'very old' village about one km further up the jeep road, near the house of a man named Islam, but I didn't check this out.

Trout Fishing Streams and lakes all over northern Pakistan are stocked with trout. Good reaches near Gilgit are Kargah Nala, Naltar Valley and Singal Nala up the Gilgit Valley. The Northern Areas season is 10 March to 9 October.

Information and licences are available at the hard-to-find Fisheries office on the east side of Bank Rd, 100 metres up from the bank (down a short alley between some wooden stalls). They may soon move up the road, near the government buildings.

Tackle can be hired from the Fisheries office (Rs 10 per day plus Rs 300 deposit) or at the shop of Raja Haji Ismaili, on the west side of Bank Rd, 40 metres down from the bank (no English sign, just ask around). Pamir Tours, Adventure Pakistan, Chinar Inn, Serena Lodge and others have package deals that include licence and tackle.

Longer Trips Overnight and longer excursions are described under Trips Beyond Gilgit, with suggestions on guides, equipment and transport.

Places to Stay – bottom end

For rock-bottom accommodation (Rs 20 or less per person) the most agreeable choices are the dormitories (or your own tent) at *Golden Peak Inn* or *Tourist Cottages*. The Golden Peak Inn also has a tent-site on Babar Rd about 400 metres west of the airport, Rs 20 a bed in their tents, or pitch your own. The centrally-located *Jubilee Hotel* (the sign says 'Jublee Hotal') has doubles for Rs 30 (no toilet) to Rs 50, on a noisy, willow-shaded yard. Travellers say it's wall-to-wall cockroaches.

In a former villa of the Mir of Nagar on Bank Rd is the *Golden Peak Inn*. The old verandahed house is still vaguely elegant and the sunny garden is a great place to nurse a pot of tea. Maintenance and food are sketchy, but offset by the easy, helpful manner of manager Latif Anwar Khan. Doubles are Rs 50 and Rs 60 (the latter with toilet and cold shower), dorm beds are Rs 20 or pitch a small tent for Rs 15.

On Babar Rd above the park, the quiet *Hunza Inn* has maps and information, a trekkers' log, bicycle rental, on-call Suzuki, jeep and wagon hire and, oh boy, hot showers. Dorm beds are Rs 25 and Rs 30, doubles (with toilet) Rs 60, and fancy doubles (carpets and shower) Rs 150 and up. Food and service get mixed reviews from travellers.

Tourist Cottages (tel 2376), on the road to Jutial, has a reputation for cheap rooms, good food and travellers' help (including a KKH 'rumour book') although when manager Abdul Karim is away, food and service slip. Sparsely furnished doubles and triples are both Rs 60, dorm beds are Rs 20, and they have tents too. They serve a set Hunza-style dinner for Rs 20 (call ahead if you're not a guest). It's three km from the middle of town but Suzukis to Saddar Bazaar pass by all day.

A large *NAPWD Rest House* is on Bank Rd at Punial Rd. Clean, comfortable doubles are Rs 60, but are usually booked out in the summer. Contact the Administrative Officer (tel 2515), Office of the Chief Engineer, NAPWD, up Bank Rd opposite the bank.

In Cinema Bazaar the *Indus Hotel & Restaurant* (no English sign but it's just left of Masherbrum Tours) has overpriced, noisy doubles (Rs 60) on a dirt yard behind the restaurant. The seedy *Karakorum Inn* on Airport Rd has noisy rooms for Rs 25 to Rs 35 a bed.

Places to Stay – middle

The most convenient location in town probably belongs to the *Mt Balore Motel*, a quiet complex of buildings and gardens right off Cinema Bazaar, run by several sons of Colonel Hassan, hero of the 1947 Uprising. Singles/doubles are Rs 100/150, negotiable in the off-season; camping is possible. They also offer guides and jeep hire.

On Airport Rd near NATCO, the slightly run-down *Vershigoom Inn* has quiet doubles/triples (with toilet) for Rs 80/100, on

a courtyard with a mountain view. The big, dark restaurant in front is popular with local people.

East of the park on River View Rd is the small *Riverside Lodge*, which gets high marks for tranquillity and good food, but is a long way from town. A double is Rs 120; camping is possible. Further east, past the bridge, is the far less cozy *Gilgit View Hotel*, with doubles for Rs 150.

The *Lahore Hotel*, opposite the cinema in lower Hospital Rd (outer Jamat Khana Bazaar), has clean, plain rooms on a tiny courtyard. Doubles/triples (with toilet) are Rs 80/100; quads (no toilet) are Rs 100.

The *Mountain Movers Inn* is across the river, but five minutes from the bazaar over the Pull Rd bridge. Carpeted singles/doubles with toilet and hot shower are Rs 90/130. They also run a jeep-rental service on Airport Rd.

On the road to Jutial, about 1/2 km past the airstrip, is the little *Sargin Inn*, with a weedy garden, a pleasant screened porch in the back and plain doubles for Rs 50.

Places to Stay – top end

The *Park Hotel* near the east end of Airport Rd has clean doubles with attached hot showers for Rs 185 and up, and a fairly good restaurant. PTDC's *Chinar Inn* (tel 2454, 2562), beside the park, has luxury singles/doubles for Rs 225/300; this is also the PTDC Tourist Information Centre.

The *Serena Lodge* (tel 2330, 2331), with doubles at Rs 560, is obviously not a place to stay but, with free video movies, all-you-can-eat dinners three times a week and a free shuttle bus, it might be a good place to visit if you're road-weary.

Places to Eat

It's hard to find the proverbial cheap and tasty, clean and well-lit place here. Most hotels have food of some sort and the bazaar is full of dark, nondescript meat-and-chapatti cafes (often called 'hotels'), but there's lots of room for improvement.

Vegetarians can get by, but normal fare is

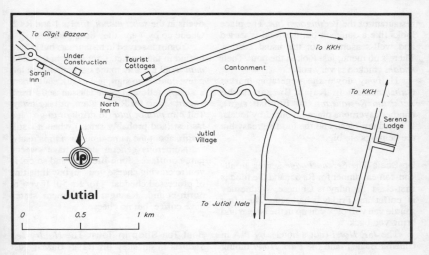

Jutial

0   0.5   1 km

dreary. Some hotels will stir something up by request, especially if you buy the ingredients.

Hygiene can be a problem if you have to eat with your fingers or scraps of chapatti, but even the lowliest places have a washstand somewhere, and something on the menu that's steaming hot. Probably a bigger risk is drinking tap water from communal tumblers.

Throughout Pakistan, Tuesday and Wednesday are theoretically 'meatless' days, when mutton and beef may not be sold at market (for economic, not religious, reasons). Restaurants often stock up on Mondays, and there's chicken in any case. In this angler's paradise, it's a pity nobody serves fish (commercial fishing is illegal), although they'll cook it if you catch it.

Cheap & Good The *Tourist Cottages* serves a filling Hunza-style dinner (thick noodle soup, rice, vegetable, meat and dessert) every evening at 7.30 pm, for Rs 20. If you're not a guest, call them early in the day (tel 2376). Take a Jutial-bound Suzuki from the bazaar for Rs 2; it's three km from Saddar. Return transport thins out in the evening, especially in autumn.

Some (but not all) travellers claim the *Hunza Inn's* food is top-notch. Try their roast chicken, which costs Rs 80 and feeds four, but they need several hours' notice.

One of Gilgit's most visible eateries is the *Pathan Hotel* (no English sign), the 'hamburger palace' on the south side of Cinema Bazaar serving *chapli kebabs*, spicy mutton-burgers. They also have good braised chicken, *kadahi* ('kah-DYE') *murghi*, enough for two for about Rs 20. It's friendly, popular and crowded at lunchtime. It's medium-clean, so stick to the fresh hot items.

About 150 metres west, beside the alley into the Masherbrum Tours yard, is a tiny, nameless cafe serving one item: *kadahi gosht*, mutton braised with vegetables and spices, served in its own cooking pan (very hygienic) and eaten with chapattis.

Diagonally opposite JSR Plaza on Airport Rd is *Baig's Restaurant*. Though dark and gloomy even in broad daylight, it's clean, with a selection of good Pakistani dishes – all very nearly ruined by non-stop videos (imagine chicken jalfrazi with screaming Japanese lady wrestlers).

Further east on Airport Rd is the big, dark

restaurant of the *Vershigoom Inn*. The place looks like a dungeon but the food is varied and well-seasoned, not the usual curries. There's no menu; just look in the pots. Their *kadahi* chicken is very good.

Halfway down the vegetable market (*sabzi mandi*) in Rajah Bazaar is the *Turkistan Restaurant* (no English sign), another cavernous place favoured by locals. It's medium-clean and the food's greasy but the helpings are big.

Up-Scale The *Serena Lodge* serves an all-you-can-eat dinner for Rs 65, and the food is first-class. Monday is Chinese, Wednesday is 'buffet' and Friday is barbecue. Their free shuttle van will pick you up in the bazaar and bring you back.

The *JSR Hotel* (not a hotel), by PIA in Cinema Bazaar, and the *Park Hotel* dining room are clean and well-run, with a fair selection of Pakistani, western and some Chinese dishes. They're both a bit over-priced; for a complete meal you could run up an almost-Serena-sized bill for small helpings of ho-hum food.

Self-Catering The best selection of fresh fruit and vegetables is at four stands in the wholesale area, on Airport Rd just west of NATCO. A smaller vegetable market (*sabzi mandi*) is along the west side of the main mosque in Rajah Bazaar. Fruit sellers prowl the streets.

Apricot season is in July and early August. The best dried apricots are not in the big-volume wholesale shops (which bring out their best only after the rest have gone to down-country buyers) but in small general stores. Good ones are at least Rs 20 a kg. It's a good idea to soak them in boiling water for a few minutes; soggy apricots are no fun but wholesalers sort them on the floor and walk over them. Apples, pomegranates, walnuts and Gilgit's own peaches appear in September and October.

Fresh rounds of *nan* bread (stout and eggy like bagels) are sold right out of the ovens in the *sabzi mandi*, for Rs 1 and Rs 2. Queue up by 7 am; they disappear fast.

Yogurt is served in restaurants but is hard to find in the market. I got mine in the *sabzi mandi* (all the way to the back, then turn left a few doors): no sign, just a dark stall where a sleepy fellow named Hassan sells fresh yogurt (*dahi*) for Rs 2 a glass, or take-away. Tell him *pita* or *jata* (to drink or to go). It's tastiest (and probably safest) when it's still warm, about the same time the *nan* is ready.

Numerous general stores have sweets, jam, cornflakes, long-life milk and so on. If you're craving cheese you can buy little tins of processed cheddar – for Rs 50! If you're north-bound, Kashgar department stores have coffee, but no cheese.

Best Tea Shop in Town The *Haidry Tea Shop* is in an alley off Rajah Bazaar, just around the corner from Bank Rd. This tiny one-man operation serves fresh black tea with milk, sugar, cardamom and ginger, in meticulously washed glasses, for Rs 1.

Alcohol None, even in the top-end hotels.

Things to Buy

A bargain you won't find elsewhere is the coarse, durable wool (*patti* or *pattu*) of Hunza and Nagar. Near the intersection of Jamat Khana Bazaar and Cinema Bazaar, several 'handicraft' shops have big selections of ready-made hats, waistcoats and *choghas* (long, embroidered cloaks) – at tourist prices. Unfortunately a lot of it is cheap, machine-woven wool (and even synthetics) from Swat and Chitral, and some shopkeepers will tell you anything.

Good handmade local wool is thick and tightly woven, with an uneven grain. Brown and white are best; colours fade quickly. If you're serious about it, look in the smaller shops of Jamat Khana and Rajah Bazaar, Bank Rd and Punial Rd. If you buy your own wool and take it to a tailor you'll get a better garment but you won't save any money. Good local wool is at least Rs 45 per metre.

A ready-made waistcoat is Rs 125, a *chogha* Rs 400, and good tailor-made ones are twice that.

You can also have a *shalwar qamiz* (the standard baggy trousers and long shirt) made, or your own clothes copied. Depending on the cloth you buy, a *shalwar qamiz* will be Rs 150 to Rs 300.

A few curios and antiques are among the books at G M Baig's Mohammad Book Stall in lower Jamat Khana Bazaar, and in Dad Ali Shah's Hunza Handicrafts by the Park Hotel on Airport Rd.

Getting There & Away
Air From Gilgit PIA flies to Islamabad and Skardu - possibly the two most spectacular (and bargain-rate) civil air routes in the world - around the shoulders of Nanga Parbat in propeller-driven Fokker Friendships.

Both are very weather dependent; a moderate wind or a hint of overcast can lead to cancellations, right up to the last minute, so in effect all bookings are standby. Buy tickets in the PIA booking office in JSR Plaza. Then, confirm your reservation by leaving your ticket at PIA by 12.30 pm on the day before you're scheduled to go. At 2 pm they give it back and tell you the check-in time. The decision to fly, and seat assignments, are only made next morning.

The flight to Islamabad goes down the Indus to Chilas, then south above the Babusar Pass and the Kaghan Valley. A left-side seat looks straight out at Nanga Parbat. It's Rs 255 (government subsidies make it Rs 175 for locals) and takes 1 1/4 hours. There are one to three flights a day; schedules are seasonal.

The 40-minute flight up the Indus to Skardu is equally spine-tingling. There's only one a week, on Mondays, for Rs 175. Nanga Parbat is out the right side.

PTDC keeps two priority seats on each flight, so if PIA says it's full, go to PTDC at the Chinar Inn and ask for a special booking (a letter of confirmation to take back to PIA). If you don't want to be here a day early, someone else can take the ticket in and pick it up. Pamir Tours, a few doors away, will do it for a small fee.

Unless you arrange something with your hotel, the only way to get to the airport is a Jutial-bound passenger Suzuki from Saddar to the roundabout near the Park Hotel (Rs 1), and a 15-minute walk to the terminal. If you happen to find an idle Suzuki in the early hours, Rs 20 would be reasonable from Saddar Bazaar.

Buses, Vans, Wagons For long-distance transport, NATCO is 250 metres east of JSR Plaza and Masherbrum Tours is about 300 metres west; private bus operators are along Airport Rd.

Regional transport usually starts from neighbourhoods where people from outlying towns have shops: Jamat Khana Bazaar for Hunza; lower Bank Rd for Nagar; Punial Rd for Punial, Ishkoman, Yasin and Chitral; Garhi Bagh (the little slice of park at the east end of Saddar Bazaar) for Haramosh and Bagrot valleys. The general bus stand, a dirt yard 150 metres north up a link road from JSR Plaza, has buses and wagons for Nomal and Chilas.

Be sceptical of departure times; vans and wagons tend to hang around until they're full.

Chilas A bus (Rs 20) and various Datsun pickups (Rs 27) go each day from the general bus stand.

Rawalpindi This takes about 15 hours in a bus, a little less in a van. Schedules are seasonal so check for yourself. Calculate your arrival time: Rawalpindi's no fun at 3 am.

In summer NATCO buses go daily at 4 and 9 am, 1, 4 and 10 pm (others were told 5, 6, 7 pm) to 'Pindi's Pir Wadhai General Bus Stand. The 9 am bus is 'deluxe' (softer seats, marginally cleaner) and costs Rs 120; the others are Rs 90. A 50% student discount is available on all but the deluxe bus, but a maximum of four discount tickets are sold for each departure.

Masherbrum Tours has daily buses for Rs 90 at 11 am and 3 pm, and Toyota vans for Rs 120 at about 10 am and 4 pm; all go to Pir Wadhai. Sargin Travel Service, in JSR Plaza, has three vans a day (in summer) to Rawalpindi's Saddar and Rajah bazaars, for Rs 120 plus a baggage fee. Prince Tours, at the Taj Hotel just west of the plaza, has two vans a day at the same price.

Hunza Sust-bound vehicles stop at Ganesh (Rs 15 to Rs 20, about 2½ hours) but it's a dusty, two-km climb or a Rs 50 jeep ride from there to Karimabad. In Jamat Khana Bazaar, wagons go directly to Karimabad at least twice a day starting at mid-morning, for Rs 20. You can also hire a Suzuki (seats eight to 10) from the Hunza Inn, Rs 400 to leave you in Karimabad, Rs 500 to bring you back the same day.

Nagar From lower Bank Rd, a NATCO 4WD pickup and several wagons go via Ganesh to Nagar village every day for about Rs 25. They leave when they're full, some time after 9 am. Other wagons and jeeps go on an irregular basis, some of them on to Hopar; ask Bank Rd merchants or at the Golden Peak Inn. For Chalt, random jeeps and vans go from Bank Rd early in the morning, and a beat-up red wagon goes in the afternoon for Rs 10.

Sust This takes four to five hours. A NATCO bus goes at 9 am, for Rs 30. The Karakorum Inn has an early-morning van for Rs 30. Hunza-Gojal Travels, in the Khunjerab Hotel just east of the Vershigoom Inn, has vans three times a day for Rs 40.

Skardu This takes six to eight hours. A daily NATCO bus (Rs 40) leaves at 6 am. Masherbrum Tours has a bus at 7 am for Rs 40, and vans at 10 am and 2 pm for Rs 60. Karakoram Travels (east of the Vershigoom Inn) and the Karakorum Inn (across the road, further east) each have two vans a day for Rs 60.

Trucks There's no yard, but trucks unload all over the bazaar. Atop the cab in fine weather is an unbeatable way to see the scenery; inside is very comfortable if you're not sharing it with five of the driver's 'brothers'! Most drivers hope for a few rupees, a fair fraction of the equivalent bus fare.

Hire Your Own Following are places to rent your own wheels. Availability and prices fluctuate with the season.

Vans: Sargin Travel Service, Hunza Inn.

Jeeps (Rs 6 per mile or about Rs 3.7 per km, plus Rs 150 per overnight stop): PTDC (Chinar Inn), Adventure Pakistan, Mohammad Book Stall, Hunza Inn, Park Hotel, Mountain Movers Inn, Mt Balore Motel, Khunjerab Hotel, Karakorum Inn, Prince Tours. Pamir Tours offers Rs 600 per day with unlimited mileage.

Suzukis: Pamir Tours, Hunza Inn, Karakorum Inn.

Car: Pamir Tours will rent a Toyota Corona, with or without a driver, for Rs 600 a day plus fuel and oil. To drive it yourself you need an International Driver's Licence and a Rs 5000 security deposit.

Getting Around

Suzukis Passenger Suzukis to Jutial and Dainyor start in Saddar Bazaar and can be flagged down in Cinema Bazaar and Airport Rd. They're Rs 1 within the bazaar, Rs 2 beyond. To signal a stop while you're riding, stomp twice on the floor. Dainyor Suzukis are a handy ride to Babar Rd near PTDC, Chinar Bagh and the Hunza Inn. Suzukis also run west from Punial Rd.

Serena Shuttle The Serena Lodge runs a free shuttle from the bazaar to the hotel. At 1, 5.30 and 7 pm the van, with a Serena logo, swings by four pick-up points marked with small brown signs (JSR Plaza; by the Patti Centre handicrafts shop at the corner of Cinema Bazaar and Jamat Khana Bazaar; further up Jamat Khana Bazaar; and by Sunshine Traders, west of the bank in Saddar Bazaar). In the afternoon the van comes back whenever you like; in the evening it comes back at 9 pm.

Bicycles Bikes can be hired for about Rs 6 an hour (plus, in some cases, a security deposit) from shops in Jamat Khana Bazaar (opposite the Mohammad Book Stall), Bank Rd (opposite the bank), Punial Rd and Cinema Bazaar, and from the Hunza Inn. Check the brakes.

Trips Beyond Gilgit

These overnight or longer excursions can start from Gilgit. All are approachable by public transport, or you can hire a jeep.

The small NAPWD Rest Houses in the Naltar, Astore and upper Gilgit Valleys should be booked ahead, even in the off-season. Some caretakers will admit un-booked guests, some won't. Contact the NAPWD Administrative Officer in Gilgit.

Guides

You don't need a guide for any of these places, although the less-visited valleys (Bagrot, Haramosh, Sai and upper Gilgit) might be easier – and more interesting – with someone who speaks some English and is known in the area. A guide is essential for high-country treks.

Finding a good guide without help is a matter of luck; nearly everyone claims to be what you need. For basic services (trail-finding, local transport and accommodation, finding food and cooking it, elementary translation) figure Rs 150 to Rs 200 a day. You may find local people who will show you trails and do some carrying and cooking for around Rs 100 per day.

A middleman can reduce the uncertainty, for a price. Try your own hotel *wallah*. Local agencies such as Pamir Tours (JSR Plaza, tel 3939) or Mohammad Book Stall (Jamat Khana Bazaar, tel 2409) use local guides and can accommodate low-budget customers.

Larger outfits like PTDC (at the Chinar Inn, tel 2454, 2562) or Adventure Pakistan (Babar Rd near the airport, tel 2663; and a desk in the Serena Lodge lobby) are versatile, reliable and more expensive. Their guides are experienced and speak good English, but they don't always know the local valleys well.

Professional guides charge up to Rs 300 a day, but tend to prefer long trips or large groups.

Equipment

Hotel managers and guide agencies can often come up with camping gear (although sleeping bags seem hard to find). If you want to buy something, Dad Ali Sha's Hunza Handicrafts (in front of the Park Hotel) has occasional pads, stoves, shoes, clothing, even ropes and crampons, among the curios.

NALTAR VALLEY

This is the final tributary of the Hunza River. Most guides who know the valleys around Gilgit call Naltar the loveliest. Its perfect alpine scenery is very accessible, for overnights or as the start of a fine trek to Chalt, or even on a fast day-trip by jeep from Gilgit. It's crowded in the summer.

The mouth of the valley is on the west side of the Hunza River at Nomal, 25 km north of Gilgit. From there a jeep road climbs 16 km (five to six hours on foot, two hours in a jeep) to Naltar village, where the valley opens up. From Naltar it's a beautiful 1/2 day (12-km) hike up to Naltar Lake and dense pine forests, a good overnight or a very long day-hike from Naltar. Near Naltar is a Pakistan Air Force winter survival school.

Beyond the lake, a day's walking takes you to the summer pasture area called Shani, where you may meet Gujar shepherds, the last real nomads in Pakistan. Another half-day up is the foot of the 4500-metre pass to Daintar and down the Chaprot or Garmasai Valley to Chalt (take a guide on this crossing, five to six days from Nomal to Chalt). A longer trek goes west to Chatorkhand in the Ishkoman Valley.

Places to Stay & Eat

Nomal has a run-down *NAPWD Rest House* with two doubles at Rs 60; you can pitch a tent on the lawn for Rs 5. The simple *Prince* and *Aliar Hotels* are open in summer.

Naltar has two *NAPWD Rest Houses* (both heavily used) with doubles at Rs 60, or pitch a tent for Rs 5. There is a stone hut above Naltar Lake. Local people may let you camp on their land, though some are said to be greedy.

During the summer light food can be found in a few Nomal and Naltar cafes. The NAPWD Rest House caretakers can do meals with whatever's available in the village, or you can bring your own food for them to cook.

Getting There & Away

From Gilgit's general bus stand, at least one bus goes to Nomal around 2 pm, for Rs 5. A jeep to Naltar is about Rs 600 return, plus Rs 150 to Rs 200 a night.

An interesting alternative is to get off any north-bound KKH bus at Rahimabad, just north of the KKH monument; climb down to

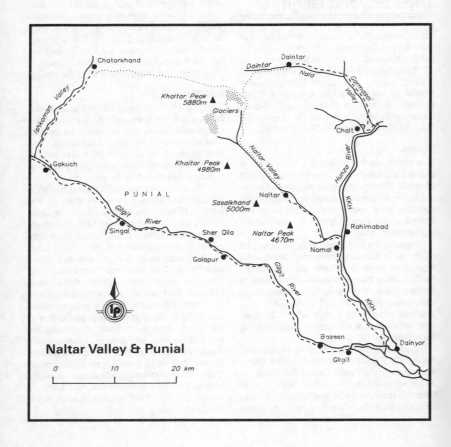

Naltar Valley & Punial

0   10   20 km

the river and walk back (south) along the bank about 1 1/2 km, and catch an ox-skin raft across to Nomal for Rs 4 (set the price before you go!). If you can't find it, 'raft' is *jalo* in Shina.

From Nomal, local jeeps come back to Gilgit early in the morning. A bus leaves about 8 am.

GILGIT RIVER WATERSHED

This is not a 'place' but a network of the Gilgit River and its broad, relatively undeveloped tributary valleys to the north and west. Close to Gilgit the scenery is unspectacular and summer weather is hot for walking, but government rest houses put the upper valleys within reach by jeep for fishing, some trekking, and overland passage into northern Chitral.

Shina and some Urdu are spoken, but almost no English. The people are Ismailis (since the 14th century, much longer than Hunza) and women are un-veiled and relaxed in public. Poverty here seems to blunt even the Muslim instinct for hospitality, and food and lodging are scarce beyond the government rest houses.

The main regions are Punial ('poon-YAHL'), along the Gilgit River between 25 and 75 km upstream; the Ishkoman ('ish-KO-man') Valley, entering the Gilgit Valley from the north at about 80 km upstream; the Yasin ('yah-SEEN') Valley, entering at about 110 km; and the upper Gilgit Valley, stretching over 200 km west to the Shandur Pass into Chitral.

Ishkoman and Yasin are said to be good trekking country. A week-long hike climbs to 4900 metres from Chatorkhand (in Ishkoman) to Nomal at the bottom of the Naltar Valley, or to Chalt. Well-known fishing reaches are at Singal Gah (Canyon) and Gakuch in Punial. For help with food, lodging and trails, a local guide is a good idea; ask around in Gilgit's Punial Rd.

Places to Stay & Eat

Three small *NAPWD Rest Houses* in Punial (Golapur, Singal and Gakuch) are within a half-day by jeep from Gilgit. Within a day's drive are others in Ishkoman (Chatorkhand and Imit) and Yasin (Gupis and Yasin village). Rest houses in the upper Gilgit Valley are at Phander and Teru. NAPWD says those at Singal and Gakuch are heavily used and hard to get. Travellers give high marks to the one at Chatorkhand.

There seem to be few restaurants, and only snacks in the shops. Especially toward the end of the season, it's wise to bring your own food, even to government rest houses.

Getting There & Away

Cargo jeeps go to most up-valley villages every day in summer, from Gilgit's Punial Rd. Ask in the shops west of the polo field, and in the lane off Bank Road on the south side of the cemetery. If you're going to Chitral (two days by jeep), ask at the shop of 'Mr Pakistani' on the corner of the alley at the west end of the polo field.

The trip itself is sure to be an adventure. If you get a seat at all, you'll share it with lumber, live goats, slabs of mutton and lots of cheerful people. Approximate fares are Rs 25 to Punial, Rs 50 to Ishkoman, Rs 70 to Rs 80 to Yasin and the upper Gilgit Valley, Rs 100 to Shandur Pass.

Jeep-hire prices vary wildly, so shop around. Return rates include a stopover charge of Rs 150 to Rs 200 a night plus a flat fee of Rs 500 to Rs 800 (Punial), Rs 1200 to Rs 2000 (Ishkoman and Yasin), Rs 3000 to Rs 6000 (Chitral).

BAGROT VALLEY

About 15 km down-river from Gilgit on the other side, a broad alluvial fan marks the Bagrot ('bah-GROTE') Valley. Its lower reaches are like a marbled moonscape, and a ride up the narrow, perched road in an over-loaded cargo jeep is unforgettable. The upper valley is huge, rugged and densely culti-vated. Bagrotis are Shina-speakers and Shia Muslims, and see few foreigners except trekkers and expeditions passing through.

Of the valley's half-dozen villages, the main one is Sinakkar, two hours from Gilgit.

About 1½ hours further, at the end of the jeep road, is Chirah, the last year-round village and site of the only rest house, with a direct view of the grey Hinarche Glacier and a series of ridges culminating in Diran Peak (on the other side are Nagar and Hunza).

Half a day's walk above Chirah are 'summer villages' where a large part of the valley's population goes with their goats and sheep each year. Seven to eight hours from Chirah are shepherds' huts and good camping, and the start of a 4600-metre crossing past the Barche Glacier and into the Haramosh Valley. The prominent peak to the south-east is 6130-metre Dubanni.

A local guide might be useful for information and translation in the valley, and is essential for treks to Haramosh or toward Diran. Ask among the Bagrot and Haramosh shopkeepers at Garhi Bagh, the small square at the east end of Gilgit's Saddar Bazaar.

Places to Stay & Eat

Best bet is to camp out, at the head of the valley above Chirah. The only hotel is a two-room *NAPWD Rest House* at the end of the jeep road in Chirah, with barren doubles for Rs 60. You may have to ask in the village for the caretaker. Bring your own food, even to the rest house. Unboiled stream water is suspect unless it's straight from a glacier.

Getting There & Away

Cargo jeeps to Chirah leave from Garhi Bagh around 2 pm, stuffed beyond belief (mine had 24 people and their cargo). The ride itself is worth the price (Rs 20) for the jolly company, the valley view and the adrenalin rush. Don't take the bus to Jalalabad, as there are no connections up-valley from there. The jeep returns in the early morning.

A hired jeep is about Rs 500 for the day or Rs 600 overnight.

HARAMOSH VALLEY

An hour south of Gilgit the Skardu Road leaves the KKH, crosses the Gilgit River and joins the Indus River. After arcing north the road and canyon turn south to skirt

7400-metre Haramosh Peak; this region is locally called Haramosh Valley. Even more than neighbouring Bagrot, Haramosh is poor and undeveloped. The Shina-speaking people in its remote canyons are unaccustomed to foreigners except as passing trekkers. There's no food or lodging, but alpine meadows and the glaciers of Haramosh Peak are a strenuous day's walk from the highway.

The village of Sassi (or Sasli) is a bus stop on the Skardu Rd, 1½ hours from Gilgit. Just before Sassi a jeep track climbs north. Take the right (lower) fork; after seven or eight km of level walking a bridge crosses to the east side of the canyon. Ask the way to Dasso village, a lung-busting climb to the bluff above.

From Dasso a footpath climbs steeply east into a side-canyon, four km to the 'summer village' of Iskere ('ISS-keh-reh') at 2500 metres, where most of Dasso's population lives from May until December, grazing goats and cutting timber. About one km above Iskere, near the toe of the Mani Glacier, are good tent sites and views of Haramosh (source of the glacier), Lyla Peak across the glacier, Baska Glacier and Malubiting Peak (7450 metres) to the north. Three km above Iskere there are shepherds' huts.

A local guide, while not essential, would be a big help here. Talk to the Bagrot and Haramosh shopkeepers at Garhi Bagh, the little square at the east end of Saddar Bazaar. A professional guide who lives in Dasso is Qurban Ali (PO Box 519, Gilgit).

Places to Stay & Eat

There are none beyond the highway. Sassi has a meat-and-chapatti cafe and several seedy road-houses with rope beds for about Rs 8.

Getting There & Away

Skardu-bound buses and vans (see Gilgit – Getting There & Away) stop at Sassi; the fare is Rs 15. Because of the long hike from Sassi, the 6 or 7 am buses are the best way to be in

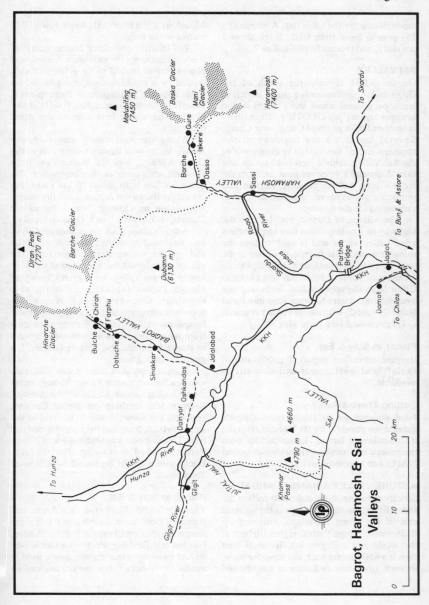

Bagrot, Haramosh & Sai Valleys

the high country the same day. A wagon (Rs 15) goes to Sassi from Garhi Bagh about 3 pm daily, and returns from Sassi at 7 am.

SAI VALLEY

On the KKH 10 minutes south of the Gilgit-Indus confluence is a shady stretch of teashops, general stores and a petrol station in upper Jaglot ('jah-GLOTE') village (there is another Jaglot north of Gilgit, near Chalt). Several km down the highway at the southern end of the village is the mouth of the Sai Valley, with a jeep road up its east side. Although I've never gone in, from the air it's long (about 50 km), remote and tempting to explore. Apparently most visitors go for the fishing.

The village of Damot, visible from the highway on a hilltop about four km in, offers good valley views and is said to have the ruins of a medieval fortification. Sai is the next valley south from Gilgit, and maps show a variety of possible multi-day treks back to Gilgit from the upper valley, including one over the 4600-metre Khomar Pass into Jutial Nala. Obviously a guide, or further research in Gilgit, would be a good idea.

Places to Stay & Eat

Bicycle travellers report a grotty inn at Jaglot, and basic meat-and-chapatti is available.

Getting There & Away

Ford wagons go to Jaglot from Gilgit's general bus stand for Rs 10. You can also take a Chilas-bound bus or Datsun pickup from the general bus stand, or a Rawalpindi-bound NATCO or Masherbrum bus.

ASTORE VALLEY & NANGA PARBAT

Strictly speaking, the Karakoram ends at the Indus River. On the other side is the western end of the Great Himalaya, crowned by 8126-metre Nanga Parbat, eighth highest in the world and still growing. Its south-east face is a 4500-metre wall, too steep for snow to stick (its name is Kashmiri for 'Naked Mountain'); the north side steps down 7000 metres to the Indus.

Pre-Islamic traditions blame many of life's misfortunes on mountain fairies, and Nanga Parbat is said to be a fairy citadel, topped by a crystal palace and guarded by snow serpents. The caprice of these spirits is manifest in the mountain itself: more climbers have died here than on any other mountain.

Along the mountain's east side, the Astore Valley was Britain's main link to the Gilgit Agency, over the Burzil Pass from Kashmir, and a caravan route before that. The cease-fire line with India, 70 km away, has closed the Burzil but Astore is still the easiest way to get up close to Nanga Parbat (or Diamar, 'DYAH-mir', as it's known locally).

Astore village is six hours south of Gilgit, on a jeep road down the far side of the Indus and up the Astore River. West from the village is the broad, thickly forested and very lovely Rama Valley, with grand views of Nanga Parbat (actually its north-east shoulder, Chongra Peak). Rama has abundant camping, and a small government bungalow six km (and 800 vertical metres) from Astore, from which it's an easy day-trip to Rama Lake and the Sachen Glacier. No guide is needed here.

Longer trips start from Rama and from villages further up the Astore Valley, including Gurikot (about 12 km above Astore), Rampur and Tarshing (up Rupal Canyon, about 40 km above Astore at the end of the jeep road). A long day-trip up the canyon from Tarshing puts you within sight of Nanga Parbat's naked south-east (Rupal) face. Local guides might be found in Astore or Tarshing.

Places to Stay & Eat

There are *NAPWD Rest Houses* at Astore and Rama (Rs 60 for a double) and there are allegedly other small inns at Harchu, Astore, Gurikot and Tarshing. Pitch your tent beside any of these for a few rupees. Some food is available in Astore but unless you are booked

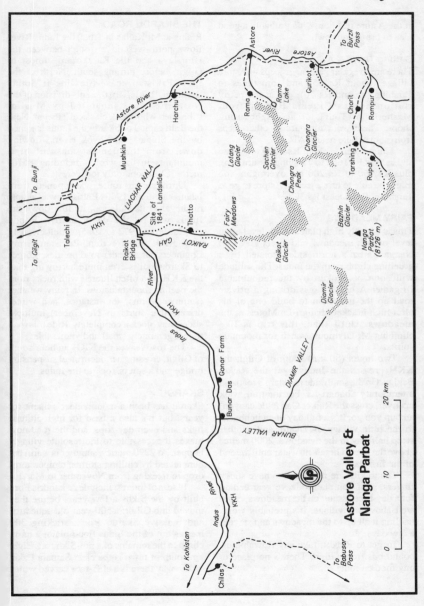

Astore Valley & Nanga Parbat

at the Astore rest house it's probably a good idea to bring your own.

Getting There & Away

There are irregular passenger jeeps to Astore village (about Rs 35) and sometimes to Tarshing (around Rs 70); ask at the petrol station across from Cinema Bazaar from Masherbrum Tours, or at neighbouring shops. There were rumours of other jeeps from somewhere near NATCO.

A hired jeep is about Rs 1200 to Astore and at least Rs 1600 to Tarshing (return trip), plus Rs 150 to Rs 200 per overnight. You might be able to hire a jeep in Astore to go to Tarshing, for at least Rs 300.

FAIRY MEADOWS

This is a lovely high plateau with level upon level of lush meadows and direct views up Nanga Parbat's north side, isolated by a gruelling climb from the Indus. The solitude will soon be broken by the redoubtable Brigadier Aslam, who is driving a private road up the mountain to build one of his ultra-high-bracket Shangri-La Motels at the meadows. Until then, this trip is like climbing Mt Olympus; watch for mountain spirits.

Two hours (80 km) south of Gilgit the KKH crosses the Indus over the Raikot Bridge. On the south side is Aslam's road and a temporary Shangri-La. For the trail, walk up-river, cross the Raikot Gah (side canyon) and up you go. It's a full day of switchbacks to the little village of Thatto, and another steep half-day to the meadows, 2000 metres above the river. There's no water until the end of the first day.

Thatto kids are rumoured to have sticky fingers, so if you plan to leave gear behind for a day-hike assault on the meadows, camp well above the village. It's probably worth hauling it all up to the meadows and staying a few days.

To get to Raikot, take any Rawalpindi-bound bus from Gilgit. There's no place to buy food en route.

THE SKARDU ROAD

Rising at Mt Kailas in Tibet, the Indus River flows north-west in a trough between the Himalaya and the Karakoram almost to Gilgit, before turning south. North of the India-Pakistan cease-fire line it drains Baltistan, 'Little Tibet', a sub-division of the Northern Areas inhabited by Muslim tribesmen who speak classical Tibetan. Near the Balti capital of Skardu the Indus is joined by the Shigar and Shyok rivers, flowing down from the densest mass of high mountains in the world, including 8610-metre K2, second only to Everest.

Until an air route was opened from Islamabad in the 1960s Baltistan was almost medieval in its isolation. Its link down the Indus was by the deep, narrow Rondu gorges. From 1972 to 1985, simultaneously with KKH construction, Pakistan Army Engineers cut a feeder road up these gorges to Skardu that is even more harrowing than the KKH, and often littered with rocks from the peeling mountainsides. In rainy weather (summer storms, for instance, and winter drizzle that starts in November) multiple slides may block it completely. Ride this road to feel genuinely small and vulnerable.

The road leaves the KKH an hour south of Gilgit, crossing a modern steel suspension bridge and a spit of rock to the Indus.

SKARDU

Skardu has been a mountaineer's haunt for years, but it's also a base for high-altitude treks and even day-trips, and the road now makes it accessible to the resolute village-hopper. At 2290 metres, summer is warm but punctuated by chilling storms; temperatures drop to freezing from November to March.

Places of interest include Askandria Fort, built by the Sikhs a few years before they moved into Gilgit; a 500-year-old aqueduct; and massive Skardu Rock, sticking 300 metres out of the Indus flood plain, a nasty climb to the remains of a pre-Sikh fort. Eight km south of town is the clear Satpara Lake; on the way there is a cliff-face carved with a

Top: The Gilgit River at sunrise (JK)
Left: Musician, Gilgit (JW)
Right: Decorated truck, Gilgit (JK)

Top Left: Head man and son in Dasso Village, Haramosh Valley (JK)
Top Right: Man in traditional wool topi (hat) and chogha (cloak), Gilgit (JK)
Bottom Left: Chilas Fort, Chilas (JK)
Bottom Right: Goatherd from Thalpan Village, along the Indus River (JK)

sitting Buddha in the same style as the one at Kargah near Gilgit.

A good primer for trekking here is Hugh Swift's *The Trekker's Guide to the Himalaya & Karakoram* (Hodder & Stoughton, London, 1982; Sierra Club books may publish a new edition). Numerous agencies (some with offices in Skardu) offer guides, support services and package expeditions of all sizes (see Treks & Tours, page 35).

Information & Orientation

The airport is 14 km from town. Landmarks along Skardu's one-road bazaar are a traffic roundabout and, eastward, the old aqueduct. A PTDC Tourist Information Centre is at the K2 Motel (tel 104), east of the aqueduct. PIA (tel 30) is just west of the roundabout and the NATCO bus station is just east of the aqueduct.

Places to Stay

Several bottom-end inns are near PIA, with middle and top-end accommodation at the east end of town; camping is said to be available near PTDC and near the polo ground. The bazaar is adequate for basic supplies during the summer.

Getting There & Away

The 250-km road trip from Gilgit takes six to eight hours (if there have been no rockfalls), with a meat-and-chapatti stop en route. Buses leave Gilgit at 6 am (NATCO) and 7 am (Masherbrum Tours) for Rs 40, and half a dozen vans go during the day for Rs 60.

The weekly, 40-minute PIA flight from Gilgit in propeller-driven Fokker Friendships, and daily flights from Islamabad, are as awesome as the road, with the adjacent peaks often above the plane. The Gilgit flight is Rs 175; Islamabad is Rs 310. These are subject to last-minute cancellation if the weather doesn't look just right. You confirm by turning in your ticket to PIA by mid-day of the day before you go; the decision to fly is only made on departure day.

GILGIT TO CHILAS

Ten minutes south of the Skardu turn-off, say hello to the Indus River, one of the longest in the world; the KKH runs beside it for the next 340 km, through Kohistan to Thakot.

Just below the confluence is the Parthab Bridge, on the old jeep (and pre-jeep) road to Skardu. Ten minutes on at **Jaglot** is the bridge across the Indus toward Astore. Across the river is **Bunji**, once a garrison of the Maharajah of Kashmir's army; above it is the Matterhorn-like Mushkin Peak.

A good place to keep your eyes open is about 1 1/2 hours south of Gilgit (or about the same distance up-river from Chilas) at **Talechi** ('TAH-la-chee') village, the only place on the road where both Rakaposhi and Nanga Parbat are visible. Along here are the best views of the largest number of snowy peaks anywhere on the KKH. From the north, the prominent ones are the Karakoram peaks of Rakaposhi (7790 metres, a sharp point above a broad white base), Dubanni (6130 metres, a blunt pyramid) and Haramosh (7400 metres, a series of glaciated ridges); and the Himalayan massif of Nanga Parbat (8126 metres, 8th highest in the world). From here, the closer you get to Nanga Parbat the more it hides behind its own lower reaches.

Opposite Talechi is the deep Astore Valley, which winds around to Nanga Parbat's sheer south-east (Rupal) face.

Soon the gorge closes in, the vistas abruptly disappear and about five minutes later (or five minutes north of the Raikot Bridge) the small Liachar Nala enters the Indus across from the highway. In 1841 an earthquake caused an entire valley wall to collapse into the Indus here, damming it up and making a lake that stretched nearly to Gilgit. When the dam broke, a wall of water roared down the canyon, washing away scores of villages and drowning thousands of people, including an entire Sikh army battalion camped at Attock, almost 500 km downstream.

By now the Indus has turned west, deflected by Nanga Parbat. At a narrow spot the KKH crosses the Raikot Bridge. On the south side is a Shangri-La Motel 'transit station', a holding pen for visitors to the resort being built at Fairy Meadows, beneath the north (or Raikot) face of Nanga Parbat.

Except for road-weeds, the river and a few irrigated plateaux, the Indus Valley west for 100 km is 'a barren dewless country; the very river with its black water looks hot', in the words of the late-1880s *Imperial Gazetteer of India*. In a series of landslide zones beneath eroded sandstone cliffs that look like they would dissolve in a drizzle, the highway resembles the little make-believe roads that kids make in dirt-piles.

Forty minutes west of the bridge is a small tree-lined bazaar at Gonar Farm. The police fort and check-post here are reminders of the long-standing antagonism between the government and the anarchic tribes down-river. Five minutes further (1/2 hour east of Chilas) is the new village of Bunar Das (Bunar Plain), on a plateau below the Bunar Valley, the main access to Nanga Parbat's western (Diamar) face.

A jeep-size suspension bridge crosses the Indus a little over an hour west of Raikot Bridge and just east of Chilas. On both sides of the river here are the best-known of the extraordinary rock inscriptions made by 2000 years of travellers through the Indus Valley and the Karakoram. About three minutes westward, near an old petrol station, look up for a dramatic view of Chilas Fort in the distance.

CHILAS

Most visitors to Chilas have come to see the petroglyphs, or are on their way to Babusar Pass. There aren't many other good reasons to stop here. The atmosphere is sullen, the scenery is barren and summer is viciously hot. Western women who do visit are virtually the only women on the streets, and the tension is enough to make many of them uneasy.

Until Kashmiri-British rule was imposed a century ago the Indus Valley west of Chilas was a hornets' nest of tiny republics, one in every valley, each loosely guided by a *jirga* or assembly but effectively leaderless, all at war with one another and feuding internally. Administratively lumped with Gilgit, Chilas is temperamentally more like Kohistan, possibly owing to a similar hostile environment and the same Sunni Muslim faith (their ancestors were forcibly converted six centuries ago by Pathan crusaders, while hardly anyone beyond Gilgit is Sunni).

The huge Chilas Fort was first garrisoned to protect supply lines to Gilgit, and beefed up after local tribes, in a rare case of collective action, nearly overran it in 1893. Now a police post, it has put a lid on Chilas, though not on the Darel and Tangir Valleys to the west.

Chilasis are Shina-speakers, with some Pathan settlers speaking Pushto. Urdu and some English are also spoken.

Orientation

There are several top-end hotels on the KKH, but the town itself is three km up a feeder road. If you arrive on a through bus, get off at the police check-point by the turn-off, not at the customary lunch stop two km east. Flag a Datsun passenger truck (Rs 1) or a tractor up to the bazaar.

Arrow-straight Ranoi Rd is the axis for the new bazaar. At the west end is the road from the KKH, and an isolated NAPWD Rest House. In the middle is the bus-yard and a turn-off to the old bazaar, which is clustered around the fort. At the east end Ranoi Rd enters Buto Gah (Buto Valley); a left fork drops to tree-shaded government offices (about 1 1/2 km past the fork) and the right fork climbs toward Babusar Pass.

Information

The post office is opposite the entrance to the fort. The town's police post is the fort itself. A small government hospital is at the bottom of a road meandering down through the bazaar from west of the fort.

Petroglyphs

The ancient routes through the Karakoram

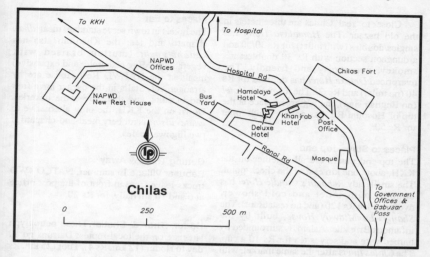

Chilas

0   250   500 m

are dotted with places where travellers pecked graffiti into the rocks: pictures, prayers or names, in thanks (or hope) for a safe passage, to acquire merit in the afterlife or good luck on the next hunting trip, or just to boast. The desolation around Chilas surely moved many to special fervour, and several sites by the highway are rich with inscriptions on the dark, 'desert-varnished' stones.

Near the KKH check-point is a sign to the 'Chilas II' site, and a jeep track toward the river. About 3/4 km along the track a huge rock is covered with hunting and battle scenes and Buddhist stupas. A common image is the long-horned ibex, an ancient symbol of fertility and abundance and an elusive trophy animal even now. Near the river-bank, on a rocky hill facing the river, are the area's oldest inscriptions, scenes of conquest and stories of the Buddha's life from the 1st century AD.

Almost four km east on the KKH, at the jeep bridge to Thalpan, is the 'Chilas I' site, on both sides of the highway and the river. The most striking pictures are a large stupa with banners flying, close to the highway, and across the river on dozens of rocks west

of the track, mythical animals, battle scenes, royal lineages and Buddhist tales. The serene, 2000-year-old Buddha figures seem incongruous at this goatherds' crossing in the middle of nowhere.

Other petroglyphs are at Hodur, Thor and Shatial (see Chilas to Shatial); all can be reached by local passenger Datsuns. Details of these and other sites are in two books you might find in Gilgit or Islamabad bookshops: Dr A H Dani's *Human Records on Karakorum Highway* and Dr Karl Jettmar's *Rockcarvings & Inscriptions in the Northern Areas of Pakistan*.

Take water; in summer the banks of the Indus are like an oven.

Places to Stay – bottom end
Definitely the best for your money is the *NAPWD New Rest House*, on a spur road west of town (an older rest house east of town was closed when I visited). Large, clean doubles with attached toilet and shower, on spacious grounds with a great view, are Rs 60. It's popular in summer; you can book ahead at the NAPWD office in Gilgit; coming from the south, ask PTDC.

Closer to 'real' Chilas are three hotels in the old bazaar. The *Hamalaya Hotel* has singles/doubles (with toilet) for Rs 30/50 and a dungeon section with Rs 30 doubles; it's smokey, very noisy and friendly. The overpriced *Deluxe Hotel* has doubles for Rs 40 (no toilet) and Rs 60. The *Khanjrab Hotel* (no English sign), the big green place at the top of Hospital Rd, has doubles with toilet for Rs 50.

Places to Stay – top end

The top-end places are all together on the KKH, about one km east of the check-point. The small, tidy *Rehman's Candle Hotel* has doubles with toilet and cold shower, overpriced at Rs 120 (and no restaurant). The *Shangri-La Midway House*, built by the infamous Brigadier Aslam, is surrounded by barbed wire and serves tea for Rs 10 a cup. The *Chilas Inn* is after the same market, with plush doubles at Rs 300 and up.

Places to Eat

The hotels in town serve standard meat, *dhal*, chapatti and tea; the Khanjrab also has *kadahi gosht* (mutton braised with vegetables). More elaborate (and expensive) meals at the NAPWD Rest House are by arrangement. Stalls in the bazaar have fruit and biscuits, and there are some bakeries. Down on the KKH, the only alternative to *haute cuisine* is rubbery meat-and-chapatti at two highway cafes.

Getting There & Away

Babusar village In summer, NATCO 4WD trucks leave from in front of the post office at 6 and 10 am daily, for Rs 20.

Hodur, Thor & Shatial These petroglyph sites are on the local routes; Datsuns go all day to Hodur (12 km, Rs 4), Thor (25 km, Rs 7) and Shatial (65 km, Rs 15).

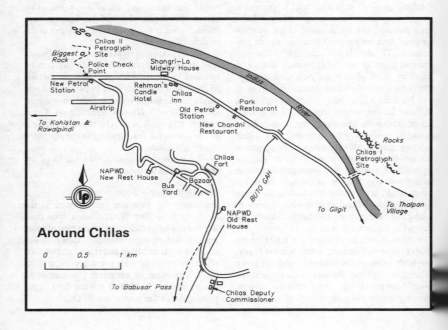

Around Chilas

Rawalpindi Flag a through bus on the KKH, or go by local jumps: Datsun to Shatial, wagon from there to Besham, and so on.

Gilgit Wagons leave from the bus-yard every two to three hours starting at 7 am. Fare is Rs 27; buy a ticket in the shack at the corner of the lot. Or flag a through bus down on the highway.

Skardu Go to Jaglot, where you can pick up a bus or van going to Skardu from Gilgit. Datsun passenger trucks leave for Jaglot (Rs 20) at least every two hours from 7 am until mid-afternoon; get a ticket in the shack at the corner of the lot.

Getting Around
Local Datsuns will take you between the bus-yard and the KKH for Rs 1; or flag a tractor.

BABUSAR PASS
A very rough jeep road crosses the Babusar Pass (4145 metres) from Chilas into the Kaghan Valley, a challenging alternative to the KKH for going south. The pass is normally open to 4WD traffic from mid-July through August. A crossing on foot is possible as early as mid-June (though you'll still find snow) until early October (though by then most villagers en route will have come down for winter). Snow starts in November.

It's 35 to 40 km from Chilas to **Babusar village** and 13 km from there to the pass. On the Kaghan side the nearest village of any size is **Battakundi**, 60 km beyond the pass. Most jeep trips go to **Naran**, 16 km past Battakundi.

Get some local advice before making this crossing. PTDC or Adventure Pakistan in Gilgit would be the best bet. In Chilas try field officers at the NAPWD office on Ranoi Rd, or the NATCO drivers on the Babusar village run. Allow for wide variations in seasonal changes noted here. See also Hazara – Babusar Pass.

Places to Stay & Eat
In the summer at Babusar village there are some shops, several small inns where a rope bed is Rs 5, and a spartan *NAPWD Rest House* with two doubles at Rs 60 (it probably helps to book ahead; ask at the NAPWD Rest House in Chilas). Battakundi has a *Pakistan Youth Hostel* (dorm beds at Rs 15 or pitch a tent) and a *C&W Rest House* (Communication & Works, the North-West Frontier Province's equivalent of NAPWD). Naran has shops, cafes, a *Pakistan Youth Hostel*, a *C&W Rest House*, cheap inns and up-scale places, but things get booked out in the summer.

Getting There & Away
NATCO 4WD pickup trucks go to Babusar village daily (in summer) from in front of the Chilas post office, about 6 and 10 am, for Rs 20. Jeeps can sometimes be hired in Chilas; ask at the bus-yard. Approximate rates are: Rs 900 to Babusar village and back; Rs 1200 to the pass and back; Rs 2000 plus overnight charges to Naran, no return. From Gilgit a jeep to Naran is about Rs 3000, including one overnight stop.

CHILAS TO SHATIAL
West of Chilas the Indus is flat and meandering. On the KKH side the Lesser Himalaya stretch 80 km south toward the Punjab. On the other side of the river are the Hindu Kush.

From **Hodur**, 20 minutes west of Chilas, take your last (or first) look at Nanga Parbat. Across the river, the remains of a 1000-year-old fort are on a ridge to the right of a side canyon (Hodur Gah), and the rocks below the fort are covered with old inscriptions. Twenty minutes on (or an hour east of Shatial) is **Thor** ('tore'), site of more inscriptions, below the bridge over Thor Gah.

Fifteen minutes further on, the KKH crosses from the Northern Areas into the North-West Frontier Province, passing a line drawn on a map by Sir Cyril Radcliffe in the feverish fortnight before Partition in 1947. This was the intended border between India and Pakistan, disarranged by the Gilgit Uprising. Ten minutes west another line, an ominous string of little white markers, prefigures 'Basha Dam', according to a sign.

Shatial, 1 1/2 hours from Chilas, was once a little Indus Valley republic of its own. Now it's just a collection of cafes, wagons, and men standing around. If you're on local transport you may have to change here; Datsun pickups go up-river to Chilas, Ford wagons down-river to Besham (five to six hours away), all day. This is also the transfer point for Darel and Tangir.

Stash your bags in a teahouse and have a look at the petroglyphs east of the bazaar, near the bridge over the Indus. They include a detailed Buddhist tableau and lots of travellers' names (imagine: *Yaqub Qarim of Yarkand was here, 21 June 346. What a dump!*).

West of Shatial the landscape darkens as the Indus cuts a deep gorge into Kohistan.

DAREL & TANGIR

Two of the old unruly valley-states that have stayed unruly are Darel ('dah-REL') and Tangir ('tahn-GEER'), which meet the Indus across from Shatial. They only voluntarily joined Pakistan in 1952, and even today have the Northern Areas' worst reputation for lawlessness. 'Administration' from Chilas mostly means police garrisons to keep the customary blood feuds from boiling over.

Reports of gun-battles between locals and police are common, and well-worn travellers' stories tell of thefts and even rape. It's hard to separate fact from legend but this doesn't seem like a good place to go, and outsiders aren't warmly welcomed. It's a pity, because the valleys are said to be among the richest of all in natural beauty and archaeological remains. Darel was the site of some important Buddhist monasteries.

Oddly enough, despite their murderous reputation the valley men didn't always measure up to the standards of colonial macho. One official wrote in 1907:

Their dislike for bloodshed is most marked: where amongst Pathans the disputants would betake themselves to their rifles, [here they] throw a few stones at each other or indulge in a biting match. If this does not settle matters, recourse is had to ... entertaining the community to dinner on alternate days.

At your own risk, you can hire a Datsun at Shatial or a jeep at Chilas, but your first stop might well be the Assistant Commissioner or the Chief of Police at Tangir village, or their counterparts at Gumari, the main village of Darel. Both are about 20 km from Shatial.

Indus Kohistan

Skirting the western end of the Himalaya, the Indus River cuts a gorge so deep and narrow that some parts see only a few hours of sunlight in a day, and so inhospitable that even the caravan routes bypassed it. When the forerunner of the KKH was driven into the remote canyon in the early 1960s, highway engineers were offered hay to feed their jeeps.

Kohistan means 'Land of Mountains' and refers to the expanse of sub-6000-metre peaks enclosing the upper Swat and Indus valleys, from the Northern Areas to the southern foothills. In administrative terms Indus Kohistan includes the Kohistan District of the North-West Frontier Province (NWFP) and a stretch below Besham where the KKH briefly enters Swat District.

Its yawning, crumbling terrain made Kohistan one of the most harrowing passages in Asia. The intrepid Chinese Buddhist pilgrim Fa-Hsien, having already crossed most of China, the Tarim Basin and the Karakoram on foot, was awestruck. In 403 AD he wrote about the passage down the Indus from Darel to Swat:

The road is difficult and broken, with steep crags and precipices in the way. The mountainside is like a stone wall 10,000 feet high. Looking down, the sight is confused and there is no sure foothold ... In old days men bored through the walls to make a way, and spread out ladders, of which there are 700 in all to pass. Having passed these, we proceed by a hanging rope bridge to cross the river.

Kohistanis live, literally and figuratively, in the shadow of their surroundings. Nanga Parbat in its slow upheaval has dealt them a steady stream of catastrophes. The worst in modern times were the flood following the 1841 landslide near Raikot Bridge (see Gilgit to Chilas) and a massive earthquake at Pattan in 1974 that buried entire villages and killed more than 7000 people.

The region's old nickname was *Yaghistan*, 'Land of the Ungoverned'. Outlaws could hide here without fear of capture; tribal warfare and blood-feuds were commonplace. Stone watch-towers and fortified houses can still be seen in the older villages. The Sikhs, the British and then the Pakistanis left Kohistan alone.

But in 1976, as the KKH was nearing completion, Pakistan took an interest in these semi-autonomous areas and a Kohistan District was created from them, probably as much to protect the new road from local xenophobes as anything else. The district government relies heavily on the police and the NWFP's Frontier Constabulary, whose large forts dot the valley. Away from the KKH, outside authority diminishes quickly.

Not surprisingly, travellers tend to rush through, grabbing a quick meal in a shabby bazaar, marvelling from the bus at the magnificent gloom and swallowing hard when the road gets narrow. In fact the roadside bazaars *are* depressing and the road *is* occasionally terrifying, and the setting does seem to induce a kind of nihilistic insanity in bus drivers. Hard work for the innocent visitor.

But in its austere way the canyon is magnificent and, as usual, the best is off the highway. It would be foolish to go off at random into the hills, but there are some safe and beautiful detours. Hospitality turns up everywhere.

Ironically, Kohistan may not have a living Indus River in it much longer. Near Komila, Kayal and several other spots, signs identify future dam sites that could turn the narrow canyon into a chain of lakes.

The People

Kohistanis are an ethnic hodge-podge and the faces are as varied as those in the Gilgit bazaar. But most are said to be Shins, descendants of invaders from the lower Indus Valley at least 1000 years ago,

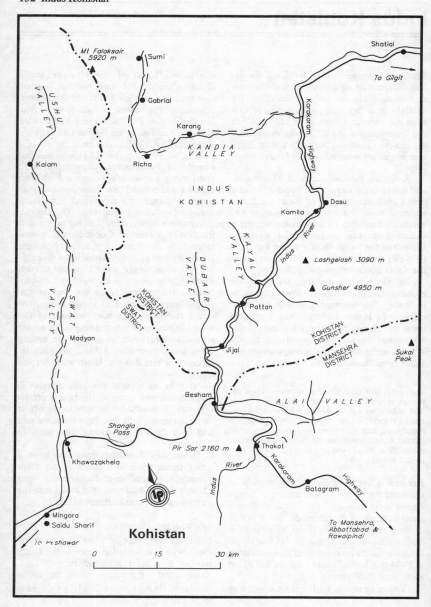

Kohistan

0   15   30 km

converted to Islam by Pathan missionaries from the 14th century onward. The Pathans themselves ('pah-TAHN'), whose tribes straddle the Pakistan-Afghanistan border and who had ruled in lower Swat since the 15th century, expanded into Kohistan in the 1700s and 1800s. Along the KKH they predominate around Besham, where Swat District touches the Indus.

Nearly everyone is Sunni Muslim, and five times a day you'll see men setting out their prayer mats wherever they happen to be – in cornfields, motel courtyards, by the roadside; you may find your own bus driver stopping at a local mosque. It's a man's world. Buses are the scene of frequent minor (often unintentionally hilarious) traumas as men rearrange themselves so as not to sit next to strange women.

In their harsh environment the Shins eke out a living where others can't, by a strenuous hybrid of nomadic and sedentary lifestyles. In most mountain valleys of south Asia shepherds drive their animals to high meadows in summer. But here, nearly everyone moves up and down, to farmland as well as pasture; many river-side villages are effectively just places to wait out the winter. A typical cycle takes villagers from the river to higher farmland (maize is the staple crop) in April-May, on to lower pastures in early June, to high pastures (as much as 3000 metres above the river) in July, then down starting in mid-September.

The Kohistani 'language' is a mixture of Shina, Pushto, Urdu, and even Arabic. Pushto, the speech of the Pathans, is spoken around Besham and in the upper Kandia Valley. Beyond the Komila and Besham bazaars, little English is spoken except by officials.

Note to Cyclists & Other Explorers

Some locals advise visitors not to go into the hills alone. The police advise them not to go at all, and tell stories of assault and robbery (and a lone woman cyclist said to have been raped near Dasu). Indeed, many travellers find the vibes in Kohistan very bad –

especially cyclists, who are highly exposed, dependent on local good-will, with obviously expensive gear and those funny rubber suits, and more apt to explore where others can't.

The risks you take are obviously up to you, but it's worth noting that solo travel off the KKH (and for women, even *on* the KKH) in Kohistan is not 100% safe. On top of a reputation for anarchy, it's populated by men with some skewed ideas about western women. It's easy to view the police as just another occupying army, but if they weren't there, we couldn't go. If you plan to get off the KKH, especially between Shatial and Pattan, consider informing the local Chief of Police or District Officer of the Frontier Constabulary.

That said, there are some lovely (and apparently safe) valley trips, some with government rest houses, described in the sections on Pattan and Besham.

SHATIAL TO DASU & KOMILA

West of Shatial the Indus suddenly turns south. Ten minutes south of the bend (40 minutes north of Dasu) is the confluence with the 80-km-long Kandia Valley, a major Indus tributary and until the 1800s a prominent kingdom of Kohistan. For almost a km the Kandia River runs parallel to the Indus behind a razor-sharp ridge before emerging, emerald-green. Hidden by the ridge, the valley begs to be explored, and might make a fascinating day-trip on the frequent passenger Suzukis that go there from Komila.

North of Dasu the road clings to increasingly vertical canyon walls, until in places it's just an amazing horizontal notch in a sheer granite face. Highway workers became mountaineers here, often lowered on ropes to drill and set charges. Massive blasting loosened the mountains for several km up and down the valley. This stretch took a year to carve and cost more workers' lives per km than any other part of the KKH.

Strangely enough, across the river are broad, shallow slopes where a highway would be much easier to build. In fact, that was the original plan. But villagers whose marginal landholdings were threatened put up such fierce resistance – sabotaging equipment, stealing supplies, harassing workers – that in the end the road was realigned.

DASU & KOMILA

A century ago, a fugitive from one side of the Indus only had to cross to the other side to be safe, and even 20 years ago towns like Dasu and Komila were worlds apart. Since being linked by the KKH bridge they have become a single extended town, the biggest between Chilas and Besham.

On the east side Dasu, headquarters of the Kohistan District, has government offices and rest houses (and officials on long, lonely postings from their homes in western NWFP). Komila has the bazaar, most hotels and all transport. Opposite Komila, tiny Jalkot was once the main village of the area but has faded away since the KKH arrived.

According to a sign in a local cafe, Kashgar is 882 km from here, Rawalpindi 341 km.

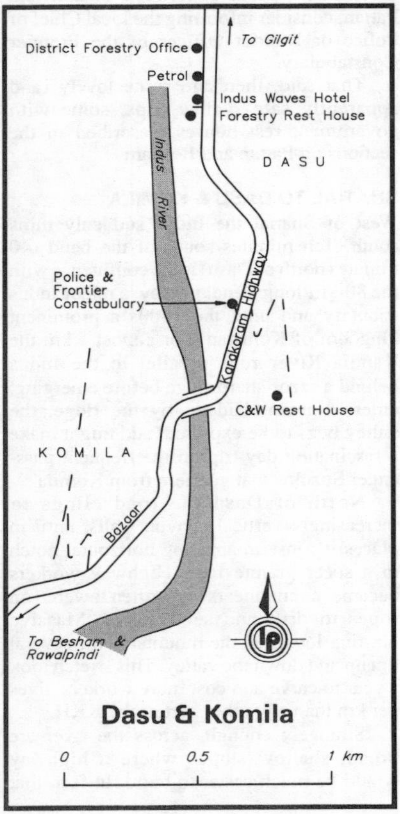

Information

Komila has a tiny post office, left of the Kandia Hotel, set back from the road and upstairs. Police Headquarters and the Frontier Constabulary are in Dasu, on the KKH 300 metres north of the bridge. The District Forestry Office, where you can book Forestry Rest Houses, is 100 metres north of the petrol station in Dasu.

Places to Stay & Eat

Dasu Possibly the best deal on the KKH is the *C&W Rest House* – quiet, cool in the summer, with high views and a first-class Kohistani cook. Carpeted, air-con doubles with hot showers are Rs 60. It's 1 1/2 km up a jeep road starting 100 metres north of the police station (no English sign on the highway). If you don't like the climb you can hire a Suzuki from Komila bazaar for Rs 10 to Rs 20 (for a ride down, make arrangements on the way up). The cook can prepare meals with half a day's notice, but he speaks no English. Book ahead if you can at the Office of the Executive Engineer, NWFP Communication & Works, (tel 52), Besham.

About 1 1/4 km north of the bridge, past some white-washed government buildings, is a *Forestry Rest House* with clean, boring doubles for Rs 80 (book it at the District Forestry Office up the road, past the petrol station). Next door, the *Indus Waves Hotel* has bare triples, overpriced at Rs 100. It's isolated, but a passenger Suzuki to Komila bazaar is Rs 1.

District Forestry Office
To Gilgit
Petrol
Indus Waves Hotel
Forestry Rest House
DASU
Indus River
Police & Frontier Constabulary
Karakoram Highway
C&W Rest House
KOMILA
Bazaar
To Besham & Rawalpindi

Dasu & Komila

0   0.5   1 km

Komila The best budget accommodation is the huge green place on the east side of the bazaar, the *Azim Hotel & Restaurant* and general store. Basic, noisy triples are Rs 40 and they have plans for up-scale Rs 60 doubles; the boisterous cafe has better food than anywhere else in the bazaar.

About 25 metres uphill from the Azim, the *Al-Mashriq Hotel* has grotty, toilet-less doubles for Rs 30. Downhill, the *Kandia Hotel & Restaurant* and the *Karakorum Hotel* said they would 'soon' be fixed up to serve foreigners, and another hotel was under construction. Other small *serais*, where a rope bed in the open is around Rs 10, aren't eager for foreigners.

There are numerous teahouses and meat-and-chapatti cafes in the bazaar. Waiters sometimes ask women travellers to use the family section (ie the back room) but they'll serve you even if you refuse.

Getting There & Away

Most transport goes from Komila. Catch regional wagons and Datsun pickups, and local Suzukis, at the top end of the bazaar. Be sure it's a passenger vehicle, not a 'special' (for hire), before you zoom off. Scheduled long-distance buses and vans use a wide space in front of a cafe just downhill from the Azim Hotel. North-bound buses may also stop at the petrol station in Dasu.

Rawalpindi & Gilgit To estimate arrivals of through buses, figure eight to nine hours from Rawalpindi and six to seven hours from Gilgit, but don't count on a seat.

Pattan & Besham Wagons and Datsuns leave when they're full, all day long. Pattan takes one hour and costs Rs 8; Besham takes two hours and costs Rs 15. The Government Transport Service (GTS) runs their phlegmatic, bashed-up old buses to Besham at 5.30 and 6 am, for Rs 13.

Chilas Take a wagon or Datsun to Shatial (2½ hours, Rs 15) and change there (1½ hours and Rs 15 more).

Kandia Valley Datsuns and Suzukis leave all day long and go as far as Sumi, at the head of the valley (four hours, Rs 30).

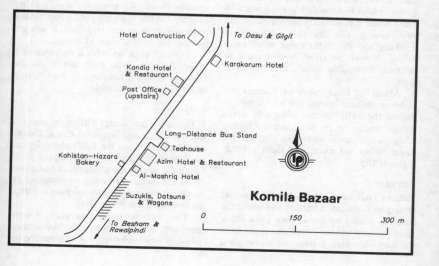

Hotel Construction

To Dasu & Gilgit

Karakorum Hotel

Kandia Hotel & Restaurant

Post Office (upstairs)

Long–Distance Bus Stand

Teahouse

Kohistan–Hazara Bakery

Azim Hotel & Restaurant

Al-Mashriq Hotel

Suzukis, Datsuns & Wagons

To Besham & Rawalpindi

Komila Bazaar

0   150   300 m

KANDIA VALLEY

This deep tributary valley was an independent princely state until the 1800s, when Pathan influence and Sunni orthodoxy began percolating in from lower Swat. In 1939 Swat annexed it, but lost it in 1976 to the new Kohistan District.

Kandia has a scattering of villages, the largest of which is Karang, 30 km from the Indus. From Gabrial, 65 km in, a track crosses westward to the Ushu River in upper Swat. From Sumi, near the head of the valley, another potential trek into Swat is a loop north around 5920-metre Mt Falaksair.

Multi-day trips should *not* be attempted without a guide who is known in the valley, and without at least informing the police or Frontier Constabulary at Dasu. But a long day-trip looks feasible in one of the passenger Suzukis that leave all day from Komila bazaar (Rs 30 to Sumi). Start early to allow enough time to get a ride back; Sumi is four hours away.

DASU & KOMILA TO PATTAN

The pyramid peak south of Dasu is Lashgelash (3090 metres); soon saw-tooth Gunsher (4950 metres) looms beyond it. In spring or after rain the dark gorge lined with white peaks is powerfully photogenic – and hair-raising: the crumbly walls slide regularly and the Indus looks miles away below. Across the river, houses cling to isolated, impossible slopes as if banished there.

About 3/4 hour south of Komila the highway slithers several km into a nala so narrow the traffic on the other side seems within reach. At its head are a Chinese bridge, a few shacks and a jeep road into the **Kayal Valley**, an excellent, short off-the-highway trip.

PATTAN

Pattan ('PAH-tahn') surely has the loveliest setting in Kohistan, a fertile bowl where the Indus is joined by the Chowa Dara River from the west and the little Palas River from the east. It's also a base for some good exploratory trips. The Indus snakes through a cross-grain of ridgelines, making for multi-layered scenery and many tributaries.

This was the centre of the catastrophic earthquake of 1974 in which entire sections of valley wall collapsed, burying whole villages and killing thousands of people. A vast amount of relief money poured in, which accounts for the 'new' look of the place. There are no ruins; arable land is too scarce (it comprises only 4% of the Kohistan District) and everything has been redeveloped.

According to one government worker, the quake was followed by a noticeable upsurge in virtue among God-fearing locals, so that even today Pattan is a safer area for travel than, say, Dasu.

Orientation

The village is well below the highway. A feeder road descends from near a KKH memorial, but through buses drop you almost a km further south, by a teashop on a bluff above the village. It's a three-km walk to the feeder road and down (you might find a passenger Suzuki going there for Rs 1, or hire one for Rs 10). Or you can short-cut straight down like everyone else, making roughly for the big grey police fort among tin-roofed government buildings. If you get lost just say 'rest house?' to someone.

The trip back up with a rucksack is a killer. A hotel under construction on the highway about 1/2 km north of the bus stop could save you the trouble.

Information

A Forestry Dept Range Office, where you can book their rest houses at Kayal, Dubair and Sharakot, is on the KKH about 1/2 km south of the bus stop, near the bridge. A small hospital is next to the government rest house below the bazaar. For other emergencies go to the Assistant Commissioner's office north-west of the police fort.

The overworked Assistant Commissioner and magistrate, Mr Mohammed Yusuf, is a helpful source of information on

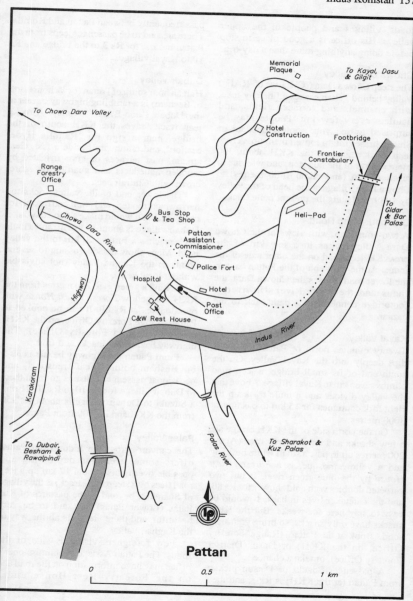

To Kayal, Dasu & Gilgit

Memorial Plaque

To Chowa Dara Valley

Hotel Construction

Footbridge

Frontier Constabulary

Range Forestry Office

Chowa Dara River

Bus Stop & Tea Shop

Heli-Pad

Pattan Assistant Commissioner

To Gidar & Bar Palas

Police Fort

Hospital

Hotel

Post Office

C&W Rest House

Indus River

Highway

Karakoram

To Dubair, Besham & Rawalpindi

Palas River

To Sharakot & Kuz Palas

Pattan

0   0.5   1 km

roads, villages and people in the upper valleys. His office is a good place to stop before doing anything more than a day-trip.

Chowa Dara Valley

The steep Chowa Dara ('CHO-wa da-RAH') Valley behind Pattan makes a fine day-hike, with channels and terraced fields, and hamlets every few km. People may be surprised to see you; some Kohistani or Shina phrases might loosen them up. A new jeep road begins at the KKH about 300 metres north of the bus stop, and was due to reach 15 km (and climb 1400 metres) to Chowa Dara village at the head of the valley by 1989, replacing the present mule track.

Old Indus Jeep Road

A two-hour loop, with views of the Chowa Dara Valley, takes in a few km of the pre-KKH jeep road on the other side of the Indus. At the west end of the Pattan bazaar, the lower road crosses the Chowa Dara, the Indus and the Palas River. Up-river, a footbridge connects to a path back to the bazaar.

Kayal Valley

Twenty minutes north of Pattan the KKH dips deeply into the Kayal Valley. On the south end of its small bridge, a jeep road climbs seven km to Kayal village. Above that the valley divides and a mule track up the right fork continues for 15 km to pastures at 3000 metres.

On the north side of the KKH bridge are a few shacks and another jeep road. About 200 metres up it, past a small white building and a yellow mosque, is a *Forestry Rest House* by the blue-green river. It has two carpeted doubles with cold shower for Rs 80, and the caretaker lives in back. It would be easy to stay here for weeks. But the KKH shacks have only snacks, so bring your own food. Book it in Pattan (Range Forestry Office, on the KKH) or Dasu (District Forestry Office), or take a chance.

A passenger Suzuki or Datsun pickup from Pattan (at the KKH) is Rs 3, and they pass frequently between Pattan and Komila. There are said to be passenger jeeps from the Pattan bazaar, for Rs 3 to the bridge and Rs 10 to Kayal village.

Dubair Valley

Half an hour south of Pattan (or 3/4 hour north of Besham) is a rambling highway bazaar at the Dubair ('doo-BARE') Valley. A rocky jeep track leaves the KKH south of the bridge, near a sign for 'Ranolia Hydel Station', and climbs up beside a fast, clear stream, past terraces of corn irrigated by wooden aqueducts and guarded by scarecrows with Chitrali hats.

The lower end of the valley looks too narrow, cultivated and well-trafficked for camping, but it would make a good day-hike. Dubair village is about 15 km in, and a mule track reaches a further 20 km to the valley head. Maps show tracks crossing to several points in the Kandia Valley (not advisable without local help).

Behind a green gate 200 metres from the KKH is a yellow *Forestry Rest House* with two doubles at Rs 80. It can be booked in Pattan (Range Forestry Office, on the KKH) or Dasu (District Forestry Office). The highway bazaar has snacks and fruit.

From Pattan the highway bazaar is Rs 5 on Besham-bound local transport, and occasional passenger Datsuns go from there to Dubair village for Rs 10 to Rs 20. Hiring a Suzuki to Dubair village is about Rs 150 from the KKH and Rs 300 from Pattan.

Palas Valley

The canyon across the Indus from Pattan offers some strenuous day-hiking and possible overnights. About 12 km up a jeep road (less by a steep mule track) is the village of Sharakot; beyond it, the pastures of Kuz Palas (Lower Palas) are said to be very beautiful, and there are trails all the way to the Kaghan Valley.

Few foreigners visit this side of the Indus. The Pattan Assistant Commissioner's office may have information on the road and on the Forestry Rest House under

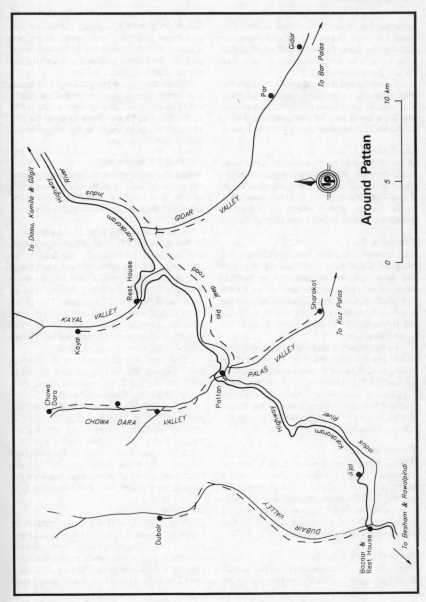

Around Pattan

construction at Sharakot, as well as advice on local protocol. If you are serious about exploring the area, paying a call on Sharakot elders might be a big help; in any case, stop by the police post there.

Cross the Indus on the road west from the Pattan bazaar or by the footbridge up-river. Occasional jeeps from the bazaar are around Rs 20; a hired jeep (if you can find one) is about Rs 250 one way. Bring your own food.

Bar Palas

A longer jeep trip on the east side of the Indus looks possible. About 15 km north on the old road a track turns up into the Gidar ('guh-DAHR') Valley. It's 20 km more up to Gidar village, above which are meadows beneath a glacier at Bar Palas (Upper Palas).

Places to Stay

The only decent place to stay in Pattan is a peaceful *C&W Rest House* on the banks of the Indus below the bazaar. Comfortable doubles with attached hot shower are Rs 40. It's popular, so book if you can (Office of the Executive Engineer, NWFP C&W, Besham, tel Besham 52). The caretaker lives to the right of the gate.

In the bazaar a multi-storey, green *serai* with rope beds shows no interest in foreigners. A hotel is under construction up on the KKH. The *Forestry Rest Houses* at Kayal and Dubair are easy to reach by passenger Suzuki. Book them at the Pattan Range Forestry Office, on the KKH near the Chowa Dara bridge.

Places to Eat

This is Pattan's weak point; food is limited, especially late in the season. The *chowkidar* at the rest house will fix lunch or supper for around Rs 15 – meat, chapatti and any vegetables he can find. Shops in the poor bazaar have biscuits and occasional fruit, and a few scruffy tea-houses have meat.

Getting There & Away

Theoretically you can leave from the bazaar, but I never had any luck. The rare passenger

Suzuki up to the KKH is Rs 1, or hitch a ride on a cargo jeep for a few rupees; hiring one is about Rs 10. Occasional passenger jeeps go from the bazaar to Kayal village (Rs 10) and to Sharakot (about Rs 20).

From the highway, passenger Suzukis and Datsuns go down-river to Dubair (Rs 5) and Besham (Rs 8), and up-river to Kayal (Rs 3), Komila (Rs 8) and Shatial (about Rs 25). Through buses to Gilgit or Rawalpindi will stop if they have seats.

PATTAN TO BESHAM

Across the Indus south of Pattan are several villages with stone watch-towers, reminders of the inter-valley warfare typical of pre-KKH days and still common in the high country.

At Jijal (or Jajial), 20 to 25 minutes south of Pattan, the KKH crosses onto the Indian subcontinent, geologically speaking. The Himalaya and Karakoram were born some 55 million years ago in a cataclysmic slow-motion collision between a drifting 'Indian plate' and the Asian landmass. The green rocks at Jijal were part of a chain of volcanic islands trapped against Asia, and the contorted white and grey material 100 metres south belongs to the subcontinent.

The canyon walls are very slide-prone here. Frontier Works Organisation crews in their tan overalls are a common sight, endlessly rebuilding the scarred road.

A few minutes south of Jijal a startling plume of bright blue liquid in the river is actually the clear Dubair River entering the muddy Indus. The Dubair Valley makes a good short trip from Pattan or Besham (see Pattan). Across the Indus are your last (or first) road views of permanent snow on the angular summits of the Lesser Himalaya.

BESHAM

Besham ('beh-SHAHM') is the prototype highway bazaar, a slapdash lot of shacks and stucco buildings, sprung from almost nothing in just a few years, trying madly to keep up with the surge in KKH use. But most travellers race right through and most locals

Top: Pattan Village on the Indus River, Indus Kohistan (JK)
Left: Man from Alai Valley, Indus Kohistan (JK)
Right: Men from Alai Valley, Indus Kohistan (JK)

Top: Street photographer, Mansehra (JK)
Left: Dyer's shop in Gurdwara Bazaar, Abbottabad (JK)
Right: Mansehra police station, formerly a Sikh temple (JK)

seem to wish they would, so there's no incentive for amenities.

Mostly Besham is a long-distance road junction and transfer point, with all-night shops, mediocre hotels and cheap *serais* (the common man's rest stop, quick meals and rope beds in the open). It's choked with trucks and buses at all hours, sounding their horns in self-advertisement. This is no place to catch up on your sleep or to enjoy the scenery.

Still, there are excursions of historical interest; the pleasant Dubair Valley is a short Suzuki-ride away and Besham is the base for visiting the high and beautiful Alai Valley.

Besham is actually in Swat District, which reaches east to the Indus here. Swat, once a princely state like Hunza, was conquered during the 15th to 17th centuries by Pathans, the flinty, independent-minded tribesmen from the border regions of Pakistan and Afghanistan. Along the KKH you'll only see large numbers of them between here and Mansehra. The common speech is Pushto, and Pathans call the Indus *Abaseen*, 'Father of Rivers'.

In its earliest form the KKH was the Indus Valley Road, meant to link Chilas, not south to Hazara but west to the Swat Valley. Besham is the transfer point for buses over the scenic Shangla Pass to Swat.

Orientation

Nearly everything is right on the KKH. The Swat Road fork marks the bazaar's north end, where you'll find most of the transport in every direction, and a line of teahouses and *serais*. Next are hotels, and shops with snacks, fruit and basic supplies. Most other useful services are strung southward along the highway.

Information

Tourist Offices The PTDC Tourist Information Centre (tel 92) is 2½ km south of town at the PTDC Motel, but you can get there on a local passenger Suzuki for Rs 2 (you may have to ask for it by its old name, the KDB Rest House). Manager Ijaz Ali has

current information on roads and accommodation.

Nearby is the office of the Executive Engineer, Kohistan Division, NWFP Communication & Works Dept (tel 52), where you can book the C&W Rest Houses in Besham, Alai, Pattan and Dasu.

Post Office & Telephone Exchange Both are on the KKH about 300 metres south of the Hotel International.

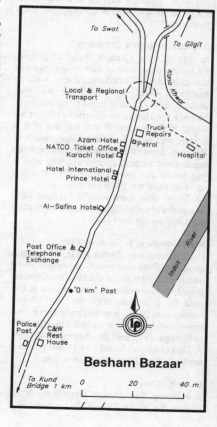

Besham Bazaar

To Swat

To Gilgit

Kana Khwar

Local & Regional Transport

Truck Repairs

Azam Hotel
NATCO Ticket Office
Karachi Hotel
Petrol

Hospital

Hotel International
Prince Hotel

Al–Safina Hotel

Indus River

Post Office & Telephone Exchange

'0 km' Post

Police Post

C&W Rest House

To Kund Bridge 1 km

0   20   40 m

Police A police post is oddly located outside the town limits, almost one km south of the Hotel International.

Hospital A District Hospital is 250 metres east down a side road near the Swat junction.

Besham Qila
Some maps refer to Besham as 'Besham Qila'. *Qila* ('keela') is Pushto for 'fort', and the old name refers to a fortified villa built here by the former Wali of Swat around 1945, before there was much of a village. Now used as private homes, it's on the west side of the KKH about 400 metres north of the Swat junction.

Site of Fa-Hsien's Crossing
In 403 AD the Chinese Buddhist pilgrim Fa-Hsien described a harrowing passage through Indus Kohistan, ending with 'a bridge of ropes, by which the river was crossed, its banks there being 80 paces apart'. In 1941 the Hungarian-English explorer Sir Aurel Stein concluded that the site of this bridge was near Kunshe village, south of Besham, where the Indus squeezes between equal-sized vertical rock walls. The spot is just below the new Kund Bridge and just up-river from the PTDC Motel.

Stein also mentions the ruins of a watch-tower on an outcrop above the bridge, probably on the west side.

KDB Memorial & Road-Marker
On a promontory by the KKH, 20 minutes south of Besham, a self-important white obelisk honours the Kohistan Development Board, which oversaw development of this area for a decade after the 1974 Pattan earthquake. Below it at the roadside is a great stone road-marker that includes the distances to Kashgar (975 km) and Beijing (5425 km). A Thakot-bound Suzuki will drop you here for Rs 1; flagging a ride back is easy.

Dubair Valley
A *Forestry Rest House*, just off the KKH beside the clear Dubair River, makes a peaceful base for exploring this long valley (see Pattan). It's about ¾ hour north of Besham, Rs 3 by Suzuki or pickup, Rs 5 by Ford wagon. To book the rest house from Besham, ask at PTDC.

Places to Stay – bottom end
Several *serais* near the Swat junction have open-air rope beds and lots of noise and flies, for Rs 5 to Rs 15. Two that welcome foreigners are the *Azam Hotel* and the *Karachi Hotel*.

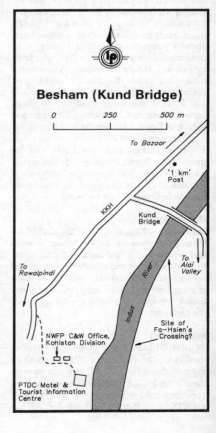

Besham (Kund Bridge)

But you can do better for the same price at the *Hotel International*. Triples and quads are Rs 30; fairly clean doubles are Rs 40 and up. All have showers and 'flushsistom'. Service is sleepy. Next door the *Prince Hotel* has small, dark doubles for Rs 35 (no shower), somehow arranged so everybody disturbs everybody else. Both hotels are handicapped by a very loud music shop between them.

The *Al-Safina Hotel*, 150 metres south, is marginally quieter and cleaner; doubles/triples are Rs 50/60. About 3/4 km south, up a short track opposite the police station, is a *C&W Rest House* (no sign in English) with doubles for Rs 40.

The *Abasien Hotel* on the Swat Road is a residential hotel for local people.

Places to Stay – top end

The only place to hear the sound of the Indus flowing by is the *PTDC Motel*, with clean bed-linen, tiled bathrooms, service like home and prices to match (doubles for Rs 300). For equal serenity at a lower price, try the riverside rest houses at Dubair, Pattan and Kayal, which can be booked here with PTDC's help.

Places to Eat

There's cheap food – meat, vegetables, rice, 'omelettes' – at the little rough kitchens of the *serais*; fill up for Rs 10. In the morning try the Pakistani equivalent of danish pastry: light, deep-fried *puri* pastry with *halvah*.

Besham's only restaurants are in the hotels. Food and selection are fair at the *International* and *Prince*, dreary at the *Al-Safina*. Dinner is about Rs 15.

Getting There & Away

Long-distance buses pass through but may not always have seats. NATCO stops at the NATCO ticket office (between the Azam and Karachi hotels) and Masherbrum Tours stops at the Azam Hotel. Schedules vary with the season so check at these places for current arrival times.

Most local transport starts near the Swat junction.

Thakot ('tah-KOTE') Suzukis and pickups from the junction, and wagons from the Azam Hotel, are Rs 6.

Alai Valley Take a Suzuki or wagon to Thakot for Rs 6. From there, buses (Rs 8) and many passenger pickups (Rs 10) climb to Alai. With good connections the trip from Besham is about three hours. The road from Kund Bridge to Alai, soon to be completed, will generate direct service from Besham. To be certain of a ride back you could hire your own Datsun (holds 10 to 12) from Besham or Thakot.

Mansehra Wagons go from the Azam Hotel all day, for Rs 22. Rawalpindi-bound buses also stop there, for Rs 18.

Rawalpindi NATCO and Masherbrum Tours buses come through eight to 10 hours after leaving Gilgit (see Gilgit – Getting There & Away). All go to 'Pindi's Pir Wadhai Bus Stand, and are Rs 35 (except the NATCO 'deluxe' around 5 to 6 pm, which is Rs 50). For a sure seat, several Toyota Coaster vans start from the Prince Hotel late at night, for Rs 50, going to Committee Chowk and Liaquat Chowk along Murree Rd.

The trip takes six to seven hours, so departures between 5 and 11 pm will arrive in the middle of the night. Pir Wadhai especially is a drag at that hour.

North-bound Local Suzukis, pickups and Ford wagons leave from the Swat junction, whenever they fill up, for Dubair (Rs 3), Pattan (Rs 8) and Dasu (Rs 16). Wagons go to Shatial for Rs 30.

Gilgit NATCO and Masherbrum Tours buses come through about six to seven hours after leaving Rawalpindi (see Rawalpindi – Getting There & Away). All are Rs 60 (except the NATCO 'deluxe' around 3 to 4 pm, which is Rs 70). For a sure seat, several Toyota Coaster vans start from the Prince Hotel late at night, for Rs 80.

The trip takes eight to 10 hours so

departures between 3 and 8 pm will put you into Gilgit in the wee hours. With any night-time departure you'll miss seeing the Indus gorge.

Swat Everything goes to Mingora, from the junction. Ford wagons (Rs 15) and buses (Rs 12) leave frequently, from 6 am on through the evening. The square, ox-like GTS (Government Transport Service) buses leave hourly, from 6 am until early afternoon.

ALAI VALLEY

Alai ('ah-LYE') epitomises the Indus highlands: tightly-knit, self-reliant, religiously conservative farmers and herders living in a network of beautiful (and in this case bountiful) high valleys, aloof even from the Indus.

You get to Alai from Thakot on a road barely one bus-width across and so lofty and exposed that near the top you can see 20 km of the Indus in a single sweep, as if you were airborne. The ride is reason enough to go, with the Alai Valley as a bonus, lush with rice terraces, cornfields and apple orchards, and rising to pine-clad mountains.

Some 15,000 people, all Pathans and devout Sunni Muslims, live in the valley system. Until the late 1970s they had their own ruler, *Nawab* Ayub Khan of Alai, and were mostly left alone. Then Alai was brought under NWFP control (symbolised and enforced by the huge Frontier Constabulary stockade in the middle of the valley) and the nawab was demoted to a National Assembly delegate. In spite of the Pathans' love of independence, and the fact that everyone here is armed to the teeth, the change apparently came without bloodshed. In fact Ayub Khan (who lives in the village of Behari) remains the valley's effective leader.

People are understandably uneasy about outsiders (non-Muslims in particular) but are instinctively hospitable. Most will wonder what you are doing here. Be prepared to smile a lot in the face of initial suspicion; try out 'asalaam aleikhum' and a few Pushto words. If you show your respect for their orthodoxy, especially by dressing modestly (shorts are roughly equivalent to walking around in your underwear, even short sleeves are a little scandalous, and women are judged more ruthlessly than men), you may enjoy some legendary Pathan hospitality. Otherwise you'll just be an intruder.

Most adults do not read or write, and only the present generation of children – mainly boys – are learning English. If you need a translator, watch for the schoolboys in their berets.

Down in Besham people may advise you to avoid Alai, or at least to call on the police when you get there. The government, willing to let foreigners visit the high country but unwilling to guarantee their safety, leaves the police with a *de facto* liability for problems. Thus the police prefer that you either stay away or accept an escort, which is sound advice in many parts of Indus Kohistan but questionable for a respectful visitor here.

The valley has two government rest houses and a few tea-shops but no hotels or restaurants. The optimum visit is probably an early, long, self-catered day-trip from Besham, with a few hours of walking around the valley. Transport is unpredictable, however, so a back-up booking at the C&W Rest House in Banna would be a good idea, and would give you an official-looking bit of paper to show to any officials you meet.

Alai is cool even in summer, so take an extra layer. From November to April it's very cold, with snow by December.

Information & Orientation

A road to Alai from the Kund Bridge, 1 1/2 km south of Besham, is due for completion soon. Meanwhile all transport goes from Thakot, on the east side of the KKH bridge 28 km south of Besham.

The 29-km Thakot-Alai jeep road rises more than one vertical km. A single hamlet, Kanai, is about halfway up. Don't waste your film on pictures from the lurching bus. From the end of the line at Kurg, walk about 1/2 km back for good views of the Indus Valley. A

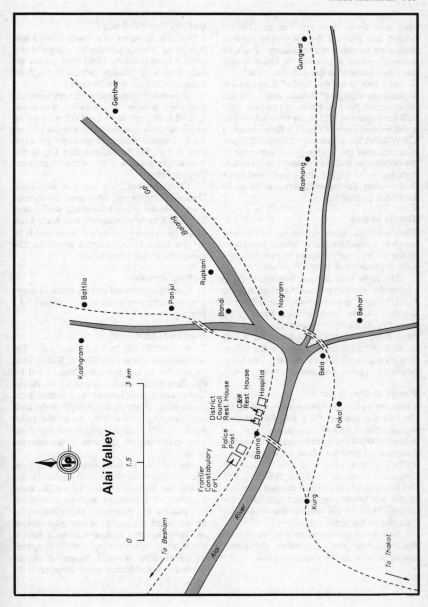

Alai Valley

long way down-river you can see Thakot bridge, and above it the flat-topped Pir Sar, according to some the legendary 'Rock of Aornos', where Alexander the Great fought the tribes of Swat in the 3rd century BC.

At a fork at the east end of Kurg, go left to the main village of Banna, about two km away across the Alai River. If you turn right in Banna after the bridge, on your left will be a red-roofed District Council Rest House, a C&W Rest House and a small hospital. If you turn left after the bridge you soon come to the police post and the Frontier Constabulary fort on your right; this road continues down-valley, the future direct route (about 30 km) back to Besham.

Things to See

The road from Banna up the north branch of the river, toward Battila, offers the best views of the valley. Just upstream from Banna is a tiny, old water-mill below the road.

The right fork at Kurg eventually takes you up the middle branch of the river, Balang Gai (Balang Canyon), toward the village of Ganthar. At its head is Sukai Peak (5000 metres?). At the first bridge, three to four km from Kurg, look up toward Behari, which locals say is the prettiest village in the valley. The Nawab Ayub Khan lives here. One stone house has a prominent watch-tower.

Places to Stay & Eat

There are no hotels or restaurants in Alai. Of the two rest houses, the *C&W Rest House*, with doubles for Rs 40, is easiest to book; ask at the PTDC Tourist Information Centre in Besham (tel Besham 92) or a few steps from PTDC at the office of the Executive Engineer, Kohistan Division, NWFP C&W (tel Besham 52). If you get stranded here, one of the rest house caretakers might take pity on you. There are no obvious possibilities for camping in the main valley.

Rest house guests can arrange meals with the caretaker; the only other alternative seems to be bringing your own food.

Getting There & Away

When it's finished, the road from Kund Bridge to Banna is sure to spawn direct service from Besham. Until then, go via the ratty bazaar at Thakot (which is Rs 6 by wagon or Suzuki from Besham).

Schedules from Thakot are very loose. At least two private buses (after 9 am and around mid-day) and one GTS bus go up every day; it's two hours to Kurg and costs Rs 8. Datsun passenger pickups go when they're full, for Rs 10, and take 1 1/2 hours. You might hitch a ride on the occasional logging lorry.

Coming back, the last bus and most Datsuns leave by mid-afternoon. Everybody seems to know when, but nobody really does. The best way to guarantee a ride back down might be to hire your own Datsun (holds 10 to 12); from Thakot, figure about Rs 150 each way, less if you bargain.

Getting Around

In Alai the occasional rickety truck or cargo jeep will take you to the upper villages for a few rupees.

SWAT VALLEY

Swat parallels the Indus on the west. The northern end of the valley, Swat Kohistan, is known for its rough natural beauty and for excellent trekking, fishing and winter skiing. Government rest houses and a few local hotels make it fairly easy to explore the area, and camping is feasible. As in the Indus Valley you'll find the police uneasy about your exploring off the road in the extreme north.

In contrast to Kohistan, southern Swat was cosmopolitan almost two millennia ago. It was the furthermost end of the Buddhist empires of Gandhara and an important destination for pilgrims. The tireless Fa-Hsien noted some 500 active monasteries, and holy sites that include a stone at Tirat in the northern valley said to bear the footprints of the Buddha himself. Ruins of stupas, monasteries and fortifications are open to the public, and the Swat museum has artefacts dating from the 2nd century BC.

Swat's traditional administrative seat, Saidu Sharif, now shares those functions with its big sister city, the market town of Mingora. With three dozen hotels between them this is probably the most tourist-developed area in the northern mountains.

The passage from Besham, four hours over the grand Shangla Pass, is a trip in itself. This was the ancient route from the Indus Valley to Peshawar and the plains. In fact, if you're bound for Peshawar, Swat is quicker and more dramatic than going via Rawalpindi.

Information & Orientation

Buses go to Mingora's general bus stand on the Peshawar Rd, or to a smaller station on New Madyan Rd. There are said to be decent mid-range hotels on New Madyan Rd, within 1/2 km of either station (turn right out of the general bus stand, then left into New Madyan Rd; or turn right out of the smaller station).

Saidu Sharif is a short ride south of Mingora, and passenger Suzukis are plentiful. A PTDC Tourist Information Centre at the Swat Serena Hotel (tel 4215 or 4604) in Saidu Sharif has information on hotels, transport, local archaeology, the Swat museum and the upper valley.

Places to Stay & Eat

Travellers' recommendations include the bottom-end *Rainbow* and *Mehran Hotels* on New Madyan Rd, the *National Hotel* opposite the bus station and the *Holiday Hotel* at the Mingora end of Saidu Sharif Rd, all with doubles at about Rs 40. Adequate Pakistani food can be found in the hotel restaurants.

Getting There & Away

Government and private buses (Rs 12) and Ford wagons (Rs 15) leave Besham for Mingora from 6 am through early afternoon, with some evening departures. PIA has flights between Saidu Sharif and Islamabad six times a week, for Rs 155.

BESHAM TO PIR SAR

Forty minutes south of Besham the KKH crosses the Indus on an elegant suspension bridge decorated with stone lions and a big sign, 'Welcome to the Karakoram Highway'. In 1976 a lively party was held here, with Pakistani and Chinese music and dance, to open the bridge and celebrate the completion of the Indus Valley Road. On either side are seedy roadside bazaars, **Dandai** on the west and **Thakot** on the east.

This is the last of the Chinese bridges, and in many respects Thakot is the real southern end of the KKH, not the railhead at Havelian. Since the first trickle at the Khunjerab, the highway has run beside one or another branch of the Indus; a few km from here it leaves the wide and heavy 'Father of Rivers' behind, and soon climbs down out of the mountains as well.

Five minutes south of the bridge a Kohistan Development Board sign proudly identifies **Pir Sar**, a nondescript mountain across the river. The explorer Sir Aurel Stein associated Pir Sar with Aornos, where Alexander the Great routed the Assakenoi tribes of the Swat Valley in 327 BC. However, recent evidence apparently undermines this claim, so the KDB's good 'historical view point' may be a red herring.

Hazara

Below Thakot the KKH leaves the Indus Valley and for 180 km descends through progressively gentler countryside to the upland plateau of Rawalpindi and Islamabad. This is a region of forested mountains below 4000 metres, with a series of broad, fertile valleys up its middle. Ease of travel through these valleys has for centuries made this a kind of gateway from the south into the mountains, toward Kashmir, Gilgit and the Northern Areas.

The region's historical name is Hazara. Its natural boundaries are the Indus River on the west, the Margalla and Murree Hills on the south and east, and the peaks of the Lesser Himalaya to the north. In administrative terms it includes the Abbottabad and Mansehra Districts of the North-West Frontier Province (NWFP).

Your response to Hazara may depend on which way you're going. South-bound, you may feel you've left the real KKH behind — no more Chinese bridges, no more outlaws, no more fickle, harrowing high-road. But it may come as a restful change, and a chance to ease slowly back into civilisation. North-bound, it spells the end of city comforts, but it's the first escape from the thick air of the Punjab.

History

The towns of Hazara still show the imprint of Sikh rule. As the strength of the Moghul Empire waned in the 1700s the region was for a time under the control of various Afghan chieftains. One of them in 1799 granted the governorship of Lahore to Ranjit Singh, a Sikh chieftain from the Punjab. Ranjit proceeded to expand his domain into a small empire that, by the time of his death in 1839, included most of the Punjab, Kashmir, Hazara and Peshawar.

An early treaty with the British had barred Ranjit's expansion south-east, but in 1845 this was violated by the regent who

succeeded him. Following the short and bloody Sikh Wars of 1846 and 1849 the British annexed the entire state, including Hazara. At Partition in 1947, Hazara's Sikhs fled to India.

Many Hazara and Punjab towns still have old buildings from this time, including fortifications from before the Sikh Wars and *gurdwaras* (temples) built in this century. Some have names from this period: Haripur and Mansehra, for example, were strongholds of Hari Singh and Man Singh, two of Ranjit's governor-generals.

BATAGRAM

Tiny Batagram straddles the Nandhiar River about 20 km above its confluence with the Indus. The town hasn't much to offer except picturesque walks in the surrounding fields and some hard-to-find Buddhist ruins in the hills near Pishora.

The people are Pathans and Sunni Muslims, but despite the Pathan reputation for truculence, they seem cordial and easy-going. The local language is Pushto; little English is spoken.

Pishora & Kala Tassa

According to archaeological researchers, there are some Buddhist ruins by a spring near the village of Pishora, eight km north of Batagram on the KKH. With local help, I found a narrow hole in a hillside that — according to someone who allegedly went in — leads to a deep underground grotto containing two large stone figures, one sitting and one standing. Unfortunately, getting into such a place would be an all-day caving expedition.

In the same area, which is called Kala Tassa, there is a rock overhang beneath which are inscriptions depicting hunters, animals and a Buddhist stupa. The writing next to the stupa refers to a monastery in the time of a Kushan king of the 1st and 2nd

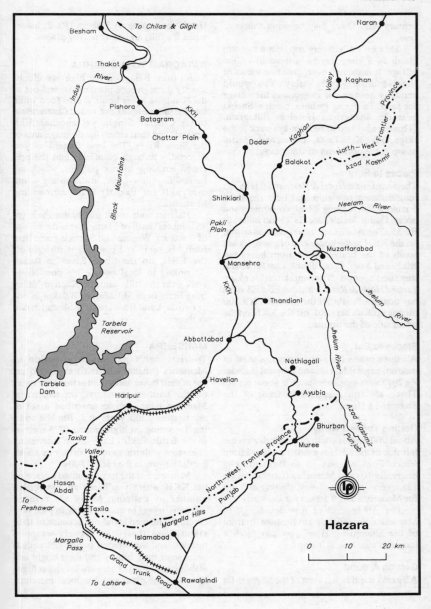

To Chilas & Gilgit

Besham

Thakot

Indus River

Pishora

Batagram

Chattar Plain

Dadar

Balakot

Shinkiari

Pakli Plain

Mansehra

Thandiani

Abbottabad

Nathiagali

Havelian

Ayubia

Haripur

Bhurban

Tarbela Reservoir

Taxila Valley

Muree

Tarbela Dam

Hasan Abdal

To Peshawar

Taxila

Margalla Hills

Margalla Pass

Islamabad

Grand Trunk Road

To Lahore

Rawalpindi

Black Mountains

KKH

KKH

Naran

Kaghan Valley

Kaghan

Kaghan River

North-West Frontier Province

Azad Kashmir

Neelam River

Muzaffarabad

Jhelum River

Jhelum River

Azad Kashmir

Punjab

North-West Frontier Province

Punjab

Hazara

0   10   20 km

century AD. There may be other things to find.

This isn't a leisurely trip, but a two-km climb in a steep ravine just south of the village. It does, however, give fine views of the Nandhiar River Valley. You would certainly need to ask someone in the village for help. To get to Pishora, catch a Suzuki near the Shangri-La Hotel in Batagram. (There is also said to be a six-km track to the ridge above Kala Tassa, starting at the petrol pump at the north end of Batagram.)

Places to Stay
The *Shangri-La Hotel & Restaurant* is by the long-distance bus stop and near the local Suzuki stand, making it both convenient and noisy. Damp doubles are Rs 25 (no toilet) or Rs 35. The *Al-Fakhar Hotel & Restaurant*, on the KKH at the upper end of town, 1/2 km south of the bridge, is far from buses but shady and quiet. Clean doubles are Rs 40 and the food's good. The unfinished-looking *Tarand Hotel & Restaurant* (no English sign) has doubles for Rs 30 (negotiable). It's 200 metres up Kutchery Rd, off the KKH on the south side of the bridge.

Places to Eat
All three hotels have restaurants; a meal of mutton, vegetable, rice and chapatti is under Rs 20. Street-side cafe lunch is about Rs 10. There are fruit vendors in front of the Shangri-La Hotel.

Getting There & Away
About 200 metres south of the bridge on the left side of the KKH is a small bus-yard from which Ford wagons go to Besham (1 1/2 hours, Rs 10) and Mansehra (two hours, Rs 12), every 1/2 hour all day, starting at 5 am for Mansehra and 6.30 am for Besham.

For Abbottabad or Rawalpindi, go to Mansehra. For Gilgit, go to Besham. In front of the Shangri-La Hotel you can catch a long-distance bus, if it stops.

Getting Around
A Suzuki stand is just west of the Shangri-La Hotel, for getting to Pishora (Rs 2, leaves when it's full) and other nearby places.

BATAGRAM TO MANSEHRA
South from Batagram the highway climbs steeply through pine plantations, and out of the Nandhiar River basin. It dips for a while into the picturesque bowl called **Chattar Plain** (after Chattar Singh, yet another Sikh general) and then enters the drainage area of the Siran River. The land flattens as you descend – through cornfields and the precision terracing of rice paddies, which are luminous yellow-green in the spring – into the Pakli (or Pakhal) Plain surrounding Mansehra.

Half an hour south of Chattar Plain (or 45 minutes north of Mansehra) is the village of **Shinkiari**. Wagons and Suzukis come here from Mansehra and continue northward off the KKH, up the Siran River to **Dadar**. According to local people it's possible to walk over the hills into the Kaghan Valley from here: from Shinkiari to Balakot in one or two days and from Dadar to Sharan in two or three.

MANSEHRA
Tourists don't pay much attention to Mansehra ('mahn-SEH-rah') except to get out of their buses and squint at three big rocks on the northern outskirts, on which the Mauryan King Ashoka inscribed a set of edicts over 2200 years ago. But the town itself – sitting on high ground (975 metres) in the fertile Pakli Plain – is an interesting place too, with traces of its history as a Sikh garrison town in the early 1800s.

Mansehra is the most southerly place on the KKH where you'll see an appreciable number of Pathans. Many are refugee Afghans, trying to make a living in their host country. The men stand out because of their stature and their big, loosely-wrapped turbans, and the women (when not veiled) because of their beauty and their bright and elaborate clothing. There are several refugee camps in the area, and one local merchant estimated that, of Mansehra's 30,000 population, about 10% are refugees.

Most people in Mansehra are willing to be photographed, but the Afghans seem camera-shy (not surprising, considering the sensitivity of their situation and the demeaning work they must often settle for), so ask before you shoot.

There haven't been any Sikhs in Mansehra since India was partitioned. The local Muslims are mostly Sunni, with some Shia. The most widely spoken language is Pushto, the speech of Pathans; some Hindko Punjabi (similar to Urdu) is also spoken. Urdu and English are mostly used as administrative languages.

Mansehra and Abbottabad together form the transportation hub for all of northern Pakistan: Rawalpindi and Islamabad, the hill-stations around Murree, Azad Kashmir and its administrative capital of Muzaffarabad, the Kaghan and Swat Valleys, and destinations north along the KKH.

Orientation

The KKH goes around Mansehra, but before it was built, the local roads came right through. The three main streets are named for their colonial-era destinations (Abbottabad, Shinkiari village, and the Vale of Kashmir), and they converge on the bridge in the middle of town.

Arriving buses stop at either the government or general bus stand, both about 100 to 200 metres from the bridge on Abbottabad Rd. Some long-distance buses only stop on the KKH near the Ashoka Rocks, a one-km walk into town along Shinkiari Rd.

A convenient landmark is the Friends Hotel, the tall, crumbling, green and white hotel overlooking the north end of the bridge.

Information

There's a red post-box just to the left of the Friends Hotel and a little stationery shop right behind it (with a big green sign in Urdu) that sells stamps. I couldn't find a post office.

None of the banks here will change foreign money into rupees. If you're broke in Mansehra, spend your last Rs 3 on the 1/2-hour bus trip to Abbottabad and change money there.

A small newsstand by the bridge sells Pakistani English-language newspapers.

Ashoka Rocks

On the northern edge of town is Mansehra's tourist attraction, three large granite boulders on which 14 edicts were engraved by order of the Mauryan King Ashoka in the middle of the 3rd century BC. Apparently appalled by the suffering his early military campaigns caused, Ashoka became interested in the new philosophy of Buddhism and attempted to dictate a new public morality based on piety, moderation, tolerance and respect for life. Though he was greatly revered, his reforms – and indeed the Mauryan Empire – didn't last long after his death. The inscriptions have survived longer, but they too are fading away; in spite of canopies built over the rocks, the ancient Kharoshthi script is now almost impossible to see.

Sikh Temple

Up Kashmir Rd about 200 metres from the bridge is a gaudy old three-storey building, which is a funny pastiche of colours and architectural styles. Built in 1937 as a Sikh *gurdwara*, it's now the home of the Mansehra Police Department. Much of the original interior is still visible, if you can persuade the guard on duty to let you have a look.

Sikh Fort

About 300 metres beyond the temple/police station, on a side-street east off of Kashmir Rd, is a fort, originally built in the early 1800s by the Sikh governor-general Man Singh (after whom Mansehra is named). Following the Second Sikh War and the annexation of the Sikh state, the British rebuilt the fort in 1857. It now houses government land offices and the district jail. A few traces of the original mud-and-rock structure can be seen inside. Further up the side-street, under pine, eucalyptus and maple trees, are old British garrison buildings,

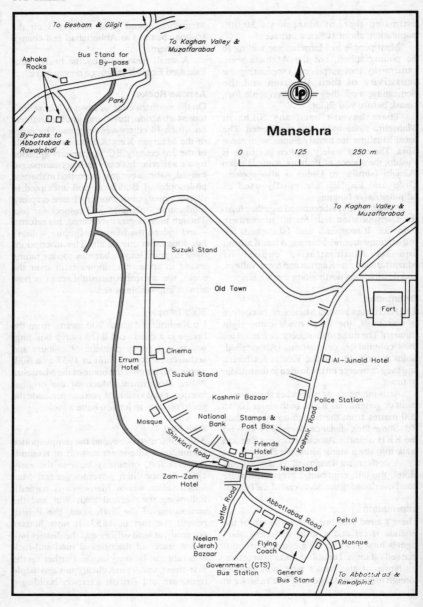

To Besham & Gilgit

To Kaghan Valley &
Muzaffarabad

Ashoka
Rocks

Bus Stand for
By-pass

Park

By-pass to
Abbottabad &
Rawalpindi

Mansehra

0   125   250 m

To Kaghan Valley &
Muzaffarabad

Suzuki Stand

Old Town

Fort

Cinema

Errum
Hotel

Suzuki Stand

Al-Junaid Hotel

Kashmir Bazaar

Police Station

Mosque

National
Bank

Stamps &
Post Box

Friends Hotel

Kashmir Road

Shinkiari Road

Zam-Zam
Hotel

Newsstand

Jaffar Road

Abbottabad Road

Petrol

Neelam
(Jerah)
Bazaar

Flying
Coach

Mosque

Government (GTS)
Bus Station

General
Bus Stand

To Abbottabad &
Rawalpindi

advocates' offices, the district courts and the homes of government officials.

Bazaars

Shinkiari Rd and Kashmir Rd curve round a big hill in the middle of town, and the Kashmir Bazaar sprawls across the top. It's a rabbit warren of a place, full of shops and living spaces tucked everywhere, most of its narrow lanes in permanent shadow. The wares are less interesting than the people shopping for them.

The smaller Neelam Bazaar (also called Jerah Bazaar), along Jaffar Rd on the other side of the bridge, seems to have older buildings, older people and more personality. It smells good, too, being full of spice vendors and confectioners.

Other Things to Do

If you're feeling active, there appear to be some good hill walks, with views of the Pakli Plain and the Black Mountains, about two km out Kashmir Rd.

If you're not feeling active, the Friends Hotel is a good place for people-watching (and Mansehra is a good town for it) or reading the newspaper over tea; climb up the narrow stairs on the right. It's a grotty, baroque old place full of little rooms, and beds on the landings. Women may be asked (but not required) to go to the 'family' area on the top floor.

Places to Stay – bottom end

The Zam Zam Hotel is on Shinkiari Rd, 50 metres west of the bridge, down a path under a tiny English sign. They have doubles with toilet for Rs 48, a windowless single for Rs 25, and a communal cold shower. The white-bearded wallah may tell you the single is booked when it's not; apart from that it's an honest place with good service and good, reasonably priced food.

There are many cheap serais or muzaffar khanas (literally 'rest places') where a rope bed, without privacy or security, is about Rs 10. The Friends Hotel is one. But none seem willing to take in westerners. Most are near the bus stands or on Kashmir Rd, recognisable by their big upper-storey balconies.

Some hotels are also skittish about foreigners, convinced that all western travellers have upper-class tastes. One such place is the Al-Junaid Hotel on Kashmir Rd, with doubles for Rs 50.

Places to Stay – middle

The Errum Hotel, 350 metres up Shinkiari Rd from the bridge, has quiet, clean singles/doubles with toilet and shower for Rs 40/65 (and a VIP suite with a genuine bath for Rs 95), a good restaurant and a rooftop patio.

Other hotels are too far out on the Abbottabad Rd to be worth it unless you have your own transport. The Nain Sukh Hotel, about 1 1/2 km away, has singles/doubles for Rs 50/70.

Places to Eat

Food is cheap and good here. Many small cafes on Abbottabad Rd serve basic gosht (curried mutton) or kadahi ('ka-DYE') gosht (spicy mutton braised and served in a tiny iron pan), daudoh (thick northern-style noodle soup), vegetables and omelettes. Fill up for Rs 10 to Rs 15.

In the early morning these places serve deep-fried paratha ('pah-RAH-tah') bread. Some may have the wonderful Pakistani equivalent of the continental breakfast: sweet, light deep-fried puri pastry, topped with a bright orange confection called halvah, and a cup of tea.

The best restaurants seem to be in the hotels. My favourite is the Zam Zam's; the selection is large and a good dinner is Rs 20 to Rs 25.

Getting There & Away

There are two long-distance bus stations on Abbottabad Rd. One is for the big grey buses of the Government Transport Service (GTS), which depart on a fixed schedule, full or not; buy your ticket at the back of the yard. The other is the chaotic general bus stand for private buses, wagons and Suzukis. Some have departure schedules but most go when they're full. Buy tickets on board or in one of the little rooms at the front of the yard.

West of the general bus stand is a separate ticket office, called Flying Coach, with air-conditioned Toyota Coaster vans to Rawalpindi and Lahore.

Abbottabad From both stands there are many, all day long, for Rs 3 in a bus, Rs 3.50 in a wagon.

Rawalpindi The journey takes three to 3¹/2 hours. From GTS to 'Pindi's Pir Wadhai Bus Stand buses leave from 5 am to 5 pm at ¹/2-hour intervals, for Rs 16. From Flying Coach to Liaquat Chowk in Rawalpindi there are five to 10 departures a day during tourist season, for Rs 35.

These all go via Havelian; a slower, more scenic alternative is to go to Abbottabad and catch a bus via the hill-station towns around Murree.

Muzaffarabad Wagons take two hours and leave from the general bus stand: wagons all day long, for Rs 9.

Balakot (Kaghan Valley) From GTS buses depart roughly hourly, from 8.30 am to 2.30 pm, for Rs 6.50; some continue to Naran. From the general bus stand there are about six departures a day in summer, from 5 am until about 3 pm; Rs 6 by bus, Rs 8 by hair-raising wagon.

Besham Buses take four hours and leave from GTS at 8.30 and 9.30 am, for Rs 19. From the general bus stand there are over a dozen departures daily, Rs 22.

Gilgit There's no direct service. NATCO and Masherbrum Tours bypass Mansehra, depositing passengers near the Ashoka Rocks at the north end of town. You can get on there if they stop; figure three to 3¹/2 hours to Mansehra. The alternative is a hop to Besham where there are local and direct options to Gilgit.

Getting Around
Local transport is by Suzuki pickup. Passenger and 'special' (for hire) Suzukis start from the general bus stand on Abbottabad Rd and from two small yards along Shinkiari Rd.

MANSEHRA TO BALAKOT
The road to Balakot and the Kaghan Valley is both beautiful and exciting; depending on your driver, you'll remember it one way or the other. It's narrow and rutty and winds like a snake for 50 km through richly forested mountains.

Buses (but not wagons) make a 10-minute stop at **Garhi Habibullah**, a collection of food stalls, fruit vendors and trinket shops about an hour from Mansehra. It is mainly a transfer point for Muzaffarabad. While you're there your bus may be boarded by various itinerant vendors of snacks, patent medicines, political causes and religious deviations.

At the end of this roller-coaster ride into the mountains you may be surprised to learn that Balakot (982 metres) is only seven metres higher than Mansehra.

BALAKOT
This is the gateway to the beautiful Kaghan Valley: embracing mountains, with pine and scrub on gravelly slopes above patchwork corn and wheat fields. From a distance Balakot is a pretty village straddling the Kunhar River. Up close, its recent haphazard growth is a blight on the landscape. But you probably didn't come all this way just to see Balakot (unless you have an interest in leprosy clinics; there's one here). Its chief asset is the information and transport available.

The normal Kaghan Valley tourist season is early June to mid-September, though the monsoon can bring daily rains and temporary roadblocks in July and August. If you don't have a sleeping bag, it's risky to come in the 'high season' without hotel bookings. Out of season, on the other hand – in May or late September, when the weather is cold but not impossible – you'll find some of the best hotel deals in Pakistan, if you're willing to negotiate.

Information & Orientation

The Tourist Information Centre is at the PTDC Motel at the south end of town, about 50 metres beyond a small stream crossing. Here you can get information on weather, road conditions and jeep availability in the upper valley. The post office, telephone exchange, civil hospital and police post are within a 200-metre walk south of the PTDC Motel. There are no banks that will exchange foreign currencies.

Things to See & Do

There's a popular 'swimming hole' on the east bank of the river, and a footpath to it from the first bend in the road. The Kunhar is glacial meltwater, and it's damn cold!

A young Balakoti told me it takes three to four hours to walk west over the mountains to Shinkiari village on the KKH. It might be a good idea to get some local advice before attempting this, however. Shinkiari has no obvious hotels but it's a 30-minute bus or Suzuki ride to Mansehra.

If you're short on time but want to have a look at the Kaghan Valley, you can hire a Suzuki 'special' for a day-trip, or a jeep for a longer journey.

Places to Stay – bottom end

A 50-bed *Pakistan Youth Hostel* is down a path just south of the hospital. A bed is Rs 15. Theoretically you must belong to the Pakistan Youth Hostels Association (PYHA) or the International Youth Hostel Association (IYHA). To book ahead call PYHA (tel Lahore 881501). Outside tourist season you may find it shut.

The *Mashriq* is the cheapest regular hotel in town, though it's overpriced like the rest; a barren double (no toilet) is Rs 40. There are some *serais* on the main road, with rope beds in open rooms for Rs 5 to Rs 10; none have English signs, nor any apparent interest in foreigners.

Places to Stay – middle

In summer these places tend to be booked up. Before and after the season they'll fall all over themselves for your business, and may drop their rates by 50% or more.

The *Koh-i-Toor Hotel* has clean, simple doubles for Rs 74. Carpeted doubles at the *Balakot Hotel & Restaurant*, *Taj Mahal Hotel* or *Park Hotel* (the tangerine-coloured palace across the river) are Rs 100 to Rs 150.

Places to Stay – top end

The *PTDC Motel's* prices are not negotiable; a single/double is Rs 200/250 plus 7$\frac{1}{2}$% excise tax. They have a restaurant, jeep rental and the PTDC Tourist Information Centre.

Places to Eat

Most hotels have their own restaurants, with food quality in line with room quality. Aside from toast-and-eggs breakfasts it's mostly Pakistani food, except by arrangement at the PTDC Motel. A modest dinner at the Balakot or Taj Mahal Hotel would be Rs 15 to Rs 25. South of the bus station are cafes and kebab shops where you can get lunch for under Rs 10 and dinner for under Rs 15.

Getting There & Away

There are two bus stands, both near the Mashriq Hotel. Government Transport Service (GTS) is just uphill from the petrol station; buy your ticket from the shack at the front of the yard. The general bus stand is down a dirt lane below the petrol station. Buy tickets at the back of the yard or on board the bus. Outside tourist season the frequency of departures drops off.

Kaghan Takes 3$\frac{1}{2}$ to 4$\frac{1}{2}$ hours. From GTS: 12.30 pm only, Rs 9. From the general bus stand: five to 10 departures daily; buses are Rs 10, wagons or pickups about Rs 20.

Naran Half an hour past Kaghan. Buses are an extra Rs 5, wagons or pickups an extra Rs 10. They normally go beyond Kaghan only in July, August and September; at other times you may have to hire a jeep or Suzuki.

Mansehra From GTS: six departures between 6 am and noon, for Rs 6.50. From the general bus stand: at least six a day until mid-afternoon; bus for Rs 6, wagon for Rs 8. Some private buses go to the Ashoka Rocks on Mansehra's north end and then finish at an isolated yard several km out of town, without ever going into town. If this happens to you, Mansehra is a one-km walk from the Ashoka Rocks, or a Rs 1 Suzuki ride from the yard.

Muzaffarabad There's no direct connection; you must catch a bus (Rs 2) or Suzuki (Rs 2.50) at the general bus stand, to Garhi Habibullah ('GAH-ree hah-bee-BOO-luh'), a transfer point near the junction of the Mansehra and Muzaffarabad roads. There you catch a private wagon coming from Mansehra.

Abbottabad, Rawalpindi, Besham Go to Mansehra.

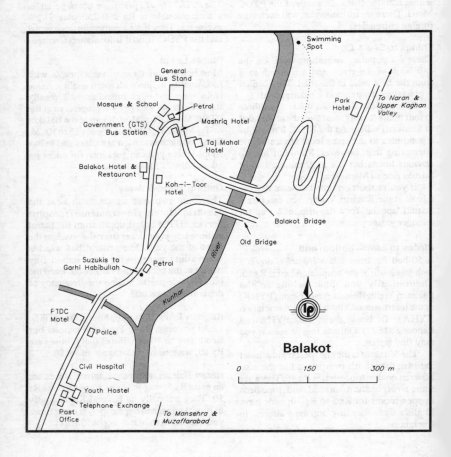

Balakot

Top: Rajah Bazaar bus stand, Rawalpindi (JK)
Left: Rajah Bazaar, Rawalpindi (JK)
Right: Saddar Bazaar, Rawalpindi (JK)

Top: Street vendor, Rawalpindi (JK)
Bottom: Pir Wadhai general bus stand, Rawalpindi (JK)

Hire Your Own Typical PTDC rates for a jeep (holds five or six) are: Shogran, Rs 200 return; Naran, Rs 500 one-way, Rs 800 return; each overnight, Rs 200 more. For trips beyond Naran in summer it's cheaper to take a bus to Naran and hire a jeep there.

You can hire Suzukis from the general bus stand or off the street. Because it holds eight to 10 people the per-person price can be less than a jeep. Suzuki drivers, however, tend to be less reliable in the face of problems and dislike waiting around while you enjoy the view. Prices are variable, so shop around. I was offered Rs 1000 to Naran and back.

THE KAGHAN VALLEY

The Kaghan Valley is beautiful and accessible, and it links the KKH at two very distant places. For about six weeks each summer the 4145-metre Babusar Pass is open, and the jeep road beside the Kunhar River and over the pass is a challenging alternative to the KKH between Mansehra and Chilas.

In 1892 the British established the pass as a supply line to their Agency at Gilgit, one of only two links to the outside world. After Partition it was Pakistan's only reliable overland route to the Northern Areas until the KKH was built. Even today, as if in imitation of history, PIA's flight to Gilgit goes right up the valley.

The population of the 155-km-long valley consists of a string of villages along the river, and a bi-annual migration of Gujars, the rootless 'cowboys' of northern Pakistan. After wintering in Kashmir and the Punjab, these poverty-line nomads fan out with their animals to the high pastures of Kohistan and Hazara. In Kaghan you'll find the roads full of them, heading up in May and June and back down in September.

Information & Orientation

The road from Balakot is paved to Kaghan village (61 km away) and gravelled to Naran (24 km more). From there to Babusar Pass it's a gradually deteriorating jeep track.

From late November till mid-April snow blocks the road beyond Kaghan; all up-valley villages, including Naran, are deserted. In May Naran and the Shogran Plateau are accessible by 4WD vehicles, though delays are likely because of encroaching glaciers, flooding and slides. June has prime tourist weather and booked-out hotels. Late July and August monsoons bring mud and slides again, but up-valley travel is possible; in fact, this is the only time for a jeep crossing of Babusar. Tourist weather returns in September. By October the upper valley is inaccessible, and travel beyond Kaghan is by 4WD. These conditions vary widely from year to year.

Shogran Plateau

At Kawai, 24 km north of Balakot, a jeep track turns east for 10 km to Shogran, 1300 metres above the valley. With immense views and prize-winning sunsets, this is a fine place to snooze away a few days. The big peak to the north is Malika Parbat (Queen of Mountains), tallest in the Kaghan Valley at 5290 metres.

A *Forestry Rest House* at Shogran can be booked through the Conservator of Forests, District Forestry Office (tel Abbottabad 2728); or inquire at Balakot PTDC. The *Lalazar Hotel* has singles/doubles for Rs 74/161. To beat the crowds, pitch a tent in higher pastures, two to three hours on.

Sharan

At Paras, eight km north of Kawai, a track winds 11 km through dense pine forest to isolated Sharan. From here you can take day-hikes, or a longer journey over the mountains to Dadar or Shinkiari, north of Mansehra.

There's a *Pakistan Youth Hostel* at Sharan, with beds for Rs 15. Theoretically you must belong to PYHA or IYHA but if beds are available (this has 25) it seems unlikely you'd be turned away. To book, call PYHA (tel Lahore 881501). A *Forestry Rest House* here can be booked with the Conservator of Forests, District Forestry

Office (tel Abbottabad 2728); or inquire at Balakot PTDC.

Shinu

Just beyond Paras, at Shinu, is a NWFP Fisheries Department trout hatchery, from which the Kunhar River (above Kaghan village) and Lake Saiful Muluk and Lake Lulusar are stocked with brown and rainbow trout. You can buy a fishing licence here.

Jared

A government-run gift shop sells local handicrafts, including wood carvings and hand-made woollen shawls.

Kaghan

This is as far as you can go in winter. The big *Lalazar Hotel* is open all winter, weather permitting; singles/doubles are Rs 74/161.

Naran

Naran is the summertime base for exploring the valley. A Tourist Information Centre is at the PTDC Motel, where you can also hire jeeps, guides and fishing tackle. The Fisheries Department office sells fishing licences.

Accommodation is dicey unless you have your own gear. On the road several km south of town is a *Pakistan Youth Hostel*; a bed is Rs 15, or pitch a tent in the yard. *Serais* have rope beds in the open for Rs 5 to Rs 10. Several small hotels catering to Pakistanis have rooms for Rs 20 to Rs 40. Some will let you pitch your tent and use their water and toilets for a small fee.

There is a *C&W Rest House*, bookable through the Executive Engineer, NWFP Communication & Works Dept (tel Abbottabad 4511); or inquire at Balakot PTDC.

The *Shaheen Hotel* and *Vershigoom Hotel* have doubles for about Rs 100. The *Cottage Motel* has singles/doubles for Rs 200/250. The *PTDC Motel* complex has tents (Rs 70 for a two-bed tent, communal toilet and shower), rooms (singles/doubles for Rs 240/300, attached bath) and separate cottages (Rs 625 to Rs 950).

Lake Saiful Muluk

Among Pakistanis, one of the most popular travel destinations in the country is this picture-postcard alpine lake, an easy uphill walk two to three hours east of Naran. At 3200 metres and surrounded by snowy mountains, it's said to be inhabited by fairies; legend has it that in ancient times a mortal, Prince Saiful Muluk, fell in love with and married a fairy. The best way to have it to yourself (you and the lake fairies and the Gujars, anyhow) is to camp here.

There's a *C&W Rest House* at the lake; book it through the Executive Engineer, NWFP C&W (tel Abbottabad 4511), or inquire at PTDC in Balakot.

Beyond Naran

All travel beyond Naran is by foot or 4WD. Leaving the main road at **Battakundi**, 16 km up the valley, you can trek to summer pastures at Lalazar Plateau. The final *Pakistan Youth Hostel* in the valley is at Battakundi, with beds at Rs 15 each and room to pitch a tent. There's another *C&W Rest House* too; book through the Executive Engineer, NWFP C&W (tel Abbottabad 4511), or inquire at Balakot PTDC.

The main road degenerates to a barely jeepable track 40 km beyond Battakundi, near **Lake Lulusar**, the biggest natural lake in Hazara and the source of the Kunhar River. A further 20 km brings you to the top of Babusar Pass and, if the weather is clear, views of the Kaghan Valley behind you and Nanga Parbat to the east.

A day-trip by jeep from Naran to the pass is usually feasible from mid-June until mid-September, but don't count on an easy time of it during monsoon season.

Getting There & Away

GTS has one bus daily from Naran to Balakot, four to five hours away, for Rs 14. There are at least five to 10 daily departures to Balakot by private bus (Rs 15) and wagon

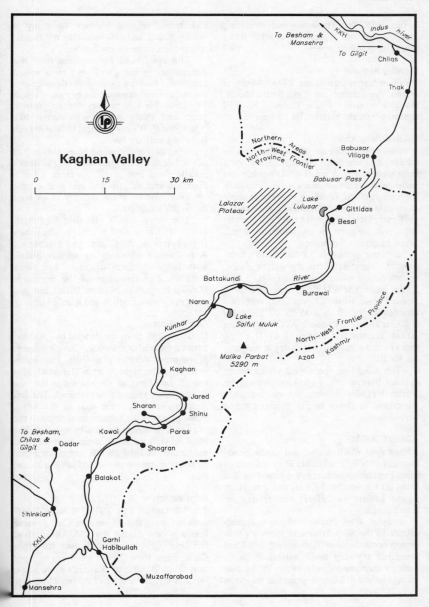

Kaghan Valley

0   15   30 km

or pickup (Rs 30). These only operate during July, August and September; at other times you'll have to hire a jeep.

Getting Around

You can hire a jeep at the PTDC Motel in Naran. Typical rates are: Lake Saiful Muluk, Rs 250 return; Lalazar Plateau, Rs 350 return; overnight haltage, Rs 200 per night.

BABUSAR PASS

It's possible to cross the pass and continue to Chilas, 130 km from Naran, but it's not a light-weight trip. A small 4WD vehicle can manage the narrow track from mid-July through August. Trekking may be feasible from mid-June (though there's still snow) until early October (though most villagers en route will be gone for the winter by then). Snow begins in November.

Babusar village is 13 km north of the pass. In summer there are a few shops, several *serais* where a rope bed is Rs 5, and a very basic *NAPWD Rest House* (Northern Areas Public Works Department) with two doubles at Rs 60. It's 35 to 40 km from Babusar village to Chilas. NATCO (Northern Areas Transport Company) 4WD cargo pickups make this trip twice a day in summer, for Rs 20.

You should get some local advice before making this crossing; a good source might be Naran PTDC's drivers. Allow for wide variations in the seasonal changes noted here.

ABBOTTABAD

Abbottabad ('AB-it-uh-bahd'), the headquarters of NWFP's Hazara Division and its main population centre, is the most pleasant town on the southern KKH, and a relaxing pause before (or after) the frenzy of Rawalpindi.

Named after James Abbott, a British officer in the Sikh Wars and Hazara's first deputy commissioner, Abbottabad is by local standards a young town, established as a military cantonment only in the 1850s. But its continuing military importance (home to Pakistan's National Military Academy at nearby Kakul, and to several elite regiments) maintains a colonial-era flavour.

The raw, loud atmosphere near the general bus stand gives way to a robust bazaar and then to a cantonment that – except for the internal combustion engine – seems lifted from the 19th century with its gardens, parks and shady streets with names like 'Club Road'. It's not unusual to hear church bells or a military band.

Not as accessible as Murree, Abbottabad never became a playground for Pakistan's middle class. But, at 1220 metres, it has a cool hill-station climate, and one of the loveliest retreats in the country is an hour away, at Thandiani.

The town has a sizeable Christian minority, and three active churches (Presbyterian, Anglican and Catholic). Abbottabad's Muslims are mostly Sunni, with large numbers of Shias and some Ismailis. The language of the region is Hindko Punjabi (similar to Urdu), but you can get by with English and a little Urdu.

Orientation

Down the hill from the general bus stand is a traffic roundabout, Fowara Chowk (*chowk*, pronounced 'choke', is Urdu for 'intersection'). The right fork is The Mall, also called the Havelian or Mansehra Rd, the thoroughfare through Abbottabad. The left fork is Jinnah Rd, the axis of the town, passing beside the bazaar, then through the old British cantonment, finally rejoining The Mall. Id Gah Rd is the main cross-street in the bazaar, and the middle-range hotels are all near the intersection of Id Gah and Jinnah Rds.

Information

Tourist Office The PTDC Tourist Information Centre (tel 2446) is at Club Annexe (once a rest house for the Abbottabad Officers' Club), across Jinnah Rd from Cantonment Park. Hours are 9 am to 1 pm and 2 to 4.30 pm Saturday through Wednesday, and 9 am to 1.30 pm Thursday.

Post The post office is at Club and Central Rds, at the north end of the bazaar.

Telephone Overseas calls can be placed, and cables sent, from the Telephone Exchange at the west end of Pine View Rd.

Banks The main office of the National Bank of Pakistan (near the courts) and the Pine View Rd office of United Bank will exchange most currencies for rupees. Habib Bank does no foreign exchange. Banks here (and northward) are a little allergic to travellers' cheques because of past incidents of fraud by foreigners, but if you're well-armed with identification you should have no problems. If you're north-bound Abbottabad is your last chance to change money until Gilgit.

Bookshops The only English-language bookshop is Variety Book Stall, south of the post office, with miscellaneous foreign magazines, novels and postcards.

Emergency The main police post is on Jinnah Rd near the bazaar. There are two hospitals: the small Cantonment General on Pine View Rd and the large District Headquarters Teaching Hospital on Id Gah Rd 1/2 km east of The Mall.

Adventure Foundation This private organisation promotes Outward-Bound-style adventures for young Pakistanis. Although they're already attempting a lot on a small budget, there's talk of opening a centre, perhaps in Abbottabad, for the sale or rental of outdoor gear. So far it's just talk, but you can call (tel 6224) or visit them at No 1 Gulistan Colony, at the corner of College Rd about 1/3 km east of The Mall.

The Cantonment

The historical heart of this military town is its cantonment, the original British garrison with its orderly streets, European architecture and grand parade ground. A flower-filled but melancholy old Christian cemetery is 1/2 km up Circular Rd.

The Bazaar

Abbottabad's other persona is its bazaar, 10 square blocks of crumbling colonial architecture, full of noise and the smells of incense and lime. The narrower and darker the alley, the older and more interesting the shops. In Gurdwara Bazaar is a former Sikh *gurdwara*, or temple, built in 1943, abandoned four years later at Partition, and now used as municipal offices. It's beneath the arch just off Jinnah Rd.

South of Kechehri Rd are the District Courts (*kechehri* is Urdu for 'courts'). The grounds are thick with petitioners and dealmakers, and the lane up from Kechehri Rd is lined with advocates' offices.

Shimla Peak

The hills that cradle Abbottabad are Shimla Peak to the north-west and Sarban Peak to the south. Shimla's summit is covered with trails through pine forest, and offers fine panoramas of the town and its surroundings. It's also blessedly cool in the summer. You can walk up (three steep km from Central Rd) or hire a Suzuki on Kechehri Rd.

Parks

There are two slightly unkempt parks, one in the cantonment and one by city hall, south-east of the bazaar. In warm weather you might find itinerant performers or a travelling circus in Cantonment Park.

Thandiani

Thandiani ('tahn-dee-AH-nee') is a series of 2700-metre forested peaks north-east of Abbottabad, fairly remote until the recent completion of a paved road. The air is cool and clean, and development is minimal – a few cafes and guest houses and a TV rebroadcast antenna, silently beaming soap operas from Islamabad. There are splendid views east across the Pir Panjal Range (beyond which lies the Vale of Kashmir) and north even to Nanga Parbat in clear weather.

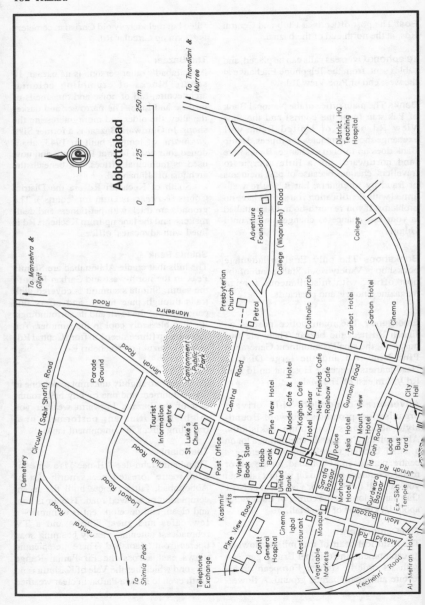

Abbottabad

0   125   250 m

To Thandiani &
Murree

To Mansehra &
Gilgit

To Shimla Peak

District HQ
Teaching Hospital

College (Wiqarullah) Road

Adventure
Foundation

College

Presbyterian
Church

Petrol

Catholic Church

Zarbat Hotel

Sarban Hotel

Cinema

Mansehra Road

Cantonment
Public Park

Central Road

Parade
Ground

Jinnah Road

Circular (Sabir Sharif) Road

Cemetery

Tourist
Information
Centre

St Luke's
Church

Post Office

Club Road

Liaquat Road

Central Road

Pine View Road

Kashmir
Arts

Variety
Book Stall

Pine View Hotel

Model Cafe & Hotel
Kaghan Cafe
Hotel Kohisar
New Friends Cafe
Rainbow Cafe

Police

Asia Hotel

Mount View
Hotel

Gumani Road

Id Gah Road

Local
Bus
Yard

City
Hall

Habib
Bank

United
Bank

Contt
General Hospital

Cinema

Iqbal
Restaurant

Sarafa
Bazaar

Marhaba
Hotel

Mosque

Vegetable
Markets

Gurdwara
Bazaar

Ex-Sikh
Temple

Bazaar

Masjid
Rd

Main

Telephone
Exchange

Kechenri Road

Al-Mehran Hotel

You could take a day-trip, but you might want to stay longer. It's an hour's ride on a snakey road beside the Kalapani ('Black Water') River, through terraced fields and pine and deodar forest. *Thandiani* means 'cool place', so bring an extra layer for the day, and more for the night. There are snack shops near the bus terminus but you'd be better off with your own food.

To stay cheaply, bring a tent or take a Rs 10 rope bed at the tiny *Far Pavilions Hotel* near the bus terminus. Two government rest houses are near the summit. One km south on a jeep road from the bus stop, by the TV tower, is a *C&W Rest House*, Rs 100 for a double with attached bath. One km further is a *Forestry Rest House*, more isolated, Rs 60 for a double. They're available if officials aren't using them but they must be booked ahead in Abbottabad. Contact the Executive Engineer, NWFP Communication & Works Dept, Shimla Peak Rd (tel 4511), or the

Conservator of Forests, District Forestry Office, Jail Rd (tel 2728).

Ilyasi Mosque

The village of Nawan Sheher, five km east of Abbottabad on the Murree road, is the site of this striking mosque, which includes a complex of spring-fed bathhouses and pools. A small bazaar nearby has tea-shops and cafes.

Places to Stay – bottom end

There are some ultra-cheapos, Rs 15 to Rs 20 for a single, across from the general bus stand, but they're noisy, a bit sleazy, and not recommended unless you're going broke.

A *Pakistan Youth Hostel* is at Mandian, north of Abbottabad. It's very isolated unless you're biking. A bed is Rs 15 for PYHA or IYHA members. To book ahead call PYHA (tel Lahore 881501). Get there on a Suzuki to Mandian. At the end of the line, turn left at the 'Ayub Medical College' sign, go 700 metres to a T-intersection and turn left again; 300 metres on, the road is now a footpath and the hostel is beyond a green gate on your left. That Suzuki might take you all the way for an extra Rs 5.

Places to Stay – middle

The *Bolan Hotel* is handy if you're leaving next morning as it's near the general bus stand. Basic, clean singles/doubles with hot showers are Rs 50/70, and there's a restaurant downstairs. But it's a long walk into town.

The best bargains are three hotels in Id Gah Rd. The *Mount View* and *Asia* have singles/doubles for around Rs 35/70; the *Marhaba*, at Rs 40/80, has a nice old atrium, rooftop access and hot showers in cold weather. The road's a madhouse of Suzukis and hawkers during the day, but quiet at night. All have decent cheap food, the rooms have toilets, and staff speak a little English.

Others in this range are north on Jinnah Rd: *Hotel Kohisar* with singles/doubles for Rs 55/80, *Pineview Hotel* at Rs 30/60 and *Model Cafe & Hotel* at Rs 35/40. The

Al-Mehran Hotel in Kechehri Rd charges Rs 35/60 but doesn't seem keen on foreigners.

Places to Stay – top end

The ones with carpets, big beds and hot running water are all on The Mall: the *Springfield* with singles/doubles for Rs 200/260, the *Sarban* at Rs 200/260 and the *Zarbat* at Rs 85/160.

Places to Eat

Selection is good in the restaurants and cafes: curries, braised chicken or mutton, *pulau* (fried rice), potatoes, spicy spinach, little tomato-and-onion salads. Each place has a butcher stall out front – not very appetising, but it keeps the flies outside. The hotels have their own restaurants, with food prices in line with room prices, and menus in fractured English. Among the mid-range hotels (dinners Rs 20 and up) I like the Marhaba best.

The *Kaghan*, *New Friends* and *Rainbow Cafes* on Jinnah Rd near Pine View Rd serve decent food in fairly clean surroundings. In the bazaar the *Iqbal Restaurant* has an elegant wood-panelled interior but so-so food, from a menu with no English. It always seems to be full of glowering Pathans watching the television.

In the bazaar you can 'self-cater' cheaply with kebabs, *samosas*, fresh fruit and sweets.

Before certain restaurants you'll see a sign, 'Inbound All Ranks' (or funny variations like 'Inbond All Rinks'), which means military personnel from the cantonment are allowed to eat there.

Things to Buy

The local handicrafts speciality is Hazara embroidery. The best deals are in obscure shops in the bazaar, but better selections (and higher prices) are said to be in two tourist shops: Kashmir Arts near United Bank and the cinema, and Threadlines Gallery about two km out on the Mansehra Rd. A look in these shops will at least tell you what to look for in the bazaar.

Tailors in Sarafa Bazaar can make a

shalwar qamiz in two days for under Rs 5 but you must bring them the cloth, which yo buy elsewhere in the bazaar (about s metres) for Rs 80 to Rs 150. Or buy o off-the-shelf in a general store.

Getting There & Away

There are two bus stations at the south end town. The Government Transport Servi (GTS) station is on Jinnah Rd 100 metr north of the Fowara Chowk junction. GT buses run on fixed schedules, and tickets a at a window at the back of the yard. Th general bus stand is 200 metres south Fowara Chowk on the Havelian R Generally you buy a ticket on board. Priva buses tend to leave when they're full, and r less often and less late in autumn and wint

Rawalpindi Takes 2½ to three hours. Fro GTS: to 'Pindi's Pir Wadhai Bus Sta roughly every ½ hour from 6 am to 6.30 p for Rs 13. From the general bus stand: to F Wadhai, all day long starting at 5.30 am (b a ticket in the room in the middle of t station); the bus is Rs 12, the quicker wag Rs 15. Air-con Toyota vans go from the lit plaza in front of the Springfield Hotel, Rawalpindi's Liaquat Chowk, five to times a day during the tourist season, for I 30; you can book ahead by telephone (52 or 5714).

These all go via Havelian; a slow a scenic alternative is by way of the hill-stati towns around Murree.

Mansehra From both stands there are ma departures, all day long; buses are Rs wagons Rs 3.50. Rawalpindi-bound air-c Toyota vans also stop in Mansehra, for Rs

Murree Takes five hours. From GTS there one bus at 7 am, Rs 10.50. From the gene bus stand there are six departures every d Rs 10.

Besham Takes five hours. From GTS bus leave at 7.30 and 8.30 am, Rs 22.

Gilgit There's no direct service. The red and white NATCO buses and the Masherbrum Tours buses pass through, and you may be able to flag one down at Fowara Chowk. Figure 2 1/2 to three hours from Rawlapindi to Abbottabad; it's at least 12 hours more to Gilgit. The alternative is to go to Besham, where there are local and direct options to Gilgit.

Balakot (Kaghan Valley) Takes three to 3 1/2 hours. GTS buses leave roughly every 1/2 hour from 7.30 am until 2 pm, for Rs 9.50. From the general bus stand there are wagons and buses all day long, for Rs 9.

Muzaffarabad Takes three hours. From the general bus stand there are about five buses (Rs 10) and 10 wagons (Rs 12.50) a day.

Getting Around

Short-haul passenger Suzukis clog Id Gah Rd all day, with kids calling out destinations. For longer trips there's a local bus yard, down an alley 70 metres east of the Mount View Hotel on Id Gah Rd. Hire a Suzuki (holds eight to 10) in upper Kechehri Rd.

Shimla Peak In summer you might find passenger Suzukis in upper Kechehri Rd, for Rs 1, or you can hire one for Rs 15 to Rs 20. Ask for *Shimla Pahari* ('pah-REE').

Ilyasi Mosque Catch a Nawan Sheher Suzuki in Id Gah Rd for Rs 1; ask for *Ilyasi Masjid*.

Mandian To get near the PYHA Youth Hostel, catch a Mandian Suzuki in Id Gah Rd and go to the end of the line (Rs 1).

Thandiani The one-hour trip is Rs 12 by Toyota pickup, Rs 8 by bus; catch them at the right rear corner of the local bus yard. Departures are frequent from 8 am until mid-afternoon. They return on the same schedule so don't count on a late ride back.

HAVELIAN

This dusty, nondescript market town has only one claim to fame: it's the official southern end of the KKH, 790 km from the Chinese border and 1200 km from Kashgar. There are no markers of any kind; the nearest one is 130 km north at Thakot. And there was already a road here, to Mansehra and beyond, before the KKH was even an idea. It's an odd choice, except that Havelian is a railhead.

But there actually is a kind of geographical boundary here. The road falls abruptly out of the hills to the banks of the Dor River north of Havelian, dropping nearly 1/2 km in the 15 km from Abbottabad. Southward, the road and railway proceed almost horizontally to Rawalpindi. This is certainly the southern end of the mountains.

There's no reason to stop here unless you want to go on to Rawalpindi by rail.

Places to Stay & Eat

If you must stay the night, the tall, skinny *Indus Hotel*, 100 metres down the left fork, has singles/doubles for Rs 30/40 and a little cafe. Nobody speaks much English.

Getting There & Away

Pleasant, creaky old trains leave for Rawalpindi at 10.05 and 11.50 am and 5.50 pm, for Rs 7, and take three hours. If you've come from 'Pindi on the train, you'll probably find an Abbottabad or Mansehra bus right at the station; it's 1/2 hour and Rs 2 to Abbottabad, one hour and Rs 5 to Mansehra. Or go out the door, keep right at the fork, and at the end of the bazaar you'll find more buses, leaving about every 30 minutes. Buses to Rawalpindi stop at the petrol station down the left fork.

HAVELIAN TO THE GRAND TRUNK ROAD

From Havelian southward it's flat and warm. Half an hour away is **Haripur**, once the centre of Hazara. It was founded in 1822 as the headquarters of the Sikh General Hari Singh, after whom it's named. In 1853 its administrative functions were all moved to

Abbottabad and now it's just a big market town.

From Haripur the road crosses the wide, sandy **Taxila Valley**. It's odd to reflect that this quiet plain was for almost five centuries a world centre of Buddhist philosophy and art, the Buddhist 'Holy Land'. Taxila was the cultural capital of the Mauryan and Kushan Empires – from the 3rd century BC to the 3rd century AD – and the valley still has abundant evidence of this extraordinary period, at archaeological sites and in a fine

museum. This makes a worthwhile one or two day trip from Rawalpindi, as described in the next chapter.

At Taxila town or at Hasan Abdal (there are several routes from Haripur) you arrive at the **Grand Trunk Road**, the old axis of the Moghul Empire and the British Raj, Rudyard Kipling's 'broad, smiling river of life' that once ran 2500 km from Kabul to Calcutta. Now the GT Road is a thunderous stream of chrome-plated trucks and buses, and the Karakoram Highway seems pretty far away.

Rawalpindi & Islamabad

This is the business end of the KKH. Going or coming, you're likely to pass through but unlikely to linger. However, there's plenty to do while waiting for your visa, trekking permit or plane out.

Rawalpindi was the headquarters of the Sikh army in the late 1700s, but it only came into its own after the Sikh wars of the 1840s, as the largest cantonment in Asia (cantonments were the tidy residential-military-administrative enclaves built next to – never quite *in* – major British colonial towns). Astride the Grand Trunk Road, Rawalpindi 'Cantt' is today the headquarters of the Pakistan army and was the home of President Zia ul-Haq until his death in 1988. Islamabad may be the capital, but in a country with a nearly unbroken line of military rulers since 1958, 'Pindi is still the centre.

By contrast, where Islamabad stands there was nothing 30 years ago. The old capital of Karachi was too far away from everything and so it was decided to build a new one, centrally located near the GT Road, Rawalpindi and the appealing summer climate of the foothills. Construction began in 1961 and will probably go on for years. As conceived by architect-planner Konstantinos Doxiades, Islamabad is to avoid inner-city decay by growing in only one direction at a time, in a series of 'sectors' across a grid, each with its own residences, shops and open space. So far only a half-dozen of these units have been developed, but in the long term Islamabad is expected to swallow up Rawalpindi itself.

Orientation

Just 15 km apart, the two cities couldn't be more different: noisy, kinetic old Rawalpindi and subdued, suburb-like Islamabad. For the shoestring traveller they form a single mega-town with budget hotels at one end, bureaucrats at the other and plenty of cheap transport in between.

Most paperwork begins in the capital. But Islamabad is expensive (except the ultra-bottom-end Tourist Camp), spread out, awkward by bus and just a little boring. Rawalpindi bazaars are cheap, compact and interesting, and buses into Islamabad are tedious but straightforward. Outside transport (air, bus and rail) clusters around Rawalpindi.

Saddar Bazaar is the sensible area to stay in Rawalpindi, with hotels in every price range, PIA's Northern Areas booking office, railway station, GPO, banks, shops, travel agents and easy transport to Islamabad, the airport and the Pir Wadhai Bus Stand.

Rawalpindi 'Pindi's north-south axis is Murree Rd, which is also the road to Islamabad. It's split in two by the east-west railway line. Middle and bottom-end hotel concentrations are at Saddar Bazaar, south of the railway; Rajah Bazaar, north of the railway and west of Murree Rd; and along Murree Rd at Liaquat ('LYAH-kut') Rd and at Committee Chowk. The airport is north-east of town, the Pir Wadhai General Bus Stand north-west and the railway station at the edge of Saddar Bazaar.

Rawalpindi's biggest bazaar is Rajah, a patchwork of dozens of smaller speciality markets. At its centre is Fowara Chowk, the six-way intersection with 'spoke' roads to Saddar, Pir Wadhai and Murree Rd.

South of Saddar is the Cantonment, with top-end hotels, city offices, army barracks, churches and other traces of colonial life, and big Ayub National Park. The city's growing end is the sprawling 'Satellite Town' to the north. It touches Islamabad at the local transport junction and market of Faizabad.

Islamabad By design, Islamabad has no axis or centre. Most of it is a grid-work of rectangular 'sectors', each with residential areas around a central *markaz* or commercial

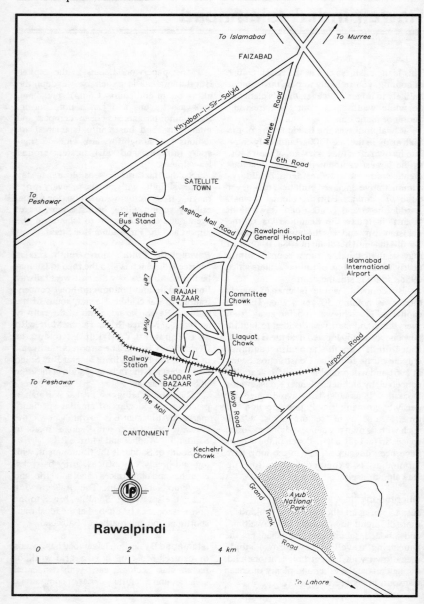

To Islamabad

To Murree

FAIZABAD

Murree Road

Khyaban-i-Sir-Salyid

6th Road

SATELLITE
TOWN

To Peshawar

Asghar Mall Road

Pir Wadhai
Bus Stand

Rawalpindi
General Hospital

Islamabad
International
Airport

Leh
River

RAJAH
BAZAAR

Committee
Chowk

Liaquat
Chowk

Airport Road

Railway
Station

SADDAR
BAZAAR

To Peshawar

The Mall

Moyo Road

CANTONMENT

Kechehri
Chowk

Grand Trunk Road

Ayub
National
Park

Rawalpindi

0   2   4 km

To Lahore

centre and a few government offices. The topmost government offices (including the cluster of ministries called the Secretariat) and most foreign embassies are at the eastern end of the grid.

Each sector has a letter-number designation, like F-7, and each sector is further divided into quarters and numbered clockwise, eg F-7/1 in the south-west corner, F-7/2 in the north-west corner, etc. Numbered streets run within sectors, while avenues and *khyabans* (boulevards) run between sectors. These Orwellian coordinates also have formal names; F and G, the letters of the main residential-commercial sectors, are Shalimar and Ramna, so F-7 is also Shalimar-7, and so on.

As a practical matter, however, most people refer to sectors by the names of their markets. The main ones, in their sequence on the bus lines, are Aabpara ('AH-pa-ra') (south-west G-6), Melody or Civic Centre (central G-6), Super Market (F-6), Jinnah or Jinnah Super (F-7) and Ayub Market (F-8).

Aabpara, the budget traveller's home in Islamabad, was there before the city was, just a bus stand and a small shabby market. South of Aabpara is a huge, jungly park, Shakarparian. Running east-west between the Fs and Gs is a strip called the 'Blue Area', to be developed as a commercial belt. Several offices once conveniently located at Aabpara have been banished to the Blue Area. North of the city are the beginnings of the Margalla Hills.

Information
Pakistan Visa Extension or Replacement
Islamabad is the only place to extend a visa or transit permit or deal with an expired visa or lost documents. The procedure is described in the Facts For The Visitor chapter – Visas, Permits & Regulations.

Foreigners' Registration If you register here, do it in the city where your hotel is. The Foreigners' Registration Office in Rawalpindi is in the Civil Courts area, beside the Senior Superintendent of Police (SSP).

Catch an airport Suzuki on Adamjee Rd at Murree Rd and get off just past the big intersection called Kechehri Chowk ('kuh-CHEH-ree choke'; *kechehri* means 'courts'), for Rs 1. Take the first right beyond the intersection and ask for 'SSP'; it's about 200 metres down. The registration office is open from 7.30 am to 2 pm Saturday to Wednesday, and till noon on Thursday.

The Islamabad office is also by the SSP, in Ayub Market (F-8) at the end of the inter-city bus line. It's on the east side of the market area. Their hours are 8 am to 1 pm and 2 to 4 pm, Sunday to Thursday, and 9 am to noon on Saturday.

Bring two passport-size photos and the Temporary Certificate of Registration ('Form C') if you got one when entering Pakistan. There's no fee.

China Visa A three-month, single-entry Chinese visa takes three working days and costs Rs 100. There's no requirement to be in a tour group or show China hotel reservations, although in the high season (May, and August through October) it's probably wise not to list too many over-crowded tourist destinations (like Beijing, Xian, Shanghai and Guilin) on your application. Don't list Tibet.

Bring your passport and two passport-size photos to the Chinese Embassy (tel 826667) in the Diplomatic Enclave. The visa office is open from 9 am to 1 pm, daily except Fridays and major *Chinese* holidays. From Aabpara, catch a passenger Suzuki out 'Embassy Rd' for Rs 1, or a taxi for about Rs 12.

India Visa Three-month single-entry Indian visas can be obtained in one day. The cost reflects how well your government treats Indian visitors; about Rs 70 for Canadians, Rs 250 for Americans, Rs 540 for UK citizens (some of whom report getting only 15-day visas).

Bring your passport and two passport-size photos to the Indian Embassy (tel 826387) on the east side of G-6. Take a bus to the GPO; walk south past Melody Cinema

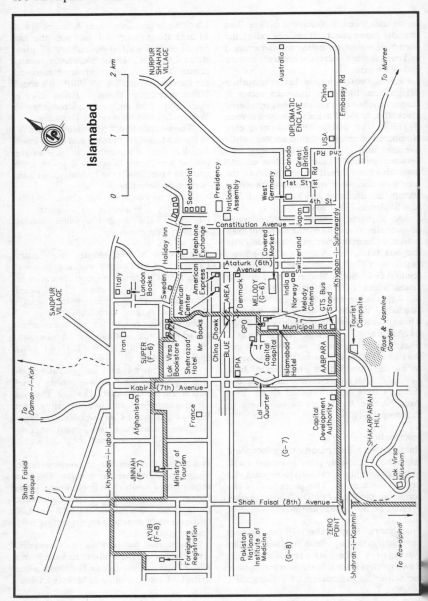

Islamabad

2 km
1
0

NURPUR
SHAHAN
VILLAGE

Australia

China

DIPLOMATIC
ENCLAVE

Embassy Rd

To Murree

Canada
Great
Britain
USA
2nd Rd

West
Germany
1st St
1st Rd

4th St

Japan
Khyabn-i-Suhrawardy

Presidency
National Assembly
Secretariat

Constitution Avenue

Covered
Market

Holiday Inn

Telephone
Exchange

Ataturk (6th)
Avenue

American
Express

Denmark

Switzerland

MELODY
(G-6)

India
Norway
Melody
Cinema
GTS Bus
Stand

Sweden
London Books
American
Center
AREA

Italy

SAIDPUR
VILLAGE

Iran

SUPER
(F-6)

Lok Virsa
Bookstore
Shehrazad
Hotel
Mr Books

China Chowk
BLUE
GPO

Municipal Rd
Tourist
Campsite

Rose & Jasmine
Garden

Capital
Hospital
PIA
Islamabad
Hotel
AABPARA

Kabir (7th) Avenue

To Daman-i-Koh

Afghanistan
France

Lal Quarter

Capital
Development
Authority
(G-7)

SHAKARPARIAN
HILL

Shah
Faisal
Mosque

Khyaban-i-iqbal

JINNAH
(F-7)
Ministry of
Tourism

Lok Virsa
Museum

Shah Faisal (8th) Avenue

AYUB
(F-8)

Foreigners
Registration

Pakistan
National
Institute of
Medicine
(G-8)

ZERO
POINT

Shahrah-i-Kashmir

To Rawalpindi

to the third left, Bazaar Rd; go east past Siraj Market; and then a block south on Ataturk Avenue. You must apply in the morning; if you're there by 9.30 am you can get the visa at 5.30 pm the same day.

Liquor Permit You can get a liquor permit from the Excise & Tax Office, next door to Foreigners' Registration in both Rawalpindi and Islamabad. You sign a form saying you aren't a Muslim and pay a small fee; the paperwork takes a day or less. The Rawalpindi permit is good throughout Pakistan (though you won't find much beer on the KKH until you're in China). If you go into one of the foreigners-only special lounges in the top-end hotels you sign the same form.

Tourist Offices In Rawalpindi, the Pakistan Tourism Development Corporation (PTDC) has a Tourist Information Centre (tel 64811, 66231) in Flashman's Hotel, open from 9 am to 4.30 pm Saturday to Thursday. It's a good place for maps and brochures but not much else. For information on KKH destinations you're better off visiting the local offices, eg Abbottabad, Balakot, Besham and Gilgit.

Islamabad has another PTDC Tourist Information Centre at the Tourism Division of the Ministry of Culture, Sports & Tourism, at the west end of Jinnah Market (F-7); it's about the same calibre as the 'Pindi office. The Tourism Division is also the starting point for trekking permits (see Facts For The Visitor – Treks & Tours).

City Maps & Other Information PTDC's tourist map, good for Islamabad but useless in Rawalpindi, is for sale at the Tourist Information Centres. The Survey of Pakistan's *Islamabad & Rawalpindi Guide Map* is more detailed but dated; it's Rs 20 at the Book Centre (Saddar), London Books (Islamabad) and other shops.

The Capital Development Authority (tel 828301) has a good map-brochure, *Trekking in the Margalla Hills*, describing walks and rest houses in the hills behind Islamabad. PTDC may have it, or go to CDA on

Khyaban-i-Suhrawardy (south edge of G-7, west of Aabpara) and ask for the Public Relations Office, room 31.

The Asian Study Group (see Libraries) has a file of hand-drawn maps of local trails, available for photocopying at your expense. Isobel Shaw's *An Illustrated Guide to Pakistan* (Collins, London, 1988) is a good source of information on the Islamabad area, by someone who used to live here.

Banks – Rawalpindi In Saddar Bazaar, Pakistani banks best prepared to do foreign exchange are Habib Bank's 'SDV' (Safe Deposit Vault) Branch, on The Mall between Canning and Kashmir Rds; and National Bank of Pakistan's Cantt Branch, behind the shops on either Bank or Haider Rd, east of Saddar Rd. Public hours are 9 am to 1 pm Monday to Thursday, 9 to 11 am Saturday and Sunday.

American Express (tel 65617), on Murree Rd north of Saadi Rd, will cash their own and other travellers' cheques (the latter for a fee) and major currencies. They're open from 9 am to 1 pm and 2 to 4.30 pm, Monday to Thursday, and 9 am to 1.30 pm Saturday and Sunday. Other overseas banks include Citibank, at Adamjee Rd east of Murree Rd; Grindlays, Canning and Haider Rds; and Bank of Credit & Commerce International (BCCI), The Mall between Saddar and Kashmir Rds.

Cash by overseas transfer or through major bank credit cards can be arranged at Habib's SDV Branch. Grindlays can do direct transfers from Australian and New Zealand banks.

Banks – Islamabad The main offices of the Habib and National banks, at Melody Market behind the Islamabad Hotel, do foreign exchange. At Aabpara, Bank of America will exchange only US dollar cash or travellers' cheques, and can arrange cash by direct transfer or with major US credit cards. American Express, far away at the Blue Area, will cash their own and other travellers'

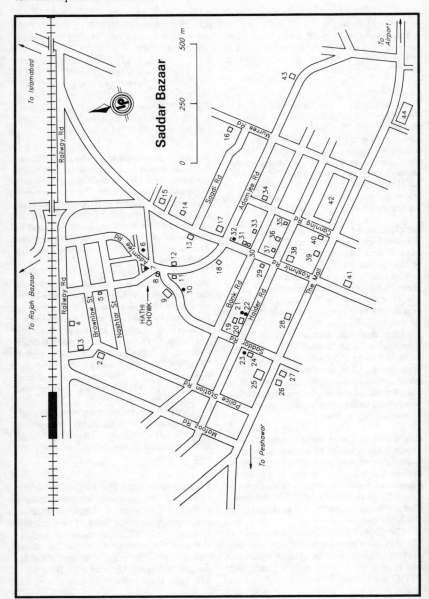

1 Railway Station
2 Police Station
3 Aurangzaib Hotel
4 Bolan Hotel
5 Cafe Khurshid
6 Breakfast Cafe
7 Al-Azam Hotel
8 Cantt View Hotel
9 Cantonment General
   Hospital
10 'Freshlime'
11 Al-Khalil Hotel
12 Hotel Shah Taj
13 Marhaba Hotel
14 New Kamran Hotel
15 Kamran Hotel
16 American Express
17 Mosque
18 Al-Falah Hotel
19 National Bank
20 Ciroz Cinema
21 Cafe
22 Cafe
23 Ice Cream
24 Book Centre
25 PIA
26 Cinema
27 Cinema
28 BCCI Bank
29 Pak-American Bookshop
30 Bakery
31 Burger Express
32 Breakfast Cafe
33 Kamran Cafe
34 Rohtas Travel
35 Grindlays Bank
36 Shakil Express Travel
37 Capri Bookshop
38 Post Office
39 Habib Bank
40 Bhatti Studio
41 Telephone & Telegraph
42 Flashman's Hotel & PTDC
   Tourist Information Centre
43 Citibank
44 Pearl Continental Hotel

The Rawalpindi GPO is at Kashmir and Haider Rds in Saddar Bazaar. For Poste Restante go inside the gate and round the left side of the main building; it's just inside the rear building. In the main building, buy stamps in the foyer (at a window that stays open till 9 pm). Stamped letters can be franked at once by asking at the left end of the main counter.

The Islamabad GPO is at the north end of Melody Market in G-6, facing away from the road. Poste Restante is at a desk at the right end of the main counter; the man at this desk will also answer queries and frank your outgoing letters.

Telephone & Telegraph For overseas calls and cables, the main telephone exchange (tel 65854 or 65809) is in Rawalpindi, half a block south of The Mall on Kashmir Rd. The Islamabad exchange is near the main government buildings, on Ataturk Avenue. Both are open 24 hours a day. For local directory information the telephone number is 17; for time it is 14.

Business Hours Nearly everything is closed Friday, though street sellers are out in droves then. Shops are open from at least 9 am to 6.30 pm daily except Friday. Private offices open from 9 am to at least 5 pm (except lunchtime, 1 to 2 pm) Saturday to Wednesday, and 9 am to 1 pm Thursday.

Ministries and other central government offices are open Sunday to Thursday, allegedly six to seven hours a day, but varying with the season and the department. The surest time is between 9 am and 1 pm.

Bookshops – Rawalpindi The best is the Book Centre (tel 65234) on Saddar Rd just south of Haider Rd. Manager 'Monnoo' has maps, overseas newspapers and magazines, travel and history books, and lots of second-hand paperback novels. He's open Fridays and holidays too.

Pak-American Commercial Ltd, upstairs on the west side of Kashmir Rd between Bank and Haider Rds, has books on Pakistan,

cheques (to get there, get off the inter-city bus at the Blue Area).

Post The main post offices (GPO) are open from 9 am to 2 pm Saturday to Wednesday, and morning hours on Thursday.

Islam and military subjects, and a bizarre assortment of foreign magazines. The Capri Bookshop, across Haider Rd from the GPO, has magazines and a few English-language books.

Bookshops – Islamabad For serious book junkies, the best in either city is the London Book Company (tel 823852) in a far corner of F-6. Manager Laiq Ahmad Khan has a big Pakistan section, survey maps, overseas newspapers and magazines, guidebooks, western best-sellers and used books. Take a bus to Super Market; from the east end of the shopping area walk five minutes north on 14th St, turn right at 10th St to a tiny strip of shops known as Kohsar Market.

The Lok Virsa Bookstore, run by the National Institute of Folk & Traditional Heritage, has books on Pakistan's unique cultural groups, and folk-music and oral-history cassette tapes. Unfortunately, only a few books are in English. It's at the west end of Super Market and stays open most evenings.

Mr Books, also at Super Market, has a fair selection of overseas newspapers and magazines, and some books on Pakistan.

Libraries The American Center, in the Blue Area, has a posh library of Americana – newspapers, magazines, novels, videotapes, exhibits and plenty of US Information Service propaganda. They're a suspicious lot, but it's an air-conditioned stop if you're in the neighbourhood. The British Council Library (tel 822205) offers the same thing for UK folks; it's in Melody Market (G-6) just left of Melody Cinema. Both are open Sunday to Thursday.

The Asian Study Group was started in 1973 to help expatriate residents get acquainted with the area. They have programmes on history, art, music, wildlife and so on, and a tiny but well-used library. They're certainly the best source of local information through western eyes. Run by volunteers and not geared to transients, they're nevertheless available to help with specific interests.

Contact them through your embassy (they have no formal office but every western embassy has at least a few members); their address is PO Box 1552, Islamabad.

Police In 'Pindi's Saddar Bazaar, the Cantonment Police Station (tel 64760) is on Police Station Rd near Railway Rd. There's a police post (tel 75009) at Pir Wadhai Bus Stand.

In Islamabad, the Civic Centre Police Station is in Melody Market (G-6), near Melody Cinema. The Margalla Police Station is at the south-west corner of the Ayub Market (F-8) shopping area.

Hospitals In Rawalpindi, major hospitals open to foreigners and within easy reach are Rawalpindi General (tel 840381), Murree Rd at Ashgar Mall Rd, right on the bus lines; and Cantonment General (tel 62254), off Saddar Rd in Saddar Bazaar. The Combined Military Hospital (tel 617448 or 616755), Tamizuddin Rd in the Cantonment, may admit foreigners. There is a private clinic called Healthways near American Express on Murree Rd.

In Islamabad, Capital Hospital (tel 825691 or 825695) is near Melody Market (G-6), a few blocks west of the GPO. The Government Poly Clinic is on the north side of G-6, near the Blue Area and on the bus lines. Further away, the Pakistan National Institute of Medicine is on the north-east corner of G-8.

Photographic Film & Processing A good place for film, processing and competent help is Bhatti Studios (tel 68771), Canning Rd opposite Flashman's Hotel in Rawalpindi. There's also a Fuji lab on Murree Rd near American Express. Photo shops in every market can do passport-size pictures for your visa paperwork. In Saddar try Quick Foto Service, next to the Al-Khalil Hotel on Adamjee Rd.

Luggage Storage The left-luggage room at the railway station will store baggage at Rs

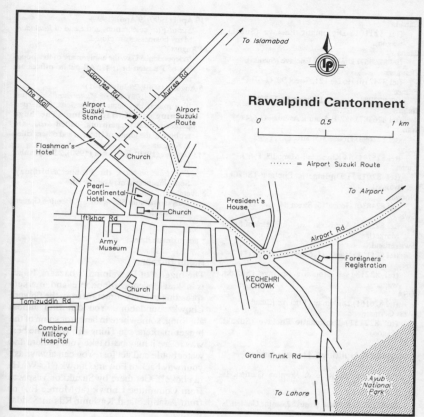

Rawalpindi Cantonment

0   0.5   1 km

...... = Airport Suzuki Route

To Islamabad

Adamjee Rd

Murree Rd

The Mall

Airport Suzuki Stand

Airport Suzuki Route

Flashman's Hotel

Church

Pearl–Continental Hotel

Church

President's House

To Airport

Airport Rd

Iftikhar Rd

Army Museum

Foreigners' Registration

KECHEHRI CHOWK

Church

Tamizuddin Rd

Combined Military Hospital

Grand Trunk Rd

Ayub National Park

To Lahore

---

1 per piece per day. They're open seven days a week.

Embassies Most are at the east end of Islamabad. From Aabpara (intersection of Khyaban-i-Suhrawardy and Municipal Rd), Suzukis go out 'Embassy Rd' past the American, Chinese and Australian embassies. The No 3 Ford wagon starts at Haider Rd in Saddar, stops at Aabpara, and passes near the British, Canadian, West German and Japanese embassies. Aabpara taxis go to the door for Rs 10 to Rs 20.

For embassies on or near Ataturk Avenue (east G-6), shown by (*), get off the bus at the GPO, walk south to Bazaar Rd, then east to Ataturk.

Afghanistan
    (tel 822566) House 176, F-7/3.
Australia
    (tel 822111) Diplomatic Enclave (Suzuki).

Canada
(tel 821101) Diplomatic Enclave (Suzuki, wagon).
China
(tel 826667) Diplomatic Enclave (Suzuki).
Denmark
(tel 824210) House 121, Street 90, G-6/3 (*).
France
(tel 823981) House 11, Street 54, F-7/4.
India
(tel 826387) 482-F Ataturk Avenue, G-6/4 (*).
Iran
(tel 822694) House 3-5, Street 17, F-6/2.
Italy
(tel 825791) 54 Khyaban-i-Margalla, F-6/3.
Japan
(tel 820181) Diplomatic Enclave (Suzuki, wagon).
Norway
(tel 824830) House 15, Street 84, G-6/4 (*).
Sweden
(tel 822557) Aga Khan Rd, F-6/3 (east of Super Market).
Switzerland
(tel 821151) House 11, Street 84, G-6/4 (*).
UK
(tel 822131) Diplomatic Enclave (Suzuki, wagon).
USA
(tel 826161) Diplomatic Enclave (Suzuki).
West Germany
(tel 822151) Diplomatic Enclave (Suzuki, wagon).

Festivals & Holidays These include:

March
Rose Festival, Rose & Jasmine Garden, Islamabad.
April
Spring Flower Show, Rose & Jasmine Garden, Islamabad.
*30 March to 29 April (1990), 20 March to 19 April (1991)
Ramadan, the Muslim month of fasting. During daylight, food and drink may be hard to find except at tourist hotels. Many shops and restaurants are closed until after sunset.
13 to 15 April
Baisakhi, a Sikh holiday. Sikh pilgrims from the Indian Punjab visit the Panja Sahib shrine at Hasan Abdal.
*1st week in May
Urs (death anniversary) of Bari Shah Latif (Bari Imam) at Nurpur Shahan village. Pilgrims come from the Punjab and NWFP; there are processions through Islamabad streets and a carnival atmosphere at Nurpur Shahan. Foreigners are tolerated.

*19 April (1990), 9 April (1991)
Eid-ul-Fitr, celebrations at the end of Ramadan. Many businesses are closed.
14 August
Independence Day, the anniversary of the founding of Pakistan in 1947. All public offices are closed.
*5 August (1990), 26 July (1991)
Ashura, the 10th day of Muharram. Shia Muslims march in solemn processions, some performing ritual flagellation. The huge papier-mache juggernauts, called tazia, are replicas of the tombs of Hussain and others killed at Karbala.
*13 October (1989), 3 October (1990), 23 September (1991)
Eid-Milad-un-Nabi, the Prophet's birthday. Some businesses may be closed.
November
Chrysanthemum Show, Rose & Jasmine Garden, Islamabad.

* approximate dates

Rajah Bazaar

The biggest of Rawalpindi's bazaars, Rajah is a kaleidoscope of people and markets spreading in every direction from the Fowara Chowk roundabout. You can find almost anything, somewhere in here; for some of the bigger markets, see Things To Buy. The best way to see it may be to take your camera and water bottle and get lost. You can always ask your way back to Fowara Chowk ('fo-WAH-ra choke'). Get there by Suzuki or Vespacar from Committee Chowk (at Murree Rd) or from Adamjee and Kashmir Rds in Saddar Bazaar.

Ayub National Park

Named after General Ayub Khan, the first of Pakistan's martial law administrators, this staid pleasure-ground south of the Cantonment has 900 hectares of paths, gardens and lakes. Catch an airport Suzuki at Adamjee and Murree Rds, get off at Kechehri Chowk and take the right fork about one km to the north end of the park. Or catch a bus to Gujar Khan on Haider Rd and get off at Gulistan Colony for Rs 1.

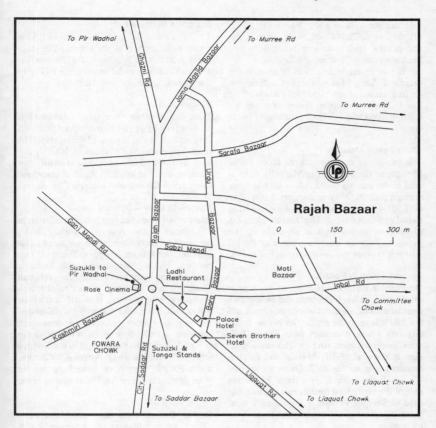

Rajah Bazaar

0   150   300 m

To Pir Wadhai

To Murree Rd

To Murree Rd

Ghazni Rd

Jama Masjid Bazaar

Sarafa Bazaar

Urdu Bazaar

Rajah Bazaar

Bara Bazaar

Sabzi Mandi

Ganj Mandi Rd

Moti Bazaar

Iqbal Rd

To Committee Chowk

Suzukis to Pir Wadhai

Rose Cinema

Lodhi Restaurant

Palace Hotel

Seven Brothers Hotel

Kashmiri Bazaar

FOWARA CHOWK

City Saddar Rd

Suzuzki & Tonga Stands

To Saddar Bazaar

To Liaquat Chowk

To Liaquat Chowk

Shakarparian

This huge urban wilderness along the south side of Islamabad has a few roads and lots of trails, 20 hectares of flower gardens, a hill with easy views of both cities, and Lok Virsa, the National Institute of Folk & Traditional Heritage. The Rose & Jasmine Garden, site of major flower shows in March, April and November, is 300 metres south of the Tourist Campsite. Lok Virsa and Shakarparian Hill are a 45-minute walk from Aabpara, or 15 minutes from the Zero Point bus stop (walk

south under the bridge, and left on a track into the park).

Museums

Lok Virsa, the National Institute of Folk & Traditional Heritage (tel 821028, 827339; PO Box 1184, Islamabad) in Shakarparian Park has a museum of traditional art, crafts and music, a tape and book library and a public events programme. This is a good source of background information on people you'll see along the KKH. From Aabpara it's a 45-minute walk or a Rs 15 taxi ride; or get off the bus at Zero Point, walk south under the bridge and follow a track left into Shakarparian, a 20-minute hike.

If you're interested in military matters, there's an Army Museum in the Cantonment, on Iftikhar Rd about 1 1/2 blocks south of the Pearl Continental Hotel. Summer hours are 8 am to noon and 5.30 to 7 pm; winter hours are 9 am to 3 pm.

Shah Faisal Mosque

The incredibly opulent, marble-faced Faisal Mosque at the foot of the Margalla Hills is said to be the biggest in Asia and is large enough for 100,000 worshippers. Most of its US$50 million cost was a gift of the late King Faisal of Saudi Arabia. The late President Zia ul-Haq is buried in the grounds of the mosque. Take an inter-city bus and get off where it crosses 8th Avenue from F-7 to F-8.

Daman-i-Koh & Saidpur

Daman-i-Koh ('DAH-ma-nee-ko') is a picnic spot in the hills, with the best views over Islamabad and, on clear days, 'Pindi and the Salt Range to the south. Get off the inter-city bus where it crosses from F-6 to F-7, walk five minutes north to a 'Daman-i-Koh' sign at the end of 7th Avenue and catch a Suzuki going up for Rs 2. Or on a cool day it's a half-hour climb on a track 25 metres east of the sign. A bit further east is a one-km road to Saidpur village, a surprisingly rural place this close to the capital, and known for its pottery.

Nurpur Shahan & Bari Imam Shrine

Nurpur Shahan village, north of the Diplomatic Enclave, is the site of a shrine to Bari Shah Latif, the Bari Imam, a 17th century Muslim Sufi mystic and unofficial 'patron saint of Islamabad'. During the first week of May the carnival-like *Urs* or death anniversary of Bari Imam is celebrated here. From Saddar Bazaar take a No 3 Ford wagon, on Haider Rd east of Saddar Rd (Rs 2); from Aabpara take the same wagon or a No 5 GTS bus (Rs 1).

Margalla Hills Hikes

The hills above Islamabad are full of hiking trails, as described in the Capital Development Authority's brochure, *Trekking in the Margalla Hills*, available from the PTDC or the Capital Development Authority.

Places to Stay

With one notable exception, Islamabad is expensive for accommodation and Rawalpindi is the logical place to stay. The main accommodation areas in Rawalpindi are around Saddar Bazaar and the Cantonment, Pir Wadhai, Rajah Bazaar, and Committee Chowk and Liaquat Chowk.

Places to Stay – bottom end

Islamabad The cheapest accommodation in either city is the *Tourist Campsite*, a 1/2 hectare of weedy open space and trees a few minutes' walk from Aabpara. There are two concrete-block 'bungalows' with lockable rooms but no beds, half a dozen concrete tent platforms and assorted places to throw a sleeping bag down. It's off-limits to Pakistanis, except for a sleepy caretaker and the manager who collects the rent each morning. A bungalow space or tent platform is Rs 15; a spot on the ground is Rs 8 with a tent, Rs 3 with just a bag. A bike is Rs 2 extra, a van Rs 10. They have locked storage for your gear, and cheap food is available in the market.

Saddar Bazaar & Cantonment Three seedy places are neighbours on Adamjee Rd in Hathi Chowk. The best of the lot is the *Hotel Shah Taj* (tel 68528), with singles/doubles (attached bath, hot water) for Rs 40/60, and you may be able to use their kitchen. Across the road the very noisy *Al-Khalil Hotel* (tel 66501) is Rs 30/50 and the cockroach-ridden *Cantt View Hotel* (tel 67863) is Rs 40/60. On Kashmir Rd the *Kamran Hotel* (old wing) is Rs 35/50. The slightly squalid *Bolan Hotel* on Railway Rd has doubles for about Rs 35.

There is allegedly a hostel in Ayub Park but I couldn't find it; in any case transport is such a nuisance it doesn't seem worth it.

Spartan 'retiring rooms' at the railway station are Rs 15 to Rs 40, but are supposedly just for Air-Conditioned class or 1st class rail-ticket holders.

Pir Wadhai This is not a fun place to stay but it has cheap hotels if you arrive late or leave early. The only ones who don't try to avoid foreigners are the *Shalimar* (tel 60813), the second hotel north of the tonga stand, with clean singles/doubles for Rs 25/40; and the sleazy *Al-Medina*, west of the long-distance buses, with grotty rooms for Rs 35/50. Little English is spoken in the hotels.

Places to Stay – middle

Saddar Bazaar & Cantonment The friendly *Al-Azam Hotel* (tel 65901) on Adamjee Rd west of Kashmir Rd has singles for Rs 48 and noisy doubles for Rs 80 (attached bath; hot water in cold weather), roof access and a decent restaurant. Nearby is the *Al-Falah Hotel* (tel 580799) with clean singles/doubles for Rs 40/80. On Kashmir Rd the quiet *New Kamran Hotel* (tel 64080) has tawdry but comfortable rooms, Rs 60/100.

Rajah Bazaar On Liaquat Rd about 150 metres from Fowara Chowk, the *Palace Hotel & Restaurant* (tel 70672) has singles/doubles for Rs 35/65 and a cheap, good restaurant. Across the street and up-stairs, the quiet and friendly *Seven Brothers Hotel & Restaurant* (tel 73132 or 71744) is Rs 75/120. Closer to the roundabout, the *Lodhi Hotel & Restaurant* isn't interested in foreigners, though their restaurant is excellent.

Committee Chowk & Liaquat Chowk Murree Rd is intersected by two 'spoke' roads from Fowara Chowk in Rajah Bazaar. Both *chowks* (intersections) have 24-hour noise and traffic, and no advantages except nearby vans to Abbottabad, Lahore and Peshawar, and inter-city transport.

Committee Chowk (Murree and Iqbal Rds) is the inter-city bus stop with the gaudy

Gulistan and Shabistan Cinemas. A block east of the intersection is the *Queen Hotel* (tel 73240) where a double with attached bath and hot water is Rs 100. There's easy access to Rajah by tonga and Vespa.

You can spot Liaquat Chowk by the huge rooftop 'Habib Bank' neon sign. On Murree Rd the small, friendly *Faisal Hotel* (tel 73210) has singles/doubles for Rs 45/65. They're Rs 35/65 at the *Al-Hayat Hotel* (tel 70979), Rs 75/100 at the *Park Hotel* (tel 73284 or 70594) and Rs 107/160 at the *National City Hotel* (tel 71411). Up College Rd, the *City Hotel* (tel 73503) has doubles for Rs 100, triples for Rs 120 and a small, good restaurant.

Islamabad Near Zero Point, the *Blue Star Motel* has rooms for about Rs 50 per person. In Super Market (F-6) the *Shehrazad Hotel* (tel 823519 or 823703) is next to the inter-city bus stop. It has overpriced but quiet doubles for Rs 108 and 162, all with hot showers. Shops of all kinds are nearby.

Places to Stay – top end

Saddar Bazaar & Cantonment The *Marhaba Hotel & Restaurant* (tel 66021 or 65178), on Kashmir Rd opposite Saadi Rd, looks a bit genteel for the neighbourhood; air-con singles/doubles are Rs 150/200.

At the venerable *Flashman's Hotel* (tel 64811), on The Mall between Murree and Canning Rds, is the PTDC Tourist Information Centre and PTDC's tours-and-transport subsidiary Pakistan Tours Ltd (PTL). Even if you could afford it, the rooms are reputedly not much of a bargain; singles/doubles start at Rs 350/475, or how about the Presidential Suite at Rs 1500?

The *Pearl Continental Hotel* (tel 66011) on The Mall east of Murree Rd is 'Pindi's primo hotel; for the price of a night here you could stay in the bazaar for a month. But if you've developed a craving for a banana split or a good cup of coffee, you can find it here.

Places to Eat

Except at the bottom end, most hotels have

their own restaurants, with slightly elevated prices. In mid-range Rawalpindi hotels an egg-toast-and-coffee breakfast is about Rs 15; a 'street' breakfast of tea, *dahi* (yogurt), *cholla* (spicy chickpeas), fried *paratha* bread or airy *puri* pastry is under Rs 10. Hotel dinners are Rs 20 and up, street dinners under Rs 20. In Islamabad everything is more expensive, except at Aabpara.

Quick-service cafes, take-outs and stalls are plentiful around markets and transport stops. Typical low-cost items are *samosas* (fried pastries stuffed with spiced potato or chickpeas), *pulao* (rice fried with vegetable bits), *sabzi* (vegetables), *tikkas* (barbecued meat pieces) and *shami kebabs* (lentil-and-mutton 'pancakes'). In the back lanes of the bazaars you can buy cheap snacks and sweets from carts, and fruit vendors are everywhere.

If you're north-bound and plan to explore Indus Kohistan, pick up some morale boosters like sweets and tinned fruit.

Saddar Bazaar Prices go up from Railway Rd toward The Mall. In the back street north of Hathi Chowk, the *Cafe Khurshid* is bright, clean, cheap and friendly. Other reasonably priced cafes include the *Rose* and *Vogue* to the right of Ciroz Cinema on Haider Rd, and the *Kamran* on Bank Rd east of Kashmir Rd. The best of the mid-range hotel restaurants are at the *Al-Azam* and *Al-Falah Hotels*, and a good but expensive one is at the *Marhaba Hotel*.

Street-side breakfast cafes (materialising at 6 am, closing by mid-morning) are opposite the mosque at Adamjee and Kashmir Rds, and in Adamjee Rd just north of the Al-Azam Hotel. A bakery with good cookies and bread is at Bank and Kashmir Rds, and next door is *Burger Express*, Pakistan's answer to McDonalds. Get good ice cream at a tacky *36 Flavours* parlour at Haider and Saddar Rds.

In the summer when 'Pindi is like a sauna, Haider and Saddar Rds are lined with vendors of fresh-squeezed sugar-cane juice, and a miraculous Rs 3 thirst-quencher called 'freshlime', consisting of crushed ice, lime, salt, sugar and soda water. The best is served with a flourish by a man with a ring in his ear at the Red & White Smoking Centre on Saddar Rd, opposite the hospital.

Rajah Bazaar Residents recommend the

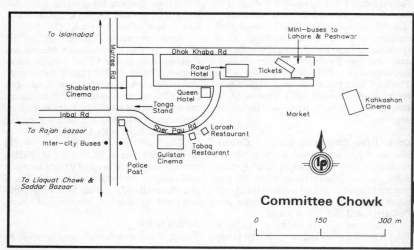

Committee Chowk

Lodhi Hotel & Restaurant, 100 metres from Fowara Chowk on Liaquat Rd (upstairs); vegetable dishes and curries are cheap and tasty. Also good is the plain but crowded restaurant at the nearby *Palace Hotel* and, across the road, the dining room at the *Seven Brothers Hotel*. The back roads of Rajah have many reasonably priced small restaurants.

Committee Chowk & Liaquat Chowk

For stepping out I like the *Tabaq Restaurant*, east of Gulistan Cinema at Committee Chowk. Prices are up-scale (a big meal is at least Rs 40) but the food's good and the choice is wide. Almost as good is the *Larosh Restaurant* next door.

At Liaquat Chowk, on Murree Rd opposite the Al-Hayat Hotel, the *Kulba-i-Khurak Cafe* is a tiny eat-there or takeaway place; a meal of rice, chicken, *shami kebabs* and salad is about Rs 20. Around the corner

on College Rd, the City Hotel's *Economy Restaurant* has similar food and prices.

Islamabad At Aabpara and Melody Market (behind the GPO and Islamabad Hotel) there are samosa and kebab stands, and cafes with cheap curried mutton and *shami kebabs*. Melody Market has a French bakery where you can ruin your budget with fresh bread, pies and chocolate cake. The *Kamran Restaurant* at Aabpara is not too pricey.

Food in other sectors is more expensive. Although the cafes of Jinnah Super (F-7) tend to be adolescent hangouts, local residents suggest *Hot & Spicy* for cheap, good food.

Alcohol If you crave a beer, the top-end hotels (Pearl Continental, Flashman's, Islamabad Hotel, Holiday Inn) have poorly-marked special lounges where you sign a form saying you're not a Muslim, and drink

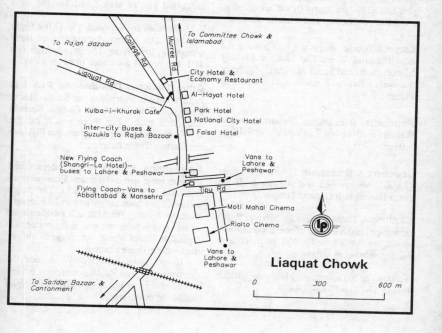

To Committee Chowk & Islamabad

To Rajah Bazaar

College Rd

Murree Rd

Liaquat Rd

City Hotel & Economy Restaurant

Al-Hayat Hotel

Kulba-i-Khurak Cafe

Park Hotel

National City Hotel

Faisal Hotel

Inter-city Buses & Suzukis to Rajah Bazaar

New Flying Coach (Shangri-La Hotel) – buses to Lahore & Peshawar

Flying Coach – Vans to Abbottabad & Mansehra

Vans to Lahore & Peshawar

Tipu Rd

Moti Mahal Cinema

Rialto Cinema

Vans to Lahore & Peshawar

To Saddar Bazaar & Cantonment

Liaquat Chowk

0   300   600 m

an overpriced lager brewed in Lahore for infidels. No alcohol is served anywhere else. You can get a liquor permit like longer-term residents do, but it's hardly worth the trouble here and isn't much use on the KKH.

Things to Buy

There are two ways to shop here. The simplest but most expensive way is in the shops for tourists and expatriates: on The Mall and around Flashman's Hotel in the Saddar-Cantonment area, along Murree Rd north of the railway, in the commercial areas of G-6, F-6 and F-7 in Islamabad and in the top-end hotel arcades. You'll find carpets, brasswork, jewellery, Kashmiri shawls, wood carvings and antiques.

The other way is by hunting in the bazaars. If you just like poking around you'll love Rajah; if you're hunting for something, Rajah's size and variety can drive you crazy. Following are a few prominent markets. You may not like bargaining, but in the bazaar you can often get $1/3$ to $1/2$ off an opening gambit if you're firm and friendly about it.

Carpets Tourist shops are on Canning Rd near Flashman's, on The Mall, at Melody Market (G-6) and Super Market (F-6), or try the street sellers on Kashmir Rd in Saddar on Fridays.

Pottery Try Bara Bazaar (Rajah), Faizabad Bazaar (north end of Rawalpindi) or Saidpur village.

Jewellery & Brasswork Try Sarafa Bazaar (Rajah), Murree Rd and Asghar Mall Rd (near Rawalpindi General Hospital).

Clothing & Tailors These are all over Rajah (cheapest) and Saddar. Off-the-shelf *shalwar qamiz* are Rs 200 to Rs 300, as much as a tailor-made set in Gilgit.

Spices The main spice area is between Rajah Bazaar and Ganj Mandi Rd.

Fruit & Vegetables Go to the Sabzi Mandi ('Vegetable Market'), Rajah.

Getting There & Away

Air The domestic carrier is Pakistan International Airlines (PIA). The Rawalpindi booking office (tel 67011) is on The Mall west of Saddar Rd. The Islamabad office (tel 825031) is in the Blue Area at 7th Avenue, near the Lal Quarter stop on any GTS bus to the Secretariat. Both are open seven days a week.

Gilgit & Skardu These cheap and spectacular flights can only be booked in Rawalpindi. Because they're very weather-dependent, subject to cancellation right up to the last minute, bookings are effectively standby. Confirm yours by leaving your ticket with PIA between 8 am and 12.30 pm the day before departure; at 3 pm they give it back. The final decision and seat assignments are only made next morning. If it's cancelled you're wait-listed for the next flight out.

Schedules are seasonal. The Gilgit flight (Rs 255, $1 1/4$ hours) departs one to three times a day in summer. The Skardu flight (Rs 310, $1 1/2$ hours) goes once or twice a day.

Other Pakistan Destinations PIA has flights almost every day to Saidu Sharif, Peshawar-Chitral, Lahore, Quetta, Karachi and other cities. For these you'll get the lowest fares from travel agents, not PIA; see the Getting There chapter.

International Flights A few international carriers have direct Islamabad connections but most stop only in Karachi. The major airlines have booking offices in Islamabad's Blue Area, along The Mall in Rawalpindi and in top-end hotels, but you'll do better at a reputable travel agent; for suggestions see the Getting There chapter.

International tickets *don't* include the departure tax – of Rs 100 on tickets bought outside Pakistan and an outrageous Rs 350 if bought in the country.

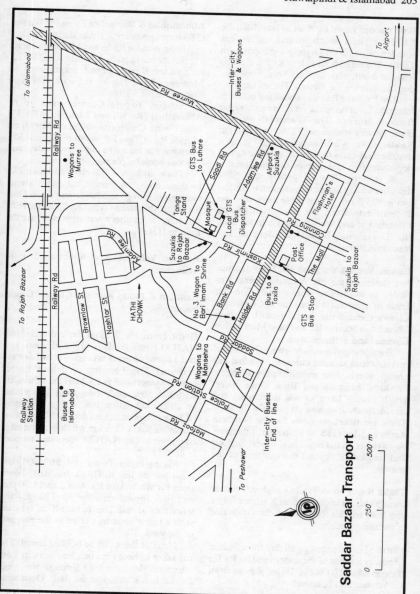

Saddar Bazaar Transport

0   250   500 m

Rail You can travel by train to Havelian, the KKH's official southern end, in ancient wooden carriages on a lightly-used spur from Taxila. The three-hour ride is Rs 7 and trains leave at 6 am, noon and 4.55 pm. For other destinations see the Getting There chapter.

The Pakistan Railways booking office in Islamabad is at Aabpara, on Suhrawardy near Bank of America. The Rawalpindi office is at the railway station (tel 72303 or 65704) in Saddar; ticket windows are open 24 hours a day. Second-class tickets are sold the day of departure; first class can be booked ahead.

A student ID card gets you a 50% discount on any ticket; non-student travellers can get 25% off. To get these discounts, get a certificate from the tourism office at Flashman's, and with this get a letter from the Divisional Superintendent at the Rawalpindi station.

Buses, Vans & Wagons The long-distance bus station is the Pir Wadhai General Bus Stand in north-west Rawalpindi. Smaller knots of vans and wagons are at Committee Chowk (behind the Rawal Hotel), Liaquat Chowk (on Murree Rd and near Moti Mahal Cinema) and in the bazaars.

Besides government-run (GTS) and private buses to most cities, Pir Wadhai has cheap hotels and swarms of travellers, hawkers, beggars and flies. Once there, you'll hardly have to ask directions; bus conductors will be all over you like the flies. There are ticket windows for the Northern Areas and for GTS to Peshawar; otherwise buy a ticket on the bus. Local buses, Suzukis and tongas are beyond the east end of the station.

Taxila Buses go to Taxila's highway bazaar from Saddar (Haider Rd near Kashmir Rd), a one-hour trip for Rs 3. A 2nd-class train ride is the same price.

Murree Ford wagons go all day from Saddar (Railway Rd east of the underpass) for Rs 13; the trip takes 1 1/2 hours. Buses also go from Pir Wadhai and Faizabad.

Abbottabad & Mansehra From Pir Wadhai GTS buses go every 1/2 hour during the day, to Abbottabad for Rs 13 and Mansehra for Rs 16; private buses go to Abbottabad for Rs 12. In Saddar Bazaar, Ford wagons go to Mansehra from Haider Rd east of Police Station Rd for Rs 18.

Air-con Toyota Coaster vans go to Abbottabad (Rs 30) and Mansehra (Rs 35) from Flying Coach (tel 70050 or 72950) on Murree Rd at Tipu Rd, south of Liaquat Rd. They have at least five departures a day, and you can book by phone.

These all go via Havelian and take 2 1/2 to three hours. A slower but more scenic alternative is to go to Murree and catch a bus there for Abbottabad (total Rs 23 and at least 6 1/2 hours). Another alternative is to take the train to Havelian.

Kaghan Valley Go to Abbottabad or to Mansehra.

Besham & Indus Kohistan Take a Gilgit-bound bus.

Gilgit From Pir Wadhai the red-and-white NATCO buses go daily at 4 and 9 am, 1, 5 and 11 pm (summer timings – schedules are seasonal). The 9 am bus is 'deluxe' (softer seats, cleaner) and is Rs 120; the others are Rs 90. A 50% student discount is available on all but the deluxe bus, with a maximum of four discount tickets for each departure. There's a NATCO ticket window at the edge of the yard. The NATCO telephone number is 860283.

Masherbrum Tours (tel 863595), the main private line to Gilgit, has daily buses from Pir Wadhai for Rs 90 at 2 and 4.30 pm, and two Toyota vans for Rs 120, leaving when they're full. The 'ticket office' is a man with a ticket-book in a chair at the east end of the yard.

None of these can be booked ahead. The trip takes 15 hours in a bus, less in a van. Late afternoon departures go through the spectacular Indus Valley in the dark. Despite its obvious drawbacks the 4 am bus allows you to see the scenery during the day.

There are also said to be wagons from Novelty Cinema and from the Mashriq Hotel in Rajah Bazaar.

Beyond Gilgit Unless you're on a package tour, onward transport is arranged in Gilgit; if you're China-bound it's done in Sust.

Peshawar Air-con minibuses go from a yard near Committee Chowk (two blocks behind Shabistan Cinema, past the Rawal Hotel). The fare is Rs 40, with hourly departures into the night. One (New Flying Coach, tel 74501) can be booked by phone, and also stops at the Shangri-La Hotel on Murree Rd south of Liaquat Rd.

Near Liaquat Chowk, vans leave all day from behind Moti Mahal Cinema and from the end of a lane beside the Shangri-La Hotel, for Rs 25. From Pir Wadhai GTS buses go every half-hour all morning for Rs 17.

Lahore All the outfits that go to Peshawar also go to Lahore; air-con mini-buses are Rs 60, vans Rs 33. GTS buses go from Pir Wadhai and from the Saddar Bazaar station (Adamjee Rd near Kashmir Rd) for Rs 31.50. Vans take five hours, GTS seven to eight (the train takes about six).

Quetta & Karachi There are no direct buses to the south. You could patch short trips together into a three-day marathon but the train costs about the same.

Getting Around

Airport Transport Suzukis go to the airport in a steady stream from Adamjee Rd at Murree Rd in Saddar. The fare is Rs 4 and they start at 6 am; earlier than that, wave one down and hire it for about Rs 15. There are Suzukis from Fowara Chowk in Rajah Bazaar, also Rs 4. Both take 50 to 60 minutes in normal traffic and drop you about five minutes' walk from the terminals. There's no airport bus service. A taxi is about Rs 50 to/from Rawalpindi, Rs 60 to/from

Islamabad. You might be able to charm your way aboard a free courtesy van at one of the big hotels.

To catch a Suzuki *from* the airport, cross the parking lot, go out the gate and turn right. Those to Rajah are about 100 metres up the road on the left, by a petrol station. Saddar Suzukis are 100 metres further, at a fork on the right.

Private Bus Private inter-city buses – gaudy Bedfords with conductors hanging out the doors – are the commonest thoroughfare transport. They have fixed routes and fares. On bad days they're smoggy, loud and maddeningly slow; on good days they're a rolling carnival with horns warbling, conductors cajoling and drivers jockeying.

GTS Bus The Government Transport Service runs drab, asthmatic buses over fixed routes. They tend to be rare and roundabout. For information in Saddar try the dispatcher's shack on Adamjee Rd east of Kashmir Rd; at Aabpara there's an office across Municipal Rd from the Kamran Restaurant. The enquiries lines (62559, 63377, 64449) are occasionally helpful.

Wagon Ford wagons have numbered thoroughfare routes. They're quicker and slightly more expensive than buses.

Suzuki Suzuki pickup trucks with seats are the commonest way to get around Rawalpindi. They have fixed fares of a few rupees; on each a boy hustles riders and collects fares (count your change). Some are for hire ('specials') and cost much more unless there are eight or 10 of you.

Tonga These two-wheeled, horse-drawn carts are the most relaxing way to get around in Saddar, Rajah, Pir Wadhai and Committee Chowk. Some ply fixed-fare routes, some are for hire.

Taxi The black-and-yellow taxis have meters but most seem to be 'broken', so settle the price before you get in; Rawalpindi to Islamabad should be about Rs 60 (less in a really broken-down one). They can be flagged on main roads, and there are stands at the big hotels, Islamabad market areas and the airport.

Vespa The little snarling Vespacar motor-rickshaws, big enough for two, operate mostly in Rajah, Pir Wadhai, Committee Chowk and Satellite Town. They're not much cheaper than a taxi, a lot less comfortable and five to 10 times the cost of a passenger Suzuki.

Inter-City Private buses link Saddar Bazaar (Haider Rd), Murree Rd, Aabpara and all the market areas of Islamabad in one tedious but handy line. Saddar to Aabpara takes 45 minutes (twice that at peak times). It's Rs 1 in one city or the other or Rs 2 between them, and an extra Rs 1 to the remoter Islamabad markets. Recognise them by the conductors' call: *bindeh-bindeh* or *slaambaad-slaambaad*.

The No 6 Ford wagon follows the bus route as far north as Super Market (F-6), then turns east to the Secretariat. The No 30 GTS bus goes from Saddar (Adamjee Rd station) to the Secretariat.

Pir Wadhai Bus Stand Local transport at Pir Wadhai is past the east end of the station. Taxis on the main road go to Saddar Bazaar for about Rs 40, Islamabad for Rs 60. The three-wheel Vespa motor-rickshaws go anywhere in Rawalpindi only.

The cheapest way to 'Pindi is a passenger Suzuki to Rajah Bazaar, then another to Saddar or other points; Rs 1 for each ride, tedious but fascinating. For the same price and a better view try a horse-drawn tonga. Change Suzukis or tongas at the six-way intersection called Fowara Chowk, at the centre of Rajah

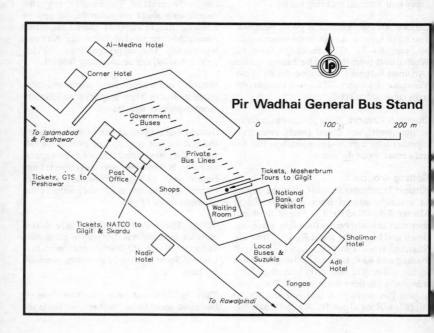

Pir Wadhai General Bus Stand

Al-Medina Hotel

Corner Hotel

Government Buses

To Islamabad & Peshawar

0   100   200 m

Private Bus Lines

Post Office

Tickets, GTS to Peshawar

Shops

Tickets, Masherbrum Tours to Gilgit

National Bank of Pakistan

Waiting Room

Tickets, NATCO to Gilgit & Skardu

Nadir Hotel

Local Buses & Suzukis

Shalimar Hotel

Adil Hotel

Tongas

To Rawalpindi

Bazaar; in peak traffic hours you may be dropped a block short of it. Hire your own tonga direct to Saddar for about Rs 15.

The cheapest ride from Pir Wadhai to Islamabad is Rs 2 by bus. Going to Pir Wadhai from Saddar Bazaar (Kashmir Rd at Adamjee Rd) Suzukis and tongas go to Fowara Chowk in Rajah Bazaar. At Fowara walk to the right side of Rose Cinema for Suzukis and tongas on to Pir Wadhai. The Suzuki trip from Saddar takes 25 to 50 minutes.

From Islamabad, take an inter-city bus to Faizabad; down the right fork (Sir Saiyid Rd) almost any west-bound bus goes to Pir Wadhai for Rs 1. Or ride the inter-city to Committee Chowk and hire a Vespa. From Aabpara a No 17 GTS bus goes all the way for Rs 2.50 but you may grow old and die waiting for it.

Rajah Bazaar From Saddar take a Suzuki (Rs 1) from Kashmir Rd at Adamjee Rd. From Islamabad, get off the inter-city bus at Committee Chowk and take a tonga, Suzuki or Vespa.

Blue Area Get off the inter-city bus at China Chowk. Also from Aabpara, get any Secretariat-bound GTS bus on Municipal Rd and get off at Lal Quarter or China Chowk.

Secretariat Go to the end of the line on a No 6 Ford wagon (Rs 2.25 from Haider or Murree Rd; Rs 1 from Aabpara) or a No 30 GTS bus (Rs 2 from the GTS stand on Adamjee Rd, or from Murree Rd).

Around Rawalpindi & Islamabad

TAXILA

The broad plain north and east of Peshawar, known historically as Gandhara, has attracted invaders since the 6th century BC.

In 326 BC Alexander the Great lingered for three months at the Gandharan capital of Takshasila – he called it Taxila – at its eastern end. Half a century later the Mauryan Emperor Ashoka, a patron of Buddhism, built a university in Taxila, and pilgrims and scholars came to Gandhara from all over Asia. Under the Kushan Dynasty in the 1st to 3rd centuries AD, Taxila was the cultured capital of an empire stretching across the subcontinent and into Central Asia. It was from here that Buddhism followed the Silk Road into China. The city was destroyed by the Huns in the 5th century.

Excavations at Taxila have revealed three separate cities spanning its 1000-year heyday; the ruins are open to the public, along with many smaller sites over a 25-square-km area. Artefacts in a striking fusion of Greek and Indian styles, including serene Buddha-figures with Mediterranean faces, are on display in the excellent Taxila Museum, open daily (except the first Monday of each month) from 9 am to noon and 2 to 6 pm in summer, 9 am to 4 pm in winter. The whole area seems strangely evocative.

Good background information is in a PTDC booklet, *Gandhara, An Instant Guide to Pakistan's Heritage*; other PTDC brochures have maps of the Taxila sites.

Places to Stay

Opposite the museum is a Tourist Information Centre and a *PTDC Rest House* with two doubles for Rs 70 and food by arrangement (best to book this at Rawalpindi PTDC). Nearby is a large *Pakistan Youth Hostel* with beds for Rs 15. Some travellers say you don't need PYHA or IYHA membership to stay. There are two spartan 'retiring rooms' at the Taxila railway station, which can be used by passengers with 1st-class tickets only, for about Rs 20.

Getting There & Away

A great way to go is by train from the Saddar Bazaar station, a lazy one-hour trip that tunnels under the Margallas into Taxila

Valley. A ticket in old wooden 2nd-class cars on the un-crowded Havelian run is Rs 3; 1st class on the Peshawar train is Rs 6. Buses (Rs 3) go from Haider Rd near Kashmir Rd in Saddar, to Taxila's raucous highway bazaar, where a tonga or Suzuki to the museum is about Rs 5.

Getting Around
Passenger Suzukis and a few tongas ply the roads connecting the museum and the excavation sites.

MURREE & THE GALIS
North-east on a twisting road into the Murree Hills is a string of old, pine-forested, colonial 'hill stations', now weekend resorts for middle-class Pakistanis and expatriates trying to beat the heat. The area is packed and expensive in summer, but it's lovely, and there's some cheap accommodation.

The original settlement is Murree, which still has a few prim buildings from its days as Punjab's summer capital. It bulges with hotels, including some cheapos; the venerable *Cecil Hotel* is too expensive to stay at, but worth a look. Ten km from Murree on a spur road is Bhurban, known for its golf course but also the site of a youth hostel.

North of Murree are half a dozen hamlets whose names end in *gali* (Hindko Punjabi for 'pass'). About 3/4 hour out, at a junction called Koozagali, a sign points to Ayubia, a recreation area featuring a chairlift, and Khanaspur, three km from the highway, with a small hotel and youth hostel. Nathiagali, half an hour on and at 2500 metres, is a miniature Murree and the most picturesque of the Galis.

To have a look you could do a two-day bus loop to Abbottabad via Murree and back

via Havelian, with a night in Abbottabad. The Murree Road is also an alternative way to get from Islamabad to the KKH, slower but much prettier than through Havelian.

Places to Stay
Summer accommodation is dicey; city folks book their weekends well ahead. There are *Pakistan Youth Hostels* at Bhurban and Khanaspur (Rs 15 per bed). Theoretically you must belong to the Pakistan Youth Hostels Association (PYHA) or the International Youth Hostel Association (IYHA) to use them. Call PYHA (tel Lahore 881501) to book ahead if you can.

Murree has a few bottom-end hotels that probably don't book out; try the *New Kashmir Hotel* on the lower Mall, with doubles for Rs 30 to Rs 40. In Khanaspur the small *Kashmir View Hotel* has doubles for Rs 40. In Nathiagali, travellers suggest the *Galliat View Hotel*, with doubles at about Rs 40. For information on other hotels and rest houses, see Rawalpindi PTDC.

Getting There & Away
In Saddar Bazaar, Ford wagons go to Murree (and back) all day, from Railway Rd east of the underpass; the 1 1/2-hour ride is Rs 13. Buses also go from Pir Wadhai and Faizabad. From Murree on to Abbottabad, a five-hour trip, there are half a dozen private buses and a GTS bus every day; and from Abbottabad literally scores of buses make the 2 1/2-hour dash back to Rawalpindi via Havelian.

Getting Around
Wagons and Suzukis provide local transport between Murree, Bhurban, Ayubia and Nathiagali.

Language

Travelling down the KKH is like passing through half a dozen tiny countries. Every few hundred km the local speech changes, not just to another dialect but to a new language. Although they run together at the edges and borrow each other's words, there are at least six widely-spoken languages — representing three different linguistic families — in addition to the two 'national' languages of Urdu and Mandarin Chinese. Persian is also spoken to some extent throughout the region.

You can get by with a little basic Urdu and Chinese, and they're useful in official situations. But neither is native to Xinjiang or the Northern Areas and they're often used grudgingly. A few words of local speech have marginal practical value but even the most garbled attempts can reward you out of all proportion to what you're actually saying; people *like* you for trying their mother tongue.

The prominent local languages are Uyghur (Kashgar and the Tarim Basin); Wakhi or Tadjik (Tashkurghan, Khunjerab and Gojal); Burushaski (Hunza); Shina (lower Hunza, Gilgit, Chilas); Kohistani (Indus Kohistan); and Pushto (Besham, Swat and northern Hazara). Included here are glossaries of common words and phrases in Urdu, Mandarin Chinese, Uyghur, Wakhi, Burushaski, Shina, Kohistani and Pushto.

English is rarely used in western Xinjiang, except by a few educated officials. But it's quite common in the larger towns of the Northern Areas, and widespread in Rawalpindi and Islamabad.

In addition to pronunciation suggestions in each list, the following sounds are common to all of them: r with a brogue or snap of the tongue, in all but Chinese; u as in 'put'; i is like 'ee'; a is 'ah'.

Entries are arranged like this: English phrase *translation* (pronunciation if necessary).

Writing

The written characters (Chinese and Arabic in Xinjiang; Persian in Pakistan) are beautiful to look at but impossible to learn, although numbers and the words for 'men' and 'women' might come in handy.

	Chinese	Persian (Urdu)
1	一	١
2	二	٢
3	三	٣
4	四	۴
5	五	۵
6	六	۶
7	七	٧
8	八	٨
9	九	٩
10	十	١٠

	Man	Woman
Chinese	男	女
Arabic (Uyghur)	ەر	مايال
Persian (Urdu)	مرد	عورت

URDU

Urdu is the 'national language' of Pakistan, although fewer than 10% of Pakistanis speak it as a first language. In spoken form it's roughly the same as Hindi, the speech of north India, but written in Persian script. Some words and pronunciations listed here reflect Northern Areas speech.

Urdu is an unrepentant scavenger language, swallowing up words and whole phrases verbatim from Persian, Arabic, Sanskrit, English, wherever. You'll have no trouble with the meanings of *plet, bohtel, machiz* and even the word for you, the foreigner, *angrez* (no matter where you're from). It's funny to listen to officials on the telephone, popping in and out of English (Urdlish?), or Urdu TV commercials for things like *'kvaliti numbir vun chai'*. A more detailed language and pronunciation guide is Lonely Planet's *Hindi/Urdu phrasebook*.

Grammar

Grammar is obscure and full of special cases. If you do feel like phrase-building, one useful form is 'postpositions', like prepositions except they go behind; some are listed here. And, roughly speaking, you can make a phrase into a question by adding 'is it?' (*heh?*) to the end.

A grammar book with a small glossary is the little *Teach Yourself Urdu In Two Months* (Anjuman Press, Karachi, 1981), available in Gilgit, Rawalpindi and Islamabad bookshops and probably overseas.

Numbers

Urdu number-words don't have a simple regularity like those in English, so try to do things in round numbers! Don't confuse 25 and 50, and 7 and 60. To add 1/2 to a number precede it with *sardeh* (thus 3 1/2 is *sardeh-teen*); exceptions are 1 1/2 and 2 1/2. This form is common in prices and clock-times.

1	ek
1 1/2	dhir
2	doh
2 1/2	dhai
3	teen
4	char
5	panj
6	cheh
7	saht
8	aht
9	nau
10	das

11	gyara
12	bara
13	tera
14	chuda
15	pandra
16	sola
17	sahtra
18	ahttara
19	unnis
20	bis
25	pachis
30	tis
40	chalis
50	pachas
60	sa-aht
70	sahttar
80	assi
90	nubbeh
100	sau
1000	hazar
100,000	lakh
10,000,000	kror

Pronouns

I/my	meh/mera
you/your (sing)	tum/tumhara
you/yours (pl & polite)	ab/abka
he (she)/his (hers)	wo/ooska
we/ours	ham
they/theirs	weh/oonka

People & Relations

man	admi (ahd-MEE)
woman	orot (oh-ROHT)
father	pita
mother	mata
husband	shawarh
wife	bivi
brother	bhai
sister	behen
friend	dost
foreigner, outsider	angrez
person (occupational suffix)	wallah

Accommodation

cheap travellers' inn	serai or muzaffar khana
room	kamira
rope bed	charpoi
key	chabi (cha-BEE)
toilet	latrin
caretaker	chowkidar

Food

food	khana

bread	roti
unleavened flat-bread	chapatti
fried bread	paratha
meat	gosht
mutton	bakri
beef	gay ka gosht
chicken	murghi
vegetable	sabzi
lentils	dhal
potato	alu
spinach	palak
peas	muttar
rice	chawal or pulau
plain rice	sadha chawal
egg	anda (ahn-DAH)
yogurt	dahi (nasal 'dai')
cheese	panir
apricot	khubani
dried apricots	sukha khubani
sugar	chini
salt	namak (NUM-uk)

Drink

water	pani
tea	chai
milky tea	dudh-wali chai
green tea	khawa
milk	dudh
soft drink	bohtel

Other Nouns

home-country	muluk
mountain/peak	pahar/pahari
tributary valley	nala
river	darya
hot spring	garem chashma
Silk Road	Shahrah-i-Resham
Karakoram Highway	Shahrah-i-Karakoram
Friday	Juma
mosque	masjid
Ismaili prayer-hall	jamat khana
hospital	shafar khana
luggage	saman (sa-MAHN)
candle	mombatti

Postpositions

to	-ko
from	-seh
of (possessive)	-ka
in	-meh

Adjectives

very	bohit
good/bad	achhah/kharab
first-rate, complete	pukka (a pukka road is paved)
inferior, incomplete	kutcha (a kutcha road is a jeep track)
beautiful	khubsurut (khoob-SOO-root)
delicious	laziz
happy	khush
hungry	bukha
ill	bimar
hot/cold	garem/tanda
expensive/cheap	mengha/sasta
left/right	bayan/dahina
more	or
another, one more	ek or
this/that	ees/oos
here/there	yeh/woh

Adverbs

enough	bas
a little	tolla
next, after this	doosri
next bus	doosri bas

Time

when? (date)	kab? (kahb)
when? (time)	kitna bajeh?
today	aj
tomorrow, yesterday	kal (according to context)
day after tomorrow, day before yesterday	parason (nasal 'n')
now	ab
immediately	abhi
how long?	kitna taim?
What time is it?	kitna bajeh heh?
(three) o'clock	(teen) bajeh
half-past (four)	sardeh-(char) bajeh ('4½ o'clock')
morning	suba

Phrases

'Peace be with you'   asalaam aleikhum
(a general greeting; the response is *wa aleikhum salaam* or, more likely outside the Northern Areas, *salaam*)

goodbye
   hudar hafiz
see you again
   pir melenge
How are you?
   kya hal heh?
fine
   tik heh (tikka)
thank you
   shukria (shu-KREE-ah)
special thanks
   mehrbani

excuse me
maf, mafki-ji (polite)
yes
han (nasal 'n')/*ji-han* (polite)
no
nahi (nasal 'nai')
God willing
inshallah
What's your name?
apka nam kya heh?
My name is (John)
mera nam (John) heh
What's the name of this place?
ees jagah-ka, nam kya heh?
Where are you going?
ab kahan jate heh? (nasal *kaha, heh*)
Is there a (Gilgit) bus today?
kya (Gilgit) bas aj heh?
What time is it going?
kitna bajeh jaenge?
Where is (the GPO)?
(GPO) keddar heh?
Do you speak English?
ab english bolteh heh?
I don't understand
meh nahi samja (sahm-JAH)
I can't read Urdu
meh Urdu nahi par sakta
Do you have (food)?
kya (khana) heh?
Is there (hot water)?
kya (garem pani) heh?
What do you want?
ab kya chahta heh?
I (don't) want tea
muje chai (nahi) chahyeh
How much does this cost?
kitna rupia? or *kitna paisa?*
He is my husband
woh mera shawarh heh
She is my wife
woh mera bivi heh

MANDARIN CHINESE

Mandarin (or *putonghua*, 'people's speech') is China's official language, the dialect of Beijing and the speech of bureaucrats. Basic spoken Mandarin is surprisingly easy: no conjugations, no declensions, word order like English, just string them together. The hard parts are pronunciation and tones.

Pronunciation

Mainland China's official Romanised 'alphabet' of Chinese sounds is called *pinyin*. It's very streamlined, but the sounds aren't always self-evident. The letters that don't sound quite like English are as follows.

Consonants: *q* (flat 'ch'); *x* (flat 'sh'); *zh* ('j'); *z* ('dz'); *c* ('ts'); *r* (tongue rolled back, almost 'z').

Vowels: *a* ('ah'); *er* ('ar'; American pronunciation); *ui* ('oi' or 'wei'); *iu* ('yoh'); *ao* ('ow' as in 'now'); *ou* ('ow' as in 'low'); *e* ('uh' after consonants); *ian* ('yen'); *ong* ('oong'); *u* ('oo') or sometimes like '*ü*': say 'ee' with your mouth rounded as if to say 'oo').

Tones

A given sound has many meanings depending on how it's 'sung'. But with common phrases you can get away without tones because the Chinese try hard to figure out what you mean. Syllables aren't stressed strongly.

Negation

Adjectives and present-tense verbs are negated by preceding them with *bu*, or occasionally *mei* (as in the all-too-familiar *mei you*, 'we don't have any').

Questions

A phrase becomes a question if you add *ma* to the end of it (you understand, *ni dong*; do you understand? *ni dong ma?*). Or make a question by juxtaposing positive and negative forms (Do you want it?, 'want-not-want?' *yao bu yao?*; do you have it? *you mei you?*; Okay?, 'good-not-good? *hao bu hao?*).

Books

If you get a phrasebook or dictionary be sure it uses *pinyin* Romanisation, not older form which are even more confusing. It's nice if it has Chinese characters too, for showing to Chinese who speak other dialects. Most phrasebooks are packed full of things you'll never be able to use ('stop or I'll scream') but Lonely Planet's *China Phrasebook* or the one from Berlitz have Chinese characters tones, *pinyin* and useful word-lists.

Numbers

The simplest way to count is (number) -ge-(object); so, for example, 'two people' is *liang-ge ren*.

1/2	*ban*
1	*yi*
2	*er (ar) (when counting)*
	liang
3	*san*
4	*si (sih)*
5	*wu*
6	*liu (lyoh)*
7	*qi (chee)*
8	*ba*
9	*jiu (jyoh)*
10	*shi (shr)*
11	*shi yi*
20	*er shi*
21	*er shi yi*
30	*san shi*
100	*yi bai*
200	*liang bai*
1000	*yi qian (chyen)*

Pronouns

I/we	*wo/women (woh-mun)*
you (sing/pl)	*ni/nimen*
he (& she & it)/they	*ta/tamen*

Possessive form Add *-de* (duh); 'our' is *nimen-de* and so on.

People & Relations

person	*ren (run)*
father/mother	*baba/mama (informal)*
husband	*zhangfu (jahng-fu)*
wife	*qizi (chee-dzih)*
son	*erzi (ar-dzih)*
daughter	*nuer (nu-ar)*
friend	*pengyou (pung-yo)*
foreigner	*waiguoren*
student	*xuesheng (shway-shung)*
tourist	*luyouzhe (lü-yo-dzih)*

Accommodation

hotel, cheaper	*lüguan (lü-gwahn)*
guest-house	*binguan*
single room	*dan-ren fangjian (dahn-run fahng-jyen)*
double room	*shuang ren fangjian*
dormitory	*sushe (su-shuh)*
key	*yaoshi (yow-shr)*
toilet	*cesuo (tsuh-swoh)*

shower	*linyü (leen-yü)*
telephone	*dianhua (dyen-hwa)*

Food

restaurant	*fanguar*
food, rice	*fan*
menu	*caidan (tsy-dahn)*
chopsticks	*kuaizi (kwy-dzih)*
steamed rice	*mifan*
fried rice	*chaofan*
fried noodles	*chaomian (chow-myen)*
bread	*mianbao*
cake	*dangao*
mutton	*yang rou (roe)*
beef	*niu rou*
chicken	*ji rou*
green vegetable	*qingcai (cheeng-tsy)*
egg	*jidan*
boiled	*zhu... (ju)*
fried	*jian... (jyen)*
soup	*tang (high tone)*
sugar	*tang (rising tone)*
salt	*yan*
hot chillies	*lajiao*
MSG	*wei-jin*
melon	*gua*

Drink

tea	*cha*
boiling water (for tea)	*kai shui (ky-shway)*
milk	*niu nai*
beer	*pijiu (pee-joh)*
wine	*putaojiu*
white spirits	*baijiu*

Transportation

bus	*qiche (chee-chuh)*
bus station	*qiche zhan (chee-chuh jahn)*
truck	*dakache (da-kah-chuh)*
train station	*huoche zhan (hwoh-chuh jahn)*
airport	*feiji chang*
ticket to (Turfan)	*dao (Turfan) de piao*
bicycle	*zixingche (dzih-sheeng-chuh)*

Around Town

post office	*you-ju (yoh-jü)*
stamp	*you-piao (yoh-pyow)*
airmail	*hang-kong (hahng-koong)*
bank	*yinhang*

police, Public Security Bureau	*gong-an ju* (goong-ahn jü)
hospital	*yiyuan*

Countries

Australia	*Ao-da-li-ya*
Canada	*Jia-na-da*
China	*Zhongguo* (joong-gwoh)
England	*Yingguo*
France	*Faguo*
Hong Kong	*Xiang-gang*
New Zealand	*Xing-xi-lan*
Pakistan	*Ba-ji-si-tan*
United States	*Meiguo*

Other Nouns

home-place	*jia* (jyah)
Silk Road	*Sichou Zhi Lu* (sih-cho jr lu)
Karakoram Highway	*Zhong-Pa Gong Lu*; 'China-Pak Big Road'
Mandarin	*putonghua* (pu-toong-hwa)
Uyghur language	*weizuhua* (wee-dzu-hwa)
money	*qian* (chyen)
RMB	*renminbi*
FEC	*wai hui* (wy-hway)
US dollar	*meiyuan*
Hong Kong dollar	*gangbi*
map	*ditu*
toilet paper	*weisheng zhi* (way-shung jr)

Adjectives

very	*hen* (hun) before adjective
good/bad	*hao/huai*
beautiful	*hao-kan*
delicious	*hao-chi* (how-chr)
happy	*gaoxing* (gow-sheeng)
expensive	*gui* (gway)
cheap	*pianyi* (pyen-yee)
left/right	*zuo* (dzwoh)/*you* (yo)
open (as in open areas for travel)	*kaifang* (kye-fung)
broken	*huai-le* (hwy-luh)
here/there	*zhe-li* (juh-lee)/*na-li*

Time

when? (date)	*ji hao?*
when? (time)	*ji dian?* (jee dyen)
today	*jintian* (jeen-tyen)
tomorrow	*mingtian*
day after tomorrow	*houtian*
yesterday	*zuotian* (dzwoh-tyen)

now	*xianzai* (shyen-dzai)
(five) o'clock	*(wu)-dian*
half-past (eight)	*(ba)-dian ban*
(three) hours	*(san)-ge xiaoshi* (...shyow-shr)
half an hour	*ban-ge xiaoshi*

Days of the week Use *xingqi* (shing-chee) plus a number (Monday = 1 through Saturday = 6; for example, *xingqi wu* is Friday); Sunday is *xingqi tian*.

Verbs

buy	*mai*
go	*qu* (chü)
live, reside	*shenghuo* (shun-hwoh)
work	*gongzuo* (goong-zwoh)
like	*xihuan* (shee-hwan)

Prepositions

from	*cong* (tsoong)
to	*dao*
in, on, at	*zai*

Phrases

hello ('are you well?')
  ni hao
goodbye
  zaijian
thank you
  xiexie (shyeh-shyeh)
please
  qing (cheeng)
excuse me
  dui bu qi (dway-bu-chee)
yes (correct)
  dui (dway)
no
  bu dui or *bu shi*
Where is (the toilet)?
  (cesuo) zai na li?
Do you have (hot water)?
  (kai shui), you mei you? (yo-may-yo)
I (don't) have rice
  wo (mei) you fan (may yo...)
I (don't) want tea
  wo (bu) yao cha (bu yow...)
How much does it cost?
  duo-shao qian? (dwoh-shao chyen)
Too expensive!
  tai gui-le! (tie gway-luh)
Enough!
  gou le! (go-luh)
Where are you going?
  qu na li? or *qu nar?* (chü...)
Is it allowed?
  ke bu keyi? (kuh bu kuh-yee)

Wait a moment		50	*ellek*
deng yi huar (dung yee hwar)		60	*otmish*
No problem		70	*yetmish*
mei guanxi (may gwan-shee)		80	*saiksen*
Where are you from?		90	*tokhsun*
ni cong nali lai de? (nee tsoong...)		100	*yüz*
I am from (America)		1000	*mung*
wo cong (Meiguo) lai de			

I am from (America)
  wo cong (Meiguo) lai de
Do you speak English?
  ni shuo Yingyu ma? (ying-yü)
A little bit
  yi dian-dian (yee dyen-dyen)
I cannot speak Mandarin
  wo bu hui shuo putonghua
Do you understand?
  ni dong ma?
I don't understand [your language]
  wo ting bu dong
I cannot read that [Chinese characters]
  wo kan bu dong

UYGHUR

Uyghur (pronounced 'WEE-gur', also called Turki) is spoken all over Xinjiang and to the west in parts of the Kirghiz and Uzbek Republics of the USSR. It's Xinjiang's 'unofficial' language; presented here is the Kashgar dialect. Uyghur is about 60% Turkish – including most nouns – with bits of Mongol, Kirghiz, Uzbek, Wakhi, Russian, Urdu, Arabic and Persian. In China, written Uyghur uses an Arabic script, although for a time children were taught a Latinised alphabet. For more words, a Turkish dictionary will help.

The symbol *ü* is pronounced by saying 'ee' with your mouth rounded as if to say 'oo'. Most words are accented on the last syllable.

Numbers

½	*yerim*
1	*bir*
2	*shkeh* or *iki*
3	*üch*
4	*turt*
5	*besh*
6	*ulteh*
7	*yetteh*
8	*saikyiz*
9	*tokuz*
10	*un*
20	*yigirmeh*
30	*ottuz*
40	*kirk*

Pronouns

I/we	*men/biz*
you (sing/pl)	*sen/siz* (*siz* is polite)
he/she/they	*u/u/ular*

Possessive form Add *-nung* after the noun.

People & Relations

person	*adem* (AH-dem)
man/woman	*er/ayal*
father	*dada, ata*
mother	*mama, ana* (old)
	apa (young)
husband	*ireh* (EE-reh)
wife	*ayaleh* (ah-YAH-leh)
elder brother	*akka*
younger brother	*hukah*
elder sister	*acha* (AH-cha)
younger sister	*singil*
friend	*dos*
head-man	*mokhtar, bashlak*

Accommodation

hotel ('guest-place')	*mihman khana*
key	*achkho* (ACH-kho)
toilet	*khala*

Food

restaurant/food stall	*tamakhana/ashkhana*
food	*tamakh*
bread	*nan*
flat-bread	*ak nan*
bagel	*gurdah*
meat	*gush*
mutton	*koi gush*
beef	*kala gush*
chicken	*toha gush*
fish	*bilekh*
vegetable	*sei*
steamed rice	*gampen*
fried rice & meat	*pulau* or *pilaf*
fried noodles & peppers	*laghman*
yogurt	*kitk*
melon	*khoghun*
grapes	*uzum*
apple	*ulmah* (OOL-mah)
peach	*shaptul*

pear	*amut*
fig	*enjü*

Drink

teahouse	*chaikhana*
water	*su*
tea	*chai*
beer	*pivo* (PEE-voh)

Transport

bus	*aptus* (ahp-TOOS)
bus station or stop	*aptus biket*
ticket	*bilet*
bicycle	*velspid*

Other Nouns

money: Chinese	
yuan or kuai	*koi*
jiao or mao	*mo*
Sunday Market	*Yekshenba Bazaar*
	Yenga Bazaar ('New Market')
home	*aileh* (AH-ee-leh)
house	*üi*
hospital	*doktor khana*
mountain	*tagh*
river	*darya*
lake	*kul*, as in Kara Kul, Bulunkul

Adjectives

good	*yakhshe* (YAKH-sheh)
bad	*yaman*
beautiful (place)	*güzel*
beautiful (face)	*cherailekh* (che-RYE-lekh)
delicious	*mizlik, tamlik*
expensive	*khummet*
left/right	*sol/ung*
this/that	*bu/u*
here/there	*buyir/uyir*

Time

when?	*kachan?*
what time?	*neech boldeh?*
	konch boldeh?
today	*bügün*
tomorrow	*atteh* (AHT-teh), *adah*
yesterday	*tünegün*
now	*hazir* (HAH-zir)
(six) o'clock	*(ulteh) boldeh*
(Beijing) time	*(Beijing) vakteh*

Phrases

hello	
salaam	

goodbye ('be happy')	
khar khosh	
How are you? ('are you well?')	
`*yakhshim siz?*	
I am well/happy	
yakhshim/khushal	
thank you	
rakhmat	
excuse me	
kechur siz	
yes/no	
dorah/dorah amas	
Where are you going?	
naga barsis? (NAH-ga BAR-sees)	
Where is (the station)?	
(biket) nada? (or *...khayerdeh?*)	
What is the name of this place?	
uyarnung ismeh nimeh?	
How much does it cost?	
nachpul?, neechpul?, konchpul?	
What's your name?	
ismengez nimeh? (ees-MENG-gez NEE-meh)	
My name is (John)	
minung ismim (John) (MEE-nung ees-MEEM...)	
How old are you?	
konch yashka kirdingez?	
I don't understand	
bilmidim or *bil mei*	
Please give me (a beer)	
manga (pivo) birsonas (...BIR-so-nas)	
I (don't) like Kashgar	
men Kashgar-neh yakhshkur (mei) men	

(With thanks to Mokimjian and Kurt Greussing)

WAKHI

Wakhi is the speech of the Tadjik people in the Tashkurghan region of Xinjiang, the Tadjik Republic of the USSR, the Wakhan corridor of Afghanistan and Gojal ('upper Hunza') in Pakistan. It probably displaced Burushaski in Gojal a century or two ago.

Numbers

1	*yew*
2	*bui*
3	*trui*
4	*tsebur*
5	*panz*
6	*sad* (sahd)
7	*hub* (hoob)
8	*hat* (haht)
9	*nau*

10	*das*
20	*wist*
100	*sad* (sahd)
1000	*hazar*

Pronouns

I/we	*wooz/sahk*
you (sing/pl)	*tu/sasht*
he/she	*yah/yah hruinan*
they	*yasht*

People & Relations

man/woman	*dai/hruinan*
father/mother	*taht/nahn*
husband/wife	*shauhar/jamat*
brother/sister	*vrut/hrui*
friend	*doost*
head-man	*arbab*

Accommodation

room	*jayi*
key	*weshik*
toilet	*tarkank* (tar-KAHNK)

Food

food, bread	*shapik* (sha-PEEK)
heavy whole-wheat bread	*kamishdoon, dildungi*
meat	*gosht*
vegetable	*ghazk*
rice	*gerangeh*
egg	*tukhmurgeh*
yogurt	*pai*
apricot	*chuan*
apple	*mur*

Drink

water	*yupek*
tea	*choi*
milk	*bursh*
buttermilk	*deegh*

Other Nouns

house	*khun*
mountain/peak	*kho/sar* (as in Borit Sar)
valley	*jerab* or *zherav*
small valley	*dur, dara*
river	*darya*
stone	*gar* (as in Passu Gar, Abdegar)
hot spring	*theen kook*

Adjectives

forming 'very': *ghafeh* before adjective

good/bad	*bahf/shahk*
beautiful	*khushroi*
delicious	*mazadar*
left/right	*chap/rost*
this/that	*yem/yah*
here/there	*drem/drah*

Time

when?	*tsoghdi?*
today	*wodeg*
tomorrow	*pigah*
yesterday	*yez*
now	*niveh*

Phrases

hello
  asalaam aleikhum
goodbye
  hudar hafiz (hu-DAHR ha-FEEZ)
How are you?
  chiz hawleh thei? (chiz HAW-lih tay)
I am (well)   *woozem (bahf) thei*
  happy   *khush*
  hungry   *merz* ('mares')
  thirsty   *wesk*
thank you
  shukria (shu-KREE-ah); special thanks *mehrbani*
What's your name?
  ti noongeh chiz thei?
My name is (John)
  zhu noongeh (John) thei
I don't understand
  majeh neh disht
I like (tea)
  woozesh (choiyeh) khush-tsaram
I want (tea)
  woozesh (choiyeh) zokh-tsaram
How much?
  tsumar?
Where is (the hot spring)?
  (theen kook) komar thei?

(With thanks to Haqiqat Ali)

BURUSHASKI

Burushaski is spoken in central Hunza, across the river in upper Nagar and in pockets elsewhere in Hunza and Nagar. Its origins are totally unknown, though some linguists think it's the oldest language in the KKH region. Its structure, like that of Navajo or Basque, make it nearly impossible for outsiders to master; there are said to be 38 plural forms, and words change form at both ends depending on context. But simple ideas are manageable. Hunza and Nagar dialects are slightly different, eg a common form of 'be' is *bila* in Hunza, *dila* in Nagar (marked * in the following).

Numbers

1	*han*
2	*alto* (al-TOH)
3	*usko* (oos-KOH)
4	*walto* (WAHL-toh
5	*tsundo* (tsoon-DOH)
6	*mishindo* (mi-SHIN-doh)
7	*talo* (tah-LOH)
8	*altambo* (ahl-TAHM-boh)
9	*huncho* (hoon-CHOH)
10	*torumo* (TOH-ru-moh)
20	*altar* (ahl-TAHR)
100	*tha* (tah)
1000	*sas*

Pronouns

I/mine	*jeh/jah*
you/yours (sing)	*um* (oom)/*umeh*
he/his	*in/ineh*
she/hers	*inegus/inemo*
we/ours	*mi/mii*
you/yours (pl)	*ma/maa*
they/theirs	*u/ueh*

People & Relations

man/woman	*hir/gus* (goos)
father/mother	*arra/mama*
(my) husband/wife	*auyar/aus* (ah-oos)
(my) brother/sister	*acho/ayas*
friend	*shugulo* (shu-GOO-loh) for men *shuguli* for women
head-man	*uyum* (oo-YOOM)
person from Hunza, Ganesh, etc	*Hunzakut, Ganeshkut,* etc

Accommodation

room	*kamera*
key	*chei*
toilet	*chukang*

Food

food, bread	*shapik* (shah-PEEK)
heavy whole-wheat bread	*phitti*
meat	*chap* (chahp)
vegetable	*hoi*

rice	*briw* in Nagar, *bras* in Hunza
thick noodle soup	*daudo*
egg	*tingan* (ting-GAHN)
yogurt	*dumanu mamu* (du-MAH-nu mah-MOQ)
white cheese	*burus* (broose)
dry cheese	*kurut*
apricot	*ju*
dried apricot	*batering* (bah-TEHR-ing)
apple	*balt*

Drink

water	*tsil*
drinking water	*minas tsil*
tea	*chai*
milk tea	*mamu chai*
green tea	*saba chai*
milk	*mamu* (mah-MOO)
buttermilk	*diltar*
grape wine	*mel*
mulberry spirits	*arak*

Other Nouns

home-place	*watan* (wa-TAHN)
house	*hah*
mountain	*chish*
valley	*har* or *bar*
river	*sinda*
channel	*gotsil*
hot spring	*garum bul* (gah-ROOM bool)

Adjectives

forming 'very':	*boot* before adjective
good/bad	*shuwa/gonaikish*
beautiful, good	*daltas* (dal-TAHS)
delicious (sweet)	*uyam* (oo-YAHM)
happy	*ayesh*
hungry	*chahmini*
thirsty	*auwa*
left/right	*ghail/doi*
this/that	*kos/es*
here/there	*kole/ele*

Time

when?	*beshal?* (BEH-shahl)
today	*kultu* or *kulto*
tomorrow	*jimale* (JEE-ma-leh)
yesterday	*sabur* (sah-BOOR)
now	*mu*

Phrases

hello	
	leh or *ajoh*

goodbye
hudar hafiz (hu-DAHR ha-FEEZ)
How are you?
behal bila* ? (beh-HAL bi-LAH)
I am (well/OK)
(shuwa/awah) bila*
thank you
shukria; special thanks *mehrbani*
yes/no
ju/baya
What is your name?
besan guik bila* ? (BEH-san gwik bi-LAH)
My name is (John)
ja ayik (John) bila*
What is the name of this place?
kuteh disheh besan ik bila* ?
Do you have (tea)?
(chai) biyah?
How much does this cost?
besan gash bila* ?
I don't understand
o dayalam (oh da-YAH-lum)

(With thanks to Latif Anwar)

SHINA

Shina is spoken in lower Hunza and Nagar (below the KKH bridge near Minapin); Gilgit and its valleys (Naltar, Bagrot, Haramosh and the Gilgit River watershed); Chilas and north-east Indus Kohistan. Meanings are often expressed by tones, so only the simplest words are given here.

Numbers

1	*ek*
2	*du*
3	*chreh*
4	*char*
5	*poin* (nasal)
6	*shah*
7	*saht*
8	*atch*
9	*nau*
10	*dai*
20	*bi*
100	*shal*
1000	*hazar*

Pronouns

I/we	*ma/beh*
you (sing/pl)	*tu/su*
he/she/they	*roh/reh/rih*

People & Relations

man/woman	*manuzho/chei* (mah-nu-ZHO)
father/mother	*malo/ma*
husband/wife	*musha* (mu-SHAH)/ *jama* (ja-MAH)
brother/sister	*zha/sah*
head-man, representative	*nambardar* (nam-bar-DAHR)
friend	*somo*
foreigner, outsider	*darineh* (da-REE-neh)

Food

food, bread	*tiki*
heavy whole-wheat bread	*chupatti*
meat	*mots*
vegetable	*shai*
rice	*briw*
egg	*haneh* (ha-NEH)
yogurt	*mutu dut* (MOO-tu doot)
apricot (common)	*jeroti*
dried apricots	*phator* (fa-TOR)

Drink

water	*wei*
tea	*chai*
milk	*dut* (rhymes with 'put')

Other Nouns

home-place	*watan* (wa-TAHN)
house	*goht*
mountain	*chirsh*
valley	*gah*
river	*sin*
hot spring	*dato uts* (DAH-toh oots)

Adjectives

good/bad	*mishto* (meesh-TOH)/ *khacho* (KHA-choh)
beautiful	*sudacho* (su-DAH-cho)
happy	*khush*
expensive	*keimeti* (kay-meh-TEE)
hot/cold	*dato/shidalo*
left/right	*kabu* (KAH-bu)/*dachinu* (da-CHEE-nu)
this/that	*anu/roh*
here/there	*athein* (ah-THANE)/ *al* (ahl)

Time

When?	*kareh?* (ka-REH)
today	*ash* (ahsh)
tomorrow	*loshteh* (losh-TEH)
yesterday	*bala* (ba-LAH)
now	*ten*; at once *dahm*

Phrases

hello
  asalaam aleikhum
goodbye
  hudar hafiz (hu-DAHR ha-FEEZ)
How are you?/fine
  jek hal hen?/shukur (SHOO-kur)
thank you
  shukria (shu-KREE-ah)i
excuse me
  mafteh
yes/no
  awah/neh
What is your name?
  tei nom jek han?
My name is (John)
  mei nom (John) han
I don't understand
  mei hir nawato (may heer NAH-wa-toh)
I like (Gilgit)
  mas (Gilgit) pasantamus (pa-SAHN-ta-moos)

(With thanks to Qurban Ali and Latif Anwar)

KOHISTANI

Kohistani is spoken in northern Swat and Indus Kohistan. It's a mish-mash of Shina, Pushto, Urdu, Persian and other languages, and it varies from one village to the next. Shina or Pushto may work just as well.

Numbers

1	*ek*
2	*du*
3	*cha*
4	*sawur*
5	*paz*
6	*shoh*
7	*saht*
8	*aht*
9	*nan, nau*
10	*dash*
20	*bish*
100	*shol*
1000	*zir*

People & Relations

man/woman	*mash (mahsh)/garyu*
father/mother	*abah (a-BAH)/yah*
husband/wife	*khawun (kha-WOON) garyu*
son/daughter	*puch/dhi*
brother/sister	*zha/bhyun*
friend	*doost*; my friend *mil doost*

Food & Drink

bread	*gwel*
meat	*masu (ma-SOO)*
vegetable	*sabzi*
egg	*anah (ah-NAH)*
yogurt	*dudi*
water	*vi, wi*
tea	*chai*
milk	*chir*

Other Nouns

name	*na*
home-place	*miwatan (MEE-wa-tahn)*
mountain	*kor*
high valley, pass	*dara*
river	*seen*

Time

today	*az (ahz)*
tomorrow	*okot*
now	*uskeh*
(two) o'clock	*(du) masmah*

Phrases

hello
  asalaam aleikhum
goodbye
  hudar hawala (hu-DAR ha-WAH-la)
good
  sugah (su-GAH), mihta
thank you
  shukria; special thanks *mehrbani*
yes/no
  ah/ni

PUSHTO

Pushto (or Pashto) is the speech of the Pathans, in Pakistan's North-West Frontier Province and in eastern Afghanistan. Along the KKH you'll hear it, heavily polluted with other dialects, in Besham, Batagram and to some extent in Mansehra.

Numbers

1	*yau*
2	*duah*
3	*dreh*
4	*salor (sa-LOR)*
5	*pinzeh*
6	*shpagh*
7	*wuh*
8	*atheh*
9	*neheh*
10	*las*
100	*sel*

People & Relations

man/woman	*nafar/khezeh*
father/mother	*plar/mur*
husband/wife	*khawun* (kha-WOON)/ *khazar* (KHAH-zar)
brother/sister	*rorh, runah/khor*
friend	*khpul*

Food & Drink

food, bread	*dodai*
meat	*wakha*
vegetable	*tarkari*
egg	*aghai* (AH-ghai)
water	*ubuh*
tea	*chai*

Other Nouns

name	*nam*
house	*kor*
mountain	*ugud* (u-GOOD)
valley	*gai*
river/stream	*rodh/khwar*

Adjectives

good	*kheh*
beautiful	*khaisteh, khesta*
expensive	*kemata* (ke-MAH-ta)

Time

today	*nunraz*
tomorrow, yesterday	*balauraz* (according to context)
day after tomorrow, day before yesterday	*dremoraz*
now	*us* (oos)

Phrases

hello	*asalaam aleikhum*
goodbye	*khudai paman* (khu-DYE pa-MAHN)
thank you	*tashakur*
yes/no	*wohli/wohli nadi*

Index

MAPS

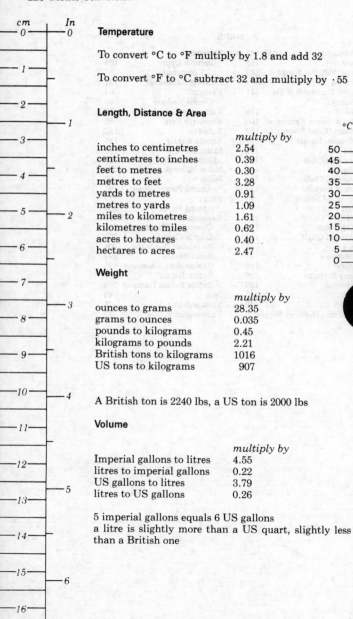

Temperature

To convert °C to °F multiply by 1.8 and add 32

To convert °F to °C subtract 32 and multiply by ·55

Length, Distance & Area

	multiply by
inches to centimetres	2.54
centimetres to inches	0.39
feet to metres	0.30
metres to feet	3.28
yards to metres	0.91
metres to yards	1.09
miles to kilometres	1.61
kilometres to miles	0.62
acres to hectares	0.40
hectares to acres	2.47

Weight

	multiply by
ounces to grams	28.35
grams to ounces	0.035
pounds to kilograms	0.45
kilograms to pounds	2.21
British tons to kilograms	1016
US tons to kilograms	907

A British ton is 2240 lbs, a US ton is 2000 lbs

Volume

	multiply by
Imperial gallons to litres	4.55
litres to imperial gallons	0.22
US gallons to litres	3.79
litres to US gallons	0.26

5 imperial gallons equals 6 US gallons
a litre is slightly more than a US quart, slightly less
than a British one

Guides to West Asia

China – a travel survival kit
Travelling on your own in China can be exciting and rewarding; it can also be exhausting and frustrating – getting a seat on a train or finding a cheap bed in a hotel isn't always easy. But it can be done and this detailed and comprehensive book tells you how.

Pakistan – a travel survival kit
Pakistan has been called 'the unknown land of the Indus' and many people don't realise the great variety of experiences it offers – from bustling Karachi, to ancient cities and tranquil mountain valleys.

India – a travel survival kit
An award-winning guidebook that is recognised as the outstanding contemporary guide to the subcontinent. Looking for a houseboat in Kashmir? Trying to post a parcel? This definitive guidebook has all the facts.

Trekking in the Indian Himalaya
The Indian Himalaya offers some of the world's most exciting treks. This book has advice on planning and equipping a trek, plus detailed route descriptions.

Trekking in the Nepal Himalaya
Complete trekking information for Nepal, including day-by-day route descriptions and detailed maps – this book has a wealth of advice for both independent and group trekkers.

Kashmir, Ladakh & Zanskar – a travel survival kit
This book contains detailed information on three contrasting Himalayan regions in the Indian state of Jammu and Kashmir – the narrow valley of Zanskar, reclusive Ladakh, and the beautiful Vale of Kashmir.

West Asia on a shoestring
A complete guide to the overland trip from Bangladesh to Turkey. Updated information on Bangladesh, Bhutan, India, Iran, Maldives, Nepal, Pakistan, Sri Lanka, Turkey and the Middle East, even Afghanistan as it used to be!

Also Available:
Hindi/Urdu phrasebook and *Nepali phrasebook*.

Lonely Planet Guidebooks

Lonely Planet guidebooks cover virtually every accessible part of Asia as well as Australia, the Pacific, Central and South America, Africa, the Middle East and parts of North America. There are four main series: 'travel survival kits', covering a single country for a range of budgets; 'shoestring' guides with compact information for low-budget travel in a major region; trekking guides; and 'phrasebooks'.

Australia & the Pacific
Australia
Bushwalking in Australia
Papua New Guinea
Papua New Guinea phrasebook
New Zealand
Tramping in New Zealand
Rarotonga & the Cook Islands
Solomon Islands
Tahiti & French Polynesia
Fiji
Micronesia

South-East Asia
South-East Asia on a shoestring
Malaysia, Singapore & Brunei
Indonesia
Bali & Lombok
Indonesia phrasebook
Burma
Burmese phrasebook
Thailand
Thai phrasebook
Philippines
Pilipino phrasebook

North-East Asia
North-East Asia on a shoestring
China
China phrasebook
Tibet
Tibet phrasebook
Japan
Korea
Korean phrasebook
Hong Kong, Macau & Canton
Taiwan

West Asia
West Asia on a shoestring
Trekking in Turkey
Turkey

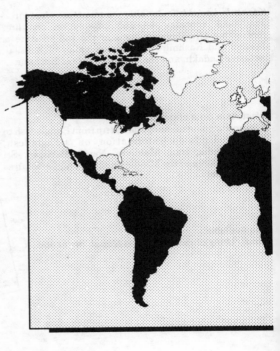

Mail Order

Lonely Planet guidebooks are distributed worldwide and are sold by good bookshops everywhere. They are also available by mail order from Lonely Planet, so if you have difficulty finding a title please write to us. US and Canadian residents should write to Embarcadero West, 112 Linden St, Oakland CA 94607, USA and residents of other countries to PO Box 617, Hawthorn, Victoria 3122, Australia.

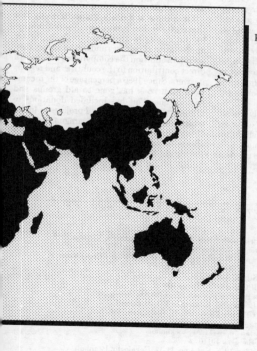

Lonely Planet

Lonely Planet published its first book in 1973. Tony and Maureen Wheeler had made a lengthy overland trip from England to Australia and, in response to numerous 'how do you do it?' questions, Tony wrote and they published *Across Asia on the Cheap*. It became an instant local best-seller and inspired thoughts of a second travel guide. A year and a half in South-East Asia resulted in their second book, *South-East Asia on a Shoestring*, which they put together in a backstreet Chinese hotel in Singapore in 1975. The 'yellow book', as it quickly became known, soon became *the* guide to the region and has gone through five editions, always with its familiar yellow cover.

Soon other writers came to them with ideas for similar books – books that went off the beaten track with an adventurous approach to travel, books that 'assumed you knew how to get your luggage off the carousel,' as one reviewer put it. Lonely Planet grew from a kitchen table operation to a spare room and then to its own office. It's international reputation began to grow as the Lonely Planet logo began to appear in more and more countries. In 1982 *India – a travel survival kit* won the Thomas Cook award for the best guidebook of the year.

These days there are over 70 Lonely Planet titles. Over 40 people work at our office in Melbourne, Australia and another half dozen at our US office in Oakland, California.

At first Lonely Planet specialised in the Asia region but these days we are also developing major ranges of guidebooks to the Pacific region, to South America and to Africa. The list of walking guides is growing and Lonely Planet now has a unique series of phrasebooks to 'unusual' languages. The emphasis continues to be on travel for travellers and Tony and Maureen still manage to fit in a number of trips each year and play a very active part in the writing and updating of Lonely Planet's guides.

Keeping guidebooks up to date is a constant battle which requires an ear to the ground and lots of walking, but technology also plays its part. All Lonely Planet guidebooks are now stored and updated on computer, and some authors even take lap-top computers into the field. Lonely Planet is also using computers to draw maps and eventually many of the maps will be stored on disk.

The people at Lonely Planet strongly feel that travellers can make a positive contribution to the countries they visit both by better appreciation of cultures and by the money they spend. In addition the company tries to make a direct contribution to the countries and regions it covers. Since 1986 a percentage of the income from each book has gone to aid groups and associations. This has included donations to famine relief in Africa, to aid projects in India, to agricultural projects in Nicaragua and other Central American countries and to Greenpeace's efforts to halt French nuclear testing in the Pacific. In 1988 over $40,000 was donated by Lonely Planet to these projects.

Lonely Planet Distributors

Australia & Papua New Guinea Lonely Planet Publications, PO Box 617, Hawthorn, Victoria 3122.
Canada Raincoast Books, 112 East 3rd Avenue, Vancouver, British Columbia V5T 1C8.
Denmark, Finland & Norway Scanvik Books aps, Store Kongensgade 59 A, DK-1264 Copenhagen K.
India & Nepal UBS Distributors, 5 Ansari Rd, New Delhi – 110002
Israel Geographical Tours Ltd, 8 Tverya St, Tel Aviv 63144.
Japan Intercontinental Marketing Corp, IPO Box 5056, Tokyo 100-31.
Netherlands Nilsson & Lamm bv, Postbus 195, Pampuslaan 212, 1380 AD Weesp.
New Zealand Transworld Publishers, PO Box 83-094, Edmonton PO, Auckland.
Singapore & Malaysia MPH Distributors, 601 Sims Drive, #03-21, Singapore 1438.
Spain Altair, Balmes 69, 08007 Barcelona.
Sweden Esselte Kartcentrum AB, Vasagatan 16, S-111 20 Stockholm.
Thailand Chalermnit, 108 Sukhumvit 53, Bangkok 10110.
Turkey Yab-Yay Dagitim, Alay Koshu Caddesi 12/A, Kat 4 no. 11-12, Cagaloglu, Istanbul.
UK Roger Lascelles, 47 York Rd, Brentford, Middlesex, TW8 0QP
USA Lonely Planet Publications, PO Box 2001A, Berkeley, CA 94702.
West Germany Buchvertrieb Gerda Schettler, Postfach 64, D3415 Hattorf a H.
All Other Countries refer to Australia address.